UNDIPLOMATIC HISTORY

RETHINKING CANADA IN THE WORLD

SERIES EDITORS: IAN MCKAY AND SEAN MILLS

Supported by the Wilson Institute for Canadian History at McMaster University, this series is committed to books that rethink Canadian history from transnational and global perspectives. It enlarges approaches to the study of Canada in the world by exploring how Canadian history has long been a dynamic product of global currents and forces. The series will also reinvigorate understanding of Canada's role as an international actor and how Canadians have contributed to intellectual, political, cultural, social, and material exchanges around the world.

Volumes included in the series explore the ideas, movements, people, and institutions that have transcended political boundaries and territories to shape Canadian society and the state. These include both state and non-state actors, and phenomena such as international migration, diaspora politics, religious movements, evolving conceptions of human rights and civil society, popular culture, technology, epidemics, wars, and global finance and trade.

The series charts a new direction by exploring networks of transmission and exchange from a standpoint that is not solely national or international, expanding the history of Canada's engagement with the world.

http://wilson.humanities.mcmaster.ca

Undiplomatic History

The New Study of
Canada and the World

Edited by

ASA McKERCHER and PHILIP VAN HUIZEN

McGill-Queen's University Press
Montreal & Kingston • London • Chicago

ISBN 978-0-7735-5694-2 (cloth)
ISBN 978-0-7735-5695-9 (paper)
ISBN 978-0-7735-5819-9 (EPDF)
ISBN 978-0-7735-5820-5 (EPUB)

Legal deposit second quarter 2019
Bibliothèque nationale du Québec

Printed in Canada on acid-free paper that is 100% ancient forest free
(100% post-consumer recycled), processed chlorine free.

Funded by the Government of Canada   Financé par le gouvernement du Canada   Canada   Canada Council for the Arts   Conseil des arts du Canada

We acknowledge the support of the Canada Council for the Arts, which
last year invested $153 million to bring the arts to Canadians throughout
the country.

Nous remercions le Conseil des arts du Canada de son soutien. L'an dernier,
le Conseil a investi 153 millions de dollars pour mettre de l'art dans la vie
des Canadiennes et des Canadiens de tout le pays.

Library and Archives Canada Cataloguing in Publication

    Undiplomatic history : the new study of Canada and the world /
edited by Asa McKercher and Philip Van Huizen.

(Rethinking Canada in the world ; 2)
Includes bibliographical references and index.
Issued in print and electronic formats.
ISBN 978-0-7735-5694-2 (hardcover). – ISBN 978-0-7735-5695-9 (softcover). –
ISBN 978-0-7735-5819-9 (EPDF). – ISBN 978-0-7735-5820-5 (EPUB)

    1. Canada – Foreign relations. I. McKercher, Asa, editor II. Van
Huizen, Philip, 1978–, editor III. Series: Rethinking Canada in the
world ; 2

FC242.U54 2019   327.71   C2018-906508-7
                                                    C2018-906509-5

This book was typeset by True to Type in 10.5/13 Sabon

Contents

Table and Figures

Acknowledgments

This project began out of our shared belief that there were important changes afoot in the field of Canadian international history, and our sense that it was important to take a snapshot of these developments and provide some sense of cohesion regarding the direction of the field. To this end we organized a symposium held in April 2017 at the L.R. Wilson Institute for Canadian History at McMaster University, where both of us were fortunate enough to spend two-year fellowships. A remarkable centre, it is supported generously by Red Wilson. Our thanks to him for championing our efforts and Canadian history more broadly. At the Wilson Institute, we benefitted from superb mentorship, first from its interim director, John Weaver, and then from its current director, Ian McKay. Enthusiastic about our project, Ian offered us considerable help, advice, and also leeway, and we benefitted greatly from his keen mind and from the intellectual environment he has created at the Wilson Institute. We were assisted too, in innumerable ways, by the indefatigable Max Dagenais and the incomparable Debbie Lobban. Overall, McMaster was enriching and fulfilling, and our thanks go to our students and our colleagues, especially Amanda Ricci, Ian Mosby, Stacy Nation-Knapper, Colin McCullough, Michael Egan, Bonny Ibhawoh, Megan Armstrong, Stephen Heathorn, Karen Balcom, Tracy McDonald, Juanita DeBarros, Nancy Bouchier, Ken Cruikshank, Ellen Amster, and Pamela Swett. The Phoenix Pub also deserves mention for providing the original liquid inspiration behind *Undiplomatic History*.

Obviously, this collection is the result of the efforts of more than just us two. First and foremost, thanks go to our contributors, each of whom took the time to prepare incisive papers, to respond to suggestions made by us and the reviewers, and to do both of these tasks on schedule. Ian McKay and Sean Mills are to be thanked for inviting us to contribute this volume to their *Rethinking Canada in the World* series. We would be remiss, also, if we did not thank Jonathan Crago, our editor at McGill-Queen's University Press. His enthusiasm for the project, and his help in seeing it through to fruition so quickly, are much appreciated. Thanks, too, to the members of the editorial and production team at MQUP: Ryan Van Huijstee, Finn Purcell, and Kathleen Fraser. Scott Howard proved an excellent copy editor, improving our prose and saving us from embarrassment. SSHRC provided financial support for the Undiplomatic History symposium, where many of the authors in this collection originally presented their papers. In addition to the contributors, we were very fortunate to have presentations and input from Tarah Brookfield, Petra Dolata, Robin Gendron, Francine McKenzie, David Meren, Alexandre Michaud, Adele Perry, Timothy Andrews Sayle, Sarah E.K. Smith, Graeme Thompson, and Ryan Touhey. Mica Jorgensen took care of all the symposium's social media needs.

Finally, our gratitude and this book's dedication go to our respective families. Phil thanks Helena, Oliver, and Sasha: my favourite three people. Asa thanks Kendall, my tireless champion, friend, and partner.

UNDIPLOMATIC HISTORY

Undiplomatic History:
Rethinking Canada and the World

ASA MCKERCHER AND PHILIP VAN HUIZEN

International history, or the historical study of international relations, is experiencing a renaissance in Canada. This volume, *Undiplomatic History: The New Study of Canada and the World,* is part of an effort that is expanding the boundaries of Canadian international history – what was once known as diplomatic history – by examining new actors, new frames of reference, and new research questions.[1] Stemming from a conference held at the L.R. Wilson Institute for Canadian History at McMaster University in spring 2017, the essays below take stock of changes in the field and chart new paths forward for Canadian international history. The ethos behind this rethinking is twofold. First, it is to place Canadian international relations into a wider domestic context, thereby showing the interconnection between foreign affairs and political, cultural, social, and economic developments. Here, the goal is to do for international history what the emergence of "war and society" did to enrich the study of military history: expand the scope of analysis and trace the societal impacts and influences of events. Just as many military historians shifted focus from the battlefield to the home front, there is now an effort among international historians to move away from an exclusive focus on embassies, dispatches, and conference tables. Second, it is to incorporate transnational and global history approaches into the study of Canadian international history. This emphasis is part of a wider trend in which the global and transnational turns have prompted re-evaluations of Canadian history. In effect, it puts on its head the self-congratulatory aphorism "the world needs more Canada"; instead,

Canada needs more of the world. The contributions to *Undiplomatic History* showcase some of the ways that the new Canadian international history is emerging and enriching the study of Canada's past.

In our view, the need to expand the scope of Canadian international history is necessary because the subfield has undergone a period of crisis and stagnation. In a recent historiographical piece, David Meren decried the tragedy of Canadian international history. Indeed, he highlighted several tragedies, the most notable of which was the lack of critical engagement on the part of Canadians with their country's foreign policy, both past and present. According to Meren, this stasis not only impeded "the emergence of a narrative capable of challenging established orthodoxies," but led both "to romanticized notions of Canada's international action" and to "the lack of an effective countervailing voice" to oppose the way in which Canadian international history was used "for reactionary ends," namely support for the war in Afghanistan.[2] In the United States, the War on Terror coincided with – or led to – a revival of diplomatic history and to historians' engagement in vigorous public debates about the nature and direction of US foreign policy and of Americans' interactions with the world. In comparison, the diminution of Canadian international history and the marginalization of its practitioners contributed to a paucity of historical input into debates about Canada's contemporary global engagement.

Meren is hardly alone in lamenting the "tragedy" of what had happened to both the practice and understanding of international history in Canada. Such laments have a long pedigree. During the "history wars" that raged in academia in the 1980s and 1990s, Canadian foreign relations history became one of the chief casualties. A result noted in 1986 by John English was that much of Canada's political history, including the history of Canadian international relations, was written by political scientists, not historians. Nearly ten years later, Robert Bothwell, the dean of Canadian international historians, quipped that the number of Canadian foreign policy historians was "by recent scientific estimate ... about the same as the digits on the feet of a three-toed sloth." More recently, Adam Chapnick asked: "Where Have All of Canada's Diplomatic Historians Gone?"[3] While Meren, English, Bothwell, and Chapnick might differ in their views on Canada's role abroad, what unites them – and us – is the sense that the historical study of Canadian global engagement is vital and that the relative inattention to this history is unsatisfactory. *Undiplomatic History* addresses this deficit. Yet as the title of our volume implies, our goal is to move away from an exclusive focus on diplomatic history, viewed (rightly, in certain ways) as hidebound, elitist, and overly concerned with the state and the small group of white males who dominated it. In truth, "diplomatic history" itself is a term seemingly used more by the field's detractors than by its proponents, who, for some time, have preferred the more expansive term "international history." In this spirit, both individually and collectively, the contributors to this volume go a step further by demonstrating how a new Canadian international history is emerging: one that blends older approaches with transnational, global, and also cultural history. To reflect wider developments in the field of international history globally, and for reasons that we expand upon below, we refer to this new Canadian international history as the study of Canada in the World.

To begin with, although it is not our intention to revisit (or worse, reignite) the history wars, it is worth briefly noting how the field has fared over the past few decades. During these conflicts, international history went by the wayside in Canada. Not that Canadian international historians disappeared – many practitioners continued to serve, albeit in interdisciplinary departments and research centres instead of history departments. Further, even as their numbers shrank, they continued publishing, training grad students, and teaching courses on international history, a subject matter that retained considerable popularity with undergraduates.[4] But they became a small, relatively insular community of scholars, relegated to the sidelines of Canadian history, rarely appearing at the Canadian Historical Association annual meetings, and publishing in highly specialized journals rather than the *Canadian Historical Review*. The passing of Canadian foreign policy history seemed to reflect a wider trend in the 1990s and early 2000s of a general disengagement from the world on the part of Canadians. The title of one polemic from the turn of the millennium put it succinctly: *While Canada Slept: How We Lost Our Place in the World*.[5]

This stagnation was concerning for two different reasons. As Adam Chapnick pointed out, "the relative paucity of scholarship on the history of foreign relations has resulted in a dearth of contrasting views" among Canada's few international historians, many of whom seemed more concerned with self-preservation than engaging in internecine debates.[6] Furthermore, the mutual ignorance of Canadian social and cultural historians and Canadian international historians meant that few critical perspectives seeped into the history of Canadian international history. This lack of debate failed to enliven interchange among historians, let alone student reading lists. Although popular with under-graduate students and vital for understanding an important and contentious facet of Canadian politics, international history was shunted aside by most Canadian history departments, if not ignored altogether.

Recently and happily, this insularity on the part of both academics and the Canadian public (if it ever really existed) is ending.[7] As Justin Trudeau announced in his first press conference as prime minister in October 2015: "I want to say this to this country's friends around the world: Many of you have worried that Canada has lost its compassionate and constructive voice in the world over the past 10 years. Well, I have a simple message for you on behalf of 35 million Canadians. We're back."[8] Perhaps it took the recent Conservative revolution in foreign policy to refocus Canadians' attention on the world and their place within it. Or perhaps the culprit was the collective impact of the war in Afghanistan, the wider War on Terror, climate change, the 2008 financial crisis, and the ongoing process of globalization, with its attendant economic, cultural, and social effects. These events and developments underscore Canada's connectivity with the world and indicate the need to study Canadians' place in it.

And things are changing in the academy as well. Canadian historians are more accepting of outward-looking scholarship, for transnational and global history have thrived over the past decade. Moreover, Canadian international historians have begun to adopt a more inclusive outlook. Just as a new political history has arisen to explore the confluence of politics, society, and culture in Canada, there has been a growing tendency toward a new, vibrant Canadian international history.[9] In *Undiplomatic History* we highlight how this field is becoming reinvigorated and point the way forward for scholars interested in Canadian foreign relations, broadly conceived. And we do mean broadly. For as is clear, or should be clear, the world matters to Canadians and to the study of Canada's past – from migration to the environment, from peace to war, from trade to human rights, and from identity formation to cultural transfer. Beyond emphasizing the obvious importance of international, transnational, and global frameworks to our understanding of Canadian history, contributors to this volume query what separates these different approaches to the study of Canada in the world, and make the case for a holistic, inclusive approach, a new international history that is reflective of the evolution that has occurred elsewhere and is now happening in the Canadian context. Given global changes to the study of international history, we begin by turning our attention to other historiographies that have been wrestling with similar questions. To do so, we look at how international history has evolved in the United States, where diplomatic history experienced a period of decline followed by a renaissance that provides lessons for Canadian historians. Such lessons are at the heart of *Undiplomatic History*. Our hope is that this volume helps to continue the process of renewing and rethinking the study of Canada in the World.

FROM DIPLOMATIC HISTORY
TO THE UNITED STATES AND THE WORLD

Canadian international history has a long pedigree, harkening back to professional history as it emerged in Europe in the nineteenth century. Here, diplomatic history was of prime importance. Concerned with Great Powers (always capitalized), with peace and war, with international treaties, and with diplomats and statesmen, diplomatic historians searched for an understanding of why conflicts among states occurred, how international crises or disputes were resolved without warfare, and how wars were brought to an end. In a Europe in which the nation-state was of paramount importance, where martial values were prized, and where a narrow elite held sway, such a limited focus on states, statesmen, and statecraft seemed natural. In many respects, then, diplomatic history was history. As Donald Cameron Watt, the leading British diplomatic historian of the 1970s and 1980s, put it in looking back on an earlier era, "to be a historian of nineteenth-century Europe and not a diplomatic historian was almost impossible."[10] Nor did two world wars seem to alter the primacy of diplomatic history, at least given its association with political history (though the political science subfield of international relations, which arose in the wake of the First World War, became of primary importance in policy-making circles).

Yet by the 1970s, diplomatic history was facing considerable criticism. Given its prioritization of the state, the field was wedded to the nation and to the archive. It was also elite-focused, largely narrative in its construction, and it prized empirical evidence over theory, all of which led critics to dismiss its "Rankean exegesis."[11] As the academy shifted away from elites, the state, and the archive, and turned instead toward common people, social forces, and theory, diplomatic history seemed outmoded and fusty. Thus, in Britain in the 1970s the field started to broaden in order to take greater account of the under-lying factors that influence state-to-state relations. What soon became known as international history tended to involve a wider focus encompassing not just diplomacy, but also economic matters, intelligence, strategy, and the domestic sources of foreign policy-making. Situating international relations into wider societal contexts also became key.[12] While this move on the part of international his-torians was a genuine effort to be more inclusive and to do more than simply recount "what one clerk wrote to another," to its critics the alteration seemed to be purely cosmetic. Thus, international his-tory remained subject to "condescension and apathy" and continued to be seen as "the most arid and sterile of all the sub-histories" – judg-ments levelled even at international historians offering the sorts of critical analyses favoured in the increasingly leftward-tilting acade-my.[13] While the concern among many international historians was that their field continued to risk "ossification," some took a more benign view. Given international history's enduring popularity with undergraduates, with book publishers, and even with the public, Jes-sica Gienow-Hecht scolded her fellow international historians for being "a global group of worriers."[14] Still, a crisis seemed evident with the field increasingly under attack from – or worse, ignored by – social and cultural historians. Furthermore, a shift was taking place, with other historians, who actively rejected the "international" label, stepping into the breach to craft outward-facing history of a differ-ent sort.

In parallel with globalization, which questioned the importance of the nation-state, the 1990s saw the emergence of transnational and global history. Largely ignoring states and the relations among them, transnational and global historians looked in broader terms at how people in one area of the globe viewed, reacted to, or were influenced by events, people, or ideas in other areas of the world. Their major pre-occupations have been with processes of migration, transportation, and communication, as well as the development of networks, imagi-naries, and identities. This type of historical analysis apparently differs from international history in an important respect. "Whereas 'inter-national' implies a relationship among nations," explains Akira Iriye, "'transnational' suggests various types of interactions across national boundaries. Extraterritorial movements of individuals, goods, capital, and even ideas would seem to be less international than transnation-al."[15] Generally, states are still present in transnational history, but what is important is to look beyond national borders. As one scholar put it, transnational historians examine "how people and ideas and institutions and cultures moved above, below, through, and around, as well as within, the nation state."[16] The state matters, but only just – and sometimes not at all.

Global historians, too, leave little room for the state. Involving a process of integrating the histories of various regions, peoples, and even time periods, global history – and its closely related kin, oceanic, imperial, and comparative history – looks far beyond the state. Some historians have likened it to globalization itself, noting that they are both processes aimed at "integrating nations and peoples – politically, economically, and culturally – into larger communities," with a focus "not on nations, but on the entire globe."[17] If transnational history is about subverting borders, then global history involves subsuming them into much larger narratives and analyses. In this area, Canadian historians might be most familiar with Atlantic history and Pacific history, as well as with the history of the British world.[18] Given that, by definition, international history is concerned with relations among states, it would seem to be deeply at odds with the transnational and global turns.

Yet international historians need not be fearful of other approaches to outward-facing history. After all, transnational history, global history, and international history draw on a similar toolkit, namely multi-archival, multi-sited research. They are each focused beyond any single state, albeit in different ways. Furthermore, many of the issues that concern these fields are similar, including migration, the environment, natural resources, global governance, trade, human rights, and the impact of warfare. There would seem, then, to be a natural fit among these three approaches to history. In regard to transnational and international approaches, for instance, many transnational historians have looked at the role of non-state actors – missionaries, development specialists, financiers, activists – whose movements and activities across borders have supplemented or frustrated the foreign policy goals of various states.

Beyond the geospatial frameworks offered by transnational and global history, over the past two decades many international historians have come to adopt cultural analyses into their work. Looking at issues connected to race, class, gender, and religion has enriched international history by allowing historians to delve into the underlying factors that influence foreign policy-making. Indeed, the American experience is instructive here, even for Canadians who might naturally be wary of something emanating from our southern neighbours.

In 1977, the Society for Historians of American Foreign Relations (SHAFR), a small professional organization, launched its flagship journal, *Diplomatic History*. The journal's mission statement had presented it as "a forum for discussion of many aspects of the diplomatic, economic, intellectual and cultural relations of the United States."[19] This was an admirable focus, but, in practice, the journal, like the field of diplomatic history writ large, concerned itself mainly with states, elites, and traditional diplomatic issues, even as the American academy shifted toward social and then cultural history. Furthermore, *Diplomatic History* and American diplomatic history were dominated by a vicious running battle between an orthodox school, a revisionist school, and a post-revisionist school over American culpability for the Cold War, and the direction of US foreign policy more generally. The result was that the field of American foreign relations history drifted into obscurity and irrelevance. It entered, as a leading diplomatic historian put it, a "long crisis of confidence" all too familiar to Canadian international historians.[20] But American foreign relations history soon revitalized itself by taking seriously the need to incorporate the transnational, global, and cultural turns. The result has been an innovative field of study (perhaps the most innovative subfield of United States history) that situates international relations within domestic, transnational, and global contexts, while highlighting and analyzing the economic, ideological, political, social, cultural, environmental, and even emotional tensions that shape foreign policy-making. Additionally, this new field of study has emphasized the role of non-state actors, including migrants, missionaries, activists, athletes, musicians, and multinational corporations.

The shift began in the mid-1990s. With transnational and global history emerging alongside cultural history, in 1997 Elizabeth Cobbs Hoffman, author of a path-breaking study of the Peace Corps, identified an emerging "New Diplomatic History" that took into account these emerging trends to make "a fuller representation of American life by portraying the interaction between the United States and the rest of the world and then tightly braiding that story together with both domestic and world history."[21] The approach that Cobbs Hoffman outlined would become better known as America in the World or the United States and the World (as Canadians, concerned as we are with not being overshadowed in our own hemisphere, our preference is for the latter): a blending of international, transnational, and global history, along with scholarship reflecting the cultural turn. In short, historians of US foreign relations took an inclusive approach that has enlivened their field.

There quickly developed a considerable literature on race and US foreign policy, which was joined by studies employing frameworks of gender and religion, as well as business and labour histories that emphasize the international role of American capital. A similar move traced development, technology, and modernization and their relation to US power. Moreover, culture itself, understood in this context as consumer goods, radio, art, music, film, and television, has been a major United States export but also a vital import, and thus historians have stressed the reciprocal nature of cultural transfer between the United States and the rest of the world. A related trend has been to look at cultural diplomacy and the ways in which Americans, both inside and outside of government, have sought to use various media and educational and cultural exchanges to spread ideals about life, liberty, and the pursuit of happiness. Of course, ideas diffuse widely, and so scholarly attention has also been devoted to how Americans have received ideas from abroad. That the field of the United States and the World could cast such a wide net may seem too much (a sign, perhaps, of the American tendency for excess?), and yet it is clear that power dynamics – the ultimate concern of diplomatic history – lie at the heart not only of typical foreign policy issues, such as peace and war, but are central to questions of gender and race, culture and economics, and modernity and religion. So, among US foreign relations scholars, it became natural to show how "beliefs about national identity, ideology, race and ethnicity, gender, and class" served to shape "the exercise of economic, political, or military power."[22]

By 2004, in the midst of this shift, leading historians of United States foreign relations could claim that their field was marked by a "healthy ferment and rich diversity" and that they were witnessing an "era of innovation" that stood in stark contrast to the dire situation of the 1980s and 1990s. In 2009, while cautioning his colleagues not to abandon the "core mission of studying state-oriented diplomacy," Tom Zeiler, then the SHAFR president, boasted that "diplomatic history is in the driver's seat when it comes to the study of America and the world."[23] Harvard's Erez Manela agreed with Zeiler that the field had enjoyed "radical, perhaps unprecedented" transformations, all the result of "a sea change in how a new generation of historians who study U.S. interactions with the wider world sees their field, and how the discipline of history as a whole views it." Yet Manela disagreed about the necessity of state-centric approaches, noting that "American historians as a whole have increasingly been seeking to transcend the nation," with foreign relations historians "eager to frame their investigations in ways that go beyond" state boundaries.[24] Clearly, tensions exist between transnational and international history approaches, but the point is that they both fit under the United States and the World banner.

It is within this disagreement over what "counts" as international history that we see the methodological and theoretical benefits of incorporating transnational, global, and cultural "turns" into international history as much as topical ones. As previously mentioned, orthodox international history approaches tend to reify state interests into something easily definable, based generally on "realist" versus "idealist" understandings of power, security, and economic interest. Thus the "United States" and "Canada" become personified, historical entities with identifiable places within a larger global system of states. New historical approaches, however, implicitly turn this understanding on its head because they force historians to ask about the sources of foreign policy decisions and to question whether there really are identifiable "interests" associated with each state, how these are identified, and, critically, who gets to define them. This has created a new debate within international history circles, one that concerns how the field actually defines itself.

If one were to take a snapshot of the United States and the World it would show that what counts in the field is not just the issue of state-level decision-making, but rather "the totality of interactions – economic, cultural, political, military, environmental, and more – among peoples, organizations, states, and systems."[25] In short, the field of international history today seemingly covers anything and everything that seeps across state borders, with the result that many diplomatic historians in the United States have begun to worry that there is no longer any cohesion to what they do. As some have contended, one of the risks associated with such an expansive definition is "the lack of complementarity among some of the methodological trends ... and the increasing difficulty in producing comprehensive and necessary historical syntheses" of US foreign relations history centred on state interests.[26] Others have disagreed, arguing for an inclusive field: "No social group should be *ex cathedra* played up or down, neither policy makers nor non-state agents."[27]

Although such disagreements are far from resolved, what is clear from this commentary is that by the end of the first decade of the new millennium, the United States and the World had become the mode of categorizing a new international history: a history that blends the more traditional, hard-power concerns of US foreign relations with cultural and social issues, and which ties these matters into analyses grounded in transnational historians' interest in the transfusion of people and ideas, as well as in global historians' concern with supranational phenomena and large-scale developments. Such expansiveness has admittedly created new problems, as some of the very underpinnings of international history have been challenged. Still, our view is that the inclusive spirit guiding the United States and the World is a model for Canadian international historians interested in revitalizing the field. Our contention, and the point of this volume, is that there is a need to adopt a Canada in the World approach. Happily, the move in this direction is already afoot.

RETHINKING THE STUDY OF CANADA AND THE WORLD

As much as international history has been relegated to the sidelines in Canadian history, other ways of looking at Canada in the world have been thriving. The topical expansion of how Canada is being thought about in global and transnational terms has begun to influence Canadian international history, but few scholars have actually queried what these different approaches to looking at Canada have to say to each other. Moreover, transnational and global approaches to Canadian history have progressed largely without attention to international history and the issues that concern international historians. As detailed below, though, this trend is now starting to shift, most recently displayed in an excellent 2017 collection, *Dominion of Race: Rethinking Canada's International History*, which reframes Canada's international relationships through the lens of race. Building on such approaches and applying them as broadly as possible to the study of Canada in the world is at the heart of *Undiplomatic History*.

Canadian transnational history in particular has grown immensely over the past decade.[28] Although there is still a tendency among Canadian historians to be rather loose with definitions, especially concerning the differences between transnational versus international history,[29] the amorphousness of what actually "counts" as transnational history means that there is a wide range of historical studies of

Canada that fall under the category, from migration history, to histories of the transfer of ideas and culture, to studies of religious and ethnic communities, to borderlands studies.[30] Thankfully, transnational history and international history in Canada are starting to mix.[31] This development is essential in many ways, from probing the degree to which borders matter, to grappling with the question of who speaks for and influences official state positions and policies in an increasingly globalized world – though as transnational history makes clear, far-flung networks and circuits of people and ideas have been a constant factor in Canada's past. As Laura Madokoro has shown, for instance, migration and refugee studies are ripe for a greater engagement with Canada's international history.[32] Along with migration, renewed attention has been focused on how peace, war, and human rights have shaped political developments within Canada and driven various forms of activism by transnational actors.[33]

Like migrants, ideas flow across borders, and considerable attention has been spent charting transatlantic currents in these areas. This of course has a very old history, going back at least as far as J.B. Brebner's North Atlantic Triangle.[34] As Henry Yu has argued, however, "Canada is as much a Pacific-oriented as it is an Atlantic-oriented nation," a view that is not necessarily geographic but rather offers "a perspective on our past" that challenges the Central Canadian dominance of national history, which frequently looks east rather than west.[35] Although Canadian-Asian relations have had a place within Canadian international historiography, more attention is being devoted to Pacific Canada, with much of the emphasis here on the role of sub-state actors.[36]

The Pacific has also played an important part in histories about Canadian links to other parts of the former British Empire, with Australia and New Zealand taking primacy of place.[37] One is tempted to state that the empire has struck back, for imperial history has come into its own. Canadian history has always involved the study of empires, but as Phillip Buckner lamented a quarter century ago, this focus, especially as it pertained to Britain, seemed to disappear in the closing decades of the twentieth century. Yet within a few short years and as part of a larger, critical re-engagement with the history of the British Empire more generally, Canada and the British world emerged as a vibrant area of study looking both at the colonial period and its legacies.[38] This subfield has drawn from transnational, global, and cultural history approaches.

As for other transnational trends, borderlands studies have added nuance to the tried and true study of Canadian-American relations, with a particular focus on non-political themes and non-state-based connections.[39] A prime example of this work is the examination of the so-called Rust Belt that runs through Canada and the United States, connecting labour, technology, and economy in a way that is influenced by Canadian-US borders and has also transcended them.[40] Such works showcase an increasing interest in regions that straddle North American boundaries, with historians using natural borders rather than political ones to delimit their studies while keeping in mind the environmental and social impacts that territorial markers have had.[41] Such efforts have paralleled an increasing interest in borderlands history between Canada and the United States, particularly in the West.[42] All of this work shows that Canadian-US histories are enmeshed, and, while there are distinct national histories, one can identify an intertwined North American history as well. Indeed, it is mostly at the borderlands level that environmental historians have started to look at the confluence of international relations and the impact of non-human nature that does not adhere to national borders – a relatively new field in international history more broadly, which Macfarlane details in this volume.[43]

Another aspect of the recent surge in studies blending transnational and international history has been the emphasis on decolonization and development, two increasingly prominent themes in the growing academic literature surrounding Canadian relations with the "Third World." Here, scholars have often emphasized the flow of ideas and people between Canada and newly decolonized regions.[44] Those historians who have focused on Canadian relationships with decolonizing or decolonized countries have reached new conclusions about the nature of Canadian foreign policy. More traditionally-minded historians interested in Canada's relationships with Britain and the United States had concentrated largely on questions of Canadian autonomy and independence, as well as the extent of Canada's sway with its Great Power guarantors. These issues are still relevant to the new scholarship, but in looking at Canadian relations with the non-Western world following the wave of post-1945 decolonization, scholars have also drawn challenging conclusions about Canada's global engagement, especially once cultural factors and economic power have been thrown into the mix.[45] Canada, these scholars have reminded us, is a Western country, with policy-makers who thought in Western terms. The point is worth stressing because many Canadians had – and have – seemingly bought too much into the rhetoric that Canada is a nation of mild-mannered, tolerant, honest brokers and peacekeepers.

Before outlining how particular chapters in this volume add to the foregoing discussion, it is worth noting one theme that the volume does not engage enough with – thus ending this foray into the budding amalgamation of different ways to study Canada in the World with a call for a new way to push the field forward. Imperial aspects of international history are not only related to Canada's relationships with areas outside of its borders. Indeed, international historians need to do a better job of looking at the relationship between international relations and imperialism as it relates to the history of the Canadian state and First Nations, Inuit, and Métis. Although transnational and global historians have made great inroads on topics as diverse as Louis Riel, Indigenous rights movements, and the comparative impact of settler societies, Canadian-First Nations relations are rarely thought about as part of Canada's international history, outside of Indigenous history circles.[46] As Canada's treaty history with First Nations communities has shown, however, this was not how actors in the past necessarily viewed it.[47] Within Canada, such an interpretation would drastically alter the timeline of Canadian international relations, which is commonly interpreted as beginning after the First World War. Furthermore, addressing Indigenous history within international relations would force Canadian international historians to reanalyze concepts such as sovereignty, and would blur the boundary between foreigner and citizen, something that Indigenous groups, as "citizens plus," have been doing for a long time, most dramatically by taking complaints against the Canadian government before the League of Nations, the British government, and the United Nations.[48]

With this lacuna acknowledged, the chapters that follow are organized according to five themes: early dominion relations, environment and health, decolonization and liberation, Cold War and peace, and human rights, corporate rights, with the understanding that there is plenty of crossover and some variance between all of them. In addition, a few of the chapters in this collection work as initial surveys of emerging or relatively ignored subfields in Canadian international history, while the rest are more detailed case studies that showcase exciting new work within these more generalized themes. Points of continuity and contrast have been highlighted by the authors throughout, but as a way to conclude this introduction it is worth briefly summarizing how everything fits together.

The first section focuses on the early stages of Canada's engagement with the world, the period from the mid-nineteenth century to the early twentieth when its colonial and then dominion status meant that Britain was nominally in charge of its formal international relations. As all three authors in this section show, however, non-state actors and transnational networks complicate this story, and cast new light on a time period long dominated by traditional foreign relations histories. Laura Madokoro's case study traces how the fallout of the United States' Civil War – an event so essential to the process of Confederation – affected early international and transnational relationships, by examining the controversy over Canada harbouring the fugitive John Surratt, who was accused of being involved in Abraham Lincoln's assassination. In doing so, Madokoro also highlights the underexamined role of religion in Canada's international relations: the Catholic Church in Quebec offered Surratt sanctuary, despite the wishes of the colonial government of Canada East, the British Colonial Office, and the United States government. Madokoro's chapter showcases the complicated confluence of church, state, and individual rights. A focus on non-state actor networks is also central to Scott Johnston's exploration of Canada's place in the implementation of global standard time during the late nineteenth century. Non-state networks, he points out, have a long history, operating as a form of "paradiplomacy" that is as old as the Canadian state itself. Thus, scientists and engineers like Sanford Fleming contributed to Canada's international relations, even when the state's foreign relations were still within the purview of the British Empire. David Webster rounds the section out, expanding on the conversation started by Madokoro about the role that religion and church organizations have played in Canada's international history. Webster's chapter operates both as a survey of religion's larger role in Canadian history and as a series of small case studies of how religion serves to further elucidate Canada's long history of engagement with Asia. This goes beyond the acknowledged role of Catholic and Protestant missionaries as unofficial state representatives (and missionary work as a diplomatic training ground), but includes, too, the ideological and theological underpinnings of state policies towards Asia in the early twentieth century. Webster shows that Christian (and often racialized) understandings of the world informed how state and non-state actors "saw" potential Canadian relationships with all parts of Asia.

The second section of the collection breaks new ground in Canadian international history, addressing themes that have not received enough attention: environment and health. Daniel Macfarlane, who has almost single-handedly carried the torch for combining environmental and international history in Canada, contributes a broad survey that details the many ways that such an approach can pay dividends for historical study. Macfarlane demonstrates that as much as Canada has been influenced by and been a part of global development and environmental networks, ultimately, when the environment is considered, its international history is still largely defined by its relationship with the United States. Indeed, this relationship has had enormous environmental implications that both countries have largely ignored until very recently, and which define an entirely new subdiscipline in international history: environmental relations. Whitney Wood, on the other hand, focuses on human health and reproduction, an emerging field within environmental history but one that has received virtually no attention from international historians, despite health itself becoming a growing area of study. By looking at Canada's experience of the globalized natural birth movement promoted by Britain's Dr Grantly Dick-Read in the mid-twentieth century, Wood shows that what "counts" as international history expands enormously when non-state scientific and medical networks are taken into account. Wood also pushes the boundaries of what can be considered part of Canada's environmental relations, applying recent insights in environmental history that show human bodies as "environments" in and of themselves, which cross borders and interact with transnational networks and ideas about medical and reproductive health.

The third group of chapters are all case studies that consider Canada's international history within the larger twentieth-century story of decolonization, liberation, and relations with the so-called Third World. Maurice Labelle examines the writings of a relatively obscure and forgotten (though extraordinarily important) Arab-Canadian activist, Jim Peters (Jameel Naseem Boutras Ahwash), to show how Peters spent a lifetime working to combat anti-Orientalism in Canada. Anticipating the work of Edward Said by more than a decade, Peters promoted positive Canadian-Middle Eastern relations in the postcolonial period. Given the current state of Arab world concerns, specifically the rise of anti-Muslim sentiment in Canada and North

America, Labelle's chapter is particularly timely and important for shedding light on the historical legacy of non-Arab-Canadian relationships with the Arab Middle East and Arab Canadians. Will Langford, on the other hand, focuses on the process of modernization overseas, outlining the history of the government-sponsored NGO Canadian University Service Overseas in Tanzania in the wake of that country's independence from the British Empire. Langford shows that, even amongst non-state actors, overseas development was fundamentally a political process tied to ideological motivations like liberal internationalism or New Left socialism – but also to Cold War considerations and Canada's relationship with the "Third World." Amanda Ricci's contribution on the United Nations' 1975 World Conference on Women in Mexico City examines a similarly racialized aspect of Canada's international policies, even while state and non-state actors attempted to address gender-based inequalities. Using a critical feminist lens, Ricci argues that the conference operated at two levels for Canadian activists: the official, state-sponsored delegation of predominantly white women and men, whose priorities were dictated mostly by gender inequalities, and the "unofficial" group of activists, comprising mostly women of colour and Indigenous actors, whose interests in gender inequality also prioritized injustices associated with poverty, racism, and decolonization.

The fourth section of this collection focuses on a more "traditional" area of study in Canadian international history: Cold War and peace. Traditional though the topic might be, these chapters all shed new light by focusing on novel lenses of analysis, time periods, and neglected areas of study. Kailey Hansson's contribution, like other chapters in this volume, explores the international role of non-state actors, showing that more than just scientific, medical, and religious networks connected Canada to the world. Citing the increasingly influential literature on cultural diplomacy, Hansson explores how "high culture," in this case ballet, influenced and was influenced by Canada's understanding of its place in Cold War relationships, particularly in relation to the groundbreaking, state-funded work of Soviet dance companies like the Bolshoi. Susan Colbourn revisits the contradictions inherent in Pierre Trudeau's 1980s global "Peace Mission" and his Liberal government's decision to allow the United States to test cruise missiles in Alberta. As Colbourn notes, activism was not relegated to non-state actors alone, and opponents of the government's plans were vehement in pointing out the hypocrisy of Canada's depiction of itself in the world. This issue of appearance and reality is a thread taken up not only by Colbourn but by other contributors to this volume, such as Stephanie Bangarth and Jennifer Tunnicliffe. Overall, Colbourn makes an important case for not neglecting to look at elite actors, whose views and actions are of fundamental importance to the study of Canada in the World. Steven Lee, on the other hand, examines non-state peace activists in the 1980s, focusing on the Canadian Peace Congress and showing that the peace movement was by no means a homogenous one. The Peace Congress navigated between a declining influence in the 1980s, particularly due to its legacy as a Soviet apologist organization, and a desire to become more mainstream in its influence.

Lastly, the closing chapters of this collection contribute to the growing literature on international human rights scholarship, albeit in very different ways. Jennifer Tunnicliffe, who explores Canada's passage of one the world's first laws against hate speech in 1970, argues that human rights activism and diplomacy have operated at domestic and international global scales, and that an understanding of both is necessary to properly assess the history of human rights and its impact on Canada's international relationships. Tunnicliffe situates the debates leading up to Canada's influential law within the confluence of domestic politics – particularly the rise of anti-Semitism in 1960s Canada – and global efforts against similar incidents under the auspices of the UN. Both sides of the debate around hate speech laws relied on different conceptions and definitions of human rights. Some promoted the rights of individual free expression, while others promoted the rights of groups to be protected from hate speech and the actions that it could incite; each side was complicated by shifting local and global contexts that influenced how such debates played out. Stephanie Bangarth explores a similarly complex definition of rights in Canadian history, arguing that the federal state has long favoured corporate over human rights. Like Webster's and Macfarlane's, Bangarth's chapter combines cases studies of corporate influences on Canada's international relations with a roadmap for future research in this area. As Bangarth argues, Canada's protection of corporate rights has manifested in many ways, with pernicious implications: selling "peaceful" nuclear technology and natural resources to dictatorial governments from the 1950s to the 1970s, which critics argued would be used to make weapons; condemning human rights violations in South Africa and Rhodesia while supporting corporate tourism to the same in the 1960s; and selling weapons to human rights violators like Saudi Arabia up to the present.

Overall, the contributions to *Undiplomatic History* seek to blur the lines dividing international, transnational, and global approaches to Canadian history. However, in blurring borders – both spatial and methodological – the papers herein have remained focused on issues connected to international relations. Here, then, is what differentiates the Canada in the World approach that we outline from other transnationally inflected histories of Canada, which often deal almost exclusively with non-state actors and issues disconnected from world politics. Like the new Canadian political history, this new Canadian international history should focus explicitly on political issues even as it brings novel transnational, global, and cultural approaches to the study of Canadians' dealings with the world.

This collection thus places traditional Canadian international history in a new context, namely a framework that takes account of the transnational, global, and cultural turns. In doing so, the United States and the World approach is our model. World politics, often broadly defined, is still our frame of reference – although international relations *per se* may not be the overriding issue for some of our contributors, and indeed some, such as Wood, push the very definition of what fits under the rubric of international relations. Ultimately, diplomats and other government officials play an important role worth examining, but they are not the only actors whose activities carry them beyond the state. As the contributors to this collection make clear, diplomacy of a kind has been practised by missionaries, migrants, corporations, students, activists, doctors, ballet dancers, and members of other networks that cross state borders. By throwing this wide variety of Canadians into the mix, *Undiplomatic History* complicates the history of how Canada and Canadians have interacted with the world.

NOTES

1 Although diplomacy is but a subset of international history, "diplomatic history" is often used interchangeably with "international history." We prefer the term "international history" for its greater flexibility and inclusiveness.

2 David Meren, "The Tragedies of Canadian International History," *Canadian Historical Review* 96, no. 4 (2015): 537–8. See also the responses to Meren's

essay by John English, Adam Chapnick, and Dominique Marshall in the
same issue.

3 John English, "The Second Time Around: Political Scientists Writing History," *Canadian Historical Review* 67, no. 1 (1986): 1–16; Robert Bothwell, "Jour-
ney to a Small Country: Only in Canada You Say? Pity," *International Journal*
50, no. 1 (1994–95): 128; Adam Chapnick, "Where Have All of Canada's
Diplomatic Historians Gone?," *International Journal* 65, no. 3 (2010): 725–37.

4 Carrying the torch for Canadian international history, Robert Bothwell,
Norman Hillmer, and John English have continued producing excellent
scholarship and providing vital mentorship to younger historians. Recent
essay collections in international history show that there are many younger
scholars active in the field as well: Colin McCullough and Robert Teigrob,
Canada and the United Nations: Legacies, Limits, Prospects (Montreal and
Kingston: McGill-Queen's University Press, 2017); Asa McKercher and
Galen Roger Perras, *Mike's World: Lester B. Pearson and Canadian External
Affairs* (Vancouver: UBC Press, 2017); Janice Cavell and Ryan Touhey,
Reassessing the Rogue Tory: Canadian Foreign Relations in the Diefenbaker Era
(Vancouver: UBC Press, 2018).

5 Andrew Cohen, *While Canada Slept: How We Lost Our Place in the World*
(Toronto: McClelland and Stewart, 2003).

6 Chapnick, "Where Have All of Canada's Diplomatic Historians Gone?," 732.

7 Critical views that seemingly form the nucleus of a revisionist school have
recently been advanced in Robert Teigrob, *Warming Up to the Cold War:
Canada and the United States' Coalition of the Willing, from Hiroshima to Korea*
(Toronto: University of Toronto Press, 2009); and Karen Dubinsky, Sean
Mills, and Scott Rutherford, *Canada and the Third World: Overlapping Histo-
ries* (Toronto: University of Toronto Press, 2016).

8 Jessica Murphy, "Canada to End Airstrikes in Syria and Iraq, New Prime
Minister Trudeau Says," *The Guardian*, 21 October 2015. It is also worth noting, of course, that Stephen Harper said almost exactly the same thing, with
opposite implications, shortly after he took office in 2006. As David Meren
points out, "Upon coming to power, the Harper Conservatives trumpeted
that 'Canada was back' on the world stage and employed the war in
Afghanistan to 're-brand' Canada and its foreign affairs, including reviving
elements of its imperial and military past as part of the national(ist) iconog-
raphy." See Meren, "The Tragedies of Canadian International History," 560.
See also Jessica Chin, "Justin Trudeau's Not the First Prime Minister to Say
'Canada Is Back,'" *Huffington Post Canada*, 1 December 2015, http://www
.huffingtonpost.ca/2015/12/01/canada-is-back-trudeau-harper_n_8688282
.html.

9 The new political history of Canada is connected to the Canadian Historical Association's Political History Group. For representative works, see Matthew Hayday, *Bilingual Today, United Tomorrow: Official Languages in Education and Canadian Federalism* (Montreal and Kingston: McGill-Queen's University Press, 2005); Marcel Martel, *Not This Time: Canadians, Public Policy and the Marijuana Question, 1961–1975* (Toronto: University of Toronto Press, 2006); Penny Bryden, *'A Justifiable Obsession': Conservative Ontario's Relations with Ottawa, 1943–1985* (Toronto: University of Toronto Press, 2013).

10 Donald Cameron Watt, "Some Aspects of A.J.P. Taylor's Work as Diplomatic Historian," *Journal of Modern History* 49, no. 1 (1977): 22.

11 Charles S. Maier, "Marking Time: The Historiography of International Relations," in *The Past Before Us: Contemporary Historical Writing in the United States*, edited by Michael Kammen (Ithaca: Cornell University Press, 1980), 357.

12 Zara Steiner, "On Writing International History: Chaps, Maps and Much More," *International Affairs* 73 (1997): 531–46. And see these excellent works reflecting this type of international history: Patrick Finney, ed., *Palgrave Advances in International History* (London: Palgrave Macmillan, 2005); Marc Trachtenberg, *The Craft of International History: A Guide to Method* (Princeton: Princeton University Press, 2006); Gordon Martel, ed., *A Companion to International History 1900–2001* (Oxford: Blackwell, 2007).

13 Gordon Craig, "The Historian and the Study of International Relations," *American Historical Review* 88, no. 1 (1983): 2; Arthur Marwick, *The Nature of History*, 3rd ed. (London: Macmillan, 1989), 94.

14 Patrick Finney, "International History, Theory, and the Origins of the Second World War," *Rethinking History* 1, no. 3 (1997): 375; Jessica Gienow-Hecht, "A Global Group of Worriers," *Diplomatic History* 26, no. 3 (2002): 481–91.

15 Akira Iriye, "Internationalizing International History," in *Rethinking American History in a Global Age: The Past, Present, and Future*, edited by Thomas Bender (New York: Palgrave Macmillan, 2012), 51.

16 David Thelen, "The Nation and Beyond: Transnational Perspectives on United States History," *Journal of American History* 86 (1999): 967. For leading theoretical and methodological explanations of transnational history, see Ann Curthoys and Marilyn Lake, *Connected Worlds: History in Transnational Perspective* (Canberra: ANU Press, 2006); Ian Tyrrell, *Transnational Nation: United States History in Global Perspective since 1789* (New York: Palgrave Macmillan, 2007); Chris Bayly et al., "AHR Conversation: On Transnational History," *American Historical Review* 111, no. 5 (2006); and Andrew Preston

and Doug Rossinow, *Outside In: The Transnational Circuitry of US History* (New York: Oxford University Press, 2017).

17 Alfred E. Eckes Jr and Thomas W. Zeiler, *Globalization and the American Century* (Cambridge: Cambridge University Press, 2003), 1.

18 As some have pointed out, transnational and global history, particularly in relation to the history of empire, has a long if unacknowledged pedigree. For a discussion of this point as it relates to Canada, see Paula Hastings and Jacob A.C. Remes, "Empire, Continent and Transnationalism in Canadian History: Essays in Honor of John Herd Thompson," *American Review of Canadian Studies* 45, no. 1 (2015): 1–7. For leading analyses of histories of the Atlantic and Pacific worlds: William O'Reilly, "Genealogies of Atlantic History," *Atlantic Studies* 1, no. 1 (2004): 66–84; Bernard Bailyn, *Atlantic History: Concept and Contours* (Cambridge, MA: Harvard University Press, 2005); Matt K. Matsuda, *Pacific Worlds: A History of Seas, Peoples, and Cultures* (Cambridge: Cambridge University Press, 2012); David Armitage and Alison Bashford, eds., *Pacific Histories: Ocean, Land, People* (New York: Palgrave Macmillan, 2014).

19 Paul S. Hulbo, "Editor's Note," *Diplomatic History* 1, no. 1 (1977): vi.

20 Michael Hunt, "The Long Crisis in US Diplomatic History: Coming to Closure," in *America in the World: The Historiography of American Foreign Relations since 1941*, edited by Michael J. Hogan (Cambridge: Cambridge University Press, 1995), 93.

21 Elizabeth Cobbs Hoffman, "Diplomatic History and the Meaning of Life: Toward a Global American History," *Diplomatic History* 21, no. 4 (1997): 500.

22 Susan Brewer, "'As Far As We Can': Culture and US Foreign Relations," in *A Companion to American Foreign Relations*, edited by Robert D. Schulzinger (Oxford: Blackwell, 2003), 17. For analyses of the historiographical, methodological, theoretical, and analytical changes to the field, see Frank Costigliola and Michael J. Hogan, eds., *America in the World: The Historiography of American Foreign Relations since 1941*, 2nd ed. (Cambridge: Cambridge University Press, 2014); and Frank Costigliola and Michael J. Hogan, eds., *Explaining the History of American Foreign Relations*, 3rd ed. (Cambridge: Cambridge University Press, 2016).

23 Michael J. Hogan and Thomas G. Paterson, *Explaining the History of American Foreign Relations*, 2nd ed. (Cambridge: Cambridge University Press, 2004), 9; Thomas W. Zeiler, "The Diplomatic Bandwagon: A State of the Field," *Journal of American History* 95, no. 4 (2009): 1053, 1072, 1055.

24 Erez Manela, "The United States in the World," in *American History Now*, edited by Eric Foner and Lisa McGirr (Philadelphia: Temple University Press, 2011), 201, 203. See also Kristin Hoganson, "Hop off the Bandwagon!

It's a Mass Movement, Not a Parade," *Journal of American History* 95, no. 4 (2009): 1087–91.

25 Merrill and Paterson, *Major Problems in American Foreign Relations*, xiv–xv.

26 Mario Del Pero, "On the Limits of Thomas Zeiler's Historiographical Triumphalism," *Journal of American History* 95, no. 4 (2009): 1080. And see, for instance, Robert Buzzanco, "Commentary: Where's the Beef? Culture without Power in the Study of U.S. Foreign Relations," *Diplomatic History* 24, no. 4 (2000): 623–32.

27 Jessica C.E. Gienow-Hecht, "What Bandwagon? Diplomatic History Today," *Journal of American History* 95, no. 4 (2009): 1086.

28 For a recent, comprehensive rundown of the transnational turn in Canada, see Karen Dubinsky, Adele Perry, and Henry Yu, eds., *Within and Without the Nation: Canadian History as Transnational History* (Toronto: University of Toronto Press, 2015).

29 Michael D. Behiels and Reginald C. Stuart, *Transnationalism: Canada-United States History into the 21st Century* (Montreal and Kingston: McGill-Queen's University Press, 2010).

30 For a sampling, see: Sean Mills, *A Place in the Sun: Haiti, Haitians, and the Remaking of Quebec* (Montreal and Kingston: McGill-Queen's University Press, 2016); Benjamin Bryce and Alexander Freund, eds., *Entangling Migration History: Borderlands and Transnationalism in the United States and Canada* (Gainesville: University Press of Florida, 2015); Maurice Demers, *Connected Struggles: Catholics, Nationalist, and Transnational Relations between Mexico and Québec, 1917–1945* (Montreal and Kingston: McGill-Queen's University Press, 2014); Harvey Amani Whitfield, *Blacks on the Border: The Black Refugees in British North America, 1815–1860* (Burlington: University Press of New England, 2006); and Karen Dubinsky, *Babies Without Borders: Adoption and Migration Across the Americas* (Toronto: University of Toronto Press, 2010).

31 Dominique Marshall, "Réponse à 'The Tragedies of Canadian International History': Un autre survol historiographique," *Canadian Historical Review* 96, no. 4 (2015): 583–9.

32 Laura Madokoro, "Family Reunification as International History: Rethinking Sino-Canadian Relations after 1970," *International Journal* 68, no. 4 (2013): 591–608; Laura Madokoro, "Not All Refugees Are Created Equal: Canada Welcomes Sopron Students and Staff in 1956," *Journal of the Canadian Historical Association* 19, no. 1 (2008): 253–78.

33 Tarah Brookfield, *Cold War Comforts: Canadian Women, Child Safety, and Global Insecurity* (Waterloo: Wilfrid Laurier University Press, 2012); Lara Campbell, Michael Dawson, and Catherine Gidney, *Worth Fighting For:*

Canada's Tradition of War Resistance from 1812 to the War on Terror (Toronto: Between the Lines, 2015); Jessica Squires, *Building Sanctuary: The Movement to Support Vietnam War Resisters in Canada, 1965–73* (Vancouver: UBC Press, 2014); Kathleen Rodgers, *Welcome to Resisterville: American Dissidents in British Columbia* (Vancouver: UBC Press, 2014); Stephanie D. Bangarth, *Voices Raised in Protest: Defending Citizens of Japanese Ancestry in North America, 1942–49* (Vancouver: UBC Press, 2008).

34 Cecilia Morgan, '*A Happy Holiday': English Canadians and Transatlantic Tourism, 1870–1930* (Toronto: University of Toronto Press, 2008); Daniel T. Rodgers, *Atlantic Crossings: Social Politics in a Progressive Age* (Cambridge, MA: Belknap Press, 2000); Nancy Christie, eds., *Transatlantic Subjects: Ideas, Identities, and Institutions in Post-Revolutionary British North America* (Montreal and Kingston: McGill-Queen's University Press, 2009); J.B. Brebner, *North Atlantic Triangle: The Interplay of Canada, the United States and Great Britain* (New Haven: Yale University Press, 1945).

35 Henry Yu, "Refracting Pacific Canada: Seeing Our Uncommon Past," *BC Studies* no. 156/157 (2007/08), 5. And see John Price, *Orienting Canada: Race, Empire, and the Transpacific* (Vancouver: UBC Press, 2011).

36 Older studies include: Steven Lee, "Canadian-Asian Experience: An Introductory Synthesis," *Journal of American-East-Asian Relations* 4, no. 3 (1995): 193–222; Paul M. Evans and Michael Frolic, eds., *Reluctant Adversaries: Canada and the People's Republic of China, 1949–1970* (Toronto: University of Toronto Press, 1991); Alvin Austin, *Saving China: Canadian Missionaries in the Middle Kingdom 1888–1959* (Toronto: University of Toronto Press, 1986). For new studies, see John Meehan, *The Dominion and the Rising Sun: Canada Encounters Japan, 1929–1941* (Vancouver: UBC Press, 2004); John Meehan, *Chasing the Dragon: Shanghai and Canada's Early Relations with China, 1858–1952* (Vancouver: UBC Press, 2011); Greg Donaghy and Patricia E. Roy, *Contradictory Impulses: Canada and Japan in the Twentieth Century* (Vancouver: UBC Press, 2008); and Kornel Chang, *Pacific Connections: The Making of the U.S.-Canadian Borderlands* (Berkeley: University of California Press, 2012).

37 Margaret MacMillan and Francine McKenzie, eds., *Parties Long Estranged: Canada and Australia in the 20th Century* (Vancouver: UBC Press, 2003); Lisa Chilton, *Agents of Empire: British Female Migration to Canada and Australia, 1860s–1930* (Toronto: University of Toronto Press, 2007).

38 Phillip Buckner, "Whatever Happened to the British Empire?," *Journal of the Canadian Historical Association* 4, no. 1 (1993): 3–34; Philip Buckner, ed., *Canada and the End of Empire* (Vancouver: UBC Press, 2005); C.P. Champion, *The Strange Demise of British Canada: The Liberals and Canadian Nationalism,*

1964–1968 (Montreal and Kingston: McGill-Queen's University Press, 2010); Katie Pickles, *Female Imperialism and National Identity: Imperial Order Daughters of the Empire* (Manchester: Manchester University Press, 2002); Phillip Buckner, ed., *Canada and the British World: Culture, Migration and Identity* (Vancouver: UBC Press, 2006); Phillip Buckner, ed., *Canada and the End of Empire* (Vancouver: UBC Press, 2004); Leigh Boucher, Jane Carey, and Katherine Ellinghaus, eds., *Re-Orienting Whiteness* (New York: Palgrave Macmillan, 2009); Kate Darian-Smith, Patricia Grimshaw, and Stuart Macintyre, *Britishness Abroad: Transnational Movements and Imperial Cultures* (Carlton: Melbourne University Press, 2007).

39 John Herd Thompson and Stephen Randall's survey of Canadian-American relations, for example, in addition to the standard political and economic approach, includes general examinations of Canadian-American labour, media, sports, and environmental relationships, including the many non-governmental actors that such activities have involved: John Herd Thompson and Steven J. Randall, *Canada and the United States: Ambivalent Allies*, 4th ed. (Montreal and Kingston: McGill-Queen's University Press, 2008). More recent works have made a valuable contribution by looking not only at the Canada-US relationship but at Canadian and United States history in parallel and in a transnational context: Robert Bothwell, *Your Country, My Country: A Unified History of the United States and Canada* (New York: Oxford University Press, 2015); and Stephen Azzi, *Reconcilable Differences: A History of Canada-US Relations* (Don Mills: Oxford University Press Canada, 2015).

40 Steven High, *Industrial Sunset: The Making of North America's Rust Belt* (Toronto: University of Toronto Press, 2003); Tracy Neumann, *Remaking the Rust Belt: The Postindustrial Transformation of North America* (Philadelphia: University of Pennsylvania Press, 2016).

41 Theodore Binnema, *Common and Contested Ground: A Human and Environmental History of the Northwestern Plains* (Norman: University of Oklahoma Press, 2001); William G. Robbins and Katrine Barber, *Nature's Northwest: The North Pacific Slope in the Twentieth Century* (Tucson: University of Arizona Press, 2011); Paul W. Hirt, *Wired Northwest*; and Lissa K. Wadewitz, *The Nature of Borders: Salmon, Boundaries, and Bandits on the Salish Sea* (Seattle: University of Washington Press, 2012). For studies that include Mexican regions as well as Canadian and US ones, see Sterling Evans, *Bound in Twine: The History and Ecology of the Henequen-Wheat Complex for Mexico and the American and Canadian Plains, 1880–1950* (College Station: Texas A&M University Press, 2007), and Richard White, *Railroaded: The Transcontinentals and the Making of Modern America* (New York: W.W. Norton and Co., 2012).

42 See, for example: Stephen T. Moore, *Bootleggers and Borders: The Paradox of Prohibition on a Canada-U.S. Borderland* (Lincoln: University of Nebraska Press, 2014); Benjamin Johnson and Andrew Greybill, eds., *Bridging National Borders in North American Transnational and Comparative Histories* (Durham: Duke University Press, 2010); Sterling Evans, ed., *The Borderlands of the American and Canadian Wests: Essays on Regional History of the Forty-Ninth Parallel* (Lincoln: University of Nebraska Press, 2006); John M. Findley and Ken S. Coates, eds., *Parallel Destinies: Canadian-American Relations West of the Rockies* (Seattle: University of Washington Press, 2002); Paul W. Hirt, ed., *Terra Pacifica: People and Place in the Northwest States and Western Canada* (Pullman: Washington State University Press, 1998); Randy William Widdis, *Permeable Border: The Great Lakes Basin as Transnational Region, 1650–1990* (Calgary: University of Calgary Press, 2005).

43 Kurkpatrick Dorsey, "Dealing with the Dinosaur (and Its Swamp): Putting the Environment in Diplomatic History," *Diplomatic History* 29, no. 4 (2005): 573–87; Kurkpatrick Dorsey, *The Dawn of Conservation Diplomacy: U.S.-Canadian Wildlife Protection Treaties in the Progressive Era* (Seattle: University of Washington Press, 1998); Wadewitz, *The Nature of Borders*; Daniel Macfarlane, *Negotiating a River: Canada, the U.S., and the St. Lawrence Seaway* (Vancouver: UBC Press, 2014).

44 Ruth Compton Brouwer, *Canada's Global Villagers: CUSO in Development, 1961–86* (Vancouver: UBC Press, 2013); Christopher R. Kilford, *The Other Cold War: Canada's Military Assistance to the Developing World 1945–1975* (Kingston, ON: Canadian Defence Academy Press, 2010); Karen Dubinsky, Sean Mills, and Scott Rutherford, *Canada and the Third World: Overlapping Histories* (Toronto: University of Toronto Press, 2016); Tamara Myers, "Local Action and Global Imagining: Youth, International Development, and the Walkathon Phenomenon in Sixties' and Seventies' Canada," *Diplomatic History* 3, no. 2 (2014): 282–93; Magali Deleuze, *L'une et l'autre indépendance: Les médias au Québec et la guerre d'Algérie (1954–1964)* (Montreal: Point de Fuite, 2001); David Meren, "An Atmosphere of *Libération*: The Role of Decolonization in the France-Quebec Rapprochement of the 1960s," *Canadian Historical Review* 92, no. 2 (2011): 263–94; David Meren, *With Friends Like These: Entangled Nationalisms and the Canada-Quebec-France Triangle* (Vancouver: UBC Press, 2012); Sean Mills, *The Empire Within: Postcolonial Thought and Political Activism in Sixties Montreal* (Montreal and Kingston: McGill-Queen's University Press, 2010).

45 Robin S. Gendron, *Towards a Francophone Community: Canada's Relations with France and French Africa, 1945–1968* (Montreal and Kingston: McGill-Queen's University Press, 2006); David Webster, *Fire and the Full Moon:*

Canada and Indonesia in a Decolonizing World (Vancouver: UBC Press, 2009); Kevin Spooner, *Canada, the Congo Crisis, and UN Peacekeeping, 1960–1964* (Vancouver: UBC Press, 2009); Michael K. Carroll, *Pearson's Peacekeepers: Canada and the United Nations Emergency Force, 1956–67* (Vancouver: UBC Press, 2009); and Ryan Touhey, *Conflicting Visions: Canada and India in the Cold War World, 1946–76* (Vancouver: UBC Press, 2010).

46 Geoff Read and Todd Webb, "'The Catholic Mahdi of the North West': Louis Riel and the Metis Resistance in Transatlantic and Imperial Context," *Canadian Historical Review* 93, no. 2 (2012): 171–95; Scott Rutherford, "Canada's Other Red Scare: Rights, Decolonization, and Indigenous Political Protest in the Global Sixties" (PhD diss., Queen's University, 2011); Penelope Edmonds, *Urbanizing Frontiers: Indigenous Peoples and Settlers in 19th-Century Pacific Rim Cities* (Vancouver: UBC Press, 2010).

47 J.R. Miller, *Skyscrapers Hide the Heavens: A History of Indian-White Relations in Canada* (Toronto: University of Toronto Press, 2000 [1991]); J.R. Miller, *Compact, Contract, Covenant: Aboriginal Treaty-Making in Canada* (Toronto: University of Toronto Press, 2009).

48 Richard Veatch, *Canada and the League of Nations* (Toronto: University of Toronto Press, 1975), chap. 7; J.R. Miller, "Petitioning the Great White Mother: First Nations' Organizations and Lobbying in London," in *Canada and the End of Empire*, edited by Philip Buckner (Vancouver: UBC Press), 299–318.

SECTION ONE

Early Dominion Relations

1

The Politics of Sanctuary: John Surratt, the Catholic Church, and the US Civil War

LAURA MADOKORO

Had it not been for the appearance of one John Surratt, a.k.a. "John Harrison" or "Charley Armstrong," in the small hamlet of St Liboire, Quebec (about 45 km north as the crow flies from Montreal), Father Charles Boucher might be unknown to the historical record beyond what remains of local nineteenth-century parish records. But in the spring of 1865 Father Boucher became part of a sanctuary incident involving Confederate sympathizers in the Province of Canada and the United States and Catholic supporters in the province. This episode revealed a difference of opinion between the members of the Catholic Church who provided sanctuary and supported the Confederate cause, and the British colonial officials and American law authorities charged with apprehending John Surratt, who was suspected as an accomplice in the assassination of US president Abraham Lincoln. It is an episode that has long captured the imagination of scholars and a general public hungry for conspiracy stories and stories of subversion, but one whose diplomatic implications have yet to be fully elaborated.[1]

Indeed, as David Webster persuasively argues in his contribution to this volume, the role of religion and religious organizations is still an under-studied aspect of the history of Canada's international relations. Although the missionary influence has been the focus of considerable study, the challenge of thinking about religious actors as central rather than peripheral to the evolution of Canada's international history remains to be overcome.[2] This chapter is concerned, in particular, with how church communities have operated with agendas and political objectives of their own, some of which had implications that are not necessarily recognized by contemporary diplomatic circles or by historians of international history.

British colonial authorities viewed the nineteenth-century Catholic Church with suspicion, feeling threatened by the influence it wielded on the daily lives of its parishioners.[3] As Steve Lee underscores in his chapter on the Canadian Peace Congress, civil society is often seen as operating at loggerheads with the foreign policy establishment when it comes to the history of Canada's international relations. Yet the nineteenth-century Catholic Church was not a monolithic actor and the offer of sanctuary could divide, as well as unite, concerned parties. This difference of opinion is akin to the variety of opinions that Amanda Ricci highlights in her contribution to this volume.

Religion is particularly important in terms of the lives of migrants and settlers, and the evolution of Canada's political and cultural landscape. Religion often caused people to think about their world differently from the way it was envisioned by colonial officials and diplomats. Historian J.S. Little describes religion as "intrinsic" to the daily lives of nineteenth-century Canadians.[4] Indeed, exploring the history of international relations through the eyes of non-state religious actors demonstrates how issues of concern to members of the church have often been ignored or marginalized in investigations of formal diplomatic relations. Yet exploring these issues is terribly important for understanding the variety of international relations that animated the lives of the residents of the Province of Canada.

The sanctuary offer to John Surratt in 1865 provides a window through which to explore relations that involved Civil War America and British colonial authorities in Canada, but which were driven by concerns about merit, loyalty, and protection on the ground, rather than concerns about state relations at the formal diplomatic level. The sanctuary offer to John Surratt, in other words, is a case of undiplomatic relations, and a neglected example of undiplomatic history of the sort to which this volume seeks to draw attention. Undiplomatic relations, in the context of the history of sanctuary, are about individuals and groups that engage in the protection of individuals with international consequences, but who do so without sanction of the state, and often in direct opposition to the wishes of colonial or state authorities.

In April 1865, John Surratt – a native of Washington, DC – was twenty-one years old. A supporter of the Confederate cause, he had recently been engaged to work as a messenger in the Province of Canada for General Robert E. Lee, the leader of the Confederate military. A number of Confederate supporters and sympathizers had taken refuge in the Province of Canada during the war, and keeping communications open and swift was considered an important element in the fight against the North.

John's mother, Mary Surratt, ran a boarding house in Washington, one that was frequented by the society actor John Wilkes Booth. On Good Friday, 14 April 1865, President Lincoln attended a performance of Our American Cousin at Ford's Theater in Washington. Approaching Lincoln from behind, Booth shot and fatally wounded the US president. His accomplice, Lewis Paine, assaulted Secretary of State William Seward, causing critical but not fatal injuries. Within days, notices appeared indicating that John Surratt was a suspected accomplice and that there was a bounty of $25,000 on his head. Surratt, who was in upper New York State at the time of the assassination, heard news of the events in Washington and promptly returned to Montreal, where he had been based for much of the spring. Confederates and their supporters, including members of the Catholic Church, sheltered Surratt in Montreal and later in St Liboire, where he was housed in the home of Father Charles Boucher, the local Catholic priest.

Political loyalty was of paramount importance during the volatile years of the American Civil War, and Catholic loyalties, though not altogether suspect, were nevertheless viewed with skepticism in both the United States and the British colony. These sentiments were compounded by Union anxieties about the Province of Canada as a site of Confederate conspiracy and a possible launching pad for Confederate attacks on Union troops – fears which materialized during the St Albans raid of 1864. Catholic actions vis-à-vis John Surratt and other Confederates undermined efforts by British colonial authorities to keep the Province of Canada neutral during the Civil War years. Attending to the role that members of the Catholic Church played in the evolving relations between British colonial authorities, Confederates, and the Union government reveals how international relations were also forged by non-state actors pursuing political objectives of their own – ambitions that were sometimes at odds with those of British colonial authorities and elected American officials.[5]

THE PROVINCE OF CANADA AND THE AMERICAN CIVIL WAR

Sanctuary, in the Judeo-Christian tradition, is the act of providing protection in religious spaces.[6] In medieval England, sanctuary was generally provided to individuals who had committed crimes and needed time to make amends or secure a pardon.[7] The modern concept of sanctuary as it has evolved over the past few decades implies the innocence of those under protection. They are being sheltered precisely because their protectors believe in their innocence, contrary to the charges and accusations of the state. The question of sanctuary is therefore one that has become inherently subversive, pitting religious and secular actors against states desirous of deporting, arresting, or detaining wanted individuals. In Surratt's time, the conceptual move to innocence was not necessarily complete.

Scholars, and a sentimental Canadian public, have used the history of sanctuary to draw distinctions between Canada and the United States, particularly from the mid-eighteenth century to the present.[8] The flight of United Empire Loyalists both during and after the American Revolution, and the movement of an estimated 30,000–40,000 slaves along the Underground Railroad, have been instrumentalized to create the impression of Canada as a natural site of refuge for individuals fleeing violence, turmoil, and upheaval in racist and revolutionary America.[9] These incidents have contributed to a myth of benign humanitarianism in Canada – one that has disguised the history of Indigenous displacement and white settler colonialism. This powerful and compelling narrative has further obscured the contentious nature of these undertakings at the time they were being pursued, and specifically the implications of sheltering individuals who were sought by legal authorities on the other side of the border.

The sanctuary provided to John Surratt emerged from the broader context of the American Civil War, the Catholic Church's position in Canadian society, and contests about merit and loyalty as imagined by citizens and subjects. The outbreak of war in the United States pitted Confederate forces in the South against Union forces in the North. At stake, among other issues, was slavery and its expansion into the Western territories. In 1860, eleven states banded together to form the Confederate States of America in order to secede from the Union, following Lincoln's election on a platform that opposed the further expansion of slavery. Lincoln's administration refused to acknowledge or grant secession and civil war erupted in 1861.[10] With the conflict, questions of loyalty came to the fore and this had particular implications for observers, sympathizers, and participants in the Province of Canada.

An estimated 40,000 British subjects volunteered on both sides of the American Civil War.[11] However, this participation was only one aspect of how the Province of Canada was implicated in the revolutionary conflict to the south. The province was also a site of Confederate refuge and plots to attack and disturb Northern forces. Confederate agents began using the Province of Canada as a significant operating base almost from the onset of the war. By 1863, the American consul John Potter was cautioning his government that steps should be taken to protect the northern border states "to prevent the consummation of contemplated deeds of wickedness."[12] Though the number of Confederates in the Province of Canada appeared to be small, their presence was keenly felt, especially after rumours about possible attacks began to circulate.[13]

Part of the Confederate strategy was to "embroil" British North America in the conflict, in order to distract and diffuse the strength of Union forces.[14] These plots took concrete form in 1864, when Confederate allies successfully orchestrated a raid on St Albans, Vermont (a short 24 km from the border), seeking to create "an atmosphere that might have induced Northern retaliation" and diverted Northern troops from the Southern front.[15] The St Albans raid began on 19 October 1864 when Confederates, who had been quietly amassing in the village posing as Canadian visitors, launched an attack. They began by robbing three banks to obtain funds to support the Confederate cause, and proceeded to hold a number of people hostage in the village green before ultimately trying to burn St Albans to the ground. One person died in the violence, though the raiders succeeded in causing only minimal damage to the town's physical structures.

Fleeing to Canada, the raiders sought physical refuge as well as legal protection. In a critical ruling, the justices determined that because the raiders or "soldiers" were under Confederate orders, and because the Province of Canada was officially neutral, they could not be extradited to face criminal proceedings in the United States. The raiders went free (and were allowed to keep the funds they had stolen from the Vermont banks), much to the outrage of the Unionists and US consular representatives in Canada. Writing from Montreal, Consul Potter deemed that "little effort" had been "made to bring them to punishment."[16]

Moreover, he determined that the Canadian government was desperately trying to avoid the extradition issue and was content to leave the issue in the hands of the court. The consul described the entire proceedings as "a mere farce."[17] News clippings reporting that the crowd in the courtroom cheered upon the dismissal were summarily dispatched to Washington, as was correspondence about how the raiders had gotten away with murder and robbery in the United States and how Montreal had become a hub for "refugees from the South, too cowardly to stay at home and fight."[18] According to Potter, in Montreal the Confederates were "entertained and treated with consideration … while they have been conspiring against the lives and property of peaceable citizens of the United States."[19]

The St Albans raid did two things. It turned many British officials in the Province of Canada against the Confederates, as they were leery of being drawn into a conflict against their wishes. It also made the Confederates more cautious about how they used the Province of Canada, particularly as the raid later proved instrumental in convincing the Colonial Office of the need to grant the province dominion status through federation.[20] Although Confederates continued to use the Province of Canada as a site to develop plans and strategies and to secure physical and material assistance, they pursued their solicitations more carefully, wary of alienating what limited support remained.[21]

This support dissipated almost entirely following news of Lincoln's assassination. American consuls at Montreal, Quebec, Toronto, and Ottawa reported of the sadness with which news of Lincoln's death attended British subjects in the Province of Canada.[22] Newspapers published numerous articles about the mourning public and their sentiments. The Canadian Methodist Episcopal Conference, for instance, expressed its "sincere and earnest sympathy," adding that "we feel ourselves called upon to denounce, in the severest terms, the unholy spirit that conceived and the human monster who executed the foul act of assassination."[23] Toronto's *Globe* newspaper lionized Lincoln, celebrating his heroic virtues. He was described as "remarkable for his kindness, generosity, and uprightness."[24] A story from the *Globe* on 17 April 1865 tracked Lincoln's life story. His politics after his inauguration were described as "moderate, but firm."[25] His battle against slavery was framed as pragmatic; Lincoln opposed the expansion of slavery, but not its outright abolition in the South until it became useful for the war. The story praised the efforts Lincoln made to offer "gradual and compensated emancipation" to states like Kentucky that were "too blind in their own interests to accept."[26] Lincoln's maintenance of social order and defence of the Union were seen as his greatest trait: "Though he had not assailed slavery as soon as some people thought he ought to have done, he took that step as soon as he could do without injury to the Union cause."[27]

Lincoln's assassination triggered speculation that Confederate agents in Canada were involved. According to historians Wilfrid Bovey and Joseph Boyko, there were grounds for these suspicions. Jacob Thompson, who had arrived in Canada in 1864 to lead the Confederate Secret Service, a loose organization whose members sided with the South, declared prior to the assassination

> that he had his friends, Confederates, all over the Northern States who were ready and willing to go any length to serve the cause of the South, that he could at anytime have the tyrant Lincoln and any others of his advisors that he wanted put out of his way, and that they would not consider it a crime when done for the cause of the Confederacy.[28]

As speculation mounted about the size of the assassination conspiracy and the people who were potentially implicated, American officials developed a number of theories about Confederates in the province. Andrew Johnson, who assumed power after Lincoln's death, suggested that Confederate agents including Jacob Thompson, Clement Clay, Beverley Tucker, and George Sanders were being "harboured" in the Province of Canada.[29] In addition to the hunt for John Surratt, detailed below, there was also an initial search for John Wilkes Booth, who had visited Canada in 1864.[30]

As historian John Boyko has suggested, the civil war in the United States was a key factor leading to Confederation in 1867. To quote: "While saving itself by creating itself, Canada was intricately involved in the war's cause and course."[31] The assassination of President Lincoln certainly had an impact on formal diplomatic relations between British colonial and American officials. There was a groundswell of support in the province for the North, calling into question notions of neutrality. When Governor General Charles Monck received news that "persons who had planned the assassination of Lincoln were on their way to Quebec," he promised his full assistance to the American government.[32] Spontaneous vigilante groups also organized themselves to patrol the border with the intention of apprehending any suspected assassins. Despite their efforts, John Surratt arrived in Montreal a few days after the assassination. His intention was only ever to stay in Canada briefly. Writing in this diary, Surratt noted that he was

> safe again on British soil, and under the protection of a neutral power. It will give them some trouble to find me here, and still more to take me; but to prevent accidental discovery I will disguise myself by dying my hair and staining my skin. I must remain here for a time, and when an opportunity offers sail for Europe.[33]

Upon his arrival, John Surratt checked into Montreal's St Lawrence Hall Hotel on St James Street, using the alias Charley Armstrong.[34] From there, he was taken to St Liboire where he was sheltered in the home of Father Charles Boucher, the local Catholic priest. Surratt himself describes his flight as follows: "Montreal not safe; left it, therefore, last evening. Detectives about everywhere." He evaded authorities by leaving his first refuge with a supporter. Each man took a separate taxi and as a result the detectives did not know whom to follow. A man "previously engaged" to take him across the river did so, and "a young lady guided him across the country to a village on the Grand Trunk railroad called San Leben (St Liboire)."[35] About idyllic St Liboire, Surratt quickly concluded, "I shall not be looked for in this retired place."[36]

According to all available accounts, Father Boucher did not know that Surratt was a wanted accomplice in the assassination of President Lincoln, understanding only that a Catholic American in ill health needed to recover from his bouts of "chills." Surratt spent most of his four months in St Liboire in hiding, "secreted in a dark room, from which he never came out except a few times, when he would go out late at night and take a walk."[37] Midway through the summer, Boucher's young maid discovered Surratt hidden away in the back room when she peeked under a crack in the door. Dr Lewis J.A. McMillan, who encountered Surratt on his later flight to Europe, recounted that "the story was immediately circulated around the village that the priest had a woman in his bed-room hiding. Then the priest told him that he could keep him no longer; that he must find other quarters."[38]

Surratt was quickly removed from the priest's house and taken to Murray's Bay (present-day La Malbaie, once a summer pleasure spot for President Taft and former governor general Viscount Byng of

Figure 1.1   John Surratt wearing his papal zouave uniform.
Surratt served in the papal guard in Italy after his refuge
in Canada.

Vimy), before he returned to Montreal where members of the
Catholic Church again supported him. On this occasion, he was sheltered at 116 Cemetery Street, "a quiet place just behind the Catholic
Bishop's Place" and the home of the father of the priest Larcille
Lapierre (canon to Ignace Bourget, with whom General Lee had associations). Despite Surratt's efforts at subterfuge, the American consul
at Quebec, Charles Ogden, was able to report to the US State Department at the end of May that Surratt was likely still in Canada. Surratt
and his supporters clearly felt that he was in danger of arrest, so it was
arranged for him to board a ship bound for the port of Liverpool. He
left Canada on 5 September 1865. In his diary, he noted that he "bade

farewell to those kind friends who have so long given me a shelter," adding, "may their safety never be endangered, or their peace and happiness disturbed."[39]

Consul Potter and others suspected early on that members of the Catholic Church were involved in sheltering Surratt. In making this suggestion to Secretary of State Seward, Potter made mention of Dr Luke Blackburn. Blackburn was a Confederate runner and one of the St Albans raiders, who was arrested on 19 May 1865 for violating the neutrality of the Province of Canada by conspiring to murder people in the United States; he was accused of mailing them clothing infected with yellow fever. Potter made pointed reference to the fact that Catholic institutions had sheltered Blackburn.[40]

Why did many Catholics, especially French Canadian Catholics, support the Confederate cause? And why did members of the church shelter John Surratt? As an answer to the first question, scholars have pointed to the Catholic Church in Canada's general "disdain" for American society, and particularly its impression (as expressed in newspaper editorials) that the United States was a nation "without cohesion" and the "most immoral country in the world."[41] Crucially, historian Preston Jones observes, "in the view of the majority of French Quebec's opinion makers, monarchies were superior to republics; parliamentary democracy was superior to what they perceived to be American democracy run amok, and working the land was superior to urban living." Jones suggests that this worldview "led French Quebeckers to sympathize with the Confederacy," given that in their general assessment of the Civil War, the North and Union Troops were "barbaric" and guilty of "all sorts of excesses."[42]

The answer to the second question is more complicated, for it is unlikely that the church hierarchy sanctioned the offer of sanctuary to John Surratt.[43] Rather, individual members of the church appear to have acted of their own volition.[44] Certainly, John Surratt's Catholicism contributed to a sense that he was someone deserving of protection. Surratt had attended St Charles College, run by members of the Sulpician Order, near Baltimore. According to historian Alexandra Lee Levin, Surratt "once entertained thoughts of becoming a priest."[45]

Levin argues that it was because Surratt was a member of the Catholic Church that supporters in Montreal, and later Father Boucher in St Liboire, sheltered him upon his arrival in Canada.

Regardless of the degree of official church sanction, the decision by certain French Catholics to protect John Surratt in his flight from the United States was an act of defiance in the face of both British and American authorities.[46] That defiance was animated by the complicated position of the Catholic Church and its followers in the United States and the Province of Canada in the mid-nineteenth century.[47] For Catholic Americans, the Civil War rep-resented, in part, an opportunity to prove their loyalties to either the Northern or Confederate cause. Approximately 200,000 Catholics served in the Union army, and dozens of priests and nuns worked in wartime hospitals. Thousands of others served and fought on the Confederate side.[48] This service had both domestic and international implications. Many Irish Catholics enlisted in the Union army, and were "socialized into Fenianism," becoming ardent nationalists and opponents of British rule in Ireland.[49]

As the war progressed, the terrible losses and violence caused many Catholics to withdraw their support for either side, demonstrating increasing support for the anti-war faction. This support invited suspicions about them as potential citizens of the republic.[50] These suspicions multiplied following the violent draft riots in New York City in July 1863, in which there was heavy Catholic participation.[51] Historian William Kurtz concludes that the war ultimately "alienated most northern Catholics and their leaders, causing them to seek refuge in a separate Catholic subculture after the war."[52] As a result, there was an enduring concern that Catholicism posed a "threat to America's republican government and institutions."[53]

The position of Catholics in the American republic, as well as the Province of Canada, where the contest over the hearts and minds of subjects was largely divided along linguistic and religious lines, created more than a Catholic subculture.[54] It fostered networks of concern across borders, entangling the Province of Canada in the turmoil of the American Civil War and the drama of President Lincoln's assassination. Historian Preston Jones notes, "between 1851 and 1871 some 105,000 Quebeckers, the overwhelming majority of them French-speaking Catholics, emigrated to the United States."[55] With friends and family immediately involved in or affected by the conflict,

French-Canadian Catholics were keenly attuned to events in the United States, and, following in the lead of church leaders, very often critical of what was transpiring south of the border.[56]

Nevertheless, upon Lincoln's assassination, French Catholics – like other Canadians – expressed outrage and grief at the shocking crime. Critically, Catholic dismay at Lincoln's assassination was not bounded by geopolitical borders as suggested by previous scholarship. Kurtz, for instance, emphasized that upon Lincoln's assassination, "pro-war and anti-war Catholics, like Democrats and Republicans, were united in their denunciation of the heinous crime. They considered Booth's actions an attack on national stability and social order."[57] There was also a transnational dimension to this response, in addition to a nationally focused one. As Kurtz further concluded, "Catholic remorse over the death of Lincoln, though sincere, did little to mitigate their reputation for opposition to the war and to the president personally."[58]

This continued mistrust can partly be explained by the trial of Mary Surratt and the flight, and subsequent trials, of her son John. Mary Surratt converted to Catholicism in her youth. Widowed at the age of thirty-nine, Mary earned a living by keeping a boarding house in Washington, DC. It was this house, and the fact that John Wilkes Booth and other alleged conspirators kept counsel there, that implicated Mary Surratt in Lincoln's murder. Charged with treason, she was tried with seven others for "maliciously, unlawfully, and traitorously, and in aid of the existing armed rebellion against the United States of America," conspiring "to kill and murder, within the Military Department of Washington, and within the fortified and intrenched lines thereof, Abraham Lincoln, late, and at the time of said combining, confederating, and conspiring, President of the United States of America and Commander-in-Chief of the Army and Navy thereof."[59]

Mary Surratt was found guilty, and when she was hanged on 7 July 1865, she became the first woman to be federally executed in the United States. There was rapt coverage of her trial in Canada, including details of her meetings with Catholic priests. The *Globe* implied her guilt from the outset by questioning her gendered behaviour, describing her as having a "masculine character" evidenced by her "control over her nerves" and her "Amazonian figure."[60] By all accounts, John Surratt, still in hiding in Quebec, had no idea about the gravity of his mother's situation. An entry in his diary from the time reads:

I find the Yankees are commencing what they call the trial with closed doors. Secret plottings to take the life of a few poor victims, and one a woman. The people and the press will cry such a thing down, or I am much mistaken. I am safe here at any rate, under the protection of those professing my own religion. I have sought sanctuary, and have found it. While here there is neither fear of betrayal, nor risk of discovery.[61]

There are hints that his hosts sheltered him from his mother's sentence and later execution in order to prevent him from returning to the United States and giving himself up in her stead – the suspicion being that both Surratts would be executed if John returned, and that there would be no trade as rumours had initially suggested.

THE DIPLOMACY OF SANCTUARY

The decision by members of the Catholic Church to provide sanctuary to John Surratt and to provide support to the Confederate cause more generally had very real, and very consequential, diplomatic ramifications; the sympathy shown to the Confederate cause, and the inability of British colonial officials to maintain a claimed status of official neutrality, ultimately contributed to the American abrogation of the Reciprocity Treaty in 1866 and Confederation in 1867. Yet the immediate diplomatic response to the offer of sanctuary was not as palatable as one might have expected given the eventual fallout.

Indeed, the American consul in Montreal, John Potter, was almost alone in his determined pursuit of John Surratt and his supporters. Consul Potter followed accounts of John Surratt's arrival and movements closely, noting that upon his arrival in the city, the hotel clerk described him as "a tall man of 24 or 25 years of age, light brown hair, without beard."[62] Yet although Potter attempted to keep a close eye on Surratt and his activities, it is clear that his efforts were futile due to the lack of coordination from authorities in the United States. Despite the fact that detectives were sent from Washington "for the purpose of arresting Surratt," the consul considered the situation to be entirely mishandled. He declared "that if the letter in the possession of these officers had been sent here, Surratt without doubt would have been arrested." He complained further that "since the death of the President I have received no instructions or communications of any kind from Washington in relation to the matter." As a result, Potter operated largely independently.

Potter was determined in his efforts because he harboured deep suspicions that some of the St Albans raiders were connected to the plot to assassinate Lincoln, and were involved in the protection of John Surratt. As Potter observed, those connected with the raid conveniently left Montreal before the "commission of the crime and have not since been seen." Nevertheless, Potter did attempt to uncover Surratt's whereabouts, notably sending out an officer to search for, and arrest, the man who drove the wagon in which it was believed Surratt left the city.

The question of Surratt's sanctuary implicated more than one person alleged to have been involved in treason and murder; it spoke to a significant Confederate presence in Canada. In correspondence with Secretary of State Seward, Potter made direct reference to the "refugees" from the South who had been "harboured" in Canada since the start of the rebellion.[63] The Consul alleged that Surratt was in close connection with the Confederate leaders in Canada – those behind the St Albans raid and the higher-ups who fled as well. Potter declared:

> It is my opinion that the Government of the United States should demand of the Canadian authorities that these men shall be expelled from Canada; and if the Canadian Govt. should refuse to take such action, that all intercourse between Canada and the United States should cease.

Not only did Consul Potter suggest that the US government be much more forceful in its demands for the extradition of Surratt and other Confederates, he recommended pulling the Reciprocity Treaty, which facilitated free trade between the Province of Canada and the United States, if Canada did not comply with such demands.[64]

The presence of Confederates in Canada, and the provision of sanctuary to John Surratt in particular, challenged the capacity of British colonial authorities to control the province's physical space. Diplomatically, however, there was – perhaps surprisingly – very little pressure for them to do something about Surratt specifically. There is no evidence that John Surratt's presence in Canada ever commanded the attention of the British minister at Washington or the governor general (though, as noted previously, Governor General Viscount Charles Monck had indicated his willingness to assist in the apprehension of Lincoln's assassins).[65] Union and British colonial officials were far more concerned with the presence of Confederates in Canada more generally. Governor General Monck, for instance, detailed concerns about Fenianism, the Civil War, and Confederates in his private and official correspondence without ever mentioning Surratt's case by name.[66]

Newspapers hint at some of the preoccupations about Surratt, beyond those of official domestic and diplomatic circles. In Toronto, the *Globe* provided rapt coverage of Lincoln's assassination with somewhat more ambiguous accounts of Surratt's sanctuary and the manhunt that resulted. Editors at the *Globe* were outraged at Lincoln's murder and the possibility that Confederate organizers and the Catholic Church had assisted Surratt and other assassins through the provision of refuge and sanctuary. Throughout the spring of 1865, the *Globe* dedicated considerable attention and coverage to the Canadian connection to the assassination plot, urging cooperation with the Union cause. The newspaper relayed the statements of American newspapers and officials including the secretary of war, Edwin Stanton asserting that the president's murder was organized in Canada.[67] People knew that Booth had visited Canada, had contact with Jacob Thompson, Larry McDonald, and Clement Clay – all Confederate organizers. One article quoted an opinion expressed by the editor of the *Montreal Gazette* that read, "we can have no hesitation in stating that it is the duty of the Canadian Government and people" to do what is necessary to capture and extradite the men accused of involvement with the president's assassination. In another article, the *Globe*'s Washington correspondent was angry that the accused had "violated our (Canada's) territory as neutrals," and argued that if Canada did not quickly extradite them, the United States should reciprocate by not extraditing bank robbers fleeing Montreal in the future.[68]

Yet despite the press coverage, there is no mention of Surratt in the records of the Legislative Assembly of the Province of Canada as the third session stopped sitting in March 1865 and only resumed at the end of August. By that time, the intensity of the manhunt had abated, and although Surratt was still in Canada, he was soon to depart. Indeed, as a result of the legislative calendar, the parliamentary record is entirely silent on Lincoln's assassination as well.[69] Yet it is clear from available records that Surratt was the subject of great interest among English and French newspaper writers, as well as to the American consul in Montreal. Combined with the anti-Catholic sentiment discussed previously, the archival record suggests that questions of

sanctuary were not necessarily illuminated or defined by official discourses, but that they wove themselves throughout the historical
record, emerging from key pressure points and evading mention
along more formal diplomatic lines.

CONCLUSIONS

After a few short months in Canada, John Surratt left for Liverpool
and ultimately took refuge in the Papal Army where he was recognized, captured, and returned to the United States in February 1867.
After a mistrial, the case against him was dismissed. He proceeded to
lead a long and some might suspect rather happy life, pursuing a number of different professional endeavours (including a public lecture
tour to promote his innocence). He married Mary Victorine Hunter,
fathered seven children, and passed away at the age of seventy-two.[70]

The provision of sanctuary by members of the Catholic Church to a
wanted fugitive further embroiled British authorities in events that
were ravaging the American republic. This, despite persistent efforts by
colonial officials to safeguard claims to official neutrality. American
consular officials followed Surratt's movements through the Province
of Canada with a keen eye, attributing responsibility for his protection
to Confederate sympathizers as well as the Catholic Church. Surratt's
presence in Canada, as well as that of other Confederates, encouraged
American officials to press for extradition, while some, such as US
Consul John Potter, wanted to hold the Reciprocity Treaty hostage to
extradition demands.

As such, there were very real implications, at the formal diplomatic
level, to the offer of sanctuary to John Surratt. In providing sanctuary
to John Surratt, members of the Catholic Church determined him to
be worthy of protection, a decision that went against the views of the
Union government in the United States and American diplomats in
Canada. The decision also undermined any claims by British colonial
officials to official neutrality. As such, the offer of sanctuary was a pro-
foundly political one, with repercussions that members of the
Catholic Church may or may not have been aware of when they provided refuge.

The challenge for historians is to reconcile this undiplomatic history with the surviving diplomatic record, which points to profound
engagement by the American consul in Montreal, but general disin-
terest in Surratt himself among more senior officials and elected rep-

resentatives in Canada. How is one to assess the impact of this single act of sanctuary in both diplomatic and undiplomatic terms? One answer lies in a reminder that the relationships between states are not governed by states alone but rather are informed and shaped by a myriad of relationships involving non-state actors. In this instance, members of the Catholic Church advanced a political agenda of their own, siding with the Confederate cause in a direct challenge to the Union government and British colonial officials.

The horror and sadness that greeted news of Lincoln's assassination made the provision of sanctuary to John Surratt unpalatable for many. At the same time, the protection of individuals was important to Confederates and their supporters who doubted the possibilities of a fair trial in the turbulent period after the assassination and President Johnson's time in office. The offer of sanctuary to John Surratt therefore created alliances among some while sowing divisions among others. Significantly, these bonds or divisions were not forged along geopolitical lines. Rather, they were the product of religious outlooks and ideological views informed by perceptions of loyalty, virtue, and righteousness in the context of the bloody American Civil War.

ACKNOWLEDGMENTS

This chapter was researched and written with generous support from the Social Sciences and Humanities Research Council of Canada. My thanks to Phil Van Huizen and Asa McKercher for their encouragement. Dexter Docherty provided superb research support and Bradley Miller provided invaluable guidance on American Consular record sources.

NOTES

1 Most recently, the story of John Surratt was featured in Robert Redford's Hollywood production *The Conspirator* (2010).

2 See for instance work by Alvyn Austin, *China's Millions: The China Inland Mission and Late Qing Society, 1832–1905* (Grand Rapids: William B. Eerdmans, 2007); Jamie S. Scott, *Canadian Missionaries, Indigenous Peoples: Representing Religion at Home and Abroad* (Toronto: University of Toronto Press, 2005); Alvyn Austin, *Saving China: Canadian Missionaries in the Middle Kingdom, 1888–1959* (Toronto: University of Toronto Press, 1986). See also works by Ruth Compton Brouwer: "When Missions Became Development:

Ironies of 'NGO-ization' in Mainstream Canadian Churches in the 1960s," *Canadian Historical Review* 91, no. 4 (2010): 661–93; "A Disgrace to 'Christian Canada': Protestant Foreign Missionary Concerns about the Treatment of South Asians in Canada, 1907–1940," in *A Nation of Immigrants: Women, Workers, and Communities in Canadian History, 1840s–1960s,* edited by Franca Iacovetta, Paula Draper, and Robert Ventresca (Toronto: University of Toronto Press, 1998), 361–83; and *New Women for God: Canadian Presbyterian Women and India Missions, 1876–1914* (Toronto: University of Toronto Press, 1990).

3 Michel Ducharme, *The Idea of Liberty in Canada during the Age of Atlantic Revolutions, 1776–1838,* translated by Peter Feldstein (Montreal and Kingston: McGill-Queen's University Press, 2014), 11; Mark McGowan, *Michael Power: The Struggle to Build the Catholic Church on the Canadian Frontier* (Montreal: McGill-Queen's University Press, 2005), 59, 205.

4 J.S. Little, *The Other Quebec: Microhistorical Essays on Nineteenth-Century Religion and Society* (Toronto: University of Toronto Press, 2006).

5 For an illuminating discussion of internal conflicts in the early American Catholic Church, see Catherine O'Donnell, "John Carroll and the Origins of an American Catholic Church, 1783–1815," *William and Mary Quarterly* 68, no. 1 (2011): 101–26.

6 Canon 1179 of the 1917 Code of Canon Law, for instance, declared that Catholic churches had the right to provide sanctuary. Specifically, "A church enjoys the right of asylum, so that guilty persons who take refuge in it must not be taken from it, except in the case of necessity, without the consent of the ordinary, or at least of the rector of the church," as quoted in Linda Rabben, *Sanctuary and Asylum: A Social and Political History* (Seattle: University of Washington Press, 2016). See also Ignatius Bau, *This Ground Is Holy: Church Sanctuary and Central American Refugees* (New York: Paulist Press, 1985).

7 Shannon McSheffrey, *Seeking Sanctuary: Crime, Mercy, and Politics in English Courts, 1400–1550* (Oxford: Oxford University Press, 2017). See also J. Charles Cox, *The Sanctuaries and Sanctuary Seekers of Mediaeval England* (London: Forgotten Books, 2017).

8 See Larry Gara, *The Liberty Line: The Legend of the Underground Railroad* (Lexington: University Press of Kentucky, 1996). There is a strong inclination to connect contemporary sanctuary incidents with historical precedents such as the Underground Railroad and the associated mythology. See Renny Golden and Michael McConnell, *Sanctuary: The New Underground Railroad* (Maryknoll, NY: Orbis Books, 1986).

9 See Maya Jasanoff, *Liberty's Exiles: American Loyalists in the Revolutionary World* (New York: Knopf, 2011). This tendency has been further amplified

through scholarship on war resisters and dodgers in the Vietnam War era. See Jessica Squires, *Building Sanctuary: The Movement to Support Vietnam War Resisters in Canada, 1965–1973* (Vancouver: UBC Press, 2013).

10 There is a robust debate about the extent to which the American Civil War can be directly attributed to the issue of slavery, as opposed to general discontent in the union. See David Potter, *Impending Crisis: 1848–1861* (New York: Harper, 1976).

11 For details, see John Boyko, *Blood and Daring: How Canada Fought the American Civil War and Forged a Nation* (Toronto: Knopf Books, 2013). See also Fred Gaffen, *Cross-Border Warriors: Canadians in American Forces, Americans in Canadian Forces* (Toronto: Dundurn Press, 1996), and Richard Reid, *African Canadians in Union Blue: Volunteering for the Cause in the Civil War* (Vancouver: UBC Press, 2014).

12 Cited in Wilfrid Bovey, "Confederate Agents in Canada during the American Civil War," *Canadian Historical Review* 2, no. 1 (1921): 46.

13 Ibid., 51.

14 Historians suggest that these were generally inept efforts, "weakened by not being pursued with sufficient tenacity." See Robin Winks, *The Civil War Years: Canada and the United States*, 4th ed. (Montreal and Kingston: McGill-Queen's University Press, 1998), 377.

15 Ibid.

16 American Consul Potter to Assistant Secretary of State, 13 April 1865 despatches from United States consuls in Montreal, 1850–1906. Washington, DC: National Archives, National Archives and Records Administration, General Services Administration, 1959–1961.

17 American Consul Potter to Secretary of State Seward, 2 May 1865, despatches from United States consuls in Montreal, 1850–1906 (NARA).

18 Ibid. See newspaper clippings included in the same series.

19 Ibid.

20 Winks, *The Civil War Years*, 301. This was partly because the St Albans raid sowed all kinds of apprehensions about future possible talk so that "the border towns were thrown into a state of turmoil that lasted until the following spring." According to Winks, there were rumours "that two thousand raiders were to descend upon Plattsburg, Malone and Ogdensburg in New York" and that Confederate agents had essentially been given a blank cheque as far as operating the border was concerned.

21 Bovey, "Confederate Agents in Canada," 55.

22 Ibid., 56.

23 "Resolutions of the Canadian Methodist Episcopal Conference," *The Globe*, 6 May 1865: 2.

24 "Assassination of President Lincoln and Mr. Seward," *The Globe*, 15 April
    1865: 2.

25 "Abraham Lincoln," *The Globe*, 17 April 1865: 1

26 Ibid.

27 Ibid.

28 Bovey, "Confederate Agents in Canada," 46. John Boyko details the presence
    of a Confederate Canadian Cabinet at length. See *Blood and Daring*, 241.

29 Winks, *The Civil War Years*, 367.

30 "The Booth Conspiracy: Various Statements Respecting It," *The Globe*, 6 May
    1865: 2. Two of Booth's trunks mysteriously appeared in Rimouski after his
    death and this fuelled speculation for years that he was, in fact, hiding in
    Canada. See American Consul Potter to Secretary of State Seward, 30 May
    1865, despatches from United States consuls in Montreal, 1850–1906
    (NARA).

31 Boyko, *Blood and Daring*, 1.

32 Winks, *The Civil War Years*, 367.

33 Entry dated 18 April 1965, John H. Surratt, *The Private Journal and Diary of
    John H. Surratt, the Conspirator*, edited by Dion Haco (New York: Frederic A.
    Brady, 1866).

34 Alexandra Lee Levin, "Who Hid John H. Surratt, the Lincoln Conspiracy
    Case Figure?" *Maryland Historical Review* 60, no. 2 (1965): 175.

35 Testimony from Lewis J.A. McMillan, *Trial of John H. Surratt in the Criminal
    Court for the District of Columbia, Hon. George P. Fisher Presiding* (Washington,
    DC: Govt. Print. Off., 1867), 472.

36 Entry dated 19 April 1865, John H. Surratt, *The Private Journal and Diary of
    John H. Surratt, the Conspirator*.

37 Testimony from Lewis J.A. McMillan, *Trial of John H. Surratt*, 474.

38 Ibid.

39 Entry dated 5 September 1865 in Surratt, *The Private Journal and Diary of
    John H. Surratt, the Conspirator*.

40 Consul Potter to William Hunter, Acting Secretary of State, 25 May 1865,
    despatches from United States consuls in Montreal, 1850–1906 (NARA).

41 Preston Jones, "Civil War, Culture War: French Quebec and the American
    War between the States," *Catholic Historical Review* 87, no. 1 (2001): 61.

42 Ibid, 63–4. These arguments are echoed by Boyko, who writes, "The destruc-
    tion of the United States through civil war and the Confederacy itself was,
    consequently, seen as a good thing by the Church hierarchy. Priests often
    equated Southerners with the Québecois – a beleaguered minority, fighting to
    preserve a unique way of life threatened by a more politically and economi-
    cally powerful enemy with no shared cultural values." *Blood and Daring*, 7.

43 Research in the records at the Catholic Diocese in Montreal reveal only
    mention of Lincoln's assassination. There is no reference to John Surratt or
    Father Charles Boucher.
44 Research on this question is ongoing, but so far, primary source research
    (including an investigation of the holdings of the Archdiocese of Montreal)
    have not revealed any decision by church hierarchies to offer sanctuary. Cer-
    tainly, rumours of Catholic involvement have been sensationalized in the
    intervening years, fuelling impressions of a self-serving and politically dis-
    loyal church in both the Province of Canada and Civil War America.
45 Levin, "Who Hid John H. Surratt," 178.
46 Writing for a popular audience about John Surratt's dramatic flight and
    refuge, the historian Michael Schein excitedly hints at a Catholic conspiracy
    to protect John Surratt and his mother Mary Surratt who was hanged for
    her alleged role in Lincoln's assassination. Michael Schein, *John Surratt:
    The Lincoln Assassin Who Got Away* (Seattle: Bennett and Hastings Publish-
    ing, 2015).
47 Historians have thoroughly documented the religious spirit that animated
    the early foundations of American nationalism and expansionism, evi-
    denced most prominently in discussions of America's "manifest destiny."
    See Matthew McCullough, *The Cross of War: Christian Nationalism and U.S.
    Expansion in the Spanish-American War* (Madison: University of Wisconsin
    Press, 2014). For much of that history, the Catholic Church occupied a
    marginal presence in American life despite its rapid growth following the
    arrival of large numbers of Catholics at the end of the Napoleonic Wars.
    Marginal, but nevertheless substantial in that the Catholic Church was a
    presence to be reckoned with. Jessica Harland-Jacobs argues that even
    though anti-Catholicism was obvious, the significant influence of the
    Roman Catholic Church meant that it had to be accommodated and
    couldn't simply be marginalized. See "Incorporating the King's New Sub-
    jects: Accommodation and Anti-Catholicism in the British Empire,
    1763–1815," *Journal of Religious History* 39, no. 2 (2015): 203–23. On the
    changing place of the Catholic Church in the United States and the
    Province of Canada, as well as the social lives of Irish Catholics, see Willie
    Jenkins, *Between Raid and Rebellion: The Irish in Buffalo and Toronto,
    1867–1916* (Montreal and Kingston: McGill-Queen's University Press,
    2013), 9. According to Stephen Kenny, "by 1860, there were 3,500,000
    Catholics in the United States, approximately 10 per cent of the popula-
    tion." Nevertheless, Catholicism continued to be vilified and Catholics
    were mistrusted as citizens of the new republic. See "A Prejudice that
    Rarely Utters Its Name: A Historiographical and Historical Reflection

upon North American Anti-Catholicism," *American Review of Canadian Studies* 32, no. 4 (2002), 649. Historian William Kurtz argues that anti-Catholic sentiment dates "back to the earliest foundations of the original colonies by Great Britain." He observes, "the colonies were overwhelmingly Protestant and seen as a means to counter Catholic French and Spanish economic and religious influence in the Western Hemisphere." *Excommunicated from the Union: How the Civil War Created a Separate Catholic America* (New York: Fordham University Press, 2015), 2.

48 Kurtz, *Excommunicated from the Union*, 4.

49 Ibid. See also Willie Jenkins, *Between Raid and Rebellion*, 5.

50 Kurtz, *Excommunicated from the Union*, 108.

51 Ibid., 109. To this, historian Stephen Kenny adds that anti-Catholicism was a "crucial and widespread societal phenomenon" in both the United States and British North America in the mid-to-late nineteenth century. See "A Prejudice that Rarely Utters Its Name," 665.

52 Kurtz, *Excommunicated from the Union*, 6. On the search for equality of treatment, see Dean Duncan, *Citizens or Papists? The Politics of Anti-Catholicism in New York, 1685–1821* (New York: Fordham University Press), 2005.

53 Kurtz, *Excommunicated from the Union*, 6.

54 As Michael Gauvreau and Ollivier Hubert underscore, the historiography on religion and social beliefs has long been divided along linguistic lines in Canada. See *Churches and Social Order in 19th and 20th Century Quebec* (Montreal and Kingston: McGill-Queen's University Press, 2006), 5. While the notion of blind followers needs to be heavily critiqued, particularly in the context of sanctuary offers where individual inclination is critical, it is still necessary to recognize the extensive social regulation and the close relationship between religion and identity in the mid-nineteenth century. As Gauvreau and Hubert suggest, "Over time, bishops controlled their clergy with growing efficiency, developed more precise ways of knowing and managing their personnel, and calibrated instruments by which to measure faith" (25). See also Michael Gauvreau and Nancy Christie, *Christian Churches and Their Peoples, 1840–1965: A Social History of Religion in Canada* (Toronto: University of Toronto Press, 2010), 6.

55 Preston Jones, "Civil War, Culture War: French Quebec and the American War between the States," *Catholic Historical Review* 87, no. 1 (2001): 57.

56 Ibid., 56.

57 Kurtz, *Excommunicated from the Union*, 125.

58 Ibid.

59 Ibid., 126.

60 "The Execution Of The Conspirators," *The Globe*, 11 July 1865: 1.

61 Entry dated 11 May 1965, John H. Surratt, *The Private Journal and Diary of John H. Surratt, the Conspirator.*

62 American Consul Potter to Secretary of State Seward, 25 April 1865, despatches from United States consuls in Montreal, 1850–1906 (NARA).

63 Ibid.

64 American Consul Potter to Secretary of State Seward, 2 May 1865, despatches from United States consuls in Montreal, 1850–1906 (NARA). The United States government cancelled the Reciprocity Treaty in 1866 in part because of the extenuating circumstances of the civil war but largely due to pressure from American protectionists.

65 A detailed study of the dispatches between the British minister at Washington and the governor general reveals no mention of John Surratt or his known aliases, John Harrison and Charley Armstrong. See Pre-Confederation despatches from the British Minister at Washington, www.heritage.canadiana.ca, accessed 24 May 2017.

66 See records preserved by Library and Archives Canada, Viscount Charles Monck. This is a preliminary assessment of the available correspondence and further research is required to determine whether Monck's correspondence contains any mention of John Surratt, a.k.a. John Harrison or Charley Armstrong, and Father Charles Boucher.

67 "The Booth Conspiracy," *The Globe*, 6 May 1865: 1.

68 "The Position of Affairs in the United States," *The Globe*, 9 May 1865.

69 This conclusion is drawn from a thorough investigation of the *Journals of the Legislative Council* and *Sessional Papers* from the fourth session of the eighth Provincial Parliament, 1865.

70 The *Globe* continued its coverage of Surratt with detailed reporting of his trials, receiving regular dispatches from the United States.

2

Making Time:
Transnational Networks
and the Establishment of Standard Time
in Canada and Beyond, 1867–1905

SCOTT JOHNSTON

The study of the past relies on a linear understanding of time: Monday before Tuesday, cause before effect, author before reader. Yet time itself has a history. How it is organized, measured, and communicated are all anchored in place, space, and, well, time. The late nineteenth-century attempt to standardize global timekeeping into hourly time zones was a highly politicized endeavour, with far-reaching social implications. The clock may know no bias or national boundary, but the transnational network of scientists, engineers, imperialists, and politicians involved in standardizing time certainly did.

Few countries took standard time more seriously than Canada. The wide longitudinal spread of Canada's geography, and the imminent completion of the Pacific railway, galvanized discussions of time reform, in which Canadian engineer Sandford Fleming played a prominent role. Fleming has since been etched into the national psyche as the mythical "inventor" of standard time – a recipient of his very own Heritage Minute – but "invention" had nothing to do with it. Time reform was a long, slow, and communal process of lobbying and activism, tugging the strings of imperial and scientific networks. The Washington Conference of 1884 acted as the centrepiece for the establishment of a universal time system, but in reality, official diplomacy took its cue from these less formal networks.[1] Canada had a seat at the conference, but no vote. Instead, Fleming relied on "soft" diplomacy and networking to represent Canada's interests. This paper explores the scope of these networks, and their ability to shape international policy. But it also demonstrates their limits, as systems and prejudices constrained their scope of action, both within Canada's borders and beyond.

The chapter is structured narratively around Fleming's efforts to make his voice, and Canada's, heard in the global time reform debate – thereby situating Fleming and Canada within the wider historiography of the standardization of time.[2] But the argument made here goes beyond the history of timekeeping, exploring the way that Canadians dealt with Canada's dominion/colonial status, navigating imperial bureaucracy and scientific networks to engage with the world. Canada's status as a dominion of the British Empire in the 1880s meant that Canada had no right to determine its own foreign policy. It could not negotiate or treat with any other nation. Yet prominent British Canadians envisioned their country as a "new Britain" or even a "better Britain," and expected to play a central part in the modernization of the "British world."[3] The underlying theme of this chapter, then, is the way in which Canada, and Canadians, interacted with their global neighbours, and understood their place in the world, at a time when Canada's individual identity was superseded by imperial realities, and yet was encouraged by the empire's promises. Canadians like Fleming had to find surrogates for diplomacy, forging alternative networks, beyond high-level diplomacy, in order to influence international policy.

This chapter has two parts. The first is an exploration of Fleming's attempt to use scientific and engineering networks – in North America, in the British Empire, and internationally – to bring about time reform. The second examines his struggle to jump though the hoops of imperial bureaucracy to earn Canada representation at the Washington Conference of 1884. Both his successes and failures in these endeavours suggest that Canadians' connections with the rest of the world relied on robust, but often unofficial, personal and professional networks. In a time period when the new dominion lacked the ability and legal authority to conduct foreign policy, these transnational and transimperial networks were a major means of Canadian interaction with the world. Still, Fleming's difficulties underscore Canada's limited influence, especially in comparison to Britain and the United

States – something that Canadians would discover, for instance, during the Alaska Boundary dispute of 1903, when London sold out Canadian interests to Washington.

The history of Canadian diplomacy is an old field of study, and one that can benefit from adopting new trends in historical writing. The transnational turn, which begs historians to look beyond the state to other actors and networks operating across, and in spite of, national borders, has the potential to remake our understanding of global relations. The prospect of a new "undiplomatic" history of global networks and relationships is an exciting one, as it promises to supplement a focus on economics and security with social, cultural, and environmental factors, recognizing that they intersect in surprising ways. This chapter contributes to that undiplomatic history by suggesting that professional networks, particularly those of science and engineering, underwrote much of the official diplomatic relationships of the late nineteenth century. The campaign to reform time measurement, examined below, is a particularly compelling case of these underlying professional networks bubbling to the surface, in the run-up to an international conference on time reform in 1884. The decisions made prior to and at the conference make little sense without examining it in the context of these unofficial networks.

Until the nineteenth century, most cities and towns used their own local time. The advent of railways and telegraphs, however, meant that the differences between these multitudes of local times became exponentially more inconvenient, and even dangerous. Given the safety concerns of rail travel without an accurate timetable, it is not surprising that it was railway workers who were among the first to suggest solutions to the problem. Sandford Fleming, a Scottish-born Canadian railway engineer, was one of these, though he should not be credited with solving the problem on his own. As Vanessa Ogle, Ian Bartky, and others have pointed out, time reform was a slow process over eight decades, and involved hundreds of personalities.[4] Fleming's influence was confined to the early years of the time reform movement in North America, and even there his influence had limits. Nonetheless, his contributions were vital to those formative discussions on time reform in the 1870s and early 1880s. Fleming published his ideas in a series of pamphlets for the Canadian Institute, in which he advocated for three main reforms. First, he wanted to replace the use of individual local times with twenty-four standardized zones around the world, each fifteen geographical degrees, and one hour, apart. Second, he wanted there to be a single prime meridian, from which to measure these zones, instead of the dozens of meridians in use in the 1870s. Fleming did not particularly care where this new prime meridian was placed, though his favourite suggestion was 180 degrees from Greenwich, in the middle of the Bering Strait. Finally, he advocated for the use of a twenty-four-hour clock, eliminating a.m. and p.m.

Proposing these ideas was one thing. Convincing national and imperial policy-makers was another. Indeed, he was most successful not with politicians and diplomats, but rather with professional engineers. Official policy-makers were not easily convinced. Through the Canadian Institute, Fleming got his paper forwarded to the governor general of Canada, the Marquis of Lorne. Lorne agreed to pass it on to the colonial secretary in London, asking for feedback.[5] But the response was not encouraging. The colonial secretary ruled out any official government action, writing in October 1879:

> It has been the custom of Her Majesty's Government to abstain from interfering with recognized usages in questions of social importance until the spontaneous use of any novel system … has become so extensive as to make it desirable that authoritative regulations should be sanctioned … and it does not appear that such a condition of affairs … has yet arisen.[6]

The British government, in other words, refused to impose any change on how the public kept time. The scientific community was as skeptical as the politicians. The Royal Astronomical Society, for example, read the paper at their council meeting, but declined to offer any feedback.[7] The Royal Geographical Society was more amenable, but doubted the feasibility of such a scheme. "There is nothing to be said against the proposal," wrote one member of the society, "except its impractibility, which is such that no scientific body is likely to urge it seriously."[8] It was not exactly a resounding endorsement. The Royal Society took a similar position, stating that although they were disposed to support the idea, "no scheme of the kind would have much chance of success unless there were a general readiness on the part of civilized nations to seriously entertain the question."[9] The astronomer royal, George Airy, and the astronomer royal for Scotland, Charles Piazzi Smyth, were also asked for their opinions. As the highest astronomical authorities in Britain, their opinions carried great weight.

Unfortunately for Fleming, neither was particularly impressed by his plan. Smyth predicted that local time would never be replaced, "no matter what beautifully-written schemes any few very learned men may propose in their closets."[10] Fleming was, according to Smyth, "running full tilt against common sense."[11] Airy wrote a similarly scathing dismissal of Fleming's ideas, noting that "as to the need of a Prime Meridian, no practical man ever wants such a thing."[12] In other words, there was a near-consensus among experts in 1879 that Fleming's plan for a universal standard time was a utopian pipe dream; laudable, but unachievable.[13]

Having been rebuffed by the scientific societies of Britain, Fleming changed tactics. He looked to the railroads.[14] The time between 1880 and 1883 saw Fleming involved in an incredible flurry of activity: letter writing, campaigning, petitioning, preparing and administering surveys, and attending conferences. In this effort, Fleming was one voice among many. Americans Cleveland Abbe, Frederick Barnard, Thomas Egleston, and William Allen all played major roles. This campaign makes it clear that standard time was not a matter of invention, but of promotion. Advocacy and activism pushed the topic from the obscurity of utopian scheming into the realm of practical possibility. And it did so largely outside the realm of official diplomacy, at least at first.

The forums for these campaigns and debates were professional societies. Fleming's Canadian Institute was involved jointly with Abbe and Barnard's American Metrological Society (AMS). But Fleming joined several other groups as well, presenting his ideas to the American Association for the Advancement of Science and the American Society of Civil Engineers (ASCE).[15] Of course, as Ian Bartky rightly points out, only a handful of members in any of these societies ever paid much attention to the issue of time reform.[16] But these individuals' voices had much more authority in the public realm with the tacit support of a professional society behind them.

Fleming convinced the ASCE to establish a Standard Time Committee, with Fleming as its chair. He set to work, using the society's distribution network to circulate a questionnaire to engineers and railway managers in Mexico, Canada, and the USA, as well as to interested academics.[17] The replies were overwhelmingly positive concerning the benefits of some sort of reform for railway time, and the survey made it clear that the railway system in North America was in dire need of a more manageable time system.[18] Armed with these results, the ASCE began petitioning the US Congress to call an international conference to establish a global time system. Meanwhile, the AMS was also lobbying Congress. At first, Abbe felt it was unlikely that the US government would call such a meeting, and hoped that the Canadian government might do it instead.[19] However, after the Canadian governor general's failure to entice any action on the part of the British, the AMS looked inward to the United States.

The AMS was undoubtedly the most respectable and politically influential of the societies pushing for time reform in the United States. As Egleston explained to Fleming in early 1883, the ASCE alone could not achieve much, as engineers had little clout. By joining with the AMS, however, they could "secure the interest and cooperation of the most powerful men in the country, which might not be so certain if we worked with the civil engineers alone."[20] The alliance paid off, and Congress did indeed call for an international conference. But it was never a sure thing, and Fleming reached overseas once more. In 1881, the International Geographical Congress met in Venice. The congress was a professional gathering of geographers, which had met twice before in the 1870s. Both times, the idea of a prime meridian for navigational purposes had been discussed but ultimately shelved for future study.[21] Time reform was not part of these discussions. Fleming and Barnard hoped to change that.

They were not very successful. At Venice, Fleming's proposals were received with mild interest, but not enough consensus to make any real impact. The resolutions that were adopted were far weaker than they had hoped. Indifference derailed the efforts of the reformers.[22] Fleming at this point turned his attention away from Europe, hoping that the planned Washington conference on an international prime meridian, which the AMS had been lobbying to set up, would render a European solution redundant.[23]

In late 1883, a second European scientific conference took place, the International Geodetic Association's General Meeting in Rome. The prime meridian was once again on the table for discussion. But Fleming looked on the Rome conference with little optimism, unsurprisingly given his past failures in Europe. As he wrote to his close acquaintance Charles Tupper, then Canada's minister of railways and canals, "from what I know of similar meetings which have over and over been held in the cities of Europe I do not anticipate any satisfactory results or any results at all beyond postponing a settlement of the question indefinitely."[24] But Rome performed better than Fleming expected. The conference passed several promising recommendations, including the selection of an international prime meridian at Greenwich, and a formal approval of the United States' proposal to hold a diplomatic conference in Washington in 1884 to ratify the new common meridian.[25] But nothing recommended at this conference was binding: it was a gathering of scientists, not diplomats. Moreover, it was a complicated road to reach that agreement. The Rome conference had suggested a controversial trade: if the rest of the world abandoned their own meridians in favour of Greenwich, Britain in return ought to abandon its weights and measures in favour of the metric system, or at least pay its share of the costs to the Metre Convention of 1875, which had set up a bureau to standardize and verify comparisons between different systems of measure. In this case, fortune favoured Fleming for once, because the British delegation, led by the new astronomer royal, William Christie, did not reject the proposal outright, and was even open to Britain paying its fair share to the Metre Convention.[26] But Christie did not have the support of his government on this question, and there was a storm of political backlash over the suggestion that Britain pay anything to the Metre Convention. Moreover, Rome's proposals had one unavoidably significant difference from Fleming's. While Fleming's plan introduced time zones universally, eliminating local time's role in everyday life for all people, Rome's proposal was for a specialized time system, to be used by railways, ships, telegraphs, and observatories. The Rome conference's recommendations meant that ordinary people would still use local time, and would have to convert to Greenwich Time or its derivative whenever they wanted to travel by rail or sea.[27] For the scientific community, Universal Time was to be a specialized tool, not a new public norm. This difference in opinion over the nature and extent of time reform would continue to plague Fleming up to the Washington conference itself, limiting his ability to sway both academic and political peers. He was an outsider not just because he represented a dominion, but also because he was not a scientist.

The time reformers had more success in North America than in Europe, although not, as an aggrieved Fleming had somewhat unfairly suggested, because North Americans were more "practical" than Europeans.[28] The notion that there was a strict continental divide, with forward-thinking North Americans being held back by Old World conservatism, is nonsense. There were Americans who opposed time reform, just as there were Europeans who supported it. Professional difference mattered more than nationality. Engineers were largely in favour of standard time. Astronomers and other scientists were more skeptical. Fleming was an engineer, and even in North America his reach was greatest with other engineers and railway officials, not academics. The vast extent of North America's railways pushed engineers to find a viable solution to the problem quickly, with or without legislation or diplomatic agreements.

Enter William Allen. An American railway worker and a latecomer to the time reform efforts, Allen learned about the AMS and its joint efforts with the Canadian Institute and the ASCE in late 1881. Allen jumped on board. While the AMS continued the slow process of petitioning the government for an international conference on time reform, Allen looked to the railroads to make more immediate changes. It was Allen who, through several meetings known as General Time Conventions, brought about Zone Time on all North American railroads. The General Time Conventions were originally designed to coordinate schedules between the various railway companies, but Allen directed their attention towards Zone Time instead. In November 1883, only weeks after the Rome conference had ended, North American railways adopted standard time, using Greenwich as a prime meridian. But for Fleming, the work was far from over. He had two larger goals. The first was to make the new railway Zone Time into legal time in the United States and Canada. The second goal was to extend Zone Time worldwide.

The first goal was not easy to achieve, and in fact Fleming made only faltering progress – a symptom of his limited political clout in American or British (or Canadian) legislatures. But the attempt to extend time zones worldwide seemed more achievable when, in August 1882, the AMS finally convinced the US government to convene a conference on the subject. A circular was forwarded to various countries with diplomatic relations with the United States, asking whether such a conference would be met with approval. When positive answers were received (it took some time; the British government was particularly slow in responding), invitations were sent out by the secretary of state in December of 1883. The conference was to meet at Washington the following October.

As one of the chief activists in the time reform movement, Fleming seemed an obvious choice to represent Canada at the conference. But just as he had been rejected by the scientific community of Europe, he found himself nearly excluded from the political sphere as well.

The vagaries of international politics, Canada's semi-colonial status, interdepartmental rivalries, and sheer incompetence nearly cost him his seat at the table. Despite Fleming's modern reputation as being instrumental to the establishment of standard time, he was, at the time, disposable. Seen from Europe, he was a wealthy but recently unemployed railwayman from the colonies, with interesting but ultimately utopian ideas. As a result, his application to join the international conference was an uphill battle – a reflection of Canada's limited influence in the world at this point.

Fleming began lobbying for his nomination as a delegate early, before the conference had officially been called. In early 1883, he asked the Canadian Institute and the Royal Society of Canada to send memorials to the governor general, requesting that Canada be represented. The governor general's reply was guarded. Canada, being a dominion, did not have direct diplomatic relations with the United States, and Canadian foreign policy was determined by the United Kingdom. As such, Canada's participation was entirely dependent on the goodwill of the Foreign Office. But the governor general did promise that if Canada managed to secure an invitation, either directly, or via the United Kingdom, a representative would certainly be sent.[29]

Not content with that answer, Fleming bypassed official channels, writing instead to Charles Tupper, a close friend, the day after receiving the governor general's reply. Tupper was then serving in London as the Canadian high commissioner to the United Kingdom. "It does not appear," Fleming wrote, "that Canada has been invited to take part in the international conference proposed to be held at Washington, but no country in the world is more interested in a satisfactory solution to the problem than Canada and as a matter of fact the movement for the solution originated in Canada."[30] Fleming asked Tupper to try and secure Canada's representation at the conference.

Fleming's problem was one of imperial hierarchies and international norms. As a dominion, Canada could not be invited unless by a specific act of the US Congress, and also by the agreement of Her Majesty's Government in Britain. A more likely solution was to have Canada represented as a part of the British delegation, hence the petitioning of Tupper and the governor general. On 9 June 1883, after a campaign of letter writing, Fleming was told that in the event of Canada being invited to the Washington conference, he would be appointed as the Canadian delegate.[31] Fleming was assured his place, but only if Canada had a place itself.

In London, Tupper set to work on Fleming's behalf. The process was a messy one, in large part because it was unclear which government department had jurisdiction. The Colonial Office (CO) was involved, as it was in all of Canada's relations with Britain, but a diplomatic conference was also a matter of foreign policy, which meant that the Foreign Office (FO) had a hand in the choice of delegates. But there was a third office: the Science and Art Department (SAD), which was a branch of the Board of Trade. The SAD was involved in all things to do with the advance of science and technology, as well as education in Britain. When British scientists were sent as delegates to the Rome conference in the fall of 1883, it was the SAD who had chosen them. As the Washington conference was to cover similar ground, it only made sense that the SAD would take part in the decision-making process once again. These three departments, each with their own agenda, existed in parallel, and without a clear hierarchy as to whose decision was final. Furthermore, all of these departments had to act under the oversight of the Treasury. This mess of bureaucracy was anything but efficient.

When the Colonial Office received word, via the governor general and Tupper, that Canada wished to be represented, they forwarded the request on to the Foreign Office. But the FO was hesitant. There were two problems. First, the USA had not yet sent official invitations; only a request to ascertain whether the UK might be interested in attending such a conference if it were held. The request, which had been received in November 1882, did not even include a date for the proposed conference. Second, the Treasury had already decided internally that they were not inclined to send any delegates to such a conference.[32] The Colonial Office made one more attempt, requesting that the FO ask the UK's ambassador in the USA, Lionel Sackville-West, to take steps to ensure Fleming's recognition as a delegate. West told the US secretary of state, Frederick Frelinghuysen, about Fleming's request for representation. Frelinghuysen replied that he would be pleased to recognize Fleming, but only after Great Britain confirmed its intent to participate.[33] In other words, Canada would not be recognized individually; Fleming was to be a British delegate or nothing. This was not promising, as at this point, given the decision of the Treasury the previous November, it seemed likely that no representative of the British Empire would attend at all.[34]

This is where personal relationships played an important role. In early July, having heard that the UK might not attend Washington,

Fleming forwarded via Tupper a letter urging the UK to participate. He stressed that Canada and the United States were willing to accept Greenwich as a prime meridian, an outcome which just might be inevitable if only the UK would attend. Fleming suggested that only with Great Britain's participation could this "problem which has long embarrassed geographers, astronomers and navigators" be settled.[35] Without his friend Tupper in a position to lobby for him, Fleming might not have succeeded.

As it was, Fleming's pleas were still greeted with indifference over the summer months. Without further details from the United States, Lord Granville at the Foreign Office was content to let the matter rest, awaiting the results of Rome before considering Washington any further.[36] Once the Rome conference was over, Fleming tried again. With help from Tupper, he emphasized the national prestige that would arise if Greenwich were named the world's prime meridian. He and Tupper pointed out that recent events concerning North American railways made the USA an ally in the fight for Greenwich, and that Russia was on board as well. "I anticipate but one result at Washington," said Fleming, "if Her Majesty's Government will only accept the invitation to participate."[37] Despite Fleming's best efforts, however, the matter was not taken up until the new year.

By then, the United States had finally sent out the official invitations, with the date set for 1 October 1884. In January 1884, the Science and Art Department sent off its report on the Rome conference. The FO, now with both the report on Rome and the USA's official invitation in hand, had to make a final decision on whether or not to attend. They reached out to the Treasury for their opinion. The Treasury, having already rejected the Washington conference once, was not particularly willing. They asked Granville whether there were any "political grounds" on which the invitation ought to be accepted.[38] The FO conceded that the political ramifications of Washington were not particularly significant, but that the Treasury ought to ask the CO and the SAD, both of which attached importance to the subject.[39] The CO, on behalf of Fleming, replied that yes indeed, delegates ought to be sent.[40]

When the Treasury at last agreed in February to provide the funds for two delegates to attend the Washington conference, it failed to specify who was supposed to choose the delegates, leading to some frustrating interdepartmental rivalry. In the end, the decision was made by the SAD. They settled on Captain Frederick Evans, the hydrographer of the Royal Navy, and Cambridge astronomer John Couch

Adams.[41] Alongside these two, the SAD suggested to the Colonial Office that perhaps the Canadian and Australasian colonies might like to send delegates as well. The CO ran the idea by the Foreign Office, but also raised some concerns about the proposal. Until now, no one had considered a delegate from Australasia. Canada was only being considered because of Fleming's activism. In the practice of fairness, inviting the Australasian colonies was a good idea. But it meant complications for the diplomatic process. The invitation from the United States was for three British delegates, maximum. With Fleming, Evans, and Adams already chosen, there was no room for more. There was also a question of whether the Australasians were interested in coming in the first place. While the CO deliberated, they sent a request to the Foreign Office to check if the US might allow a fourth British delegate from Australasia.[42]

The waters were muddied further when the SAD announced a week later that the Indian Council had nominated a delegate as well, General Richard Strachey.[43] Either the SAD was unaware of the three delegate limit, or they assumed that colonial delegates did not count as British delegates. Either way, there were now five prospective delegates vying for three seats.

In an attempt to clarify the situation, the Foreign Office asked the United States if India, Canada, and the Australasian colonies could be represented. Secretary of State Frelinghuysen wrote back with a compromise. It would be unfair, he said, if Britain and its possessions had five votes, while each other nation had three. On the other hand, involving as many of the world's geographies as possible in the conference would "add to the interest and value of its deliberations and to the weight of its conclusions."[44] Therefore, the United States would allow five delegates from Britain and its possessions, but only three of them would be allowed to vote.

From the United States' perspective, the offer was a fair one. But the British had caught themselves in a trap, which only the Colonial Office seemed to recognize at first. Fleming would expect a vote, having been involved in the process since the very beginning. But the Australasian colonies would resent their delegates have an inferior position to Canada's. The CO was stuck in an unpleasant position, a situation made worse when the SAD proposed that the Indian delegate be given the right vote.[45]

The CO was livid and sought to defend Fleming. In a flurry of internal memos, civil servants critiqued the SAD's decisions. The SAD "had

no right to appropriate the votes without previous consultation with
us, and I think they ought to be remonstrated with, for there is sure
to be unpleasantness if Mr. S. Fleming does not get a vote. Could not
private pressure be brought to bear on them?"[46] Another replied,
"They ought to treat Canada as a Dominion, as she is, and I cannot
help thinking that a little pressure brought to bear upon the U.S. Government would make then rescind the decision [to limit the number
of votes to three] … and give one more vote." Another responded,
"Write to the S and A Dept. and point out that the unfortunate result
of their acting without referring to this Dept. will be to exclude Sandford Fleming who is the originator of the whole Conference, and ask
that he may be allowed to have one of the votes." Another asked if it
was indeed true that Fleming started the whole conference. He had
talked to Donnelly (from the SAD), who seemed to think that the idea
originated in America. "It is not certain," he continued, "that India
would give way to Canada so we must be quite sure of our ground."
The other replied with a full list of Fleming's actions: Fleming was the
first to bring the topic to the attention of the British government back
in 1879, although back then the replies from the "English learned
bodies were almost entirely unfavourable to the scheme proposed –
which shows that the idea had not then commended itself to our
scientific men … The first intimation we had of the Washington Conference was the request from Canada that Mr. Fleming should represent the Dominion there." The note concluded, "But for Mr. S. Fleming the question (as far as I can judge) might never yet have attained
official prominence – there might have been no Washington Conference – we might not have been sending any representatives of this
country at all."[47]

Back in Canada, Fleming was completely unaware that his role as
delegate for Canada was in peril. In June, not having heard anything
on the subject officially since he accepted the provisional nomination
from the governor general twelve months earlier, he wrote to Tupper
and the undersecretary of state, G. Powell, asking for an update. He
wanted to make sure that he would be properly accredited.[48] Powell
replied a few weeks later, telling Fleming that they would pass his
name on to Her Majesty's Government as having been accredited as
the representative of Canada.[49] But Powell's reply did not tell the
whole story. As usual, Tupper was more forthcoming, telling Fleming
that although it was pretty much decided that Fleming would indeed
represent Canada, it was still up in the air as to whether he would be

allowed to vote. "The Colonial Office is making a hard fight for you not only on the right of Canada but on your own as the projector of the whole thing."[50]

In the meantime, the Colonial Office had heard back from the Australasian colonies. As their delegate would not be able to vote, Australia and New Zealand declined to send one. The Colonial Office was relieved, as it let them off the hook for part of the problem. With the Australasia colonies out of the way, only the issue of Canada's vote remained. The SAD justified their choice to exclude Canada from voting by saying that "the interests of Canada are not necessarily identical with the those of this country on the question."[51] They suggested that the best option might be to plead once more with the United States to agree to recognize a Canadian delegation in its own right, entirely separate from the British delegation.[52] The CO supported the idea as a last resort, and requested the FO make the request to the United States.

It was a long shot. It would mean recognizing a dominion as an equal at a table of nations. This was problematic because most countries would consider the idea to be an underhanded ploy to get the British an extra vote at the table, assuming Canada would inevitably vote in tandem with its colonizing power. It would set a "dangerous" diplomatic precedent (similar fears led to American opposition to the seating of Canada and the other dominions at the 1919 Paris Peace Conference).

Once again, the United States' reply was a compromise. The notion of a colony representing itself was rejected outright. "No colony will be separately recognized," the reply stated bluntly.[53] However, the US was willing to make a different sort of concession. The number of delegates each nation was allowed to send was raised from three to five.[54] The compromise was a satisfying one. As Mr Lowell, a member of Britain's diplomatic mission to the USA, wrote, the new limit allowed "for the representation of the diverse local interests, which might exist within the dominions of any of the powers ... H.M.G. can secure representation for all the diversified interests of the British Empire without violating the principle of giving all the powers an equal voice."[55] Britain could now send Fleming, Strachey, and an Australasian as British delegates with full voting powers, alongside Adams and Evans from Britain itself. Relieved, the Colonial Office made quick work of ensuring Fleming's place.

From the perspective of the CO, the SAD's lack of concern for Fleming's nomination was inexplicably incompetent. But that one-sided view is only partially accurate. Thus far, the SAD's perspective has been largely missing from this narrative, and their reputation for incompetence comes mainly from the prejudices of the other departments. Their silence is in large part because much of the department's papers have been lost or destroyed. However, it is possible to piece together from private papers some of what was going on in the SAD in 1884 – enough to partially rehabilitate them. The SAD was attempting to prevent an international incident involving the metric system, which was expected to be raised in connection with standard time. As astronomers had proposed at the congress in Rome the year before, the SAD feared that in Washington Britain might be pressured to accept the metric system in return for France's adherence to a Greenwich meridian. The SAD had this issue in mind when the issue of nominating delegates for Washington came up in early 1884, and the department had to ensure that any delegates chosen would have moderate views in connection with the Metric Convention. Fleming was a wild card where they were concerned. They wanted their own people in the delegation.

The SAD's decision-making about the Prime Meridian Conference was therefore based on solving an entirely separate scientific controversy, adherence to the metric system. Fleming's timekeeping schemes were immaterial to the SAD, and so he was ignored. Even had they known about Fleming's desire to attend Washington, his allegiances concerning the metric system were unknown. He was therefore nearly passed over, and would have been ignored entirely if not for the intervention of the CO. The result of this controversy was that most of the British delegates attending Washington were picked for their position on the metric system, not on the meridian question. Ironically, the tenuous link between the two concepts was deteriorating rapidly, and would evaporate entirely by the time the conference began. The metric system would only be discussed perfunctorily at Washington. The idea of a trade, Greenwich for the metric system, had lost favour. The SAD, which had tried so hard to appoint delegates who would support the Metric Convention, actually had to tell those delegates not to bring the subject up at all at Washington, and did so in their official letters of instruction.[56]

The incredible influence that the metric controversy had on an apparently unrelated subject demonstrates how unusually undiplomatic diplomacy can be. Scientific networks had an immense, if usually invisible, role in shaping international relations. Science is often a political pursuit. Preoccupations with weights and measures, rather than national interest, lay behind the choice of delegates for the British Empire. Of course, the two overlap. Britain had a national stake in maintaining imperial measures over the French metre. But Britain's position on the subject was largely authored by scientists who had broken through into the diplomatic world.

The SAD's preoccupation with the metric controversy was a real barrier to Fleming. The CO's campaign to secure a spot for Fleming ultimately paid off, but barely. Fleming got his seat alongside Strachey, Adams, and Evans, but the latter three's understanding of the meridian question as a bargaining chip in a debate over systems of measurement hardly acknowledged the notion of universal, collective timekeeping proposed by Fleming. They may have been sitting at the same table in Washington, under the same flag, but they had very different ideas about what was to be accomplished there.

Fleming received his official appointment on 25 September 1884, just six days before the conference was to begin.[57] As for Australasia, the question of their attendance was reopened in September, but at that point it was too late; they could not find a suitable delegate able to arrive in Washington in time.[58] After all the deliberations, Fleming was at last a full delegate to the Washington Prime Meridian Conference, with Strachey, Adams, and Evans. His official title was "British Delegate for Canada." But he was to be dealt one final slight. Despite the months of incessant correspondence and quibbles about how voting was to be carried out, the conference itself decided on the spot in October that voting would not occur by individual delegate after all. Votes would be cast by nation. And since Fleming was representing Britain, not Canada independently, his voice was significantly diluted among those of his British peers.

At the conference, professional fault lines continued to shape the conversation. France and Britain came into conflict over the location of the prime meridian, but these national conflicts were ultimately secondary to professional ones on the topic of timekeeping. Guided by the professional expertise of naval officers in attendance, for example, Greenwich was chosen as the world's prime meridian (70 per cent of the world's shipping already used it).[59] Astronomers then led the effort to establish a universal day for scientific purposes. But the railway engineers in the room, Fleming and Allen, failed to convince the conference to establish time zones for civic use. Fleming's proposals were repeatedly undermined, not by French delegates, but rather by his fellow British delegates, particularly astronomer J.C. Adams. Imperial unity broke down along professional lines. As a result, time zones would not become international law at Washington. These would be introduced only piecemeal, country by country, over the next half century.

The results of the conference itself reflect the same professional divisions that challenged Fleming in his attempt to be a part of it in the first place. As this chapter has shown, Canadians' access to international politics was restricted by imperial policy and international norms, but also by personal and professional relationships. The Dominion had no standing as an independent actor in high politics. Nonetheless, Fleming managed to insert his voice into the debate by working outside the normal channels of diplomacy, through established networks of science (where possible), and, more successfully, networks of engineering. It was these informal networks that were the real lifeblood of the "British world" and beyond. Imperial networks were never merely political institutions: indeed, some of the most lasting connections in the empire stemmed from the movement of people and institutions, not political ties. Furthermore, these connections were not simply one-way paths from metropole to periphery. A better conceptual tool is that of a web, with multiple nodes and smaller pathways interlocking with each other.[60] The scientific and engineering networks that both helped and hindered Fleming are good examples of these strands that linked different parts of the British world, in tandem with other interests, notably commercial ones. Professional institutions like the AMS, ASCE, and Canadian Institute were able to lobby national governments with some success. Only with their backing was the Washington conference was initiated. Even then, Fleming's ability to take part was limited by imperial bureaucracy, and by competing interests over the metric system. It took some creative advocacy and a reliance on informal networks beyond the usual diplomatic process to ensure Canadians a seat at the table, even if Canada remained subject to the whims of larger powers.

NOTES

1 Indeed, the Washington conference largely failed to achieve time standardization.

2 Vanessa Ogle, *The Global Transformation of Time* (Cambridge, MA: Harvard University Press, 2015); Ian Bartky, *One Time Fits All* (Stanford: Stanford University Press, 2007); Peter Galison, *Einstein's Clocks, Poincaré's Maps* (New York: W.W. Norton, 2003); Charles Withers, *Zero Degrees: Geographies of the Prime Meridian* (Cambridge, MA: Harvard University Press, 2017).

3 For more on the British world, see Phillip Buckner, *Canada and the British Empire* (Oxford: Oxford University Press, 2008); Tamson Pietsch, *Empire of Scholars: Universities, Networks and the British Academic World, 1850–1939* (Manchester: Manchester University Press, 2013); Carl Bridge and Kent Fedorowich, eds., *British World: Diaspora, Culture, and Identity* (London: Frank Cass, 2003).

4 Ogle, *The Global Transformation of Time*; Bartky, *One Time Fits All.*

5 Sandford Fleming, Universal or Cosmic Time, 1885, Ya.2003.a.17994, British Library (BL), London.

6 Ibid.

7 Council minutes, 14 November 1879, part 1, no. 2, vol. 8, Royal Astronomical Society Archives, London.

8 Sir John Henry Lefroy's Report on Mr. Sandford Fleming's proposals respecting a prime meridian and time reckoning, 19 November 1879, RGS/CB6/1377, Royal Geographical Society Archives, London.

9 Sandford Fleming, Universal or Cosmic Time, 1885, Ya.2003.a.17994, BL.

10 Ibid.

11 Ibid.

12 Ibid.

13 The admiralty also rejected the proposal on the basis that the public was not yet ready for such a change. Dispatch on Time Reckoning, 17 October 1879, MG29 B1, vol. 30, LAC.

14 For more on this, see Bartky, *One Time Fits All.*

15 Ibid., 70.

16 Ibid., 59.

17 Bogart to Fleming, 13 March 1882, MG29 B1, vol. 2, LAC.

18 See MG29 B1, vol. 2, LAC.

19 Abbe to Fleming, 10 March 1880, MG29 B1, vol. 1, LAC.

20 Egleston to Fleming, 20 February 1883, MG29 B1, vol. 14, LAC.

21 Bartky, *One Time Fits All*, 35–47.

22 Wheeler to Fleming, 2 March 1882, MG29 B1, vol. 53, LAC.

23 Fleming to Bogart, 26 October 1881, MG29 B1, vol. 63, LAC. See also Bartky, *One Time Fits All*, 66–7.

24 Fleming to Tupper, 20 October 1883, MG29 B1, vol. 65, LAC.

25 *Journal of the Society of the Arts*, No. 1625, vol. 32, 11 January 1884, Ac.4470/3, BL.

26 Report by the Committee, MSS Eur F127, vol. 188, Strachey Papers, BL.

27 Ian Bartky, "Inventing, Introducing, and Objecting to Standard Time," *Vistas in Astronomy* 28 (1985), 110.

28 Fleming to Tupper, 20 October 1883, MG29 B1, vol. 65, LAC.

29 Powell to President of the Canadian Institute, 8 May 1883, F1052, Container 1, Archives of Ontario.

30 Fleming to Tupper, 9 May 1883, MG29 B1, vol. 65, LAC.

31 Fleming to Powell, 23 June 1884, MG29 B1, vol. 65, LAC.

32 Letterbook, 28 November 1882, F0566/19, National Archives of the United Kingdom (TNA), Kew.

33 West to Granville, 14 June 1883, MG29 B1, vol. 27, LAC.

34 Adoption of a Common Prime Meridian, 5 June 1883, CO42/776, NA.

35 Proposed International Prime Meridian Conference, 18 July 1883, CO42/775, NA.

36 Granville to Lowell, 21 July 1883, MG29 B1, vol. 1, LAC.

37 Fleming to Tupper, 20 October 1883, CO42/775, TNA.

38 Treasury to Foreign Office, 14 January 1884, FO5/1886, TNA.

39 Foreign Office to Treasury, 21 January 1884, FO5/1886, TNA.

40 Colonial Office to Treasury, 7 February 1884, FO5/1886, TNA.

41 Donnelly to Foreign Office, 3 May 1884, FO5/1886, TNA.

42 Colonial Office to Foreign Office, 2 May 1884, FO5/1886, TNA.

43 Science and Art Department to Foreign Office, 10 May 1884, FO5/1886, TNA.

44 Lowell to Granville, 21 May 1884, FO5/1884 TNA.

45 Donnelly to Foreign Office, 21 June 1884, FO5/1887, TNA.

46 Prime Meridian Conference, 28 June 1884, CO42/779, TNA.

47 Ibid.

48 Fleming to Powell, 23 June 1884, MG29 B1, vol. 65, LAC.

49 Powell to Fleming, 18 July 1884, MG29 B1, vol. 39, LAC.

50 Tupper to Fleming, 17 July 1884, MG29 B1, vol. 50, LAC.

51 Science and Art Department to Colonial Office, 1884, FO5/1887, TNA.

52 Ibid.

53 Lowell to Legation of the United States, 29 August 1884, Microfilm M30 146, US National Archives and Records Administration II (NARA), College Park.

54 Frelinghuysen to Barnard, 18 September 1884, Microfilm M40 101, USNA; Lowell to Legation of the United States, 29 August 1884, Microfilm M30 146, NARA.

55 Lowell to Granville, September 1884, CO42/779, TNA.

56 Science and Art Department to Strachey, 24 June 1884, MSS Eur F127, vol. 188, Strachey Papers, BL.

57 Derby to Fleming, 26 September 1884, MG29 B1, vol. 27, LAC.

58 Prime Meridian Conference, September 1884, CO309/127, TNA.

59 France abstained, and did not begin using Greenwich for several decades more.

60 For more on networks and their conception as a web, see Simon Potter, "Webs, Networks, and Systems: Globalization and the Mass Media in the Nineteenth and Twentieth-Century British Empire," *Journal of British Studies* 46, no. 3 (2007): 621–46; Thomas Metcalf, *Imperial Connections: India in the Indian Ocean Arena, 1860–1920* (Los Angeles: University of California Press, 2007), 7–8. Note also that these webs were not uniform, but rather, as Frederick Cooper suggests, "filled with lumps, places where power coalesces surrounded by those where it does not, places where social relations become dense amid others that are diffuse." Quoted in Pietsch, *Empire of Scholars*, 3. For more on how racial bias underpinned international networks in the nineteenth century, see Akira Iriye, *Cultural Internationalism and World Order* (Baltimore: Johns Hopkins University Press, 1997), 13–50.

3

Rethinking Religion's Role
in Canadian Transnational Relations

DAVID WEBSTER

Religion has shaped international affairs, and continues to do so. From the great Christian missionary enterprise to Asia in the nineteenth century, in which Canadians played a major role, to the "clash of civilizations" rhetoric that informs today's "war on terror," relations between states and societies have been deeply informed by religious flows, currents, and clashes. Yet religion receives limited attention in the study of Canadian foreign relations. Few writers have addressed the question, for instance, of whether Canadian churches had their own "foreign policy" distinct from the Canadian government, and how that policy may have influenced and been influenced by state policy. There has been no Canadian equivalent to what Andrew Preston calls the "religious turn" in the study of the United States and the World.[1]

This gap leaves our understanding of Canada's interactions with the world incomplete. There is a large literature on Canadian missionaries and their role in the history of Canada-Asia relations, but it halts in the mid-twentieth century. It is almost as if Canadian foreign policy was secularized in a stroke, limited to policy, trade, and – to some newer researchers – economic development and transnational non-governmental networks. Yet Canadian churches did not suddenly withdraw from global engagement with the decline of missions, decolonization, and a deepening Cold War. They remained heavily committed overseas, even while their stress on conversion receded and terms such as "World Missions" gave way to "Global Outreach" – to cite the changing titles of the relevant division of the United Church of Canada. Canada remained a society in which religion mattered well after 1945 – and still does today. Without seeing the place of religious organizations in Canada's foreign relations, we cannot come to a full understanding of Canada's place in the world. Religion's place in Canadian foreign relations may be undiplomatic history – or churches may have been pursuing their own diplomatic strategies.

Ignoring religion's importance also leaves government policy-makers ignorant. In his overview of religion's role in US foreign policy, Andrew Preston cites the example of President John F. Kennedy, dumbfounded by Buddhist monks setting themselves on fire in South Vietnam. "How could this have happened?" Kennedy asked. "Who are these people? Why didn't we know about them before?" As Preston notes drily: "They were merely the people who made up 90 per cent of South Vietnam's population, and the fact that Kennedy and his people found their presence shocking is shocking in itself."[2]

My point is simply Preston's point: it is important to notice religious influences on foreign policy, even in the second half of the twentieth century, a period often glossed as overwhelmingly secular. "In fact, it was the very nature of the cold war that allowed religion to play a greater role in international history than ever before," Preston writes in the introduction to a recent volume on religion and the Cold War. With direct war unthinkable, the Cold War became a "contest over legitimacy," a clash of ideas. And ideas are very much religion's field of operations.[3] This chapter tries to explore a few aspects of religion's role in Canada's transnational relations by considering, in a very preliminary fashion, its implications for the way we study "diplomatic history" in Canada. It is both overview and case study. Like Laura Madokoro's chapter, which highlights the way that religious thought and anti-Catholic sentiment crossed the Canada-US border,[4] it aims to make visible the interactions between religious actors and government diplomacy. The importance of non-government diplomats and of transnational networks and ideas is also present in this volume's chapters on peace movements, anti-orientalist campaigning, development work, environmental diplomacy, and human rights. In each of these realms, from peace to the concept of nature to notions of human dignity, religious influences pervade. Understandings of Canada and the World are moving beyond the confines of diplomacy, economics, and security to also include transnational social relations, part of the global "transnational turn." This chapter aims to contribute to the greater inclusion of religious influences within the study of Canada and the World.

In her chapter, Whitney Wood describes a "gospel of natural birth" that reached Canada. The word is apt: Canada and Canadians went forth into the world to preach many gospels. Even the not-very-religious "son of the manse" Lester Pearson, the most storied figure in Canadian diplomacy, called religion a "part of our being."[5] It should be part of our understanding of Canada's foreign relations, too.

THE PRESERVATION OF CIVILIZATION

It goes without saying that Louis St Laurent's cabinet, which presided as Canada entered the Cold War, was a group containing many dedicated Christians, with the devoutly Catholic prime minister in the lead. It would be more surprising if the cabinet had *not* been made up of Christian believers, of course, and it is not remarkable to suggest that their faith may have shaped some of their actions.[6]

A speech by St Laurent at the 1950 University of Toronto convocation, riven through with images of Christian civilization under threat, serves as well as any other document as Canada's declaration of full entry into the Cold War.[7] The speech could easily be read as an attempt to bolster Canadian public support for a stronger global role. Certainly, Canadian public support for membership in the North Atlantic Treaty (signed in 1949) and a combat role in the Korean War (1950–53) was bolstered by the St Laurent government's appeal to Christian anti-communism. These themes were especially effective in harnessing support from groups that might have favoured a retreat back to Canada's shores, including in right-leaning Catholic Quebec and left-leaning circles linked to the Cooperative Commonwealth Federation (CCF, forerunner to today's New Democratic Party).[8] Yet we should at least consider that St Laurent was sincere in his religious beliefs, as most Canadians were, and that they informed his actions. Fresh from an apocalyptic struggle against a totalitarian threat, many Canadian Christians saw a new menace on the horizon. Even if his speeches on Christian civilization were merely cynical attempts to build public support for Cold War re-armament and for the hot war in Korea, his swift resort to those themes and their rapid success in building public consent testify to religion's power in the realm of foreign relations.

Titling his address "The Preservation of Civilization," St Laurent borrowed from *The Twilight of Civilization* by the French Catholic thinker Jacques Maritain, which originated as a speech delivered in Paris in 1939. Like Maritain, who spoke as the Nazis threatened France, St Laurent lamented that Western, Christian civilization (he used the two descriptors interchangeably) faced dire threat. Maritain, in the English translation of his remarks published in 1942, deplored the way that "the pagan empire is now crushing Europe." But he also evoked hope, where "the first rays of a dawn are often mingled with the twilight." For the "heathens" of the Nazi or communist "Pagan Empires," the universal love that Christ commanded stopped at national borders. To Maritain, like many Christian thinkers before him, it was self-evident that borders meant little to people of faith.[9] This type of internationalism forms a key component of the Christian influence on Canadian foreign relations.

For St Laurent, as for Maritain, the threat to civilization came from "totalitarianism, whether it takes the form of Fascism or Nazism or Communism." With Nazi Germany vanquished, communism remained the great threat, necessitating another buildup of arms: "Communism, in its Soviet form, denies the essential importance of the human being and the possibility of the individual ever influencing his own fate, in this world or in the hereafter."[10] And so, vigilance and armed strength were vital:

> If war should come between those who profess the gross material-
> ism of Communist ideology and those who accept the moral
> ideals of our Christian civilization, I am firmly convinced that
> the powers of evil, like the gates of Hell, would not prevail.
> But such a struggle, regardless of the outcome, would itself be
> a disaster.

Yet "security against the forces of barbarism from without" was simply a first step. Barbarism also lay within Western society, where spirituality was eroding. "To preserve civilization," St Laurent continued, "we have to nourish the spirit within." From that philosophical basis, he spelled out a Christian and Cold War case for foreign aid:

> We cannot neglect the less fortunate in our own midst, nor can we
> ignore the plight or nations less fortunate than our own. The
> preservation of civilization requires us to help those untold mil-

lions, most of them in Asia, to improve their standards of life and to achieve a situation they will feel it is worthwhile to defend. Despite our relatively small population, we have advantages here in Canada which fit us to contribute effectively to a combined effort to convince the less fortunate peoples that even on the material plane the free world has more to offer than Communism. It is not without significance that Canada should have furnished the first Director for the Technical Assistance Programme of the United Nations.

In addition to the material benefits there must[,] however, be a fount of spiritual values in our free societies. We in the Western world have adopted the conception of good and evil from the Hebrew and Greek civilizations. This concept has been transformed and transmitted to us through our Christian traditions. It comprises a belief in the intrinsic value of every individual human being and a sense of obligation to our neighbour.

Foreign aid, in other words, was not simply an economic transaction, nor simply charity. It was a way to tempt new nations away from Communism and to win them to the side of "Christian civilization" in its struggle against barbarism and against a totalitarian system that sought to enslave the human mind and the human spirit.[11]

St Laurent had referred to technical assistance, the sharing of Western knowledge and techniques with less developed countries in an effort to see them become more prosperous and retain their links to the West. Although the United States was far and away the largest technical assistance donor, Canadian technical assistance was also substantial. Canadian hopes flowed especially through the United Nations Expanded Programme of Technical Assistance, headed by Hugh Keenleyside, former deputy minister of mines and resources in Ottawa, and before that a top-ranking External Affairs official. Keenleyside grew up in Vancouver attending no less than four church services each Sunday, but he was not a practising Christian. Still, he painted technical assistance as "a great crusade for human progress" and gave technical advisor jobs to more than a few heirs to the "social gospel" tradition embodied in Canada's Cooperative Commonwealth Federation. Canada rapidly rose to become the largest per capita donor to UN technical assistance.[12]

THE GOSPEL OF COOPERATIVES

The case for technical assistance was laid out by Lester Pearson's parliamentary secretary (and later Quebec's premier) Jean Lesage.[13] For "hundreds of millions" of people in developing countries, Lesage told Parliament, "living conditions are not merely deplorable; they are intolerable." That required action.

> If we expect the peoples of Asia, Africa and Latin America to share
> our belief in democracy and to stand with other nations of the
> free world in defence of the democratic way of life, we must help
> them to know the benefits of democracy. We must convince them,
> by genuine and practical co-operation, that our system does not
> tend to perpetuate economic and social injustice and class privi-
> lege. It is urgent, therefore, that we should continue, through the
> United Nations and outside it, as in the Colombo Plan, to assist
> underdeveloped countries to build up, little by little, conditions of
> economic stability and social well-being.

In this, technical experts were the frontline workers, Lesage argued.

> The technical assistance mission and experts constitute the "other
> forces of the United Nations." While the soldiers of the United
> Nations are fighting in Korea to repel aggression, it is the privilege
> of these other "forces" to contribute directly to the well-being of
> the countries in which their operations are conducted and in so
> doing to help ease the present international tension.

Canada sent an entire regiment of technical advisors into the field. They were not mere foot soldiers taking orders. Rather, they influenced Canadian government thinking while they carried out government programmes for technical assistance, especially in Asia.

An example is Louis Bérubé, fisheries advisor through Canada's Colombo Plan in the 1950s and 1960s. One Canadian ambassador called him "a wonderful zealot from Quebec [who] preach[ed] the cooperative movement gospel that fishermen could largely control their own destiny if they worked together to catch and market their own produce."[14] This cooperative gospel drew from recipes Bérubé developed while working in the hardscrabble fishing villages of Quebec's Lower Saint Lawrence and Gaspésie regions. Then it simmered

in his Asian advisory career in Cambodia, Sri Lanka, and finally
Malaysia. Bérubé preached empowerment for producers through
building up co-operatives all along the production chain: organizing
fishers into co-operatives, creating credit co-operatives that could lend
them the capital they needed to escape the clutch of rapacious traders,
and capping it with marketing expertise to make sure that fish would
find willing buyers, whether domestically or internationally.[15]

As Colombo Plan fisheries advisor to Cambodia starting in 1955,
Bérubé's interest went further than the expanded production laid out
in his mandate. He also sought to promote social change in Cambodia through cooperative organization. In his reports on Cambodia,
Bérubé was explicit on this point and on the value of the Quebec fisheries cooperative model. To win government support, he appealed to
anti-communism, a theme that worked as well in Catholic networks
in Quebec as in offices in Ottawa. Cambodian fishers, he wrote, were
"the smallest of Cambodia's small people" (his translation of *petit peu-
ple*). They were dominated by ethnic Chinese traders in "the same way,
if not worse, than were our own fishermen under the iron hand of the
fish companies in the 19th century. Something has to be done, or they
will listen to the sing-song of Communist propaganda." How could
poor people be satisfied without turning to communism? "The
answer is co-operation, the organization of co-operatives in every sector of the economic activities of the nation." Cooperative education
and organization had succeeded in Quebec, he concluded. "It can do
the same here. And it must do it. Otherwise our best programmes for
technical development of the Cambodian fisheries are jeopardized
and their net result reduced to a minimum, if not entirely wasted."[16]
This was a Catholic and social-democratic vision: cooperative organization as a path towards social justice which at the same time served
the twin goals of modernization and anti-communism.

Bérubé was subsequently offered the job of director of the Canadian Fisheries Project in Ceylon (now Sri Lanka), a much larger Canadian aid effort and one that offered ample opportunity for promoting
co-operatives. There, he criticized the existing Co-operative Fish Sales
Union and called for reform of "this pseudo co-operative" – namely,
the creation of a Canadian-style marketing board for fish. All the
same, promotion of co-operatives was earning Canada points in Ceylon. For instance, high commissioner R.G. "Nik" Cavell reported to
Ottawa that one cabinet minister whom he called a "well known
Marxist trouble maker" had nevertheless offered "unqualified praise
for Canada and her association with Ceylon."[17] In a neutralist govern-

ment moving to the political left, Canadian support for the co-operative gospel helped maintain a positive image for Canada and served the interests of both donor and recipient governments.

Bérubé's subsequent work in Malaysia saw the co-operative gospel yoked explicitly to Canadian support for a pro-Western government, even at the cost of undermining a profitable commercial business. Bérubé recommended a large programme of Canadian capital assistance to the fisheries project, dismissing concerns from Canadian high commissioner to Malaysia Arthur Menzies and others that Canadian aid should not undermine arrangements then in the hands of a corporation based in Singapore.[18] Cold War skirmishes, in this context, trumped capitalist considerations – though it was a close-run contest. When Canada started providing capital aid to Malaysia (then still Malaya), funds flowed first and fastest to Malaya's East Coast Fisheries Project. The region was home to 18,000 fishers that the government in Kuala Lumpur planned to organize into a large co-operative, thus helping poorer Malays to raise their living standards and freeing them from the economic dominance of ethnic Chinese merchants. For the governing United Malays National Organization (UMNO), this played to its ethnic base and reduced poverty. For Bérubé, it evoked Quebec fishers' struggles to free themselves from English corporate domination. For the Canadian government, which was asked to provide much of the funding necessary, it was an alternative, non-communist appeal to poor Malays. Malaya's stability and allegiance to the West was at risk from a communist-led insurgency defeated only with British military assistance. Aid to fishers helped create a non-communist possibility of greater prosperity. In a small way, and in keeping with the entire Canadian aid programme, it was part of meeting the communist threat by creating "the dynamic counter-attraction of a free, prosperous and progressive society," in the words of Escott Reid, Canadian high commissioner in India.[19] In the Malayan context, communism and anti-communism were coded ethnically: the communist forces were mostly from the large ethnic-Chinese minority, while the UMNO government tried to rally Malays to the defence of their homeland on ethnic lines. Yet ethnicity was also religion: to be a Malay was to be a Muslim.[20] UMNO's brand of moderate religious nationalism in the East Coast fisheries project drew on support from Bérubé's Catholic social activism, and, at one more remove, the St Laurent government's determined defence of "Christian civilization."

When the Colombo Plan administration in Ottawa assigned Bérubé to work in Cambodia, it was a one-off contract to a country where the elite spoke and worked in French. Government reports, though, quickly noted Bérubé's "very wide background of experience and a note-worthy record of achievement in his field," and his "flair for working with people of an under-developed country."[21] This led to contracts in English-speaking contacts in Ceylon and Malaya. He earned the full confidence of the civil servants responsible for technical assistance, who continued to deploy him to areas where he could help form co-operatives. His advocacy helped shift Canadian government policy in a direction more sympathetic to cooperative organization. In this he received important backing from other technical advisors, such as fellow co-operatives advocate A.H. (Gus) MacDonald, director of the Northern Affairs Branch of Saskatchewan's Department of Natural Resources. A parallel project saw Malayan civil servants study at Nova Scotia's St Francis Xavier University, whose cooperatives training programme was one outflow of the left-Catholic Antigonish movement. Cooperatives were not the be-all and end-all of Canadian aid to Malaya, but in response to joint requests from Canadian experts and Malayan officials, and with expert reports backing up one another's recommendations, they became a significant aspect of bilateral aid relations. Technical advisors like Bérubé and MacDonald held views consistent with overall Canadian foreign policy goals, and stressed the value of cooperatives in reaching those goals. This in turn influenced the pattern of Canadian development aid. Catholic social teachings, including the promotion of co-operative organization, dovetailed with Canadian government priorities. At the same time, there was clear influence on thinking in Ottawa about what sort of aid projects were desirable and effective. From "the field," religious perspectives affected Canadian diplomacy. While the government was trying to harness socialists like MacDonald and "wonderful zealots" like Bérubé, its own development strategies were shaped by the advisors it chose.

MIDWIFE TO THE ISLAMIC REFORMATION[22]

Just "as the Roman was called to teach the world law, the Greek to teach the world art, the Hebrew to teach the world religion, so we in Canada, if true to our opportunities, may be called upon to lead the world in the work of world-wide evangelization," declared prominent Methodist layman and Liberal politician Newton Rowell at the peak of the missionary age. Rowell's was a nationalist view of Canadian missions, but missionaries were equally embedded in a "transatlantic evangelical community" that helped make real the post-1945 idea of a "North Atlantic triangle." J. Lovell Murray, head of the Canadian School of Missions, was typical in describing Canada, Britain, and the United States as "more than neighbours; their nervous system is one."[23]

The wave of European and North American missionary work in Asia and Africa faded in the later twentieth century. Yet its legacy lingered, influencing the emerging notion that peoples of faith might make common cause to resist totalitarian threats. Political leaders picked up on this legacy. "We who have faith cannot afford to fall out amongst ourselves," President Franklin D. Roosevelt said in a call to unite religious leaders in a common struggle against atheistic communism. His successor Harry Truman continued the effort, including "the top Buddhist and the Grand Lama of Tibet" among the common front of faith he dreamed of erecting. At first, Islam figured less prominently. Orientalist preconceptions saw majority-Muslim countries as weak, backwards, superstitious, and – in the case of postwar modernization theorists – trapped in the mire of "tradition." Still, there was hope that the Muslim world, properly guided into modernity, might become a shield against communism.[24] Resurgent political Islam appeared to many Western policy-makers as greatly preferable to the communist adversary or even to "radical" Third World nationalism and non-alignment. It was a potential Cold War ally. This was an idea that some Muslim activists could also pick up on, as Maurice Labelle's chapter recounts. The world situation, *Saturday Night* editorialized, had given the West "a strong reason to seek a better knowledge of and sympathy with the group of nations whose concept of the universe is at least monotheistic and spiritual and entirely opposed to the gross materialism with which we are confronted in the Communist bloc."[25] Similarly, one Pakistani newspaper invoked the same trope of civilization under threat as St Laurent had, issuing a clarion call for religions to unite against the communist menace:

> Never was there greater need for world religions to pool their
> resources than to-day, when civilisation is threatened by one of the
> darkest forces known to history, a force out to reduce man to a
> producing machine and consuming animal, with no higher des-
> tiny than a few creature comforts ... Between them, the worlds of
> Islam and Christianity can accomplish a great deal to turn the tide

of atheistic materialism and build a new and happier world on the Fatherhood of God and brotherhood of man – concepts which form the corner-stones both of Islam and Christianity.[26]

This theme of religions united against communism was picked up by McGill University principal Cyril James as he sought support for the Institute of Islamic Studies (IIS) being set up at his university in the early 1950s. James argued that there were "three great religions in the world today, Christianity, Islam, and Communism – and Islam stands halfway between Christianity and Communism ... In a strategic sense, in the struggle between Russia and the West for the minds of men, the Islamic lands are critical areas."[27]

Trans-Pacific religious connections, in other words, were not limited to Christianity: McGill's Institute for Islamic Studies shows how they could be mediated through other religions as well. The IIS role in shaping Islamic education in Asia aligned with the Canadian government's self-defined mission in its relations with Asia as a whole, acting as a modernizing agent and in keeping with Canada's Cold War goals. The institute set itself the goal of understanding Islam and shaping its future directions. Wilfred Cantwell Smith, its founder and guiding spirit as director from 1951 to 1963, had been "representative among the Muslims" for the Canadian Overseas Missions Council, a joint board of the Anglican, Baptist, Presbyterian, and United Churches. Returning to Canada in 1949, he became McGill's professor of comparative religion. Under his leadership, the IIS worked with the Canadian government: Canadian missions in six Muslim countries spread information about the IIS and asked British embassies to do so in countries where Canada was not represented. Collaboration peaked when Smith's brother Arnold served as Canadian ambassador to Egypt in 1958–61.[28] In a limited way, Ottawa was trying to harness an academic and religious institute to its global strategies, but the knowledge and approaches developed at McGill would also inform the ways in which Canadian diplomats viewed the Islamic world.

Smith dreamed of helping Islam come to terms with modernity. "The Muslims must modernize their life; but they cannot do so without thinking through their own religion," he argued in one early formulation of the IIS mission.

Amongst their (and indeed all 'orientals') immense and manifold problems, none is more fundamental than their need of re-expressing their faith in twentieth-century terms ... At its highest – if you will not smile at the exaggerated ambition – I would foresee our programme conceivably acting as a kind of midwife for the Islamic Reformation which is struggling to be born.[29]

Smith hoped to engage with the Colombo Plan, the major channel for Canadian aid to Asia. "We have assumed far too glibly that in our relations with Afro-Asia all we have to do is give and teach," he wrote in one of his best-known books, calling for 0.5 per cent of Canada's $50-million annual Colombo Plan budget to go to cultural interchange. Despite his lobbying, External Affairs replied that cultural exchange lay outside the plan mandate.[30]

In effect, the IIS was trying to push the Canadian government to broaden its Cold War strategies. That push ultimately succeeded when Smith's McGill model was picked up by Indonesian IIS graduates returning to work in their country's ministry of religion, who made it the basis for overhauling the country's "very traditional" Islamic universities system.[31] As Indonesia's religion minister, IIS graduate Abdul Mukti Ali would modernize the Islamic education system, leading a "McGill mafia" that worked with the country's military rulers to shift Indonesian Islam away from Middle Eastern models. By the 1970s, the Canadian International Development Agency (CIDA) was willing to fulfil Smith's old calls by offering scholarships to Indonesians to study at the IIS.[32] CIDA stepped up its involvement in 1990 by kicking in $6 million over five years for the IIS to strengthen the capacity of the IAIN system directly, and by bringing IAIN teachers for graduate training at McGill. It stepped up support to $12.4 million for 1995–2000, and support for McGill-IAIN partnership has remained substantial in the twenty-first century.[33]

As time wore on, the adversary was not so much Soviet-led communism as fundamentalist Islam. Based on a common understanding, the IIS – from its Presbyterian missionary founder to its modernist Muslim graduates – acted on religious impulses in ways that affected the way Canada interacted with the Islamic world. Religion and Canadian foreign policy were allied, but religious influences again shaped Canadian foreign policy.

THE "LOSS" OF THE "LITTLE CHINESE"

When in 1949 Chairman Mao Zedong declared the inauguration of the People's Republic of China, the news came as a tolling of doom

in parishes throughout Quebec. Some 400 Quebec Catholic missionaries were in China. The Missionary Sisters of Notre-Dame des Anges
of Lennoxville alone counted 105 religious sisters in the country.[34]
Another mission society, the Jesuit Procure des Missions Étrangères de
Chine, sent more than $1.1 million to China missionary work in the
two decades of the 1930s and 1940s – more than 80 per cent of that
during the Chinese civil war of 1945–49 – a sure sign that Quebec
Catholics were taking an interest in China missionary work.[35] China
missions were the vocation for the independent Quebec-based Société
des Missions-Étrangères, created to give French Canada a voice in
global missions.[36]

The presence of China was most visible through the Saint-Enfance
collections and events that were omnipresent in Quebec parishes.
Children throughout Quebec could for 25 cents "buy" a Chinese
orphan to be baptized. These "petits chinois" or "petites chinoises" –
little Chinese – were symbolized with pictures that were available in
a choice of colours.[37] Missionary work, with China as the prime mission field, represented a "great venture" for Catholic Quebec, in the
words of Canon Lionel Groulx.[38] All of this had a large element of
condescension towards "lesser races," of course, but it also helped to
make sure that Canadians were aware of China and that they saw it
mainly through a religious gaze as mission field, ripe for harvest.

Few Canadians rejoiced in the advance of communism in China –
after all, Canadian missionaries there, and many other Canadians, saw
Christianity and communism as the great rivals for the hearts of the
Chinese people. Still, there were those who saw Mao's new regime as
an improvement on the previous Kuomintang (Nationalist) government. In Canada's embassy, first secretary and chef-de-mission Chester
Ronning, the China-born son of Lutheran missionaries (and later
leader of the Alberta CCF), greeted the arrival of communist armies as
an "almost too good to be true" chance to usher in "a kingdom of genuine peace." While some in the English-speaking Protestant churches
took anti-communist stances, others agreed to accommodate themselves to the new regime, which ordered the expulsion of missionaries
and a new self-governing, socialist Chinese Christian church. One
expelled missionary even left China dressed in a Mao suit, a clear sig-
nal of his political sympathies.[39]

The dominant reaction in Quebec was more hostile. Close to Ronning in location, but a world away in opinion, an unnamed Jesuit cor-

respondent offered the following view to readers of the magazine *Relations*, published by the Jesuit province of French Canada:

> Le Christ a dit : *Je suis la Voie, la Vérité et la Vie*. Le communisme, ennemi du Christ, n'est pas une voie, mais un précipice; ce n'est pas la vérité, mais un mensonge éhonté; ce n'est pas une vie, mais la mort de l'âme humaine. Les plans communistes en éducation visent à la subjugation de la race humaine par un matérialisme sans espoir. Humblement et pleins d'espérance, nous prions et souffrons afin que le jour vienne ou le Christ, Voie, Vérité et Vie, se montrera aux masses de Chine et les conduira triomphalement sur le chemin de la vérité.[40]

The writer stressed the importance of saving China and its traditions from becoming "un immense colonie russe … non seulement en matières économiques, mais aussi culturelles et spirituelles."[41] The article and the wider reaction it exemplifies serve as good examples of the Quebec Jesuits' sense of their role as both cultural and religious mediators between Quebec and China.[42]

While Canadian Protestant missionaries agreed to leave China, and were gone by 1952, Catholics were less willing to go. In Quebec, stories of persecution of Québécois missionaries continued until the final expulsions in 1955. Quebec nuns were accused of murdering a thousand Chinese babies (most were baptized on their deathbed, which from the nuns' point of view meant saving their souls even if their lives could not be saved). Five nuns from the Missionary Sisters of the Immaculate Conception (MIC) of Montreal were sentenced to five-year prison terms (later commuted to expulsion). As Serge Granger writes: "China became Quebec's first experience of the Cold War … Quebec's Cold War had a religious tone, comparing communism to atheism."[43]

A strong "China lobby" in the United States spent much of the 1950s lamenting the "loss of China." There was no counterpart in English Canada, a difference that informs most English-language scholarship about Canada-China relations.[44] Yet in Quebec Catholic circles – meaning in most of Quebec – the "loss" of China as a mission field was felt keenly: all the more so since the Saint-Enfance collections for China continued at the parish level until the late 1950s, providing a weekly lived sense of connection to suffering Chinese children. This religious inheritance would linger and affect future Canada-China relations.

GOD'S CALL TO A NEW BEGINNING

After the fall of Mao and the gradual restoration of religious freedoms in China, Canadian government and church networks both moved, in parallel but different ways, to restore ties to China. In 1981, Montreal hosted the first large encounter between Chinese and Western Christians since the end of the missionary age. "God's Call to a New Beginning," as the conference was called, aimed to respond to the new opening in China and to restore links with Chinese churches, absent the old colonialist and racist condescension.

Canadian recognition of the People's Republic of China, followed by an exchange of embassies in 1970, eased the restoration of ties between Chinese and Canadian Christians, but it would be a mistake to ignore the religious aspects of these restored contacts. It was the end of religious persecution in China that made this restoration of contact possible. Beginning in 1976, the Canadian churches, most of them with head offices in Toronto, embarked on a new project in cooperation with Anglican, Presbyterian, and United churches sponsoring a Canada-China Programme (CCP).[45]

The CCP was part of what John Stackhouse calls "a somewhat bewildering alphabet soup of organizations" seeking to "bring Christian principles to bear on questions of public policy." From the 1970s to the 1990s, Canadian churches formed a constellation of ecumenical coalitions dedicated to a region of the world – such as the CCP, the Canada Asia Working Group, and the Inter-Church Coalition for Human Rights in Latin America – or to a specific issue, such as Project North (for Indigenous rights), GATT-fly (later the Ecumenical Coalition for Economic Justice), and Ten Days for World Development. These coalitions challenged government policy in their mandated areas, drawing on support from the Catholic, United, Anglican, and Presbyterian churches, plus smaller denominations such as the Lutherans, Quakers, and Disciples of Christ, on a case-by-case basis. In each instance, they offered recommendations to the government based on partnership with organizations in other countries that shared the Canadian mainline churches' belief in economic, social, and ecological justice – the language that the coalitions increasingly used to describe their religiously informed mandates. Ecumenical coalitions, in the China case as elsewhere, can be read as a Canadian Christian effort to build a different sort of foreign relations for Canada.[46]

The Canada-China Programme was one such coalition. Like the others, it inspired spin-off groups without formal church ties, which consequently had the moral authority of religious mandates coupled with the freedom of action that came from lack of formal affiliation to the churches. One such group was Amitié-Chine (AC), a Montreal-based NGO that aimed to break down "les frontières idéologiques" – to cross not only geographical but also ideological borders. Amitié-Chine counted three cofounders: Sister Fleurette Lagaçé MIC, Father Roland Lanueuville PME, and Father Michel Marcil SJ. The MIC sisters, Missions-Etrangères fathers, and Jesuits would also be the main financial backers.[47] Marcil stood in the intellectual Jesuit tradition; Laneuville brought the diocesan church's official mission society into the mix; and Lagaçé carried the heritage of the women's religious orders that had heavily influenced Chinese education. All three founders carried a sense of personal connection to China and the hope that the broken body of the church might be made whole – not by the pope reasserting control over the Chinese government's officially approved Chinese Catholic Patriotic Association (CCPA), but rather, on the one hand, through dialogue between the Vatican and the underground Chinese priests and bishops ordained in secret with papal approval and their "house churches"; and, on the other hand, through the Chinese government-recognized priests, bishops, and laity.

China's government allowed Buddhist, Christian, and other religious leaders to attend the triennial gathering of the World Conference on Religion and Peace in 1979, the first such overseas religious contacts permitted since Mao's days in power. "God's Call to a New Beginning," the 1981 international conference in Montreal, was the next step. It was also the occasion for the creation of Amitié-Chine. AC did not aim at changing China, the historic goal of the missionary enterprise, but rather at changing attitudes in Quebec towards China. With the door open a crack to restoring ties between Chinese Catholics and the global church, AC aimed to open doors in Quebec. It listed its objectives as sharing news from China in order to "aider a faire comprendre la realité de la Chine"; to encourage dialogue, exchanges, and cooperation between Quebec and China; and to assist targeted aid projects to China. All this should be done, Sister Lagaçé wrote, "dans un esprit de coopération, d'animation et de partage."[48]

AC was involved in the "New Beginning" conference in two ways. First, it provided local hosting and an entry into the Catholic milieu of Quebec that the Toronto-based CCP was poorly placed to offer. Second, it gave cover for Canadian Catholics to quietly break with the rejectionist position of refusing to engage bishops ordained with the Chinese government rather than Vatican approval. In 1983, the Canadian Conference of Catholic Bishops (CCCB) approved the CCP's willingness to keep "the door open for relations with the Chinese church," but rejected its "one-sided defence" of government-approved churches in China.[49] In Montreal, the doors opened for dialogue with the Chinese Catholic Patriotic Association and its Protestant counterpart, the China Christian Council. In this process, voices linked to AC were important. The conference gave unprecedented space for approved Chinese Christian leaders to publicly criticize Western intervention, and even criticize Vatican-affiliated missionary churches for not sufficiently indigenizing the church in China.[50]

AC also permitted the Canada-China Programme to gain access to China through delegations invited to tour the country and meet Christians, while ensuring Canadian delegations were ecumenical (both Protestant and Catholic). This permitted, for instance, a Canadian ecumenical delegation to visit China in 1982.[51] It was equally central in a 1985 Canadian Catholic Friendship Delegation that signalled the ascendance of the "engagement" strategy within the Canadian Catholic church. The presence of AC cofounders Lagaçé and Marcil, especially, allowed Canadian delegations to speak in both of Canada's official languages – as well as in China's official language. Contacts from the Chinese government-approved Catholic church could not go directly to Canadian Catholic groups – all of which were of course in communion with the Vatican, as the Chinese "patriotic" church was not. Amitié-Chine, with no official standing as a Canadian Catholic organization, was ideally placed to serve as the contact point for China dialogue.

In 1987, AC (rather than the Canada-China Programme) hosted the first formal Chinese Catholic visit to Canada. This was a high-powered group, led by the vice-president of the (Chinese government-approved) Chinese Conference of Catholic Bishops. AC connections enabled the delegation to meet bishops in both French and English Canada.[52] The Canadian Conference of Catholic Bishops proved willing to enter dialogue with the official Catholic Church in China even while (like the Vatican) it described government-approved Chinese bishops as "illegitimate." By 2003, Ottawa archbishop Marcel Gervais on behalf of the CCCB welcomed the visit of Beijing "patriotic" bishop Fu Tieshan, calling it a chance to open "a very positive dialogue leading to deeper mutual understanding."[53]

AC also aimed to foster a more positive view of China within Quebec society. Thus it funded a health clinic and nurse training in Gansu province and partnered with a Quebec-based adoption network and the Amity Foundation, the first Chinese Christian NGO, to assist Quebec families to adopt Chinese children – a somewhat conscious echo of the pre-war "little Chinese" orphan theme as well as a concrete manifestation of AC's aspiration to build people-to-people connections. AC began a twinning project between a school in the Montreal suburb of Laval and one in Shenzhen, the Chinese city across the border from Hong Kong. It participated in a television show, "La Voix de Chine." Website offerings also featured samplings of "Eastern wisdom" from Confucius and Chinese language lessons – some of them taught by Chinese-speaking members of the group.[54]

It is difficult to gauge the wider impact of AC. There is evidence of an active series of public events and of ties to adoption-minded families, as well as links to some Asian studies professors. The largest impact was probably within Canadian religious networks. AC access to China grew by leaps and bounds. By 1998 it was able to gain approval to send funds to assist in the formation of Chinese seminarians, the sort of foreign funding to the church that had been banned during Mao's years and for two decades afterwards. The organization was not, however, able to realize the dream of facilitating restored communion between Chinese and Quebec Catholics. "Rome ne bougeait pas": Rome did not move, as one AC member said bluntly. Nor would Canadian bishops move further than they had already. By 2005, the mission of spreading awareness of China within Quebec had also been overtaken by easier communications with a more open China, and the organization decided to close its doors. Nevertheless, it could point to a role in the rapprochement at the social level between Canada and China that followed the resumption of Canada-China diplomatic relations in 1970, and to a significant influence within Canadian religious networks.[55]

A case study of Amitié-Chine fits well into several emerging historiographical movements. Many studies richly detail the Quebec missionary enterprise in China, but fall silent about its legacy in Quebec-China relations. AC is one of what are in fact multiple

legacies left in Quebec by the missionary enterprise that loomed so
large earlier in the twentieth century. Catherine Foisy has described
the continued vigour of missions even in a time of increased secu-
larization in Quebec, illustrating the ongoing importance of missionary ties in Quebec's engagements with Asia, Africa, and Latin
America.[56] The AC case implies that, even in the absence of a Quebec missionary presence in China, the legacies of missions and individual former missionaries were important in permitting the re-
emergence of links as China began moving to re-engage with the
global community. This re-engagement was not merely diplomatic
and economic, as the literature on Canada-China relations implies.
It was also religious. This conclusion underlines similar studies
about the importance of Catholic networks in a persistent identification between Quebec nationalism (even in its more recent and
more secular forms) and Latin America, shown in the work of Maurice Demers and Catherine Legrand.[57]

Cultural transfers drawing on previous religious connections were
not unique to Quebec. Latin American liberation theology influenced the thinking of English-Canadian Catholics in the Antigonish
movement, who in turn brought their own theology to their work in
Latin America.[58] Liberation theology provided the founding note for
the Canada-China Programme, which tried to link it to the English-
Canadian Protestant "social gospel" tradition.[59] Amitié-Chine's own
efforts to take a progressive theological stance within a relatively conservative Catholic milieu serve as one example of the international
dimension of Canadian religious history.

This is truer still within a Quebec context. Newer scholarship rejects
the view of Quebec's "Quiet Revolution" as a progressive, secular
movement casting off the heavy hand of the Catholic church. Quebec
was not an "isolated," inward-looking, and "backwards" province during the years of church domination. Instead, it emerges as an open,
globally engaged society that maintained strong ties to Latin America, China, Haiti, parts of Africa, and other parts of the world. These
connections were prominent within Catholic networks open to cultural transfers between Quebec and the Global South. Again, Maurice
Demers's work linking intellectual developments in Quebec and
Latin America is exemplary. Serge Granger has argued for continuities
between early Quebec engagement with China and subsequent Canadian diplomatic history. He even connects figures affected by Quebec
Catholic social teaching to the origins of the Cultural Revolution.

Granger's argument intersects with that of Pierre Beaudet on the interplay of "red" (socialist) and "black" (Jesuit-Catholic) influences in Quebec's longstanding engagement with the wider world.[60]

In surveying the legacy of the English-Canadian missionary enterprise, Ruth Compton Brouwer argues that in many ways, "missions became development."[61] The point applies with equal force to Quebec-centred, French-speaking, Catholic cases, as the example of Louis Bérubé illustrates. From the social teachings of the Catholic Church was born one strand of Quebec's engagement with the Global South. The Amitié-Chine story, in a small way, helps to connect a time when girls from Quebec villages dreamed of saving Chinese souls and Chinese children to a time in which Quebec's engagement with China is not merely about trade missions, but also about engagement in a multitude of areas, from adoption to tourism to education to energy.[62] In tracing micro-historical studies like the Amitié-China story, we can begin to paint a more detailed picture in which engagement never really stopped.

RELIGIOUS FREEDOM, RELIGIOUS INFLUENCE

The Sri Lankan liberation theologian Tissa Balasuriya, reporting on the 1981 "New Beginning" conference in Montreal, had worried that church re-engagement with China might repeat the missionary errors of overidentification with imperialist governments. "We should be careful that our present openness to China is not a mere religious counterpart of the policies of the Western States and of business corporations that are now opening themselves to China," he wrote.[63]

Canadian Christian networks would heed that fear, working instead to ensure that church connections to China could not be seen as echoes of Canadian government or business goals. Church and government aims often dovetailed, but the churches guarded their independence. Ottawa attempted to involve churches as one aspect of its China diplomacy. In the 1990s, for instance, foreign minister Lloyd Axworthy asked Canadian churches to take part in his efforts at dialogue with China. The church response stressed that churches were in no way an arm of Canadian government foreign policy:

the Canadian churches have made it very clear that this type of ecumenical work is not something new given their many years of tireless efforts to forge, build, promote, and protect their Chinese church relationships … Though we are contributing to DFAIT's [the Department of Foreign Affairs and International Trade's] pursuit of bilateral dialogue, we do not want [Canadian church delegations to China] to be portrayed as contributing to the Canadian government's political agenda. Our relationships with China are rooted in partnership and we would not continue to pursue this initiative if it doesn't contribute to strengthening our church partners which is an essential aspect of the Canadian churches' ongoing mission.[64]

The subsequent Religious Freedoms delegation, led by senator and former moderator of the United Church Lois Wilson, was careful to stress that Canadian government follow-up be carried out in full partnership with Canadian churches.[65] With a common focus on religious freedom, the churches were willing to collaborate with the Canadian government on foreign policy – but they carefully guarded the prerogative of their own independent foreign policy.

The issue of religious freedom, like that of partnership with China, was nothing new in the 1990s, no matter what policy-makers in Ottawa might have thought. Canadian Baptists, for example, had organized a large and successful campaign for religious freedom in Romania in the 1920s, and at their 1922 congress called for "bearing witness to the cause of religious liberty." In this, they echoed a long tradition in US foreign policy which saw churches and government come together to campaign for freedom of religion overseas.[66] Church-based networks also challenged Canadian government policy on apartheid in South Africa, human rights, conflicts in Nicaragua and El Salvador, Third World debt and development, and many more issues – undiplomatic histories just beginning to be told.[67] Some analysts have suggested that Canadian foreign policy was pulled towards that of the "like-minded states," including the Netherlands and the Scandinavian countries, through a "humane internationalist impulse."[68] But to the extent that Canadian foreign policy moved in that direction, it is perhaps just as likely that the influence came from religious networks within Canada, many of which lobbied hard for a more "just" foreign policy. Religious influence on government foreign policy was normative, not determinative, but it was nevertheless real.

In the case of development aid, Canadian government and religious foreign policies coincided. Canada would begin to deliver aid partly to save Christian civilization by enfolding newly independent countries in the Western embrace. Religious efforts went towards "humanizing" aid policy, encouraging co-operatives, cultural exchange, and other aspects seen as being in tune with the Christian gospel or as making an ally of the Islamic world. In time, churches came to develop an alternative foreign policy of their own, expressed through ecumenical coalitions and drawing on associated NGOs that were religiously inspired but not explicitly religious. The churches carefully guarded their independence of action and their independent goals and relationships – key elements of a foreign policy – from becoming too tied to government goals and actions. Yet their global diplomacy, independent of government diplomatic strategies, was a significant element in how Canada and Canadians interacted with other parts of the world.

"As never before in history, our troubles are driving home upon the consciousness of mankind the truth that the whole world is one," wrote Jesse Arnup of the United Church in 1934.[69] The mainline churches, even after their missionary efforts faded, tended to be one of the most internationally minded groups in Canadian society. It may be in this internationalism, above all, that religious influence played out. Religious voices were among those in Canada who were most internationally minded, most resistant to narrow nationalism and commercial self-interest. There is scope for much future research in this area. In short: religion needs to be read back into the study of Canada and the World.

NOTES

1 Andrew Preston, "The Religious Turn in Diplomatic History," in *Explaining the History of American Foreign Relations*, 3rd ed., edited by Frank Costigliola and Michael J. Hogan (Cambridge: Cambridge University Press, 2016), 284–303.

2 Andrew Preston, *Sword of the Spirit, Shield of Faith: Religion in American War and Diplomacy* (New York: Knopf, 2012), 517.

3 Andrew Preston, "Introduction: The Religious Cold War," in *Religion and the Cold War: A Global Perspective*, edited by Philip E. Muehlenbeck (Nashville: Vanderbilt University Press, 2012), xi–xii.

4 In this, Madokoro underlines a theme in her own earlier work about the common ties of anti-Asian racism in the nineteenth century Pacific world, rooted in a "defence" of white, Christian societies in Canada and other countries. Laura Madokoro, *Elusive Refuge: Chinese Migrants in the Cold War* (Cambridge, MA: Harvard University Press, 2016).

5 Pearson cited in C.P. Champion, *The Strange Demise of British Canada* (Montreal: McGill-Queen's University Press, 2010), 97.

6 Again, this point echoes Preston, *Sword of the Sprit.*

7 Louis St Laurent, "The Preservation of Civilization," Department of External Affairs, *Statements and Speeches*, 50/43.

8 Escott Reid, *Time of Fear and Hope: The Making of the North Atlantic Treaty, 1947–49* (Toronto: McClelland and Stewart, 1977); Reg Whitaker and Gary Marcuse, *Cold War Canada: The Making of a National Insecurity State, 1945–1957* (Toronto: University of Toronto Press, 1996); John Price, *Orienting Canada: Race, Empire, and the Transpacific* (Vancouver: UBC Press, 2011).

9 Jacques Maritain, *The Twilight of Civilization* (New York: Sheed and Ward, 1943), vii–ix, 40.

10 St Laurent, "The Preservation of Civilization."

11 Ibid.

12 Hugh L. Keenleyside, *Memoirs Vol. 1: Hammer the Golden Day* (Toronto: McClelland and Stewart, 1981); Keenleyside standard welcome letter to technical experts, 1952, S-0441-1483-03, United Nations Archives and Record Management (UNARMS); Summary charts of pledges to EPTA, RG25 vol. 6090 file 5475-DU-1-40[19.1], Library and Archives Canada (LAC).

13 Canada, House of Commons, *Debates*, 25 March 1952, 764, 762.

14 Earl Drake, *A Stubble-Jumper in Striped Pants: Memoirs of a Prairie Diplomat* (Toronto: University of Toronto Press, 1999), 71.

15 "Projet de stabilization et d'expansion du movement cooperative chez les pêcheurs du Cambodge," report by Bérubé to minister of finance of Cambodia, 1 May 1956, and "Co-operative Organization of Fishermen," Bérubé's progress report #3 to Colombo Plan administration in Canada [1956], RG74, vol. 258, file 36-8C-B10[2], LAC.

16 "Co-operative Organization of Fishermen," Bérubé's progress report #3 to Colombo Plan administration in Canada [1956], RG74, vol. 258, file 36-8C-B10[2], LAC.

17 Colombo letter 723, 19 November 1956; Bérubé to A.W. Rosenthal, 1 September 1958, F.E. Pratt, chief, capital projects, to Bérubé, 15 September 1958; and Colombo letter 766, 9 December 1958, RG74, vol. 259, file 36-8C-B10[4], LAC.

18 Bérubé's report to minister Aziz, 7 July 1959, RG25, file 11038-17-A-40 [9], LAC.

19 "Canadian Foreign policy, 1947–1951," draft speech by Escott Reid, Canadian high commissioner in India, 15 February 1957, MG26 N1, vol. 12, file Reid, Escott-Canada-External Affairs 1951–57, LAC.

20 Richard Stubbs, *Hearts and Minds in Guerrilla Warfare: The Malayan Emergency*

1948–1960 (Toronto: Oxford University Press, 1989); Judith Nagata, "What Is a Malay? Situational Selection of Ethnic Identity in a Plural Society," *American Ethnologist* 1, no. 2 (1974): 331–50.

21 W.D. Mills to Finlay Sim, T&C interoffice memo, 30 Dec. 1958, RG74, vol. 259, file 36-8C-B10[4], LAC.

22 This section draws on my *Fire and the Full Moon: Canada and Indonesia in a Decolonizing World* (Vancouver: UBC Press, 2009), with some supplemental research.

23 Robert Wright, *A World Mission: Canadian Protestantism and the Quest for a New International Order, 1918–1939* (Montreal and Kingston: McGill-Queen's University Press, 1991), 9.

24 Alvyn Austin, *Saving China: Canadian Missionaries in the Middle Kingdom, 1888–1959* (Toronto: University of Toronto Press, 1986), 85–6; Preston, *Sword*, 134, 322, 351, 413; Wright, *World Mission*, 9.

25 *Saturday Night*, November 1952.

26 *Civil and Military Gazette*, 26 October 1952.

27 Rockefeller Foundation report on visit to McGill, 1 April 1954, RG1.2, 427R, box 10, file 93, Rockefeller Archives Center (RAC).

28 E.H. Norman, Information Division, Department of External Affairs, to Smith, 29 September 1952, RG25, vol. 8267, file 9455-P-5-40, LAC.

29 Smith's proposal to James, 7 May 1951, RG2, box 208, file 5586, McGill University Archives (MUA).

30 Smith, *The Faith of Other Men* (New York: New American Library 1962), 105; Smith to R.G. Nik Cavell, Colombo Plan administrator, 26 June 1953, RG25, vol. 6576, file 11038-40 [12], LAC; secretary of state for external affairs to Smith, 29 April 1955, RG2, box 180, file 6251, MUA.

31 Siaful Muzani, "Mu'tazilah Theology and the Modernization of the Indonesian Muslim Community: Intellectual Portrait of Harun Nasution," *Studia Islamika* 1: 91–131, IAIN Jakarta, *Research on the Role of the McGill University Islamic Studies Alumni in Academics, Bureaucracy and Society* (Jakarta: Centre for the Study of Islam and Society), 2.

32 IIS annual report, August 1975, RG2, box 504, file 9252, MUA; Principal R.E. Bell's notes on meeting with IIS director Charles Adams, 6 December 1971, RG2, box 457, file 8670, MUA, McGill news release, 22 June 1972, RG3, box 207, file 4039, MUA.

33 Hickling Corp., "Mid Term Evaluation, IAIN Institutional Development Project," Feb. 1992, and IIS response, Adams to Vice-Principal Roger K. Prichard, 7 July 1972; Phase II renewal agreement, [1995], RG3, box 1001, file 17381, MUA; IAIN Jakarta, "Cooperation between IAIN and McGill University: Impact on the Development and Modernization of Islam in

Indonesia" (Unpublished impact study, 2000); IAIN Indonesia Social Equity Project, "About the Project," http://www.mcgill.ca/indonesia-project /about/.

34 Austin, *Saving China,* 152; Catherine Foisy, "Des Québécois aux frontières: Dialogues et affrontements culturels aux dimensions du monde, Récits missionnaires d'Asie, d'Afrique et d'Amérique latine (1945–1980)" (PhD diss., Concordia University, 2012), 124–5; Réne Bacon et Gisèle Desloges, *Sœurs Missionnaires de Notre-Dame des Anges: Se Faire Chinoises avec les Chinois (1922–1932)* (Lennoxville: Sœur Missionnaires de Notre-Dame des Anges: 1991); Emile Gervais, *Un Mois en Chine avec les Sœurs Missionnaires de Notre-Dame des Anges du Diocèse de Sherbrooke* (Sherbrooke: Messager Saint-Michel, 1937); Emile Gervais, *Les Soeurs Missionnaries Notre-Dame des Anges: Ses Origines, son Esprit et son Oeuvre* (Sherbrooke: Messager St-Michel: 1963); Chantal Gauthier, *Women without Frontiers: A History of the Missionary Sisters of the Immaculate Conception, 1902–2007* (Outremont: Carte Blanche, 2008); Irene Mahoney, *Avec Toi Jusqu'au Bout du Monde: 30 ans de Mission Ursuline en Chine* (Sillery, QC: Éditions Anne Sigier, 1997).

35 Samuel C. Fleury, "Le financement canadien-français de la mission chinoise des Jésuites au Xuzhou de 1931 à 1949: La Procure de Chine" (MA thesis, Université Laval, 2014).

36 Claude Gillet, "Cinquante ans de réalisation: La Société des Missions-Étrangères," *Etudes Historiques* 38 (1971): 55–69.

37 Serge Granger, *Le lys et le lotus: Les relations du Québec avec la Chine de 1650 à 1950* (Montreal: VLB Editeur, 2005). For recollections of "buying" a "petit Chinois," see for instance "Acheter un petit chinois à 25 sous," from the web page "Être Chinois au Québec," 13 December 2011, http://etrechinoisau quebec.net/acheter-un-petit-chinois-a-25-sous-2/.

38 Lionel Groulx, *Le Canada français missionnaire, une autre grande aventure* (Montreal: Fides, 1962).

39 Wright, *World Mission,* 56; Chester Ronning, *A Memoir of China in Revolution* (New York: Random House, 1974), 141, 29; Peter Stursberg, *The Golden Hope* (Toronto: United Church Publishing House, 1987), 9–11.

40 Report from a Jesuit correspondent in China, *Rélations,* no. 117 (Sept. 1950), 275, available in digitized form through the Bibliothèque et Archives Nationales du Québec at http://collections.banq.qc.ca/ark:/52327 /2507176.

41 Ibid., 274.

42 Jacques Langlais, *Les Jésuites du Québec en Chine (1918–1955)* (Beauceville: Ateliers de l'Eclaireur, 1979).

43 Foisy, "Des Québécois aux frontières," 121; Serge Granger, "Quebec and

China during the First Half of the Twentieth century" (PhD diss., Concordia University, 2002), 244; Granger, "Quebec and China," 251, 258.

44 The landmark study edited by Paul Evans and B. Michael Frolic, *Reluctant Adversaries: Canada and the People's Republic of China, 1949–1970* (Toronto: University of Toronto Press, 1991), has been followed by other examples of policy-oriented analysis, such as recent articles in *International Journal* and *Canadian Foreign Policy* as well as Huhua Cao and Vivienne Poy, eds., *The China Challenge: Sino-Canadian Relations in the 21st Century* (Ottawa: University of Ottawa Press, 2011), and Pitman Potter, ed., *Issues in Canada-China Relations* (Canadian International Council, November 2011).

45 "Introducing the Canada China Program," *China and Ourselves (C&O)*, no. 1 (May 1976), 1; CCP administration committee minutes, 8 September 1976, Canada-China Programme fonds (CCP) 14–5, United Church of Canada Archives; "Catholic Roundtable on China: Introduction" (September 1992), Canadian Conference of Catholic Bishops Archives (CCCBA), box U3173, file 13. On religious developments in China see Philip L. Wickeri, *Reconstructing Christianity in China: K.H. Ting and the Chinese Church* (Maryknoll, NY: Orbis, 2007). On the Canada-China Programme's history, see David Webster and Sarah Zwierzchowski, "Inter-Church Coalitions as Site of Ecumenical Contact and Conflict: The Canada China Programme, 1971–2000," *Historical Studies* 81 (2015): 73–96.

46 John Stackhouse, "The Protestant Experience in Canada since 1945," in *The Canadian Protestant Experience 1970–1990*, edited by George A. Rawlyk (Montreal and Kingston: McGill-Queen's University Press, 1990), 223. On the coalitions, see Bonnie Greene, ed., *Canadian Churches and Foreign Policy* (Toronto: Lorimer, 1990). I have explored the interactions of two ecumenical coalitions, the CCP and CAWG, in "After the Missionaries: Churches and Human Rights NGOs in Canada's Relations with China," *Journal of American East Asian Relations* 20, no. 2–3 (2013): 216–33.

47 Confidential interview with AC member, 2015; Gauthier, *Women without Frontiers*, 386; AC website, archived version of 8 March 2005, via archive.org.

48 Lagaçé, "Amitié de Chine," *Passages*, newsletter of the fédération de professionnels chinois canadiens (Québec), tenth anniversary edition (2003), http://www.fccp.ca/fall2003.final_colour.pdf, 45.

49 CCP general committee minutes, 28 September 1983, CCP 14-5.

50 Katherine Hockin, "God's Call to a New Beginning," CCP 5-11; Bishop Tu's conference paper, CCP 4-14.

51 Theresa Chu, "Visit to Seven Dioceses in China, Sept. 23rd to Oct 20th, 1982," CCP 9-7.

52 Theresa Chu, "The First Chinese Catholic Delegation to Canada" (June

1987), ccp 7-5; Report of Canadian Catholic Friendship Delegation to China (2–27 March 1985), ccp 7-3.

53 Michael Murray sj, co-director of cccb Missions Office, to ccp, 18 March 1988, ccp 7-6; "Chinese religious delegation visits the cccb," press release from Canadian Conference of Catholic Bishops, 20 February 2003, http://www.cccb.ca/site/eng/media-room/archives/media-releases/2003/1306-chinese-religious-delegation-visits-the-cccb.

54 ac website; Lagaçé, "Amitié de Chine"; Gauthier, *Women without Frontiers*, 386; *Passages*, (2003), 2. See also the film *Alice au pays des gros nez*, directed by Nicole Giguère (2003).

55 Paul T.K. Lin, *In the Eye of the China Storm: A Life Between East and West* (Montreal: McGill-Queen's University Press, 2011; confidential interview, 2015; ac website.

56 Foisy, "Des Québécois aux frontières."

57 Maurice Demers, *Connected Struggles: Catholics, Nationalists, and Transnational Relations between Mexico and Québec, 1917–1945* (Montreal and Kingston: McGill-Queen's University Press, 2014); Catherine Legrand, "Réseaux missionnaires québécois et action sociale en Amérique latine, 1945–1980," *Études d'histoire religieuse* 79, no. 1 (2013): 93–116.

58 Catherine Legrand, "The Antigonish Movement of Canada and Latin America: Catholic Cooperatives, Christian Communities and Development in the Great Depression and the Cold War," paper presented at conference on "Catholic Activism in the Americas, 1891–1962: Comparative and Transnational Approaches," The Catholic University, Washington, dc, October 2013.

59 "Lessons from China and the Social Gospel," *Catholic New Times*, 1 July 1979.

60 Serge Granger, "French Canada's Quiet Obsession with China," *Journal of American-East Asian Relations* 20, no. 2–3 (2013): 156–74; Pierre Beaudet, *Qui aide qui?* (Montréal: Boréal, 2009).

61 Ruth Compton Brouwer, "When Missions Became Development: Ironies of 'NGOization' in Mainstream Canadian Churches in the 1960s," *Canadian Historical Review* 91, no. 4 (2010): 661–93.

62 For instance, Frédéric Mayer, "The Soft Power in the Relations of the Canadian Provinces with China"; Olga Alexeeva, ""Energy and Environmental Issues in Sino-Canadian Relationships in 21st Century"; and Éric Lefrançois, "La politique étrangère du Canada envers la République Populaire de Chine" – all papers presented at a conference on "Canada-China Relations: Past, Present, Future," University of Regina, October 2011.

63 Report of Rev. Tissa Balasuriya (director, Centre for Society and Religion) on "God's Call to a New Beginning" conference, 1981, ccp papers, 5-1, ucc.

64 Background note for 1999 Ecumenical Delegation to China, Canada Asia Working Group papers, box G-6, file 6. Note that file numbers for this private collection (consulted by the author by special arrangement) are likely to change when the collection is archived in the United Church of Canada Archives.

65 Report of the Canadian Ecumenical Delegation on Religious Freedom in the People's Republic of China, 24 October – 5 November 1999, CAWG, G-6/16.

66 Wright, *World Mission*, 93; Preston, *Sword*, passim.

67 Renate Pratt, *In Good Faith: Canadian Churches against Apartheid* (Waterloo: Wilfrid Laurier University Press, 1997) is a rare exception in centring the role of the ecumenical coalitions.

68 Cranford Pratt, *Middle Power Internationalism: The North-South Dimension* (Montreal and Kingston: McGill-Queen's University Press, 1990).

69 Wright, *World Mission*, 238.

SECTION TWO

Environment and Health

4

Natural Security:
Canada-US Environmental Diplomacy

DANIEL MACFARLANE

It has become a truism, even a cliché, to point out that Canada and the United States share the longest undefended border in the world. However, only one of these two qualifiers is actually true: it certainly isn't *undefended*, but it is indubitably the *longest* international border between two countries, bar none. But given that it traverses so much territory, what does this border divide, aside from two nations? At the coasts, obviously the oceans. In the Pacific Northwest, one of the world's major mountain ranges. Then plains and prairies, and further east the largest freshwater system in the world. And so on. The point is that Canada and the United States share many varied ecosystems. Faced with the challenge of cooperatively protecting (or, more often, exploiting) these ecosystems, the two countries have had to come up with an array of formal political and diplomatic mechanisms, some of which are now considered pioneering forms of international environmental governance.

The last few decades have seen a proliferation of studies on Canadian foreign relations with countries *other* than the United States. This has been most welcome and necessary. As the various "undiplomatic history" contributions to this volume demonstrate, the transnational and global turn has brought many previously ignored subjects, geographic areas, and issues under the aegis of Canada's international history. Nonetheless, since 1945 Canada's most important political, cultural, and economic relationship is unequivocally with the United States. This association takes many forms, including continental security, binational trade and tariffs, people flows and migrations, and cultural exchanges. But Canadian-American historians have consistently neglected one of the most important elements of this bilateral entanglement: the environment.

True, North American diplomatic historians have often addressed certain natural resources because of their economic, political, strategic, and military importance – oil is an obvious example, while fish, water bodies, and birds have been the subjects of treaties brokered between Ottawa and Washington.[1] Yet international historians generally treat these natural resources as passive, one-dimensional objects bereft of any materiality or agency, just statistics on paper, no different than widgets or chocolate bars.[2] An environmental history perspective would insist that the nature of these natural resources – whether it be smelter smoke or zebra mussels, red fife wheat or bauxite – makes an enormous difference. While defining a field is notoriously difficult, suffice it to say here that environmental history as a discipline revolves around the study of human-environmental interactions in the past; it looks at the ways that society and the natural world have mutually shaped each other by drawing on sources and approaches (for example, ecology, science, technology) that foreign affairs historians might find, forgive the pun, foreign.

I contend that a full and proper comprehension of the modern history of Canadian diplomacy, especially vis-à-vis the United States, requires the incorporation of environmental history techniques and perspectives. To capture the marriage of environmental and diplomatic history, I propose the notion of "natural security" as a twofold concept. First, to reflect the importance that the natural environment plays in what we think of as the traditional aspects of a nation's security and defence from outside aggressors – not only in terms of the geography and landscapes that must be conquered, but equally for the production of armaments and equipment (metals for tanks, planes, and bullets), and the ability to mobilize defence forces (canals for vessels, fuels for vehicles). Second, to point out that a nation without reliable access to, and control over, necessary natural resources is not "secure."[3]

This chapter will serve as a sort of reconnaissance for a more general twentieth-century study of Canadian-American relations through the lens of environmental diplomacy.[4] I will proceed by first providing some context and methodological discussion about the field of the history of environmental diplomacy in North America. I will show that the natural world has been integral to the thrust of modern

Canadian-American relations and undiplomatic history, highlighting a range of pertinent examples, and then zero in further on the Cold War period – transborder water resources in particular – to provide some detailed case studies to support my larger arguments. In doing so, I also touch on the ways that Canadian cultural views of nature, technology, and continental relations have manifested themselves in distinctive forms of environmental nationalism. Thus, although this might be considered a state-of-the-field approach, it might be better described as an argument for what the field should be, not what it is.

I'm not only suggesting that environmental history helps us better understand Canada's involvement with the wider world, for the reverse is also true: I argue that we can't fully comprehend Canada's environmental history and ecological impact without reference to Canada's foreign relationships, particularly the United States. More so than most other G-20 countries, Canada's prosperity has historically been linked to sending resources abroad (primarily to the United States), with all the attendant national anxieties about "hewer of wood, drawer of water" status that frequently crop up, perhaps most famous-ly during the 1911 reciprocity election. Cross-border trade with the US is now worth around $2 billion per day (though that level of eco-nomic interaction has recently been threatened by the Trump admin-istration), and the desires and vagaries of US markets (and other foreign markets) profoundly shape Canada's engagement with its nat-ural resources – tar sands oil or softwood lumber are only some of the most obvious current examples.

Just as the general history of Canadian-American relations reveals oscillating patterns of cooperation and conflict, the two nations alter-natively govern, or fight over, a multitude of natural resources. Even Canadian landscapes far from the shared borders are shaped by the United States: in the north, for example, through the construction of the Canol project or Alaska-Canada Military Highway during the Sec-ond World War, and then radar lines during the Cold War, to more contemporary squabbles about control of the Northwest Passage and other Arctic questions. The history of bilateral environmental diplo-macy helps explain why, despite the power imbalance, Canada does so well in negotiations with the United States government. Not only does Canada put its top officials on the US file, which the State Department does not, but they are usually much more intimately familiar with the precise flow rate of a particular border water, or, to paraphrase a Henry Kissinger quote employed later in this chapter, the vagaries of the sex life of salmon. In these cases, knowledge can be a valuable corrective to asymmetry.

Nature is a powerful historical actor. There are many cases where seemingly domestic concerns, such as pollution or fish, insert themselves into binational predicaments by disregarding the border. And even when diplomats try to preserve nature they often find themselves quickly outdated, since nature doesn't always move in identical or predictable ways – fish change their migratory patterns, wind and water currents shift. Furthermore, environmental history as an approach offers a way of understanding what is unique about a society and what is a product of environmental forces. Part of the reason that Canada and the United States have so much in common, from a global perspective, is their many shared geographies and ecological experiences. Conversely, the two nations have some very different geographic and environmental mythologies – the frontier thesis vs. the Laurentian thesis, the temperate/tropical south vs. the north – which result in different perceptions of the links between natural environments and national character/identity.

Canadian international history has been reinvigorated in recent years not only by a focal shift away from the North American continent but by a bringing together of approaches from transnationalism, borderlands, culture, gender, and race studies. At the same time, as the introduction to this volume points out, Canadian foreign affairs scholarship has been on the decline; meanwhile, according to some metrics, environmental history is among the fastest growing historical fields in North America.[5] Without incorporating environmental history, Canadian external relations as a discipline risks being further marginalized (at least within the academy).

SETTING THE STAGE

Beginning in the 1990s, scholars such as Mark Lytle and Kurk Dorsey wrote pieces that explicitly sought to define and promote "environmental diplomacy" as a field of North American historical inquiry.[6] American historians have since authored a number of works on that nation's history of environmental diplomacy. In the Canadian context, Dorsey produced what is perhaps the first scholarly monograph consciously framed as historical Canadian-American environmental diplomacy,[7] and there are a handful of other works that utilize a history of environmental diplomacy approach to varying extents, as well as a number of studies that touch on Canada-US natural resources relations to some degree.[8] Despite these various contributions, in the words of eminent environmental historian Graeme Wynn, environmental diplomacy history as a subfield "remains relatively untilled": though the existing publications have been impressive individually, Wynn continues, they amount to a "thin harvest."[9]

According to Lytle and Dorsey, diplomatic historians have ignored environmental history for a number of methodological and ideological reasons: the study of diplomatic history has traditionally been very anthropocentric while environmental history is, of course, premised on bringing in non-human actors and agencies; environmental history uses more theory; diplomatic historians tend to address subjects that are bounded by borders and nation-states, which isn't always the case with environmental history; and so on. Indeed, environmental history uses sources that might seem strange and novel to the diplomacy history crowd, which has traditionally relied on archival evidence (granted, the cultural turn in international history has been changing that for some time now).

How do we determine what counts as *historical* environmental diplomacy? Political scientists and international relations scholars have produced more research explicitly on international environmental relations than have historians. While the result has been a great deal of valuable work, a side effect is that non-historians have defined the agenda for studying past environmental relations. Scholarship focused on contemporary environmental protection – what has been called "green paradiplomacy" among other titles[10] – is probably the dominant strand in environmental diplomacy: it tends to focus on multilateral protection agreements such as UN climate change efforts. As a result, environmental diplomacy is quite often defined as contemporary (i.e., post-1970) environmental protection. But from a historian's perspective, a focus on solely post-1970s agreements about environmental protection is flawed, both because of its exclusion of diplomacy that is not aimed at *protecting* the environment, and because of its temporal rigidity.

First off, a 1970 cut-off date seems more a product of the frames of other social science disciplines. True, notions of environmental "conservation" a century ago were generally quite different from contemporary perceptions of preservation: the former was instrumental, most concerned with conserving for maximum future human exploitation, while the latter sees nature as inherently deserving protection for its own sake, regardless of the anthropogenic benefits. While there certainly has been a proliferation of multilateral environmental protection treaties since 1970, Canadian-America treaties to conserve wildlife and resources stretch back to the early twentieth century, even the nineteenth.

Second, I contend that the field of historical environmental diplomacy should not only include agreements and relations aimed at preserving or conserving habitat or wildlife. Indeed, I'm suggesting that the very opposite – agreements, practices, trade, and negotiations that degrade and despoil the environment – also need to be included under the definition of environmental diplomacy. Any form of past diplomacy dealing with natural resources, including their exploitation, is an appropriate subject for inclusion in this field. We are missing out on a large part of the historical process if we ignore diplomacy and relations that are about exploiting resources, if for no other reason than the fact that state-to-state negotiations about protecting the environment are a much more recent development. Moreover, contemporary attempts to make sustainable decisions and policies require cognizance of how we have affected and manipulated specific ecosystems in the past. Hence, for the purposes of this chapter I define historical environmental diplomacy as the study of historical international relationships and negotiations that directly involve the management or usage of natural resources, including those forms of diplomacy which result in both environmental protection and environmental degradation.

CANADIAN CONFEDERATION AND BEYOND

Kurk Dorsey breaks the existing literature on international diplomacy of the environment into three general streams: early fisheries treaties, multilateral wildlife conservation treaties, and pollution control accords.[11] We can certainly see that pattern replicated in the North American context (though we must add water development accords to the list). For example, nation-to-nation diplomacy concerning fisheries access in the territory that would become Canada long predated Canada's existence as a sovereign nation. Channeling Harold Innis, the exploitation of cod, furs, and other staples was arguably the major preoccupation of the nascent, and then fledgling, country. This involved environmental diplomacy with the First Nations, though ultimately it took the form of settler colonialism –

indeed, the subsequent history of modern Canadian-American environmental relations is only possible because of this past legacy of resource and land appropriation.

Fishing diplomacy, both in the oceans and in the Great Lakes, only intensified after Canadian Confederation – for example, fish were central to the 1871 Treaty of Washington, the new nation's first major foray into bilateral North American relations. By the first decade of the twentieth century, fish remained a central concern of government officials, joined by other forms of wildlife conservation as well as boundary waters developments.[12] To illustrate, let's consider a 1906 meeting between Prime Minister Wilfrid Laurier and US secretary of state Elihu Root. Of the five items on Root's list of subjects needing attention, all but one is "environmental": (1) pelagic sealing; (2) the North Atlantic fisheries; (3) the inland fisheries; (4) United States pecuniary claims; (5) boundary waters.[13]

The environmental elements of this list were formally settled over the following two decades, a particularly fruitful period in Canada-US relations (and US-UK relations, since Canada was not able to independently handle all aspects of its foreign relations until the Statute of Westminster in 1931). Bilateral agreements were reached regarding seals, migratory birds, and various types of fish. The seminal Boundary Waters Treaty (BWT), signed in 1909, was an initial step in the rapprochement that characterized Canadian-American ecopolitics for most of the twentieth century. Securing this treaty was a significant coup for Canada, since the much more powerful United States was agreeing to a commission within which the two countries were equal. The Boundary Waters Treaty notably granted equal navigation access to the waters covered by it, and regulations were adopted concerning water diversions and changes to water levels; essentially, outside of special agreements, any changes in the level of a border water need agreement through the International Joint Commission, a six-member body created by the treaty in which there is parity between Canada and the United States.

The Boundary Waters Treaty settled some specific festering border water disputes. The treaty is often characterized as a pioneering piece of international environmental management legislation, while the IJC has been portrayed as a model for bilateral cooperation. According to a former commissioner, the philosophy of dispute-settlement and conflict-avoidance built into the BWT and IJC was far more sophisticated than any comparable piece of bilateral machinery then existing

Figure 4.1   International Joint Commission logo.

in Western society.[14] For example, the treaty employed the word "pollution" for what appears to be the first time in the history of transborder environmental governance.

At the same time, it is important not to exaggerate the role and importance of the ijc. Though it was explicitly set up so that commissioners are technically independent from the government that appointed them, the ijc can also be limited because the two federal governments must refer an issue to the commission (and the two federal governments have at times made executive agreements outside of the ijc). Moreover, an extended analysis of the ijc's first century of operation shows that its behavior, role, and function changed significantly over time. For its initial decades it was an elite form of water apportionment that favoured industrial and government interests at the expense of environmental, recreation, and local interests. Rather than dissuading hydraulic engineering megaprojects such as those discussed later in this chapter, the ijc was in fact a chief proponent of them. The first decades of the ijc are characterized by mixed results and partial irrelevance, followed by a period from the 1940s to the 1960s defined by partisan politics resulting in large-scale endeavours with dubious environmental impacts. After this came a period of more noticeable success up to about the 1990s, then a return to a fairly marginalized position.[15]

The Canadian and American governments had definite environmental goals in mind when they created the BWT and IJC, goals that we should not disregard even if they do not necessarily match our contemporary understanding of environmental protection. Nonetheless, the BWT and IJC succeeded in providing a framework and ground rules that have, for the most part, prevented or resolved bilateral disputes over boundary and transboundary waters for over a century. In doing so, the IJC has proven to be a foundation stone for modern Canada-US environmental diplomacy, particularly in the realms of border waters and crossborder pollution.[16] Is the IJC the most important aspect of the Canadian-American environmental relationship? Perhaps. Nonetheless, the scope of this relationship is so large that a list of the most relevant issues, cases, events, processes, and accords go well beyond the IJC. I have provided such a list below for the twentieth century (see table 4.1).

The sheer magnitude of this list indicates the historical importance of environmental diplomacy issues within the northern North American relationship during the twentieth century. Granted, this list is impressionistic, generally limited to those bilateral issues that have a predominantly environmental dimension. It also isn't qualitative, in that there is no indication of each entry's relative importance or influence within the scope of bilateral relations.

Nonetheless, many of the issues on this list are of the *punctuated* variety: wars, crises, and negotiations that grab headlines and cause major concerns or controversies in the bilateral relationship. The Columbia River Treaty and St Lawrence Seaway agreement, which will be discussed below, are examples of such punctuated events. At the same time, once achieved, both of these water developments became major parts of the background infrastructure that facilitate the smooth flow of transborder relations. In that sense, the general tenor of the bilateral relationship also depends on the continuing day-to-day, often low-profile, matters. The "North American school" of Canadian-American relations points to the importance of shared continental outlooks and tendencies; highlights cooperation between the two nations without obscuring conflict; and sees the bilateral rela-

Table 4.1
Twentieth-century environmental diplomacy issues

1900–1950	1950–2000
Chicago Sanitary and Ship Canal (1900)	Niagara Diversion Treaty (1950)
Niagara water diversions (1908)	St Lawrence Seaway and Power Project (1954–59)
Milk-St Mary River disputes (1908)	Integrated Canada-US electricity networks
Inland Fisheries Treaty (1908)	Canadian-American oil trade and pipelines; MOIP status
Salmon Treaty (1909)	Various border water disputes: Richelieu, Champlain, Skagit, Garrison, Devil's Lake, Red River
Boundary Waters Treaty (1909) and IJC	Law of the Sea (1950s onward)
North Atlantic Cod Fisheries Agreement (1910)	Great Lakes basin pollution
Passamaquoddy Treaty (1910)	Radioactive fallout and the Test Ban Negotiations (1960s onward)
North Pacific Fur Seal Convention (1911)	Columbia River Treaty (1964)
IJC studies on border waters pollutions	North American environmental movements
IJC references and applications	IJC references and applications
Migratory Bird Treaty (1916)	Canada-US Auto Pact (1965)
Halibut Treaty (1923; 1930, 1937, 1953, 1977)	The *Manhattan* Affair (1969)
Trail Smelter Dispute (1927–1941)	The Arctic Waters Pollution Prevention Act (1970)
Niagara Convention (1929)	Great Lakes Water Quality Agreements (1972 onward)
International Pacific Salmon Convention (1937)	Acid rain (1970s onward)
Great Lakes and St Lawrence waterway and power project agreements (1932 and 1941)	The *Polar Sea* Affair (1985)
Ogoki-Long Lac Diversions (1940s)	Softwood lumber disputes (1982 onward)
Great Lakes Fisheries Convention (1946 and 1954)	Pacific Salmon Treaty (1985)
Alcan Military Highway and Canol Pipeline (WWII)	Canada-United States Air Quality Agreement (1991)
Metals and minerals (WWII onward)	Canada-US Free Trade Agreement (1988)
Radar lines in the north (1946 onward)	North American Free Trade Agreement (1994)

tionship as constituted not only by negotiations at the elite and executive levels, but by the everyday social, cultural, and economic interactions that generally provided the relationship with an inbuilt
momentum, balance, and continuity.[17]

These everyday interactions, I would suggest, indicate that the evolution of the Canadian-American relationship was disproportionately
shaped by environmental diplomacy. This sentiment was shared by
Henry Kissinger, who opened a meeting with the Canadian ambassador with the sarcastic query: "I hope you haven't come to talk to me
about the sex life of the salmon."[18] It should be pointed out that the
many forms of continued exports and imports that make up the transborder trade relationship cumulatively have a major ecological impact
over time, but are difficult to represent on a list. Indeed, if we were to
take stock of all the goods that have moved across the border, the environmental impact of producing, manufacturing, and transporting
these goods would be astronomical. I have already mentioned a number of the natural resources that are directly exchanged, such as aluminum or fossil fuels. But also consider manufactured or semi-fin-
ished manufactured products, such as vehicles. The 1965 Canada-US
Auto Pact, for example, is included on the above list because of the toll
automobile production takes on the natural world, making it an excellent example of the ways that conventional foreign policy and trade
issues have a very important ecological dimension.[19] Or consider a
diplomatic matter that, like many others, is more difficult to represent
on a reductive list: Canadian content anxieties about imported American magazines in the 1960s. A diplomatic matter that is usually
framed as the history of culture and nationalism, Canada-US periodi-
cal relations actually have important environmental dimensions since
American publishers relied on Canadian wood pulp to print their
wares, denuding huge swaths of Canadian forests in the process.[20]

COLD WAR CASE STUDIES

In the 1920s issues like Niagara Falls, the St Lawrence River, the Trail
Smelter, and fish dominated the environmental diplomacy to-do list.
The 1930s saw a fall-off, chiefly due to the impact of the Great Depression. But the Second World War played host to a rapid intensification
of bilateral diplomacy with clear environmental dimensions. That
pace only continued as world war gave way to cold war. It is the early
Cold War period on which I'd now like to concentrate. Given that I've

been speaking in broad strokes about the nature of environmental diplomacy, it seems useful to provide some fine-grained case studies that illustrate the rewarding ways that environmental and diplomatic history can be blended. In particular, I would like to look at three important transborder water issues. The Niagara, St Lawrence, and Columbia hydro projects all involved formal diplomatic agreements between Canada and the US, and all were among the key determinants of the bilateral relationship in an era that is often termed the "Golden Age" of Canadian-American relations – so called due to an increased level of integration and cooperation (though in recent years scholars have offered necessary correctives to the extent of the era's goldenness). All three of these projects certainly bespeak cooperation but were preceded by years, even decades, of significant and often unrecognized conflict, especially in the cases of the St Lawrence and Columbia.

Negotiations for a St Lawrence deep waterway began in the 1890s, and continued in earnest at various points throughout the first half of the twentieth century. In 1932 Canada and the United States inked a treaty to build a seaway, as well as to deal with a range of other border waters issues in the Great Lakes-St Lawrence basin; the US Senate, however, did not approve this treaty. A similar fate befell a bilateral 1941 executive agreement to construct the St Lawrence project, largely because fighting the Second World War took priority. Talks picked up again after the end of the global conflict. At a time when the Korean War was ongoing and Cold War tensions were extremely high, diplomats from both sides stated that the St Lawrence dispute was the top issue in Canadian-American relations. An American official, for example, disclosed that the St Lawrence had the potential to "probably injure our relations with Canada more than any other single incident which has occurred during this century."[21] Such a statement demonstrated the importance of the St Lawrence impasse.

Frustrated by American inaction, the Louis St Laurent government tried to forge ahead with an all-Canadian seaway, which would work in tandem with a binational power project. The prospect of "going it alone" struck a nationalist chord in Canada. This was indicative of a cultural view of the St Lawrence River as a "Canadian" possession that should be developed solely by Canada, and the connections between hydro-electric power and Canadian identity. Indeed, the St Lawrence River occupies a key perch in the Canadian national imagination because of its historic nation-building role.

However, from an American perspective, an all-Canadian route was genuinely perceived as a security and economic threat. Washington used various forms of linkage (the diplomatic relations practice of connecting the outcome of a policy issue to an unrelated issue) to stop the Canadian plan and secure American participation, essentially holding hostage the hydro-electric project that Canada, and particularly Ontario, so desperately desired.[22] In 1954, the Canadian government saw the writing on the wall and reluctantly agreed to a joint waterway via a bilateral agreement (while the hydro power aspect was approved by the IJC).

The St Lawrence Seaway and Power Project was both a hydro-electric project (power dam) and a navigation project (locks and canals). The construction of this megaproject had an enormous environmental and social impact on the St Lawrence basin. The St Lawrence power project required three dams in the international stretch of the St Lawrence dividing Ontario and New York. These dams created Lake St Lawrence, which inundated some 20,000 acres of land on the Canadian side, along with another 18,000 acres on the US shore. Communities, roads, and other infrastructure had to be moved, razed, or flattened, including trees and cemeteries.

The construction phase of the Seaway and Power Project, from 1954–59, required a wide range of constant crossborder interactions to work out the many technical, economic, and physical aspects of the shared project. Along with the Niagara project, discussed below, the involvement of non-federal state actors made seaway diplomacy an important stage in the evolution and expansion of subnational North American relations.[23] The province of Ontario and Ontario Hydro not only helped shape their federal government's St Lawrence policies – as did New York State and PASNY within the United States – but directly negotiated with their New York counterparts and lobbied the American federal government. In numerous respects the St Lawrence Seaway and Power Project established a pattern for subsequent Canadian-American environmental relations.

Like the seaway, transborder Niagara Falls discussions began around the turn of the twentieth century, and then continued sporadically over the next half-century.[24] And, similar to the St Lawrence case, there were diplomatic agreements that weren't ratified by the US Senate. Large-scale hydro-electric production and distribution had its birth at Niagara Falls in the late nineteenth century, and resulted in many industries springing up or relocating in the vicinity. Power-

Figure 4.2   Moses-Saunders power dam on the St Lawrence.

houses diverted large volumes of water from the Niagara River, which fostered public concern about the aesthetic impact of lower water levels on the falls. Legislative steps were taken, such as the 1906 Burton Act, and an article in the Boundary Waters Treaty – indeed, both the Niagara and St Lawrence cases had been prime reasons for arriving at that treaty.

In response to public worries about the scenic grandeur of Niagara Falls, Canada and the United States formed special joint boards to come up with solutions that would allow the maximum amount of water to be diverted, but with minimum impact on appearance (and, in turn, the tourism economy). Based on such studies, the Niagara Convention and Protocol was signed in 1929 by both countries; it was, however, not able to make it through the US Senate. Further transnational studies examined how to create the "impression of volume" while still feeding water to power stations and industry. Many people were also worried that the constant erosion threatened the integrity of the waterfall. Engineers recommended that the riverbed above the falls, and the falls themselves, be manipulated, and suggested remedial works. Such measures were included in the failed 1932

Figure 4.3   Niagara Falls from old Schoellkopf power station.

Great Lakes Waterway Treaty and 1941 St Lawrence executive agreement. During the Second World War the two countries ignored the legal limits on the amount of water diverted at Niagara Falls. They also shared the cost of a stone-filled weir – a submerged dam – above the falls to raise the water level in order to facilitate greater diversions.

Eager to legally enshrine higher diversion rates, the two countries decided to divorce Niagara from the seaway talks. The result was the Niagara River Diversion Treaty of 1950. This Canadian-American accord virtually equalized water diversions while restricting the flow of water over Niagara Falls to no less than 100,000 cfs during daylight hours in what was deemed the tourist season (8 a.m. to 10 p.m. from April to mid-September, and 8 a.m. to 8 p.m. during the fall). A minimum of 50,000 cfs was required to flow over the falls the remainder of the year. This meant that Canada and the U.S. could rob the falls of half of the Niagara River's flow during tourist hours, and about three-quarters the rest of the time.

The treaty also called for remedial works approved by the International Joint Commission. This commission created the International Niagara Falls Engineering Board, whose studies indicated that the

diversions outlined by the 1950 treaty would have a noticeably negative impact on the scenic beauty of the area: the Chippawa-Grass
Island Pool level would drop by as much as four feet, exposing areas of
the river bed, turning the American Falls into an unsightly spectacle,
and greatly reducing the appearance of the flanks of the Horseshoe
Falls. According to the engineering board, the point of any remedial
works and manipulations would be to create the appearance of an
unbroken and satisfactory crestline while allowing for the diversion of
water for power production. A 1,550 foot control dam was built from
the Canadian shore, parallel to and about 225 feet downstream from
the weir built in the 1940s, featuring thirteen sluices equipped with
control gates (five more were soon added). This structure controlled
water levels and facilitated the diversion of water to the huge tunnels
which fed the downstream hydro-electric stations. Along with the
other remedial measures, the control dam also spread out the water as
it approached the waterfall, partly for appearance's sake and partly
because flows concentrated in certain places caused more erosion damage. Both countries undertook excavations along the flanks of Horseshoe Falls (64,000 cubic yards of rock on Canadian flank; 24,000 cubic
yards on American flank) in order to help with the distribution of flow
and unbroken crestline. Crest fills (55 feet on the Canadian shore and
300 feet on the American side) were performed, with much of the
reclaimed land transformed into prime public vantage points.[25]

Prior to the twentieth century, Niagara Falls was not seen as a
"Canadian" natural icon in the same way as the St Lawrence. However, the great cataract came to resonate with Canadian nationalists for
a number of the same reasons as the St Lawrence – for example, both
played a role in the past expansion from colony to nation, both were
battle sites in the War of 1812, and both belonged to the commercial,
economic, and population center of Canada – but the falls' ability to
produce hydro power was particularly important. As would also prove
to the case with the Columbia River, Canadian identity became
uniquely intertwined with hydro-electricity production, for it represented a way of taking advantage of Canada's natural birthright and
setting while simultaneously offering a way to assert some economic
and energy independence from the United States. Of course, this
required undertaking joint developments, which served to further
integrate the two countries – but this tendency to pull away from the
US with one hand while simultaneously strengthening ties with the
other is a classically Canadian one.

The transborder Niagara complex became one of the largest hydro-electric conglomerations in the world. However, further state efforts in the 1960s to increase the volume of diversions from the Niagara River met with stiff public opposition. Governmental mindsets were changing too. The American Falls were dewatered in 1969 as part of a study to see whether it was feasible to remove all the rock (called talus) that had gathered at the base of the cataract, but engineers ultimately recommended, in contrast to what had been done to the Horseshoe Falls in the 1950s, that the American Falls be left alone to let nature take its course.[26]

During the same decade other parts of the continent weren't as apprehensive about remaking water bodies for power production. The Columbia agreements of the 1960s, also coming after decades of attempts and engineering studies, outlined how Canada and the US would mutually exploit the Columbia River for hydro-electricity and flood control. Before the Second World War, a number of hydro-electric stations had already been built on the Columbia River, which begins in British Columbia before entering the United States, and the river's various tributaries. But as North American planners entered the height of the high modernist era, American officials realized that damming the upper parts of the Columbia River to create storage reservoirs would allow for full electric power and flood control development in the lower portion of the basin. The catch was that these reservoirs would be in Canadian territory. In 1954, BC Premier W.A.C. Bennett struck a deal with an American firm, Kaiser Aluminum and Chemical Corporation, to develop a large storage dam on the upper Columbia River. In return for a fifty-year water licence, BC would get 20 per cent of the electricity generated downstream. Canada's federal government, however, was opposed and passed the International River Improvements Act, stipulating that a federal licence was necessary to dam an international river. Negotiations at the federal level accelerated, picking up steam after the election of John Diefenbaker in 1957. The Columbia River Treaty was signed in January 1961 and ratified by the United States.[27] It involved three dams in Canada, and another American dam whose reservoir would extend into Canada. The Canadian dams would benefit downstream American power and flood control interests. In exchange, Canada would receive cash and half of the extra US electricity that these dams made possible, plus the dams in Canada would produce electricity.

However, the treaty signing had been rushed since US president Dwight Eisenhower was about to leave office, and the Diefenbaker government thought the BC provincial government was in agreement with the terms of the accord. But it soon became apparent that this wasn't the case. Bennett envisioned a "two rivers" scheme that aimed to simultaneously replumb the Columbia and Peace Rivers for hydro development, with the resulting power sold to American entities on a long-term basis. However, this ran up against a long-standing federal policy of disallowing the permanent export of electric power. Moreover, the 1961 treaty was portrayed by many Canadian nationalists as a capitulation to Washington, and there were complaints that the terms of the treaty were unfavourable to Canadian interests.

General A.G.L. McNaughton, an opponent of the treaty who also happened to be the chair of the Canadian Section of the International Joint Commission, actively promoted an "all-Canadian" plan that included a diversion of the Kootenay River into the Columbia to create greater water flows so that more hydro dams could be built entirely on the Canadian side.[28] This was the direct result of McNaughton's IJC experience during the St Lawrence negotiations in the 1950s, where he had been a chief proponent of the all-Canadian seaway idea. Indeed, McNaughton may be the most underappreciated Canadian foreign policy actor in the post-1945 period, for, in addition to his roles at the United Nations and on the Permanent Joint Board on Defence, he was instrumental in shaping Canada's approach to border waters through his position on the International Joint Commission.[29]

By the time Lester Pearson replaced Diefenbaker as prime minister, the Columbia matter was still at an impasse. But when Pearson met with the new US president, John F. Kennedy, in May 1963, the prime minister suggested that Canada would authorize the sale of downstream benefits over a longer period if favourable changes could be made to the treaty terms. Premier Bennett was amenable to the changes since the sale of long-term downstream benefits was on the table. An elaborate series of triangular negotiations between the BC, Canadian, and US governments took up much of 1963, dealing with sticking points such as downstream benefits and the forming of an integrated continental electric grid.[30] Canada and British Columbia reached an agreement, and then in 1964 Canada and the US consented to a protocol that modified the 1961 treaty.[31] Canada would receive half the power made possible by the Canadian works (but generated in the United States), and would sell its downstream benefits for $254 million for thirty years to a group of American utilities, in turn passing the proceeds on to British Columbia.

But many Canadians attacked the revised agreement. Donald Waterfield labelled Pearson's handling of the treaty as a "pusillanimous surrender," as did others who saw the Columbia experience as evidence of American imperialism.[32] Nationalist detractors condemned the Columbia project for integrating the two countries' power grids, thereby preventing the formation of an all-Canadian grid.[33] Moreover, the "important downstream environmental and social costs were at best undervalued and in some cases ignored by the parties that crafted the final agreement."[34] Today, many see the treaty as an environmental anachronism since "the most obvious substantive elements missing from the treaty are fish and wildlife, water quality, and other environmental and ecosystem benefits."[35]

As the Columbia matter was being worked out, the environmental movement was picking up steam in North America, birthing various forms of environmental diplomacy aimed much more explicitly at environmental protection, rather than exploitation. Other shared waters attracted the attention of diplomats. Water quality in the Great Lakes-St Lawrence basin was a significant concern. Efforts to clean up pollution in the Great Lakes had been a Canada-US (as well as an Ottawa-Ontario) dispute for some time. In 1963, shortly after Pearson was elected, Ottawa and Queen's Park created a cost-sharing agreement; this allowed Canada to join with the US in 1964 to refer pollution in the lower lakes to the IJC. After more years of study, the result was the first Great Lakes Water Quality Agreement (GLWQA), signed in 1972, followed by a more comprehensive agreement in 1978.[36] The two federal governments tasked the IJC with investigating several other border issues, all of which eventually resulted in important reports: Great Lakes water level regulation; pollution in the Red River; preservation and enhancement of the American Falls at Niagara; and air pollution in the Port Huron-Sarnia and Detroit-Windsor regions.

As I've endeavoured to show, if only briefly, the St Lawrence, Niagara, and Columbia developments were contentious political and diplomatic debates. These completed megaprojects resulted in hybrid envirotechnical systems that blended the natural and the artificial into new forms of infrastructure, but they also had contentious and complex political histories that complicate the narrative of smooth Canadian-American integration in the middle of the twentieth century. Fusing together environmental and diplomatic history approaches demonstrates just how vital environmental diplomacy was to the bilateral relationship. Furthermore, I would argue that an environmental history perspective offers unique and valuable insights about Canadian nationalism, national identity, and national self-interest – all of which are quintessential concerns of political and diplomatic historians. For instance, the histories of border waters I've covered reveal how Canada's approach to engineering transborder waters was inextricably bound up in unique forms of Canadian "hydraulic nationalism" as well as American environmental imperialism.[37] In other words, the various political jurisdictions conceptualized the same water bodies quite differently.

The water bodies were themselves key historical actors in other ways, which up this point I've mostly only been able to adumbrate. Rivers are shaped by humans, but they equally shape human history. A river opens up many possibilities while simultaneously closing off many others. Aside from the connections between political decisions and the cultural meanings of these waters, the size, volume, fluvial characteristics, and seasonal nature of these rivers dictated what type of navigation or power development could be installed, as well as where these developments would need to be placed. Such factors severely constrained or significantly influenced political and diplomatic decisions – for example, the siting of a hydroelectric dam was fundamentally important for determining whether the project would require the concurrence or involvement of the other country. Indeed, remaking these large fluvial systems required types of capital, jurisdiction, and expertise that public agencies (i.e., government), rather than private interests, were best able to provide. During the construction phase of these megaprojects, the myriad ways that rivers, waterfalls, and lakes can become transnational historical actors are revealed even further. Rivers move: they shift channels, they erode, they flood. Given that the replumbing of these waters spanned the borders, transnational engineering boards and processes were needed, and both nations and their representatives had to continually negotiate with and adapt to not only each other, but to the ecosystems they were engineering.

Of course, many of the topics I've discussed are also part and parcel of energy diplomacy, particularly hydro-electricity. An entire chapter could easily be written on Canada-US energy and electricity diplomacy, but I'll restrict myself to just a few comments. Since many of the earliest sites of large hydro-electric development were along border waters with the United States, power stations needed to be negotiated between Canada and the United States, and between the Canadian federal government and provinces. As a consequence, a distinct form of energy diplomacy emerged in Canada during the twentieth century.[38] In 1920, hydro power was responsible for 97 per cent of the electricity produced in Canada, and by the 1940s it was still responsible for about 90 per cent.[39] Since the Second World War, non-firm (i.e., interruptible) power sales have dominated the Canada-US electricity trade.[40] Moreover, until the 1960s Canada-US energy relations primarily consisted of transborder electricity connections from hydro stations, rather than fossil fuel exports and imports.[41] Up to the 1960s, the majority of power exported from Canada to the US was via Ontario, and St Lawrence and Niagara power played the leading role in shaping Ontario and the federal government's approach to electricity exports, and thus also energy policy. The water megaprojects covered in this chapter therefore entrenched Canadian-US energy relations and paved the way for the development of the transborder electricity grids that proliferated in the latter half of the twentieth century, enhanced by the Canadian federal government's allowance of long-term firm power as part of the Columbia River treaty. By 1975 there were sixty-five international interconnections, with a total transfer capability of over 6,000 megawatts; even though new Canadian hydro-electric developments moved away from the border (e.g., northern Quebec), much of their product was wheeled to northern states.[42] Electricity exchange remains today a key part of energy diplomacy, and the environmental impacts of the stations that produce the electricity are therefore a casualty – or the cost of doing business, depending on one's perspective – of Canadian-American relations.

There are other, more structural, ways that rivers have agency if we draw on approaches which stress that the material environment shapes human society as much as the reverse is true. Societies are fundamentally shaped and structured by the energy forms they rely upon. Timothy Mitchell's *Carbon Democracy*, for example, outlines how the materiality of fossil fuels helped create modern democracy.[43] In the same vein, given Canada's enormous historical and contemporary reliance on a different energy source, hydro-electricity, we might ask how the domestic production of hydro power, along with the large water resources of the Great Lakes-St Lawrence and Columbia basins, shaped modern Canada. While there is not room here to probe this question in detail, drawing from a different study I'd like to suggest just a few possibilities.[44] Harnessing large rivers for hydro-electricity requires enormous state involvement and expertise – this conditioned Canadians for an interventionist state, and made them comfortable with sacrificing hinterland waters for metropolitan benefits. And until long-range electricity transmission technology was developed, industry needed to be located closely to the source of hydro power, which had important spatial ramifications for Canada's industrial and urban development (e.g., Niagara's proximity to Toronto). Moreover, long-range transmission lines, once developed, create unique path dependencies.

CONCLUSION

Looking at the Canada-US relationship through an environmental history lens offers a number of advantages. It brings into stark relief the profound ecological impact of bilateral diplomacy and trade markets: mining uranium, pulping trees, reconfiguring border waters, etc. It also shows the extent to which the Canadian-American relationship is predicated on the natural world and natural resources. The field of international history would benefit from adopting environmental history methods because the greatest international threats currently facing humanity are arguably ecological: climate change, species extinction, and water security. Though this study has been limited to the North American context, it is easy to see how an environmental diplomacy approach would be very beneficial for analyzing Canada's other international relationships: Canada's role in contributing to nuclear weapons, and then its efforts to limit their tests and proliferation; the ecological side effects of Canadian peacekeeping efforts in Asia and Africa; the environmental impacts of Canada's globalized trade regimes; the operation of Canadian mining companies around the world; Canadian positions on multilateral environmental agreements such as the Montreal Protocol or Kyoto Accord; and so on.

Climate change is of course a border-spanning process, and one to which international and transnational historians are uniquely placed to respond – provided that they can also "see" like an environmental historian. In turn, the international and diplomatic history fields offer methodologies and skills that would benefit environmental historians, since so many of their subjects span borders. The ability to unwind and uncover the inner workings of nation-states and governments, a focus of international historians, is something environmental historians could use more of, precisely because so many of their subjects involve government regulation or multiple political jurisdictions. Environmental diplomacy as I've outlined it here also provides an excellent avenue for better incorporating domestic and cultural history into diplomatic history. It is an ideal way to blend transnational and international history, fields which often aren't enough in conversation with each other, while demonstrating the ways that borders both do and don't matter. Thus, it is not a one-way street in which only international historians would benefit from environmental history.

Many of the other contributions to this volume incorporate historical actors that have usually escaped the gaze of Canadian international historians. Like other types of undiplomatic history, an environmental diplomacy perspective brings in a most unique array of foreign policy actors – though in this case, those actors range from fish to waterfalls to acid rain. Including an environmental perspective not only opens up the aperture to allow new subjects into the frame, but, just as importantly, it changes the depth of field of, well, the field, by bringing into focus important environmental aspects of the issues that have traditionally concerned Canadian foreign policy scholars. Moreover, the pressing national security issues North Americans face today and in the future may well be "natural security" issues – climate change, of course, but also pollution, water scarcity, health pandemics, sea level rise and acidification, energy sources, etc. Thus, I'm not suggesting that environmental diplomacy issues alone can explain the whole Canadian-American relationship. But I would suggest that the inverse is equally true: exploring the Canadian-American relationship without cognizance of and emphasis on environmental diplomacy, as has almost always been the case, fails to provide a full picture of the bilateral relationship.

ACKNOWLEDGMENTS

The author would like to thank Norman Hillmer and Kurk Dorsey for reading and commenting on an early draft of this paper, the participants in the Undiplomatic History symposium for their feedback, and the editors of this collection for their insights.

NOTES

1 Kurkpatrick Dorsey, *The Dawn of Conservation Diplomacy: U.S.-Canadian Wildlife Protection Treaties in the Progressive Era* (Seattle: University of Washington Press, 1998).

2 While diplomatic historians are still only beginning to see the intersections with environmental historians, military historians have long been aware of these connections (and, it should be added, so have many historians of science and technology). Kurk Dorsey, "Crossing Boundaries: The Environment in International Relations," in *The Oxford Handbook of Environmental History*, edited by Andrew C. Isenberg (Oxford: Oxford University Press, 2014), 708.

3 It is likely obvious to those familiar with political ecology and international law approaches that aspects of "natural security" as outlined here are derived from notions of "food security" and "water security" often promulgated in the United Nations.

4 In 2012, I created and taught a course on the history of Canada-US environmental relations, and I intend to turn those lectures notes into a survey volume on the subject.

5 https://www.historians.org/publications-and-directories/perspectives-on-history/december-2015/the-rise-and-decline-of-history-specializations-over-the-past-40-years.

6 Mark H. Lytle, "Research Note: An Environmental Approach to American Diplomacy History," *Diplomatic History* 20, no. 2 (1996): 279–300; Kurk Dorsey, "Dealing with the Dinosaur (and Its Swamp): Putting the Environment in Diplomatic History), *Diplomatic History* 29, no. 4 (2005): 573–87; Kurk Dorsey and Mark Lytle, "Forum: New Directions in Diplomatic and Environmental History," *Diplomatic History* 32, no. 4 (2008): 517–646.

7 Dorsey, *The Dawn of Conservation Diplomacy.* Other representative publications on the history of American environmental diplomacy works include: Kurkpatrick Dorsey, *The Dawn of Whales and Nations: Environmental Diplomacy on the High Seas* (Seattle: University of Washington Press, 2014); Jacob Hamblin, *Arming Mother Nature: The Birth of Catastrophic Environmentalism* (New York: Oxford University Press, 2013); Edwin Martini, *Agent Orange: History, Science, and the Politics of Uncertainty* (University of Massachusetts, 2013); Jason Colby, *The Business of Empire: United Fruit, Race, and U.S. Expansion in Central America* (Cornell University Press, 2011); J.R. McNeill and Corinna R. Unger, eds., *Environmental Histories of the Cold War* (Cambridge: Cambridge University Press, 2010); Erika Maria Bsumek, David Kinkela, and Mark Atwood Lawrence, eds., *Nation-States and the Global Environment: New Approaches to International Environmental History* (New York: Oxford Univer-

sity Press, 2013); Mark Cioc, *The Game of Conservation: International Treaties to Protect the World's Migratory Animals* (Athens: Ohio University Press, 2009).

8 Below is an admittedly impressionistic list of works that could be fully or partially described as Canadian-American historical environmental diplomacy, even if all the authors included wouldn't identify as such. Briton Cooper Busch, *The War against Seals: A History of the North American Seal Fishery* (Montreal and Kingston: McGill-Queen's University Press, 1987); Thomas Dunlap, *Nature and the English Diaspora: Environment and History in the United States, Canada, Australia, and New England* (Cambridge: Cambridge University Press, 1999); J.D. Wirth, *Smelter Smoke in North America: The Politics of Transborder Pollution* (Lawrence: University Press of Kansas, 2000); Margaret Beattie Bogue, *Fishing the Great Lakes: An Environmental History, 1783–1933* (Madison: University of Wisconsin Press, 2000); Kathryn Morse, *The Nature of Gold: An Environmental History of the Klondike Gold Rush* (Seattle: University of Washington Press, 2003); Brian Payne, *Fishing a Borderless Sea: Environmental Territorialism in the North Atlantic, 1818–1910* (East Lansing: Michigan State University Press, 2010); Tammy Nemeth, "Continental Drift: Energy Policy and Canadian-American Relations," in *Diplomatic Departures: The Conservation Era in Canadian Foreign Policy, 1984–93*, edited by Nelson Michaud and Kim R. Nossal (Vancouver: UBC Press, 2001); Joseph Taylor III, *Making Salmon: An Environmental History of the Northwest Fishery Crisis* (Seattle: University of Washington Press, 1999); Phil Van Huizen, "Building a Green Dam: Environmental Modernism and the Canadian-American Libby Dam Project," *Pacific Historical Review* 79, no. 3 (2010): 418–53; Daniel Macfarlane, *Negotiating a River: Canada, the US and the Creation of the St. Lawrence Seaway* (Vancouver: UBC Press, 2014); Lynne Heasley and Daniel Macfarlane, *Border Flows: A Century of the Canadian-American Water Relationship* (Calgary: University of Calgary Press, 2016); Neil Swainson, *Conflict over the Columbia: The Canadian Background to an Historic Treaty* (Montreal and Kingston: McGill-Queen's University Press, 1979); Lissa Wadewitz, *The Nature of Borders: Salmon, Boundaries, and Bandits on the Salish Sea* (Seattle: University of Washington Press, 2012); Barbara Cosens, ed., *The Columbia River Treaty Revisited: Transboundary River Governance in the Face of Uncertainty* (Corvallis: Oregon State University Press, 2012); Owen Temby, "Property, Technology, and Environmental Policy: The Politics of Acid Rain in Ontario, 1978–1985," *Journal of Policy History* 27, no. 4 (2015): 636–69; Daniel Macfarlane, "Fluid Relations: Hydro Developments, the International Joint Commission, and Canada-U.S. Border Waters," in *Towards Continental Environmental Policy? North American Transnational Environmental Networks and Governance*, edited by

Peter Stoett and Owen Temby (Albany: SUNY Press, 2017); Norman Hillmer, Daniel Macfarlane, and Michael Manulak, "The Pearson Government and Canadian Environmental Diplomacy," in *Mike's World: Lester B. Pearson and Canadian External Relations*, edited by Asa McKercher and Galen Roger Perras (Vancouver: UBC Press, 2017); William Willoughby, *The Joint Organizations of Canada and the United States* (Toronto: University of Toronto Press, 1979); Carle E. Beigie and Alfred O. Hero Jr, *Natural Resources in US-Canadian Relations*, 2 volumes (Boulder: Westview Press, 1980); John Carroll, *Environmental Diplomacy: An Examination and a Prospective of Canadian-US Transboundary Environmental Relations* (Ann Arbor: University of Michigan Press, 1983); G. Bruce Doern, *Green Diplomacy: How Environmental Policy Decisions are Made* (Toronto: C.D. Howe Institute, 1993); Peter Stoett and Phillipe Le Prestre *Bilateral Ecopolitics: Continuity and Change in Canadian-American Environmental Relations* (London: Routledge, 2006); George Hoberg, "Canadian-American Environmental Relations: A Strategic Framework," in *Canadian Environmental Policy: Context and Cases*, edited by Deborah VanNijnatten and Robert Boardman (New York: Oxford University Press, 2002), 171–89; Donald Barry, Bob Applebaum, and Earl Wiseman, *Fishing for a Solution: Canada's Fisheries Relations with the European Union, 1977–2013* (Calgary: University of Calgary Press, 2014); Don Munton, "The Provinces and Canada-United States Environmental Relations," in *The Provinces and Canadian Foreign Policy*, edited by Tom Keating and Don Munton (Toronto: Canadian Institute of International Affairs, 1985); Debora VanNijnatten, Robert Healy, and Marcela Lopez-Vallejo, *Environmental Policy in North America: Approaches, Capacity, and the Management of Transboundary Issues* (Toronto: University of Toronto Press, 2014); Carolyn Johns, Debora Van-Nijnatten, Kathryn Bryk Friedman, and Gail Krantzberg, "Transboundary Governance Capacity in the Great Lakes Basin," *International Journal of Water Governance* 4, no. 1 (2016): 7–32; N.F. Dreisziger, "The International Joint Commission of the United States and Canada, 1895–1920: A Study in Canadian-American Relations (PhD diss., University of Toronto, 1974); Robert Spencer, John Kirton, and Kim Richard Nossal, eds., *The International Joint Commission Seventy Years On* (Toronto: Centre for International Studies, 1981). The many volumes in the Documents on Canadian External Relations series also provide a wide array of primary sources on Canadian environmental diplomacy.

9 Graeme Wynn, "National Dreams," in Macfarlane, *Negotiating a River*, xxi.

10 A. Chaloux and S. Paquin, "Green Paradiplomacy in North America," in *Sustainable Development and Subnational Governments: Policy Making and Multilevel Interactions*, edited by H. Bruyninckx et al. (New York: Palgrave Macmillan, 2012), 217–36.

11 Dorsey, "Crossing Boundaries," 690.

12 Dorsey, *The Dawn of Conservation Diplomacy*.

13 This list is reproduced in Robert Bothwell, *Your Country, My Country: A Unified History of the United States and Canada* (Oxford: Oxford University Press, 2015).

14 Maxwell Cohen, "The Commission from the Inside," in *The International Joint Commission Seventy Years On*, edited by Robert Spencer, John Kirton, and Kim Richard Nossal (Toronto: Centre For International Studies, 1981), 108.

15 See Clamen and Macfarlane, 2015.

16 The IJC has been a subject of study for many non-historians, though that pattern will be broken with the release of the following edited collection: Daniel Macfarlane and Murray Clamen, eds., *The First Century of the International Joint Commission* (Calgary: University of Calgary Press, forthcoming). See also Dreisziger, "The International Joint Commission of the United States and Canada, 1895–1920"; Spencer, Kirton, and Nossal, *The International Joint Commission Seventy Years On*; L.M. Bloomfield and G.F. Fitzgerald, *Boundary Waters Problems of Canada and the United States* (Toronto: Carswell, 1958).

17 The most prominent proponents of the North American school include Norman Hillmer, Robert Bothwell, J.L. Granatstein, and Greg Donaghy. This school is in many ways an outgrowth of "continentalist" interpretations and the Carnegie Endowment for International Peace series on Canadian-American relations edited by James Shotwell and capped by John Bartlet Breber, *North Atlantic Triangle: The Interplay of Canada, the United States, and Great Britain* (New Haven: Yale University Press, 1945), which are less anti-American than "imperialist" approaches.

18 Robert Bothwell, "Thanks for the Fish: Nixon, Kissinger, and Canada," in *Nixon in the World*, edited by Fredrik Logevall and Andrew Preston (New York: Oxford University Press, 2008), 399.

19 On the auto pact and Canada-US automobile relations, see Dimitry Anastakis, *Auto Pact: Creating a Borderless North American Auto Industry, 1960–1971* (Toronto: University of Toronto Press, 2005); Dimitry Anastakis, *Autonomous State: The Struggle for a Canadian Auto Industry from OPEC to Free Trade* (Toronto: University of Toronto Press, 2013).

20 Mark Kuhlberg, In the Power of the Government: The Rise and Fall of Newsprint in Ontario, 1894–1932 (Toronto: University of Toronto Press, 2015); Michael Stamm, Dead Tree Media: Manufacturing the Newspaper in Twentieth Century North America (Baltimore: Johns Hopkins University Press, 2018).

21 FRUS Vol. 2, 1951, Canada: 916.

22 Daniel Macfarlane, "'Caught Between Two Fires': St. Lawrence Seaway and Power Project, Canadian-American Relations, and Linkage," *International Journal* 67, no. 2 (2012): 465–82.

23 See Daniel Macfarlane, "Watershed Decisions: The St. Lawrence Seaway and Sub-National Water Diplomacy," *Canadian Foreign Policy Journal* 21, no. 3 (2015): 212–23.

24 This section is derived from the author's research for a book on Niagara Falls, as well as various publications including: Daniel Macfarlane, "Dam the Consequences: Hydropolitics, Nationalism, and the Niagara-St. Lawrence Projects," in *Border Flows: A Century of the Canadian-American Water Relationship*, edited by Lynne Heasley and Daniel Macfarlane (Calgary: NICHE-University of Calgary Press, 2016); Daniel Macfarlane, "'A Completely Man-Made and Artificial Cataract': The Transnational Manipulation of Niagara Falls," *Environmental History* 18, no. 4 (2013): 759–84.

25 Press Release: Niagara Falls Preservation Program Starts, 15 January 1954, LAC, vol. 6348, file 1268-D-40, pt. 25.2, Library and Archives Canada.

26 Daniel Macfarlane, "Saving Niagara from Itself: The Campaign to Preserve and Enhance the American Falls, 1965–1975," *Environment and History* (forthcoming).

27 Robert W. Sandford, Deborah Harford, and Jon O'Riordan, *The Columbia River Treaty: A Primer* (Victoria, BC: Rocky Mountain Books, 2014), 17.

28 Macfarlane, *Negotiating a River*, 215; Hillmer, Macfarlane, and Manulak, "The Pearson Government and Canadian Environmental Diplomacy." On the general Pearson-Kennedy relationship, see Asa McKercher, *Camelot and Canada: Canadian-American Relations in the Kennedy Era* (Oxford: Oxford University Press, 2016); Greg Donaghy, *Tolerant Allies: Canada and the United States, 1963–1968* (Montreal and Kingston: McGill-Queen's University Press, 2003).

29 On McNaughton and the all-Canadian Seaway, see Macfarlane, *Negotiating a River*.

30 On the subject of a transborder grid in the Pacific Northwest, see Paul Hirt, *The Wired Northwest: The History of Electric Power, 1870s–1970s* (Lawrence: University of Kansas Press, 2012).

31 The revised terms included new procedures for the operation of flood control; reaffirmation and clarification of Canada's rights to divert water for consumptive and other uses; and the increase in Canada's entitlement to downstream power benefits. Chris W. Sanderson, "The Columbia River Treaty after 2024," in *The Columbia River Treaty Revisited: Transboundary River Governance in an Age of Uncertainty*, edited by Barbara Cosens (Corvallis:

Oregon State University Press, 2012). For documents relating to the treaty, see Canadian Departments of External Affairs and National Resources, *The Columbia River Treaty, Protocol, and Related Documents* (Ottawa, 1964).

32 Waterfield, *Continental Waterboy*, 116; Joy Parr, *Sensing Changes: Technologies, Environments, and the Everyday, 1953–2003* (Vancouver: UBC Press, 2008), 123.

33 Jeremy Mouat, "The Columbia Exchange: A Canadian Perspective on the Negotiation of the Columbia River Treaty, 1944–1964," in Cosens, *The Columbia River Treaty Revisited.*

34 Sandford, Harford, and O'Riordan, *The Columbia River Treaty*, 43. See also Tina Loo, "People in the Way: Modernity, Environment, and Society on the Arrow Lakes," *BC Studies* 142/143 (2004): 161–96; Tina Loo with Meg Stanley, "An Environmental History of Progress: Damming the Peace and Columbia Rivers," *Canadian Historical Review* 92, no. 3 (2011): 399–427; Parr, *Sensing Changes*, 103–35.

35 John Shurts and Richard Paisley, "The Columbia River Treaty" in *Water Without Borders? Canada, the United States, and Shared Waters*, edited by Emma S. Norman, Alice Cohen, and Karen Bakker (Toronto: University of Toronto Press, 2013), 147.

36 The agreement established a non-binding framework for cooperative management of water quality in Lakes Ontario and Erie. Both nations developed common water quality objectives and regulatory standards for several types of pollutants, chiefly connected to excess nutrient loading, and implemented programs to achieve these goals. For example, the US spent $10 billion on improvements in municipal sewage treatment between 1972 and 1978. In 1978, the two countries arrived at a new agreement, building upon the 1972 version. The 1978 agreement was amended in 1983 and a subsequent protocol was signed in 1987. The GLWQAs, amongst the most important North American environmental accords, led to significant improvements for the Great Lakes ecosystem. See Lee Botts and Paul Muldoon, *Evolution of the Great Lakes Water Quality Agreement* (East Lansing: Michigan State University Press, 2005), 13–15.

37 On "hydraulic nationalism" see Macfarlane, *Negotiating a River.*

38 Heasley and Macfarlane, *Border Flows.*

39 Canadian Hydropower Association, 2008; Office of Energy Efficiency and Renewable Energy, n.d.

40 Janet Martin-Nielsen, "South over the Wires: Hydroelectricity Exports from Canada, 1900–1925," *Water History* 1 (2009): 126–7.

41 See Daniel Macfarlane, "Fluid Relations: Hydro Developments, the International Joint Commission, and Canada-U.S. Border Waters," in *Towards Conti-*

nental Environmental Policy? North American Transnational Environmental Networks and Governance, edited by Peter Stoett and Owen Temby (Albany: SUNY Press, 2017); Daniel Macfarlane, "Current Concerns: Canadian-American Energy Relations and the St. Lawrence and Niagara Megaprojects," in *Energy in the Americas: Critical Reflections on Energy and History*, edited by Amelia Kiddle (Calgary: University of Calgary Press, under review).

42 Mark Perlgut, *Electricity Across the Border: The U.S.-Canadian Experience* (New York: C.D. Howe Research Institute, 1978), 11.

43 Timothy Mitchell, *Carbon Democracy: Political Power in the Age of Oil* (London: Verso, 2013).

44 Daniel Macfarlane and Andrew Watson, "Hydro Democracy: Water Power and Political Power in Ontario," *Scientia Canadensis* vol. 40, no. 1 (2018): 1–18.

5

Spreading the Gospel of Natural Birth: Canadian Contributions to an International Medical Movement, 1945–60

WHITNEY WOOD

Anticipating a "long-awaited" fourth pregnancy in the spring of 1948, twenty-seven-year-old Karen Birch[1] from rural Alberta wrote to Dr Grantly Dick-Read (1890–1959), British obstetrician and the leading figure in the burgeoning natural childbirth movement. Praising Dick-Read's influential volume, *Childbirth without Fear*, first published in North America in 1944,[2] she asked the doctor "to take on a patient 6,000 miles away," and requested "a correspondence course in intelligent parturition."[3] Though Dick-Read responded that Mrs Birch was unfortunately "just outside [his] limit for attending women in labour!"[4] she continued to correspond with the doctor for approximately eighteen months. While not his patient, Birch, like other Canadians who wrote to Dick-Read, was an active participant in the broader international campaign for "childbirth without fear," one of the first organized efforts to contest the increasing medicalization of childbirth that had gone largely unquestioned since the late nineteenth century.

Historians have examined the impact of Dick-Read's theories in Great Britain and the US, but his teachings have received little attention in the Canadian context.[5] Additionally, much of the existing literature, including Margarete Sandelowski's *Pain, Pleasure and American Childbirth*, has focused on Dick-Read's writings and other popular and medical literature.[6] As a result, the voices of childbearing women, who left "few firsthand accounts of their views and experiences," are largely silent in much of the existing historiography.[7]

This chapter begins to redress these imbalances by taking a multi-sited approach to the history of the natural childbirth movement in postwar Canada. Relying on correspondence between Canadian parents and Dick-Read to bring the voices of individual women and men into the history of an international medical movement, it focuses, in particular, on lay, bottom-up, or grassroots efforts to promote natural childbirth. At the same time, in highlighting professional responses to natural childbirth ideologies, it offers a parallel history of medical internationalism, interpreting Canadian attitudes and practices (at both the grassroots and professional levels) in light of broader transnational trends such as the migration of women and physicians, and in terms of engagement with a global medical movement that was inseparable from the growing anxieties of the Cold War.

Historians of medicine have long adopted colonial and imperial approaches in the study of the spatial distribution and spread of epidemic disease,[8] but fewer have focused on the transnational spread of medical ideas and practices. The twentieth century, in particular, marks a significant period of health internationalism, as organizations such as the Red Cross established a "nation-building mission … in the broadly defined health realm."[9] Scholars including David Arnold and Mary-Ellen Kelm have deftly demonstrated that all "modern" medicine is colonial in terms of its relation to the body.[10] In particular, colonial and imperial power dynamics have markedly shaped the movement of medical ideas, practitioners, and patients – all of which readily circulated, as Warwick Anderson has noted, "between imperial outposts and European and North American urban centres."[11]

Looking at Canadian engagement with the international natural childbirth movement – a movement that, in the immediate postwar decades, was synonymous with the ideas put forward by Grantly Dick-Read – this chapter explores each of these themes. In so doing, it builds on the work of historians including Karen Flynn, David Wright, Sasha Mullally, and Laurence Monnais, who in recent years have begun to unpack the complex histories of medical diaspora, focusing on the international migration of nurses and physicians.[12] Like many of the other contributions to this volume – David Webster's on religion, or Kailey Hansson's on cultural diplomacy – this examination of medical internationalism underscores the importance for Canada in the World scholars of incorporating approaches that, while relatively new to the Canadian historiography, have been a mainstay of transnational, global, and international history for some time. This look at natural birth provides a valuable example of how ideas, people, and practices spread across transnational networks, demonstrating that Canada existed as one of many spokes in a broader transnational medical culture.[13] Health, medicine, and gender offer valuable lenses of historical analysis for international historians, and as this study demonstrates, they have the potential to bring often overlooked non-state actors, including parents and physicians, into the "undiplomatic history" of Canada and the world.

GRANTLY DICK-READ AND NATURAL CHILDBIRTH

By the interwar period, anaesthetized birth – or, at the very least, the provision of some analgesia or pain relief for the majority of urban, "white," middle-to-upper-class patients during delivery – was increasingly commonplace throughout much of the Western world. The majority of Canadian practitioners offered some form of anaesthesia to the expectant mothers they confined. At the same time, however, the beginnings of natural childbirth movements represented some of the first significant and organized opposition to this medicalization. One of the key figures in this process was Grantly Dick-Read, who had popularized the term in his titular work, *Natural Childbirth*, published in the UK in 1933.[14] Dick-Read's fixation on the ease of so-called "primitive" childbirth echoed nineteenth-century medical folklore that consistently emphasized the hardiness and vitality of relatively "uncivilized" Indigenous bodies.[15] Fundamentally, Dick-Read concluded that fear of giving birth caused tension, and that this tension contributed to heightened contractility and spasms in the cervix, resulting in pain. He argued, above all else, for the need to overcome this fear, which he saw as a major obstacle to women's healthy fulfillment of the maternal instinct.[16] To this end, prenatal education and a close relationship between the expectant mother and her physician were the keys to overcoming pain in childbirth.

Dick-Read envisioned the ideal birth as one involving a conscious, confident, and active participant, rather than a drugged patient.[17] As growing numbers of middle-class women throughout the Western world were increasingly accustomed to receiving pharmacological pain relief when they gave birth, this vision of a drug-free birth "bucked the trend" in British and North American obstetric practice.[18] Nevertheless, Dick-Read's ideas found a captive audience during the first years of the "baby boom" that followed the Second World War, as Canadian women tended to marry at a younger age, and have more children than their counterparts a generation earlier – a new reality that, understandably, led many mothers to want to have more of a say regarding the events taking place in the birthing room.[19]

MIGRATION AND MATERNITY IN POSTWAR CANADA

Natural childbirth ideologies received some attention throughout the 1930s, but it was not until the North American publication of *Childbirth without Fear* in 1944 that the method entered mainstream medical discourses, effectively attracting expectant mothers.[20] Between 1946 and his death in 1959, more than sixty Canadians took the time to write to Grantly Dick-Read. More than three-quarters of correspondents were female, although at least fourteen men – mostly from medical backgrounds – also took the time to write. Correspondents were located across the country and hailed from all provinces, with the exception of Prince Edward Island; no correspondents wrote from the Yukon or Northwest Territories. The largest number came from Ontario, followed by British Columbia and Quebec. This suggests that natural childbirth theories had the power to cross deep-seated Canadian regional, cultural, and linguistic divides, a point also made by individual letter writers.[21] While it is more difficult to infer class and racial or ethnic backgrounds, letter writers appear to represent a select (and limited) group of Canadians. The majority of correspondents appear to have been well educated, hailing from the middle or upper-middle classes. British backgrounds appear to predominate. Most appear to have written on one occasion only, though a few did carry on lengthy correspondences with the doctor. For all letter writers, however, the "atmosphere of anonymity created by correspondence" appears to have encouraged the frank expression of intimate details concerning childbirth experiences.[22]

As might be expected, those motivated to write letters tended to respond very favourably to Dick-Read's message.[23] Letter writers sought information and clarification on Dick-Read's *Childbirth without Fear* method, as well as more generalized marriage and family advice. At the same time, in their engagement with this international movement, Dick-Read's correspondents provided their own critical commentary on the Canadian medical establishment.[24]

Enthusiastic about the possibilities of the method but unsure of where to turn, the majority of letter writers, first and foremost, asked Dick-Read for referrals to physicians who could assist them in "achieving" natural births.[25] Writing from Saskatoon in 1953 before a cross-country move, Joan Brooks asked Dick-Read if he could refer her to a new physician in Toronto. She enclosed £1 with her inquiry, which, she noted, was the going fee for an office visit to a Canadian physician. Dick-Read directed her, as he did many other correspondents, to write to Miss Miles of the Toronto branch of the Canadian Mothercraft Society, a group established in 1931 based on principles laid out by New Zealand's Dr Truby King.[26] Such advice may have been problematic for some Canadian mothers – particularly those living in and attending other provincially run prenatal and baby clinics in the Toronto area, given ongoing tensions between Toronto physicians, including leading Canadian pediatrician Alan Brown, and Mothercraft nurses trained in "foreign methods," since the association's establishment in the early 1930s.[27]

For women who had recently moved to Canada as part of the postwar immigration boom, these referrals would have been especially helpful. Many of Dick-Read's correspondents, both women and men, identified themselves as recent newcomers to Canada, with a good deal having arrived from the United Kingdom in the years immediately following the Second World War. Joy Rames, who emigrated from England the month before writing to Dick-Read in 1950, described herself and her husband as "very much 'strangers in a strange land,'" and asked for the doctor's help in securing a physician.[28] Writing from her new home in northern Ontario, Rames was advised to write to a doctor in Windsor, nearly ten hours away.[29] Dick-Read regularly recommended a select number of colleagues to his correspondents, so it is unclear whether or not he knew of the obstacles (geographic and otherwise) such referrals could have presented. Likewise, Arlene Scott of Hamilton, who had arrived from London in late 1947, asked Dick-Read for advice on finding a natural childbirth practitioner in a 1949 letter.[30] Men also sought referrals for their wives. This was the case when Samuel Mockford, who had emigrated to Canada and settled in Toronto, wrote to Dick-Read in December 1949 in anticipation of his wife's first baby the following summer.[31] Some noted that they had first encountered Dick-Read's theories prior to emigrating. Joy Rames, for example, obtained a copy of Dick-

Read's *Revelation of Childbirth* while still living in England.[32] In a 1958 letter, Fay Grabowski, then living in Toronto, noted that she first read Dick-Read's "CWF" in England in 1951, before emigrating to Canada as a widow in 1953.[33]

CANADIAN PHYSICIANS
AND THE INTERNATIONAL CULTURE OF MEDICAL PRACTICE

Canadian medical practitioners were similarly affected by postwar immigration trends, and the international movement of physicians was shaped by a number of factors. The years immediately following the Second World War saw a transnational transformation in health services across a number of European and Commonwealth countries, with France, Britain, Canada, and other nations introducing universal health insurance in the years between 1945 and 1970. The introduction of state-administered medical services, coupled with the postwar baby boom, "unleashed a pent-up demand for medical care" across North America and Europe, with many national jurisdictions finding themselves "unprepared to address this new demand with the pre-existing domestic supply of doctors."[34] In this atmosphere, many nations, including Canada, turned to foreign-trained physicians to fill the void.

David Wright and Sasha Mullally have demonstrated that the "Canadian-British nexus" marks a particularly significant – yet under-explored – site of medical migration throughout the second half of the twentieth century.[35] Indeed, this nexus played a significant role in shaping the spread of natural childbirth theories and methods in mid-twentieth-century Canada.

After the passage of the Medical Care Act in 1966, the federal Department of Manpower and Immigration was quick to classify medicine as a "high demand" occupation, one that was awarded considerable points under Canada's new immigration system.[36] The emigration of physicians from the United Kingdom was seen as especially desirable, as evidenced by the selection of the British-trained physician Dr Richard Swinson as Canada's nominal "ten millionth" immigrant in 1972.[37] The field of human health resources was characterized by a high level of mobility throughout the postwar years; persistent emigration and immigration meant that Canadian physicians were an important component of the broader "multi-national web of health-care workers" throughout the postwar period.[38]

The international movement of medical professionals, of course, has much older roots. From the early nineteenth century onwards, physicians and surgeons circulated in patterns that were "predicated along imperial and linguistic lines."[39] As M. Anne Crowther and Marguerite Dupree have shown, Scottish medical traditions – practised by growing cohorts of Glasgow and Edinburgh graduates – spread to the far corners of the British Empire.[40] Irish medical graduates, too, routinely embraced the possibilities offered by international practice, and during the first half of the twentieth century, nearly half of the graduates of Irish medical schools were practising abroad.[41]

This process was by no means one-directional. Canadian doctors, particularly in the field of obstetrics, regularly embraced international training opportunities. The place of obstetrics in Canadian medical schools was a source of ongoing discussion and debate throughout the late-nineteenth and early-twentieth centuries, with persistent anxieties surrounding the need for greater training. In this atmosphere, international educational experiences filled a critical need, and gave new Canadian practitioners the opportunity to work with some of the leading names in midwifery and obstetrics. Kenneth Neander Fenwick, who earned his MD in Kingston in 1871, undertook postgraduate training at St Thomas's Hospital in London as well as in New York before becoming professor of obstetrics and diseases of women and children at Queen's University in the late-nineteenth century.[42] Abraham Isaac Willinsky, who received his MD from the University of Toronto in 1908, undertook a six-month postgraduate course at the Rotunda Hospital in Dublin the following year, based on the advice of a fellow doctor who told him: "if you're interested in babies, Dublin's the place."[43] Medical centres including London and Edinburgh were popular destinations for postgraduate study in a variety of subjects, as were cities like Paris and Vienna, and "large surgical centres" throughout the United States.[44] Foreign credentials, particularly in specialties like obstetrics, remained commonplace well into the twentieth century. Harold Benge Atlee, a leading figure in Canadian obstetrics, undertook extensive postgraduate work in the UK during the interwar period, studying surgery, the diseases of women, and obstetrics in Manchester, Edinburgh, and London. Upon his return to Canada, Atlee was appointed staff gynecologist at Victoria General Hospital in Halifax, and took up a teaching post at Dalhousie University. Both Atlee and the president of the university, Arthur Stanley Mackenzie, expressed the belief that these international training

opportunities were of great benefit to both the individual practitioner, and the practice of medicine in "the New World."[45]

At the same time, many practitioners who were born, raised, and
trained abroad emigrated to Canada and took up obstetric practice.
Some of these physicians, particularly those emigrating from the UK,
came to occupy influential positions in Canadian medical schools.[46]
Again, these types of experiences persisted into the twentieth century.
Medical school overproduction was "deeply embedded in the culture
and economy of Irish medical education," and though rates of international practice were declining by the post-Second World War years,
Irish doctors continued to find North America an attractive option
for medical practice.[47] Some faced professional obstacles based on the
widely held view that Irish medical education failed to match the
standards of American medical schools.[48] Other physicians, however,
particularly those practising north of the forty-ninth parallel, enjoyed
long and successful careers. Patrick Beirne, a native of Galway, received
his MD from the National University of Ireland in 1946. After emigrating to Canada in 1948, he spent four years as an intern and resident at St Michael's Hospital in Toronto, and during this period,
sought out post-graduate training at Cornell University in Ithaca,
New York. He was appointed staff obstetrician at St Michael's in 1953,
and spent his career ascending the ranks both in the hospital, and
in the Department of Obstetrics and Gynaecology at the University
of Toronto.[49]

Internationally trained physicians – namely Atlee and Beirne –
were leading figures in the Canadian natural childbirth movement.
H.B. Atlee became interested in Dick-Read's ideas in the 1940s, and
was a vocal supporter of natural childbirth techniques, publishing his
own volume on the subject in 1956.[50] Dick-Read, in turn, was aware
of and interested in Atlee's work, and considered the Nova Scotia
obstetrician a Canadian leader in the field; in a 1959 letter he commented to one Waterloo, Ontario, mother who was interested in a natural birth that he wished she "could go a little further east to Halifax
and have your baby under the care of Dr. Atlee."[51] Toronto-area
women made note of Patrick Beirne's sympathy to natural childbirth
methods. One woman, writing in 1957, referred to herself as "one of
Dr. Beirne's Naturals."[52] Another, writing in 1958, made explicit note
of Beirne's Irish background and training at the Rotunda in describing the doctor's skill and patience in the delivery room.[53]

On a more general level, Canadian parents seemed to suggest that foreign-trained physicians were, to a certain extent, freed from the existing customs and constraints of the Canadian medical establishment, and, as a result, more amenable to adopting unconventional natural childbirth methods. Reverend John Mathews of Pugwash, Nova Scotia, reported to Dick-Read in a 1958 letter that his wife's "British-trained" doctor was "mildly permissive" of the ideas espoused in *Childbirth without Fear*.[54] In an atmosphere where many mainstream practitioners continued to resist women's efforts to exert control over the decision-making and events taking place in the birthing room, this "mild permissiveness" may well have been noteworthy. In a 1958 letter, Moira Kaufman of Winnipeg described a positive birth experience to Dick-Read, attributing this, in large part, to her own doctor's "understanding and cooperation" with her desire to pursue a natural birth. Noting the Winnipeg doctor's "postgraduate studies in Dublin," Kaufman suggested that "there is no doubt he could be a key figure in advancing your work here."[55] For his part, Dick-Read responded that the fact that this doctor was "not positively antagonistic [to the method] as so many doctors are" meant that he could well be an ally to which he would refer patients, and noted that his previous experiences in speaking "to one or two Winnipeg doctors at a conference in Chicago" led him to believe that most practitioners in that city "did not appear ... very keen to alter the present condition of affairs in Winnipeg."[56]

SPREADING THE GOSPEL OF NATURAL BIRTH

As Amanda Ricci shows in her contribution to this volume, taking the experiences of women into account leads to a broader and more expansive understanding of "what counts" as international history. Though women often remained at the margins of "official" high politics and traditionally defined diplomacy throughout the postwar decades, they did participate in international and transnational movements. Indeed, those women who took the time to write to Dick-Read played a key role in the movement's growth. Letter writers consistently mentioned their efforts to "spread the Natural Childbirth gospel" to friends, relatives, and, blurring the boundaries between the grassroots and professional elements of the movement, to doctors and nurses.[57]

They were pleased to report any signs that the movement was gaining momentum. After buying Dick-Read's *Childbirth without Fear* in
1947, Karen Birch, whose account opened this chapter, reported that
she lent her volume to her younger sister and two friends over the
course of the following year.[58] In a 1949 letter, she related her obser-
vations that "CWF" was "becoming a 'movement' in the USA," and she
assured Dick-Read that "if my missionary fervor can accomplish it,
said movement will start in Alberta, also."[59] As Birch suggests, men
(often the husbands of enthusiastic supporters) contributed to the
spread of the movement as well. Over the coming months, Birch lent
the "little book" to "a young pediatrician-to-be" (her husband's
cousin), and commented that she, her husband, friends, and relations
were "preaching CWF 'til it's a wonder we're not forcibly shut up."[60]
This "missionary fervor" to "preach" the method had some success,
and Canadian physicians recalled being introduced to Dick-Read's
ideas by their expectant patients in the late 1940s. Dr W. Roy Walker,
living in northern British Columbia, told Dick-Read that the fact that
he had heard of the British method, in spite of his remote location,
offered a sign of "the penetration of the 'gospel' to the 'uttermost parts
of the earth.'"[61]

Writing from Toronto in 1951, Hazel Carter reported to Dick-Read,
"your cause is spreading more rapidly than you might dream." She
commented that "you can't get your book in any of the stores …
because their [*sic*] all sold out," and she told the doctor that she and
her "few recruits" were continuing to "spread the word" on *Childbirth
without Fear*.[62] After moving to Edmonton and having a successful
natural birth in the summer of the same year, Joy Rames told Dick-
Read that as a result of her positive experience, "they now have the
nurses in the Labour rooms of the University Hospital giving instruction in relaxation." She also noted that, after giving birth, "several of
the doctors came up to ask me about it [the Read method] so maybe
they will take it up."[63] Katherine Passman of Merlin, Ontario, suggested in a 1951 letter that Dick-Read "would be glad to know" that his
work was "advancing," and noted her plans to give a copy of *Childbirth
without Fear* to her obstetrician.[64] Dick-Read responded with an offer
to send reprints of his work to the doctors Passman had mentioned,
writing that such a gesture would "tremendously augment" Passman's
"kindly efforts to help mothers, and to extend this approach to childbirth … for in reality it is the Doctors who can do so much for the
women of our time."[65] By reminding Passman of the significance

of the physician's role, Dick-Read upheld traditional doctor-patient power dynamics.

Throughout the 1950s, Dick-Read's correspondents continued to highlight their efforts, telling the doctor of how they recommended and lent their copies of his work to everyone they could,[66] and reporting, with a sense of pride, the long waiting lists they encountered in trying to check his books out of public libraries as proof that Dick-Read's theories "were spreading and gaining favour among women themselves."[67] Again, these efforts were not limited to women. Maurice Dupont of Cobourg, Ontario, noted in a 1953 letter, for example, that he hoped that Dick-Read's work would "find a wide public here," and assured the doctor, "I shall certainly tell everyone about it."[68]

At the same time, the movement enjoyed growing coverage in the Canadian popular press. American coverage of the spread of natural childbirth ideas – especially as promoted by the New York Maternity Center Association – was regularly reprinted in a host of Canadian newspapers in the years following Dick-Read's first American lecture tour in 1947, and Canadian newspapers published their own coverage.[69] A November 1952 article in support of Dick-Read's theories, entitled "No Anaesthetic for Me, Thanks," appeared in one of Canada's leading women's magazines, the *Canadian Home Journal*.[70] Beginning in December of the same year, *Childbirth without Fear*, along with the "young and pretty" Canadian mothers who gave birth following these dicta, attracted the attention of Lotta Dempsey's popular "Person to Person" column in the *Globe and Mail*.[71] The *Globe* continued to cover the method in a favourable light throughout the decade.[72] One 1957 letter printed in the *Globe*, commenting on "all the fuss" surrounding natural childbirth, took issue with the paper's viewpoint that "childbirth without fear" represented a new trend; here, Toronto mother Anna Davies argued that the method was relatively well established in many Canadian cities, and that "demand for, and interest in, the method expounded by Grantly Dick-Read is not lacking among young mothers today."[73]

By the mid-1950s, natural childbirth was a subject of increasing interest for many Canadians. Dick-Read's ideas were the subject of a CBC broadcast in May 1956.[74] Dick-Read himself answered women's questions on natural birth in a January 1958 piece in *Chatelaine*, noting that the movement had already attracted the attention of "many Canadian women," with *Chatelaine* editors stating that the Canadian Mothercraft Society (CMS) offered "prenatal instruction based directly on Dick-Read's method."[75] The fact that *Chatelaine* reached nearly 2 million Canadian readers per month during the 1950s and 1960s makes this piece particularly significant.[76] Throughout the postwar period, the Toronto branch of the CMS remained instrumental in publicizing natural childbirth techniques, providing expectant patients with information on Dick-Read's theories using a variety of methods including lectures and film screenings.[77] Toronto classes that offered instruction in natural childbirth techniques were led by Mothercraft nurses who had trained at the Maternity Center in New York, demonstrating, as scholars including Flynn have also shown, that the movement of health care professionals in the postwar decades extended beyond physicians.[78]

By the immediate postwar years, Dick-Read had lectured in the United States and expressed a desire to visit Canada.[79] It was the rising momentum of natural childbirth theories over the course of the 1950s, however, that culminated in an extensive North American lecture tour including stops in Toronto, Montreal, and Ottawa in 1958.[80] Growing public attention to the movement, particularly through such "official" channels as the CBC, may have been helped by the fact that Dick-Read counted among his Canadian supporters Dr Ernest Couture, director of the Division of Child and Maternal Health in the Department of National Health and Welfare. The two practitioners carried out an international correspondence throughout the late 1940s and early 1950s, before Couture returned to private practice.

In a 1951 letter, Couture commented that it was clear that Dick-Read was "in close touch with the obstetrical world not only locally but on an international basis," based on the number of letters he received from Canadian parents-to-be.[81] Indeed, as will be discussed, Dick-Read was a regular attendee at a variety of international conferences and congresses in the field of obstetrics, during which he met and conversed with influential Canadian practitioners. The following year, Couture was pleased to report to Dick-Read that his theories were "steadily making their way" in Canadian obstetric practice, particularly in Nova Scotia – where they were promoted by practitioners including H.B. Atlee – and the Ottawa and Toronto regions.[82] By the mid-1950s, natural childbirth techniques were practised in a number of Canadian obstetric wards. Carl Tupper, who succeeded Atlee as the head of the Department of Obstetrics and Gynaecology at Dalhousie, told Dick-Read in a 1956 letter that he and his colleagues were "quite convinced that [natural childbirth] is a very valuable adjunct to obstetrics." He reported that the new wing in Halifax's Grace Maternity Hospital was "built around the idea of natural childbirth," and asserted that "most of the doctors in Halifax are practicing this procedure."[83] Though natural childbirth was most popular in urban centres, the method found a home in a range of Canadian hospitals, including the Goose Bay Hospital in Labrador.[84]

Scholars have suggested that the fact that Grantly Dick-Read "originally planned to be a missionary may explain the intensity and fervor of his work."[85] Indeed, Dick-Read's efforts to promote natural childbirth through lecture tours, interviews, and coverage in the popular press were positively received by a number of Canadian parents, who, in turn, did their part to "spread the gospel" to other audiences. While natural childbirth was popular among the lay public, and did find its supporters within the mainstream medical establishment, the majority of Canadian physicians continued to resent lay incursions into medical decision-making processes. Marion Hilliard, head of the Department of Obstetrics and Gynaecology at Women's College Hospital in Toronto, showed some support for the method in a January 1957 piece published in *Chatelaine*, stating that she "heartily approve[d] of a woman's being conscious throughout the birth." Nevertheless, Hilliard went on to assert that "only an obstetrician" could safely make decisions in the birthing room, "not an overeager patient and her friends."[86] Other physicians were more vocal in their opposition, and spoke out against what they saw as "The Modern-Day Cult" of natural childbirth, which led to the "grossly insulting" practice of "nineteen-year old girls" attempting to advise "mature, highly trained specialists on how they want their babies delivered."[87]

THE "RED" METHOD OF CHILDBIRTH

Mounting Cold War anxieties over the course of the postwar decades also shaped responses to natural childbirth, both in Canada and internationally. As historian Paula Michaels has demonstrated in her volume *Lamaze: An International History*, at the same time that Dick-Read's ideas were gaining ground in North America in the late 1950s, "a similar psychological approach to obstetric pain was taking shape in continental Europe."[88] This approach was spearheaded by French obstetrician Fernand Lamaze. Though reminiscent of the theories and practices put forward by the British Dick-Read, Lamaze's method of psychoprophylaxis (or pain management) found its roots in the ideas of Soviet psychologist I.Z. Vel'vovskii.

Vel'vovskii had spent the interwar period researching the possibilities offered by various psychological methods of pain relief, seeking to apply this research to pain in childbirth. Like much of Soviet psychology during this period, Vel'vovskii's research involved "ritual kowtowing to Pavlovian physiology … an indispensable component of medical teaching, research, and writing" in the mid-twentieth-century USSR.[89] The fact that Vel'vovskii's principles were, in actuality, deeply rooted in Ivan Pavlov's theories of conditional response made his ideas all the more popular during the Cold War, "when the Communist Party and Soviet state demanded uncompromising loyalty," and Pavlov represented an appealing "homegrown Soviet alternative to anything linked to Western, capitalist medicine."[90] After the Second World War, Vel'vovskii refined his interwar research, publishing an initial article on psychoprophylaxis in the Soviet journal *Obstetrics and Gynaecology* in 1950.[91]

While Dick-Read's ideas on natural childbirth were introduced to French audiences in the late 1930s after he first lectured in Paris in 1939, and were practised in select Paris maternity wards from 1949 onwards, Michaels suggests that they had limited influence on the development of Lamaze's separate yet similar vision of painless birth; Lamaze remained "skeptical about the Read method's efficacy."[92] Nevertheless, Lamaze was aware of and interested in the possibilities of psychoprophylaxis by the mid-1940s. Along with a group of French physicians, he travelled to the USSR in 1951 to study advances in Soviet public health and medicine. Here, the French obstetrician insisted on observing a birth conducted according to Vel'vovskii's principles, and was permitted to witness "a thirty-five-year-old typist giving birth to her first child, 'without pain and with joy'" at a Leningrad clinic.[93] Upon his return to France, Lamaze introduced psychoprophylactic principles to the Paris maternity ward that operated under his direction, providing the Soviet psychoprophylactic approach with a major foothold in France, and bringing these ideas to new international audiences.

Though his particular method of psychological pain relief had its roots in the USSR, Lamaze revised his theories for French audiences, and psychoprophylaxis "found yet another incarnation in the United States, where its development continued."[94] Throughout much of the 1950s, Michaels argues, "the lack of US-Soviet contact and virulent anti-Soviet sentiment in America insulated the US from the movement for psychoprophylaxis."[95] Still, by the late 1950s, the Lamaze method found new and captive audiences in North America, particularly following the publication of American mother Marjorie Karmel's popular work, *Thank You Dr. Lamaze*.[96] Despite the existence of both distinct and subtle differences between Dick-Read's natural childbirth theories and Lamaze's psychoprophylactic techniques, the two methods quickly became linked in the Canadian popular and cultural imaginations.

In January 1956, the *Montreal Gazette* and other North American newspapers reported that Pope Pius XII had declared that "the Roman Catholic Church" had "no moral or theological objection to a Russian means of achieving painless childbirth." In this papal announcement, made before an international audience of over 700 gynaecologists and physicians from throughout Europe and South America, the pope discussed "the psycho-prophylactic method … developed by the followers of the Russian physiologist and Nobel Prize Winner, Ivan Petrovic Pavlov, who died in 1936." He stressed the Russian roots of natural childbirth, as well as its use "in hundreds and thousands of cases in Russia and Communist China." This emphasis incensed Dick-Read, who saw himself as the sole father of natural childbirth, but he was nonetheless pleased with the pope's recognition that he (Dick-Read) had "perfected [the] theory and technique."[97]

The papal announcement firmly linked the theories of Dick-Read, Vel'vovskii, and Lamaze, and the Canadian popular press continued to emphasize the international attributes of Dick-Read's method over the years that followed. A November 1958 *Globe Magazine* piece highlighted Dick-Read's "successful practice at a maternity hospital run by nuns near Johannesburg" while on a tour of central Africa, during which Dick-Read undertook extensive study of the birth habits of "primitive" African women. The same piece also reinforced the relationship between Dick-Read's natural childbirth theories and the practice as used in the Soviet Union, noting that "in Russia, natural childbirth is state policy."[98] At the same time, North American commentators were quick to highlight the fact that "Western" mothers-to-be received gentler treatment than their Soviet counterparts, and, as Lamaze's ideas gained popularity in the late 1950s and 1960s (particularly following Dick-Read's death in 1959), they emphasized the French rather than the Soviet roots of psychoprophylaxis.[99] Still, opponents of the method continued to make note of the "red" aspects of natural childbirth. A 1961 training manual published by the American Society for Psychoprophylaxis in Obstetrics, which was popularly known as the "Red Manual" due to its vivid red cover, provided ready fodder for such criticisms.[100]

As Scott Johnston demonstrates in his contribution to this volume, professional scientific networks have long transcended the nation-state. These networks, Johnston suggests, represent valuable sites of "soft" diplomacy, highlighting the significant role of non-state actors on the international stage. As natural childbirth gained popularity in the postwar years, a growing number of international events dedicated to psychoprophylaxis in obstetrics allowed physicians from both sides of the iron curtain to share and discuss the latest natural childbirth research. International experts in the field, including Dick-Read, were regular attendees, and from the late 1940s on, Canadian practitioners were an important part of these international discussions.

The British Congress of Obstetrics and Gynaecology was held in Dublin in 1947 to celebrate the Bicentennial Anniversary of the Rotunda Hospital, marking the first major international conference in the field of obstetrics to take place since the outbreak of the Second World War. There, Dick-Read met and conversed with William Albert Scott, professor of obstetrics and gynaecology at the University of Toronto.[101] Events abroad offered some Canadian practitioners the chance to forge transnational relationships, but these opportunities were multiplied when international conferences were held on Canadian soil. Both Dick-Read and Pierre Vellay (a prominent French physician and disciple of Lamaze) spoke at the Second World Congress of Obstetrics and Gynaecology held in Montreal in June of 1958, a major international event that devoted an entire day to papers and roundtables on "widespread psychoprophylactic techniques" in use throughout Europe and North America.[102] Canadian physicians were also present at the First International Congress of Psychosomatic Medicine and Childbirth held in Paris in July 1962, featuring approximately 400 participants from over thirty nations, with papers – including by Winnipeg's Dr A.A. Earn and Halifax's Dr N. Destounis – translated into English, French, and German.[103] In 1966, the Biennial Convention of the International Childbirth Education Association took place in Toronto, featuring a roster of keynote speakers who were recognized international experts in the field of natural childbirth, including Canada's own H.B. Atlee.[104] As natural childbirth – a term that increasingly came to refer to the Lamaze method

rather than Dick-Read's earlier theories – continued to gain both professional and lay followings throughout the 1960s and 1970s, Canadians remained an important part of these international conversations.

CONCLUSION

In her classic American study, Margerete Sandelowski writes that "in
the 1940s and 1950s, natural childbirth was the Read method and no
other."[105] Accordingly, while Dick-Read found a captive international
audience during the postwar years in those who were interested in a
new way to birth, he was in turn the natural audience for Canadian
women and men interested in alternative techniques, some of whom
felt compelled to write to a physician for the first time.[106] By writing
to Dick-Read in the immediate postwar years, lay Canadians participated in a transnational exchange. In their grassroots efforts to reform
mainstream obstetric practice, these women and men made individual contributions to the foundation of a global feminist health movement that emerged in the following decades. In responding to the
ideas of the British Grantly Dick-Read, parents-to-be demonstrated
their engagement with a global medical movement that was itself
fuelled by the international migration and communication of non-
state actors – both women (as mothers-to-be) and the physicians who
treated them. Alongside these patterns of immigration and emigration, medical ideas flowed across national borders, shaping and sus-
taining a transnational culture of natural childbirth.

NOTES

1 In accordance with the archival restrictions of the Wellcome Library, all
   names are pseudonyms. The pseudonyms I have chosen aim to reflect the
   ethnic and linguistic backgrounds of letter writers.
2 Grantly Dick-Read, *Childbirth without Fear: The Principles and Practice of Natural Childbirth* (New York: Harper, 1944).
3 Karen Birch to Grantly Dick-Read, 5 April 1948, PP/GDR/D.90, Wellcome
   Library.
4 Dick-Read went on to joke, "if I did decide to do so, it is possible that your
   infant might arrive before your obstetrician." Dick-Read to Karen Birch, 1
   September 1948, PP/GDR/D.90, Wellcome Library.
5 The Canadian medical profession's responses to natural childbirth are
   briefly examined in Wendy Mitchinson's *Giving Birth in Canada* (2002),

and Dick-Read's role in the development of the natural childbirth movement in the 1960s and 1970s is briefly addressed in Canadian histories of breastfeeding and caesarean section. See Wendy Mitchinson, *Giving Birth in Canada, 1900–1950* (Toronto: University of Toronto Press, 2002), 215–16; Tasnim Nathoo and Aleck Ostry, *The One Best Way? Breastfeeding History, Politics and Policy in Canada* (Waterloo: Wilfrid Laurier University Press, 2009); and Sally Elizabeth Mennill, "Prepping the Cut: Caesarean Section Scenarios in English Canada, 1945–1970" (PhD diss., University of British Columbia, 2012).

6	Margarete Sandelowski, *Pain, Pleasure, and American Childbirth: From the Twilight Sleep to the Read Method, 1914–1960* (Westport, CT: Greenwood Press, 1984), 139.

7	Works that aim to correct this imbalance, again, have tended to focus exclusively on the American and British contexts. See Mary Thomas, *Post-War Mothers: Childbirth Letters to Grantly Dick-Read, 1946–1956* (Rochester: University of Rochester Press, 1997).

8	Warwick Anderson, "Postcolonial Histories of Medicine," in *Locating Medical History: The Stories and Their Meanings,* edited by Frank Huisman and John Harley Warner (Baltimore: Johns Hopkins University Press, 2004), 285–306.

9	Sarah Glassford, *Mobilizing Mercy: A History of the Canadian Red Cross* (Montreal and Kingston: McGill-Queen's University Press, 2017), 5. See also Julia F. Irwin, *Making the World Safe: The American Red Cross and a Nation's Humanitarian Awakening* (Oxford: Oxford University Press, 2013); and Laurence Monnais and David Wright, *Doctors beyond Borders: The Transnational Migration of Physicians in the Twentieth Century* (Toronto: University of Toronto Press, 2016).

10	David Arnold, *Colonizing the Body: State Medicine and Epidemic Disease in Nineteenth-Century India* (Berkeley: University of California Press, 1993); and Mary Ellen Kelm *Colonizing Bodies: Aboriginal Health and Healing in British Columbia, 1900–1950* (Vancouver: UBC Press, 1999).

11	Anderson, "Postcolonial Histories of Medicine," 300.

12	See Sasha Mullally and David Wright, "'La Grande Seduction?': The Immigration of Foreign-Trained Physicians to Canada, c. 1954–1976, *Journal of Canadian Studies* 31 (2007): 67–89; Karen Flynn, *Moving beyond Borders: A History of Black Canadian and Caribbean Women in the Diaspora* (Toronto: University of Toronto Press, 2011); and Laurence Monnais and David Wright, eds., *Doctors beyond Borders: The Transnational Migration of Physicians in the Twentieth Century* (Toronto: University of Toronto Press, 2016).

13	See also Paula Michaels, *Lamaze: An International History* (Oxford: Oxford University Press, 2014).

14 Grantly Dick-Read, *Natural Childbirth* (London: William Heinemann, 1933).

15 Grantly Dick-Read, Autobiography – Unpublished Manuscript, Instalment Two, 22–24; Instalment Three, 7, PP/GDR/A.92, Wellcome Library. For nineteenth-century examples, see George J. Engelmann, *Labor among Primitive Peoples: Showing the Development of the Obstetric Science of To-Day from the Natural and Instinctive Customs of All Races, Civilized and Savage, Past and Present* (St Louis: J.H. Chambers, 1882).

16 Dick-Read was less concerned about the impacts that this fear had on women's own physical and mental health, a fact that undergirds his traditional understandings of a woman's role in both the family and society – despite what some perceived to be the "radical" nature of the approach he promoted.

17 Lecture on "Pains of Labour," Norwich, 17 October 1933, PP/GDR/C.71, Wellcome Library.

18 Paula A. Michaels, "Pain and Blame: Psychological Approaches to Obstetric Pain, 1950–1980," in *Knowledge and Pain*, edited by Esther Cohen, Leona Toker, Manuela Consonni, and Othiel Dror (Amsterdam: Rodopi, 2012), 233.

19 Demographic studies suggest that for younger groups of married women (those under age thirty), birth rates continued to climb until 1956. *Canadian Women: A History*, 2nd ed., edited by Allison Prentice et al. (Toronto: Thompson Nelson, 1996), 379.

20 The year after Dick-Read's first American lecture tour, 1948, was a key turning point in this regard: "relatively few Americans … knew of the method before Harpers published *Childbirth without Fear* in 1944. It was not until 1948 that enough Americans knew of Natural Childbirth to make it an important part of American life." Sandelowski, *Pain, Pleasure, and American Childbirth*, 89.

21 Lorraine Blair, for example, told Dick-Read that his work had value for all Canadians, writing, "Your book was very inspiring even for a young girl and although a French speaking Canadian, I did not have any difficulty in reading it." Lorraine Blair to Dick-Read, 28 November 1950.

22 Mary Thomas, *Postwar Mothers: Childbirth Letters to Grantly Dick-Read, 1946–1956* (Rochester: University of Rochester Press, 1997), 19.

23 Karen Birch, for example, wrote that both she and her younger sister were immediately pleased with Dick-Read's "damn good sense," and went as far as to state her intent to name her next child in honor of the doctor. Karen Birch to Dick-Read, 12 October 1948, PP/GDR/D.90, Wellcome Library.

24 See Whitney Wood, "'Put right under': Medicalisation, Anaesthetisation, and Harm in Post-war Canadian Obstetrics," *Social History of Medicine* 31, no. 4 (2018): 796–817.

25 See, for example, Mrs George Spark to Dick-Read, 5 January 1947,
    PP/GDR/D.93, Wellcome Library; Hilda Garner to Dick-Read, 26 September
    1947, PP/GDR/D.92, Wellcome Library; Edith Zimmerman to Dick-Read,
    PP/GDR/D.93, Wellcome Library. For more on the construction of "achieve-
    ment" and "success" in natural childbirth discourses, see Whitney Wood,
    "Disappointment, Shame, and Women's Struggles to Achieve Natural Child-
    birth in Postwar Canada," in *Affect and Activism: Second-Wave Feminism and
    the History of Emotions*, edited by Catherine Gidney, Lara Campbell, and
    Michael Dawson (UBC Press, forthcoming).
26 Joan Brooks to Dick-Read, 21 April 1953, and Dick-Read to Brooks, 27 May
    1953, PP/GDR/D.90, Wellcome Library.
27 Cynthia Comacchio has argued that the "Mothercraft controversy" was
    essentially a struggle for control between Canadian physicians and Mother-
    craft nurses, with the former taking issue with nurses' role "in prescribing
    for their infant patients, a role that held serious portents for physicians
    involved in child welfare." Cynthia Comacchio, *Nations Are Built of Babies:
    Saving Ontario's Mothers and Children, 1900–1940* (Montreal and Kingston:
    McGill-Queen's University Press, 1993), 150–2.
28 Rames wrote: "We are very much 'strangers in a strange land' at present and
    I wondered if you could tell me of any hospital in Eastern Canada, or of any
    individual doctor who shares your belief. I think I shall find it rather diffi-
    cult if I was under the care of a doctor who was antagonistic to the theory
    and I should be very grateful if you could help me at all." Joy Rames to
    Dick-Read, 8 March 1950, PP/GDR/D.92, Wellcome Library.
29 Dick-Read to Joy Rames, 28 March 1950, PP/GDR/D.92, Wellcome Library.
30 Scott asked for advice as to how she should "go about solving the problem
    of medical aid sympathetic to [the natural childbirth] viewpoint," and wrote
    that the method "was certainly not applied in a number of recent maternity
    cases I know of personally." Dick-Read instructed her to get in touch with
    the Toronto branch of the Canadian Mothercraft Association. Arlene Scott
    to Dick-Read, 6 July 1949, and Dick-Read to Scott, 1 August 1949,
    PP/GDR/D.93, Wellcome Library.
31 S. Mockford to Dick-Read, 27 December 1949, PP/GDR/D.92, Wellcome
    Library.
32 Grantly Dick-Read, *Revelation of Childbirth: The Principles and Practice of Nat-
    ural Childbirth* (London: William Heinemann, 1942). This volume was
    republished in North America as *Childbirth without Fear.*
33 Fay Grabowski to Dick-Read, 28 August 1958, PP/GDR/D.95, Wellcome Library.
34 Laurence Monnais and David Wright, "Doctors beyond Borders: Entangle-
    ments and Intersections in the Modern History of Medical Migration," in
    Doctors beyond Borders, 11.

35 David Wright, Sasha Mullally, and Mary Colleen Cordukes, "'Worse Than Being Married': The Exodus of British Doctors from the NHS to Canada, c. 1955–1975," *Journal of the History of Medicine and Allied Sciences* 65, no. 4 (2010): 546–75.

36 Mullally and Wright, "'La Grande Seduction?'"

37 "Immigration: An Ideal Family," *Time Magazine Canada*, 12 June 1972.

38 Wright, Mullally, and Cordukes, "Worse Than Being Married," 569, 573.

39 Monnais and Wright, "Doctors beyond Borders," 5–6.

40 M. Anne Crowther and Marguerite W. Dupree, *Medical Lives in the Age of Surgical Revolution* (Cambridge: Cambridge University Press, 2007).

41 Monnais and Wright, "Doctors beyond Borders," 6–7.

42 Kenneth Neander Fenwick, *Manual of Obstetrics, Gynaecology, and Pediatrics* (Kingston: John Henderson and Co., 1889), preface.

43 A.I. Willinksy, *A Doctor's Memoirs* (Toronto: Macmillan, 1960), 35.

44 See Samuel S. Peikoff, *Yesterday's Doctor: An Autobiography* (Winnipeg: Prairie Publishing Company, 1980); Willinsky, *A Doctor's Memoirs*, 24, 41–2, 105; Wilfred Abram Bigelow, *Forceps, Fin & Feather: The Memoirs of Dr. W.A. Bigelow* (Altona, MB: Frieson and Sons, 1970), xvii, 34, 41.

45 Writing to Mackenzie in 1922 while working at a variety of London-area hospitals, Atlee noted that upon his return to Dalhousie, he could easily fill his yearly lecturers "with stuff I have collected over here that is practical and of vital importance to the would-be doctor." Atlee later wrote to request a letter of introduction from Mackenzie, to distribute to additional hospitals, and asked the president "to stress the fact that Medicine in the New World would be greatly benefitted by me being given the opportunity to study at close quarters the methods of the English gynaecologists." H.B. Atlee to Arthur Stanley Mackenzie, 29 October 1922 and 23 November 1922, President's Office Correspondence, Box 87, Folder 10, President's Office Fonds, UA 3, Dalhousie University Archives.

46 Professor John Clarence Webster, for example, trained in Scotland and taught in the Department of Midwifery and Diseases of Women at the University of Edinburgh before being appointed lecturer in gynaecology at McGill in 1896. John Clarence Webster Fonds, P 011, Osler Library for the History of Medicine.

47 Monnais and Wright, "Doctors beyond Borders," 7.

48 Greta Jones, "'A mysterious discrimination': Irish Medical Emigration to the United States in the 1950s," in *Doctors beyond Borders*, 96–117.

49 Irene MacDonald, *For the Least of My Brethren: A Centenary History of St. Michael's Hospital* (Toronto: Dundurn Press, 1992), 261.

50 H.B. Atlee, *Natural Childbirth* (Springfield, IL: Charles C. Thomas, 1956). See also Wendy Mitchinson, "H.B. Atlee on Obstetrics and Gynaecology: A Sin-

gular and Representative Voice in 20th-Century Canadian Medicine," *Acadiensis* 32, no. 2 (2003): 3–30.

51 Dick-Read to Beverley Sawyer, 1959 [n.d.], PP/GDR/D.98, Wellcome Library.

52 Pamela Strong to Dick-Read, 14 April 1957, PP/GDR/D.98, Wellcome Library.

53 Fay Grabowski to Dick Read, 24 August 1958, PP/GDR/D.95, Wellcome Library.

54 John Matthews to Dick-Read, 29 January 1958, PP/GDR/D.96, Wellcome Library.

55 Saul Kaufman to Dick-Read, 22 March 1954, PP/GDR/D.92, Wellcome Library; Moira Kaufman to Dick-Read, 12 March 1958, PP/GDR/D.96, Wellcome Library.

56 Dick-Read to Moira Kaufman, 24 March 1958, PP/GDR/D.96, Wellcome Library.

57 In seeking to align themselves with select mainstream medical practitioners, these women challenged what Sandra Morgen has identified as an artificial binary or dichotomy between "feminist and patriarchal" or "grassroots and professional" women's health activism. Sandra Morgen, *Into Our Own Hands: The Women's Health Movement in the United States, 1969–1990* (New Brunswick: Rutgers University Press, 2002), 117.

58 Karen Birch to Dick-Read, 12 October 1948, PP/GDR/D.90, Wellcome Library.

59 Karen Birch to Dick-Read, 24 May 1949, PP/GDR/D.90, Wellcome Library.

60 Karen Birch to Dick-Read, 30 August 1949. In the same letter, Birch told Dick-Read, "My husband paid you a tribute which I must pass on to you. It is the more unusual in that Fred is reserved and reticent even for the quiet Canadian he is, our race not being given to high flowery speeches much. I remarked that you were probably one of the greatest men living, at least the most influential. Fred said, 'Dr. Read is the greatest man since Jesus Christ.'"

61 W. Roy Walker to Dick-Read, 15 March 1948, PP/GDR/D.192, Wellcome Library.

62 Hazel Carter to Dick-Read, 8 June 1951, PP/GDR/D.91, Wellcome Library.

63 Joy Rames to Dick-Read, 22 July 1951, PP/GDR/D.92, Wellcome Library.

64 Katherine Passman to Dick-Read, 11 May 1951, PP/GDR/D.92, Wellcome Library.

65 Dick-Read to Katherine Passman, 3 July 1951, PP/GDR/D.92, Wellcome Library.

66 Anne Weston to Dick-Read, 8 April 1953, PP/GDR/D.93, Wellcome Library.

67 Laurel Rice to Dick-Read, 24 April 1955, PP/GDR/D.92, Wellcome Library. In a 1956 issue of the London-based *Parents* magazine, Mrs J.C.T. of

Saskatchewan reported, "I try to spread the good word around." "Parents in Canada," *Parents*, October 1956.

68 Maurice Dupont to Dick-Read, 15 April 1953, PP/GDR/D.91, Wellcome Library.

69 "Education, Dr. Read Says Key to Painless Childbirth," *Toronto Star*, 20 January 1947; "Says Fear Causes Childbirth Pains: Dr. Grantly Read, London Obstetrician Expounds Controversial Theory," *Montreal Gazette*, 1 February 1947.

70 "No Anaesthetic for Me, Thanks," *Canadian Home Journal* (November 1952), 20, 68–9; Geraldine Stowe to Dick-Read, 5 March 1953, PP/GDR/D.93, Wellcome Library.

71 Lotta Dempsey, "Person to Person," *Globe and Mail*, 2 December 1952, 13. See also *Globe and Mail*, 5 January 1955; 22 January 1955; 11 February 1955; 10 May 1956.

72 See, for examples, "More Mothers Get Prenatal Instruction," *Globe and Mail*, 18 February 1953, 10; "Mothercraft Works for Family Life," *Globe and Mail*, 7 March 1956, 13; Florence Schill, "Group Is Enthusiastic about Natural Birth," *Globe and Mail*, 28 March 1956, 16.

73 "Readers' Comment: A Mystery What All the Fuss Is About," *Globe and Mail*, 31 January 1957, 18.

74 Helen Scoles to Dick-Read, 28 May 1956, PP/GDR/D93, Wellcome Library.

75 Evelyn Hamilton, "Dr. Grantly Dick Read answers your questions on NATURAL CHILDBIRTH," *Chatelaine* (January 1958).

76 Valerie Korinek, *Roughing It in the Suburbs: Reading Chatelaine Magazine in the Fifties and Sixties* (Toronto: University of Toronto Press, 2000), 3.

77 Dick-Read to Betty Daniels, 23 December 1955, PP/GDR/D.91, Wellcome Library.

78 Schill, "Group is Enthusiastic About Natural Birth," 28 March 1956, 16. The same article reported on St Michael's "plans to send a nurse to New York for training in the Read relaxation method."

79 Dick-Read to Mrs George Spark, 5 January 1947, PP/GDR/D.93, Wellcome Library; Dick-Read to L.B. Miller, 23 October 1947, PP/GDR/D.91, Wellcome Library.

80 American and Canadian Tour 1958, PP/GDR/C.99, Wellcome Library.

81 Ernest Couture to Dick-Read, PP/GDR/D.189, Wellcome Library.

82 Ernest Couture to Dick Read, 15, June 1952, PP/GDR/D.189, Wellcome Library.

83 Carl Tupper to Dick Read, 11 July 1956, PP/GDR/D.192, Wellcome Library.

84 Olive Dickason, "Birth Rate High: Goose Bay Hospital Uses Natural Childbirth," *Globe and Mail*, 2 January 1955.

85 Donald Caton, "Who Said Childbirth Is Natural? The Medical Mission of Grantly Dick Read," *Anaesthesiology* 84 (1996), 957.

86 Marion Hilliard, "Your First Baby," *Chatelaine* (January 1957), 46.

87 June Callwood, "The Modern-Day Cult of Childbirth," *Chatelaine* (March 1964), 46.

88 Michaels, *Lamaze*, 26.

89 Ibid., 38.

90 Paula Michaels, "Comrades in the Labor Room: The Lamaze Method of Childbirth Preparation and France's Cold War Home Front, 1951–1957," *American Historical Review* 115, no. 4 (2010): 1031–60.

91 Michaels, *Lamaze*, 33.

92 Ibid., 47.

93 Ibid., 43.

94 Ibid., 95.

95 Ibid., 93.

96 Marjorie Karmel, *Thank You Dr. Lamaze: A Mother's Experiences in Painless Childbirth* (New York: Lippincott, 1959).

97 "RCs Accept Red Finding for Birth," *Montreal Gazette*, 9 January 1956.

98 Joanne Strong, "The Tempest One Man's Created about Birth," *Globe Magazine*, 3 November 1958, 28.

99 Michaels, *Lamaze*, 100. Though Lamaze himself had died in 1957, the Lamaze method continued to be promoted by his disciples, including Pierre Vellay, with Paris becoming a major international capital in the natural childbirth movement.

100 Elisabeth Bing, Marjorie Karmel, and Alfred Tanz, *A Practical Training Course for the Psychoprophylacitc Method of Childbirth* (New York: American Society for Psychoprophylaxis in Obstetrics, 1961).

101 Dick-Read to Alex Agnew, 14 October 1947, PP/GDR/D.188, Wellcome Library.

102 Congress attendees seemed to agree on the existence of two main camps in terms of the practice of psychoprophylaxis in obstetrics – "the method known as 'natural childbirth', in use in the United Kingdom and the United States, and the method based on Pavlovian principles first introduced in Russia and now widely used on the continent in Europe." "Medical Meetings: The Second World Congress of Obstetrics and Gynaecology," *Canadian Medical Association Journal (CMAJ)* 79 (1 August 1958): 206.

103 "Medical Meetings," *CMAJ* 86 (1 September 1962): 522.

104 "Medical News in Brief," *CMAJ* 94 (19 March 1966): 50.

105 Sandelowski, *Pain, Pleasure, and American Childbirth*, 98.

106 Edith Zimmerman to Dick-Read, 17 July 1950, PP/GDR/D.93, Wellcome Library.

SECTION THREE

Decolonization and Liberation

6

Jameel's Journal:
Jim Peters, Anti-Orientalism, and Arab
Decolonization in 1960s Canada

MAURICE JR. LABELLE

Khalas, Jim Peters told himself; he had had enough. Upon peeping at Joseph Rosenfeld's freshly published *The Orgiastic Near East* (1968), the first-generation Arab Canadian leader could not hold back his irritation at the latest addition to a growing body of texts and images in Canada that blatantly dehumanized Arabs. Nor could he resist the urgent need to defend "the Arab cause" anew.[1] In the hope that he was "not writing into a void," Peters immediately penned a protest to the Arab desk at the United States' State Department. *The Orgiastic Near East*, it read, was "not just one of the many pornographic works that flood unhindered in Canada from your country, but it is a deliberate and sustained attempt to vilify and calumniate the Arabs."[2]

Joseph Rosenfeld's text claimed to present the "hard reality" of sex, sexuality, and sexual behaviour in the Arab world.[3] Yet, more importantly, *The Orgiastic Near East* represented and empowered a long-standing Orientalist tradition in the world that misrepresented Arab peoples, societies, and cultures by marrying "the Orient and the freedom of licentious sex."[4] Amid its orgy of demeaning falsities, the book's description of sexual desires and habits in Syria likely culminated Peters's reading of Rosenfeld's "ethnopornography."[5] Its Orientalist depictions of both Syrian men as rapists and the bestial sodomy of Syrian women, among others, offended Peters and, surely, his paternal Syrian family. Syrians, it asserted, "are among the most sex-minded in the world."[6] An "old Syrian saying" evidenced this fact: "Not all women are alike to the eye, and not all men are similar in size." So did the Syrian "Tale of the Vizier's Son and the Bathkeeper's Wife." This "special tale" recounts the story "of a masseur's lament when he sees that the son of the prime minister has a penis diminutive in size." *The Orgiastic Near East* recounts, then:

> The bathkeeper calls his wife and says to her: "I was rubbing a handsome boy when all of a sudden I saw his prickle wasn't like that of other males, for its size did not exceed that of a peanut and it was well-nigh hidden between his thick thighs. So come, O wife, and see if you can rub it and revive it and start it growing again."
>
> The woman was very successful. She began masturbating the boy ... "Whereupon the boy's prickle stirred and swelled, for its smallness was in appearance only, since it was one of those which retire almost entirely into belly when at rest. Suddenly it sprang erect, rising up on end as huge as that of an elephant or a jackass, a powerful sight to see. Then he mounted her with his magnificent member and thrust its greatness between her thighs; and for three hours he rode her and futtered her ten full times, while she sobbed and sighed, and writhed and wriggled under him."[7]

According to Jim Peters, Rosenfeld's panoply of "filthy lies" symbolized "the character assassination of the Arab peoples from the Atlantic to the Arabian Gulf."[8] A decade prior to the publication of Edward Said's seminal text *Orientalism* and its ensuing travels to Canada, an affected Peters understood full well the linkages between anti-Arab prejudices, transnational hierarchy, and power. Without question, Orientalism's "worldliness" involved myriad Canadian frontiers – a point developed in David Webster's contribution to this volume.[9]

The same situation applied to the "traveling theory" of anti-Orientalism, as Jim Peters's pen reveals.[10] The critique against Orientalism and its (mis)representations, eloquently popularized by *Orientalism*, was not new in 1968, let alone 1978. Collectively and individually, it developed at different times, in myriad places, and in a globalizing context.[11] Edward Said himself openly acknowledged this both in,[12] as well as after, *Orientalism*: "At the bottom of what I said ... had been said before me." Arab anti-imperialists who "had suffered the ravages of imperialism and colonialism, and who, in challenging authority, provenance, and institutions of the science that represented them in Europe, were also understanding themselves as something more than what this science said they were." This historical anti-Orientalist perspective represented a "challenge to Orientalism, and the colonial era of which it is so organically a part," and "was a challenge to the muteness imposed upon the Orient as object."[13]

This paper explores Jim Peters's anti-Orientalism during its apogee in the 1960s. By using his extensive private correspondence, writings, and activities, it (re)orients Canada's place within the transnational circulations of anti-Orientalist thought. Despite being slow out of the gate, anti-Orientalism and similar decolonial interventions are now enmeshed within the Canadian scholarly mosaic, be it diplomatic, immigration, or Indigenous histories. Far from a mere footnote, Said's tour-de-force serves as a mandatory passage – albeit often quite brief – along the bumpy roads of re-storying modern Canada within and beyond its geographical borders.[14] Contemporary historical narratives about Canada unearth the interconnections between racial prejudices, cultural discriminations, political exclusions, and socio-economic inequalities. Revised analyses and syntheses, moreover, include the voices and agency of Others, citizens, temporary residents, and foreigners alike.[15] Yet anti-Orientalist activisms, disconnected from their unsettling contexts, remain in the peripheries of Canadian and non-Canadian imaginations. The personal journal of Jameel Naseem Boutras Ahwash, Jim Peters's Arabic name,[16] is an essential chapter in transcending this structural (in)difference, continuing critical reconciliation, and decolonizing both Canadians and Arabs.[17]

*   *   *

Jim Peters was born in 1917 in Toronto, amid the early period of Arab immigration to Canada. According to the census of 1921, a mere 8,282 Arabs lived in the Canadian *mahjar* (diaspora) at that time. When contemplating accessible North American destinations, Arab intellectuals and professionals fixed their gaze to the south of the forty-ninth parallel. Those who moved to Canada "were largely peasant and worker stock which in Arab terms means that they came from small villages in which Arab farmers live."[18] Many, like Peters's Lebanese mother, were illiterate. As such, Arab activism in the Canadian public sphere was limited. The internationalizing question of Palestine represented the sole matter of collective political interest. And, in such local and national conversations, early Arab Canadians experienced Orientalism first hand.[19]

Jim Peters was not immune to such cultural and socio-political discrimination. Prior to serving as an armourer for almost five years in the Royal Canadian Air Force during World War II, Peters edited Toronto's *Syrian-Lebanese Mercury* in the late 1930s, the only Arab Canadian newspaper at the time. "Arab affairs," especially those of British Palestine, occupied much space in his mind and columns.[20] In the wake of the Holocaust, Zionism – the global settler-colonial *mentalité* that supported the establishment of a Jewish state in Palestine and simultaneous dispossession and forced relocations of indigenous Palestinians – did not relent in its dehumanization of Arabs. Arabs were "lazy, primitive, fanatical, and barbaric" in popular Canadian imaginations.[21] The Canadian government, to the consternation of Peters and many other Arab Canadians, framed a Palestine policy that reflected this racialized logic, treating Zionist Jews and indigenous Palestinians unequally to the tragic detriment of the latter. Ottawa, far from being even-handed at the United Nations and elsewhere, was decisive in facilitating the creation of what would become the state of Israel in 1948, which engendered the Arab *nakbah* (catastrophe) and roughly 750,000 Palestinian refugees.[22]

The Arab-Israeli conflict unsettled Peters. Refraining from activist political involvement during the 1950s, he entered the Canadian fray at decade's end. A linguistics professor at Ryerson Polytechnical Institute, Peters joined ranks with post-*nakbah* Palestinian refugees and other Arab nationalists across the globe who publicly denounced the continuation of imperialism – that is, its cultural ways of seeing Arabs and resultant socio-political structures of inequality – in the Middle East. Arab critiques of Western imperialism thus flowed to Canada, alongside migrants like Issa Fahel. Upon arrival, the Palestinian Fahel immersed himself within the Canadian public sphere. Before too long, in response to Canadian experiences with the Suez Crisis of 1956–57, he formed the Canadian Friends of the Middle East (CFME) in London, Ontario. Its core objectives were twofold: "counter pro-Israel bias in the media" and empower Arab perspectives in Canada.[23]

Peters's and Fahel's paths crossed at the CFME, which recruited the former to serve on the organization's national committee. Peters's intellectual penchant for language and communications, alongside his Arab politics, made him an ideal candidate to present "the Arab view point" to Canadians through "literature, letters to the editor, [public speaking], letters to MPs, and deputations to Parliament [that] combat lying Zionist propaganda." Fahel firmly believed that Canadian Orientalism and Ottawa's subsequent Middle East policies were tainted by "Zionist pressures groups" and their discriminatory ways of seeing Palestinians. Arab Canadians, he explained to Peters, had "a special duty towards our respective countries" to globalize – in their case, Canadianize – Arab decolonization. The flow of Arab information into Canadian mindscapes was key. "True" knowledge, Fahel insisted, was power. And "our combined efforts would be a hundred or a thousand times more effective than the sum of our individual efforts."[24]

Peters agreed, joining CFME's executive committee and launching an affiliated Toronto chapter in the fall of 1960 from his home in Don Mills. As the president of the Canadian-Arab Friendship Society (CAFS), he led the charge of reorienting Canada-Middle East relations in the nation-state's largest metropolis. Membership was far from robust, initially numbering a mere twenty-seven. The CAFS, under Peters's leadership, welcomed all: Arabs, Arab Canadians, and "other Canadians who sympathized with the Arab cause and appreciated Arab history and its contributions to western civilization." Its initial goals were social and educational. Yet, rather quickly, the Toronto group realized that both aims merged into an anti-Orientalist mandate that sought "to correct the Arab image in the media."[25]

Peters's CAFS was not left alone in the face of this daunting task. Through its connection to Fahel's CFME, it quickly linked up with a nascent anti-Orientalist network of like-minded activists, intellectuals, and institutions across North America and the Middle East. Its most important ally was the League of Arab States's Arab Information Office (AIC) in Ottawa. Set up in January 1960, the AIC's primary aim was to "contribute in some measure towards a better understanding by the Canadian [public] of the legitimate and just aspirations of the Arab people." It did so by disseminating historical and contemporary information about Arabs, forging relationships with organizations and communities dedicated to the Arab world, working with the Canadian media, and facilitating Canadian access to qualified, appropriate public speakers. The Middle Eastern-run AIC, moreover, served as a decolonial linchpin, connecting Peters's CAFS and Fahel's CFME with the likes of the Quaker-led American Friends in the Middle East, anti-Zionist US rabbi Elmer Berger's American Council for Judaism, Arab student organizations and public intellectuals, and Middle Eastern governments. This network ensured a steady flow of anti-Orientalism between communities, countries, and continents.[26]

Peters formed a strong relationship with the AIC's founding director, Khalid Babaa. Upon first contact in late 1960, the Palestinian Babaa and the president of the CAFS hit it off. They shared a common cause: the Arab decolonization of Canada. To be remotely successful, the AIC director stressed, Peters's organization "cannot be an 'honorary' one, rather it must be an efficient, effective, and productive one." Haunted by pre-*nakbah* Arab information efforts in North America, Babaa warned: "We have had an enough deep slumber and it is time for us to be fully aware and do whatever we can to promote a just cause."[27] Babaa, like Peters, was no stranger to Canadian Orientalism. Two months in, the *Ottawa Citizen* welcomed the AIC director as "Ali Babaa's grandson." The "tall, dark, and tense" character it described came straight out of the well-known but controversial *One Thousand and One Nights* folk tale, "Ali Baba and the Forty Thieves." A romanticized thief's grandson, not an experienced Palestinian public relations officer, represented "the Arab view point" in Canada, insinuated Ottawa's leading English-language daily.[28]

Peters, Babaa, Fahel, and other anti-Orientalists predominantly focused their activities on Canadian misunderstandings of the Arab-Israeli conflict, especially the perceived cultural inferiority of Arabs in relation to Ashkenazi Jews. Peters, for his part, strongly felt that Zionism "created a press that neglects the Arabs when it does not malign them outright."[29] Cinema and its "reel bad Arabs" were no different.[30] The North American anti-Orientalist network was up in arms about Leon Uris's 1958 novel *Exodus* and Otto Preminger's ensuing 1960 film – Israel, we now know, influenced the making of both.[31] A month ahead of Preminger's movie release, New York City's AIC branch published a fault-finding pamphlet that denounced Uris's book as "an extension of the ruthless war of propaganda that has been waged by the Zionists since the forceful usurpation of Palestine." *Exodus* celebrated the creation of Israel and romanticized Zionist settler colonialism, defaming Palestinians and Arabs more broadly in the process. Replete with "untruths, half-truths, deliberate omissions and distortions of events," Uris's "strong bias against the Arabs color every word and line of the book." The AIC pamphlet contended that the historical novel portrayed "all Arabs as treacherous, cruel, ignorant, filthy, and completely immoral." Furthermore, it erased historical indigenous connections to the land, Zionist dispossessions of Palestinians, and resultant humanitarian crises.[32]

Acknowledging that Uris's book almost instantaneously achieved "cultural authority" in the United States, Peters and his fellow Canadian anti-Orientalists prepared for their inevitable public confrontations with Zionism and its misrepresentations. The CAFS and CFME organized a demonstration during *Exodus*'s Toronto premiere at the Tivoli Theatre. Preminger's film, as expected, grossly disappointed those picketing outside. Following in the book's footsteps, the movie sentimentalized the imperial binary of "Israelis as heroes" and "Arabs as villains." It North Americanized Zionism by connecting fantasies of Israeli settler colonialism with Canadian and US myths of so-called Western expansion.[33]

The protest was Peters's first. Overall, he thought it went well. "At first there's a little fright before the battle," he confided to a friend, "and then exhilaration as the enemy is discomforted." Both the Tivoli's manager and *Exodus*'s film company agent pleaded with the Arab Canadian leader to abrogate the demonstration. Preminger's take was much different than Uris's, they argued. The film "was kosher" and "didn't attack anybody except the British a little." Peters refused to step down, confessing to both men "that [he] hadn't seen the movie, but any movie based on a such a horrible book had to be picketed."[34]

Jim Peters's encounter with *Exodus* led him to cross the Rubicon. Being "the only one who speaks for the Arabs in Toronto" earned him credibility amongst anti-Orientalists in North America.[35] Contrary to Zionist myth-making, the Arabs were the David – not the Goliath – in the global story of Israel; Toronto, he felt, was no different from Tel Aviv. "The very idea, the temerity of fighting the Zionist of this city is a bit ridiculous," Peters confided, "but we must do what we can if we want to live with ourselves."[36] In both numbers and resources, Zionists exceeded Arabs in Ontario's capital and elsewhere. To be remotely successful, he understood the need to "always distinguish between the Jew and the Zionist," even if "it is not always easy to make the distinction when nearly every Jew one meets is a Zionist of some degree." Before an audience at the Unitarian Church of South Peel in late 1961, Peters insisted that the "West must see the Arabs through their own eyes (purged of imperialism), not thru Zionist eyes."[37]

"Unable to say no" to Babaa, Peters took on the editorship of the new *Middle East Digest and Newsletter*. This quarterly platform, whose readership spanned Canada and the United States, permitted him to refine his anti-Orientalist ideas by bringing distant peoples closer to each other and connecting Canada to the global scale of Arab decolonization. As editor, he knew that the empowerment of marginalized Arab perspectives was central to fomenting cross-cultural empathy. In his first editorial, Peters declared that the "continued alienation of Arab feeling for the West must be arrested, and this can only be done by presenting Western readers (and to Canadians especially) the normalcy of Arab and Middle East aspirations and efforts for self-determination and self-fulfilment."[38]

Peters's post-introductory editorial in the following issue did not hold back. His anti-Orientalist critique of Western misrepresentations of Arabs was on full display, singling out a recent *Saturday Evening Post* article entitled "Seething Arab world."[39] In the eyes of Peters, Harold Martin's piece was Orientalism *pure laine*; it represented a "specific genre" designed "to denigrate the Arab character." Overflowing with pejorative photos, derogatory clichés about "the ferocious, nomadic Arab," and "worn out phrases and anecdotes" about political instabilities in the Arab world, he concluded that the January 1962 piece was cut from the same cloth as Rudolph Valentino's infamous 1921 film, *The Sheik*. Such features of Arabs, the article intimated, explained an unchanging Arab "hatred for the Jews." Peters wanted "to be clear" to his readers: "Arab hatred is directed at the Zionist, not at the Jew." Martin's logic in the *Post* was both flawed and out of place. "Antisemitism," the Arab Canadian leader explained, "is not an Arab tradition: a word for it does not exist in the Arabic language." Rather, antisemitism "is a Western phenomenon, and now that the West has relieved its rather insensitive conscience by giving Palestine to the Zionists, it is not cricket to project Western antisemitism on to the Arabs."[40]

In the summer of 1962, Babaa and the Arab League offered Peters an intimate look at the Middle East. He could not refuse the opportunity "to touch the face of the Arab world with [his] own hands, to smell the smells of the East with [his] own nose, and to feast [his] eyes on the colorful tapestry of Arab life." Welcomed as an official delegate, the six-week pilgrimage took him to Egypt, Jordan, Lebanon, and Syria. Upon setting foot in Cairo, Peters's first leg culminated in a scheduled meeting with Arab League Secretary General Abdel-Khalek Hassouna that frankly "discussed conditions in Canada in relation to Zionism and the Arab world." From there, encounters with Palestinian refugees in Jordan and Lebanon took center stage. These visits, Peters noted, "heightened my sense of outrage at the success of Zionism at the cost of a million Arab refugees." He witnessed first-hand "the squalor of the refugee camps, the poverty and hurt in their lives."[41]

Tragedies aside, the "intelligence and the ambition of the Palestine refugees" struck Peters.[42] An hour outside Nablus in the Jordanian West Bank, he was introduced to Al Hajj Abd Hafiz Shanti, a local Palestinian elder. Upon shaking Peters's hand, Shanti politely shook his head and said: "Ah! Canada, the country which helped to give our lands to the Zionists." The Palestinian refugee opened his home in the village of Qalqilya to Peters for a few days. Shanti shared his personal *nakbah* experience with the Arab Canadian leader and showed him his ancestral land on the Israeli horizon, which overlooked the Mediterranean. To the right, Shanti explained, the "land you see between here and the sea was owned by this village … now we have only these hills of stone." The sight of "the finest orange grove in the world" in the distance imprinted on Peters. Zionist settler colonialism dispossessed these from the Palestinian people of Qalqilya. Overcome with emotions, Peters asked Shanti: "But how do you make your living now that you have lost all your life's work?" The Palestinian elder walked him over to the east of the village and "pointed proudly to the young orange trees on the [other] side of the hill." Peters was awestruck. But how, he asked. With their bare hands, Shanti replied. Qalqilya residents carried soil to the new location, formed a co-operative, and dug wells. As his Canadian guest departed a few days later, Shanti asked Peters to "tell the people of North America when they say the Zionists have made the desert bloom that the desert they talk about was our orchards … Tell them that without one dollar of help, we Arabs have made the stones bloom."[43]

Peters returned rejuvenated from his Middle Eastern sojourn. "More determined than ever to bring the political and moral truths of the Arab world to the attention of the Canadian peoples," the Arab Canadian leader expanded his anti-Orientalist gaze beyond the media. Canadian foreign policy, as Shanti said in the West Bank, was equally accountable for the plights of Palestinians and Arab self-determination more broadly. Both Ottawa and Canadian society writ large needed to critically reconcile their connections to Western imperialism and its Orientalist ways of seeing. Zionism coloured Canadian decision-making.[44] Upon hearing news that Lester B. Pearson intended to address a Zionist convention in Toronto, Peters denounced the official leader of the opposition. Far from being even-handed vis-à-vis the Arab-Israeli conflict, the head of the Liberal Party "alienate[d] Arabs from the West." As he explained in an ensuing issue of his *Middle East Digest and Newsletter*, "Israel symbolizes everything that the Arab came to hate in colonialism."[45]

Meanwhile, Peters's anti-Orientalist network continued to expand. Babaa's sudden relocation to Dallas, Texas, resulted in a life-long, "close relationship" with his temporary replacement, the experienced Arab public relations officer Sami Hadawi.[46] A prolific writer,[47] the Palestinian Hadawi put Peters in touch with prominent Arab anti-Orientalists in the United States, like Mohammed Mehdi, the secretary general of New York City's Action Committee on American-Arab Relations. Mehdi's "zealous efforts to rout Arab inertia and foil Zionist lies" mirrored that of the Arab Canadian leader. Signing off in their correspondence as Jameel, rather than Jim, Peters complained that "our people are so dead in combatting the Zionist blight." Toronto, like New York, was a "great Zionist city."[48]

Discontent with Arab Middle Eastern leadership in North America arose as a byproduct of anti-Orientalist correspondence and activisms. Peters's developing misgivings matched those of the US public intellectual Alfred Lilienthal. The anti-Zionist American Jew's latest book, *The Other Side of the Coin*, lamented that Arabs in the United States possessed a mere "scintilla of public relations sense."[49] Middle Eastern government funds for anti-Orientalism in North America dwindled. Peters, based on his experience in Toronto, agreed. Arab Middle Eastern representatives in North America, Lilienthal confided to Peters, "know so little about public relations." The more daunting task at hand was "to make them realize this." The Arab Canadian leader did not sit idly by, contacting the AIO-contracted and Montreal-based Brakeley Public Relations Limited. Notable exceptions aside, a general Arab Middle Eastern approach of indolence and incapability frustrated him, as did a lack of Middle Eastern-initiated leadership. The Arab *mahjar* in North America did not have the means, resources, and energies to simultaneously fill local, national, and continental voids. "The Zionists," Peters asserted in a letter to the firm, "have dealt deadly blows at the reputation of the Arabs, and have managed with genius to reverse the role of victim and aggressor." His faith in the globality of Arab decolonization waned, as he felt "that the righting of the imbalance and injustice relative to the Arab reputation is well-nigh hopeless."[50]

Peters's anti-Orientalist activism waxed with the advent of the 1967 Arab-Israeli crisis. With war on the brink in the Middle East, a powerful current of character assassination toward Arabs resurfaced in the Canadian public sphere. Canadian Orientalism contradicted the national self-image of peacekeeping in the region. Far from being exceptionally nice and polite toward Arabs,[51] alarmingly large strands of Canadian society showcased their racialized core and their direct linkage to the legacy of Western imperialism in the Middle East. Canadians rallied en masse behind Israel, against Arabs.[52] Arabs, Peters charged in his *Middle East Digest and Newsletter*, were faced with and resisted a deluge of undiplomatic "images falsified by design, or by ignorance, misunderstanding and romantic invention."[53] Amid Arab Canadian protests against Canadian perceptions and policy concerning the Arab-Israeli conflict, Peters's CAFS issued its own press release. Non-Arab Canadian reactions to Arab "annoyance and resentment" were misplaced, Peters wrote. Contrary to popular belief, Arab Canadians did not misunderstand Ottawa's so-called even-handed, neutral approach. According to Peters, Canadians "must realize that we have been rubbing the Arabs the wrong way for the last 20 years." After listing eleven political and cultural grievances, the statement affirmed:

> We have not been neutral, neither at the governmental nor at the popular level, while deceiving ourselves with our imagined self-image of neutrality. Our failure to be neutral at the governmental level particularly has compromised our effectiveness as a peace-maker. We should not be surprised at the cumulative reaction of Arabs, nor at the growing mistrust of the non-aligned nations.[54]

A view through an Arab lens, however brief, would illuminate the myth of Canadian diplomacy in the Middle East. Anti-Arab cultural prejudices sanctioned a Canadian foreign policy that supported Israel's perpetual cycle of unlawful violence against Arabs during the fateful month of June 1967.[55]

Canada required a new approach in the wake of the Arab-Israeli war of 1967, Peters felt. Arab Canadians could no longer depend on Middle Eastern governments, nor the Arab League, to lead Arab decolonization in North America. Israel's rapid annihilation of Arab forces, illegal occupation of the Jordanian West Bank, the Egyptian Gaza Strip, the Sinai Peninsula, and Syria's Golan Heights, in addition to its brazen unification of West and East Jerusalem, exacerbated Peters's opposition toward the apparent synergy between Canada's Zionist media bias and Ottawa's supposed even-handedness.[56] Humiliated by both the Arab debacle and "the partisan behavior of many Canadian politicians and clergyman," he responded to outstanding calls to form a national organization. Greater inter-cultural dialogue between Arabs, Arab Canadians, and Canadians necessitated coast-to-coast mobilization. "Arab-Canadian relations have never been poorer as a result of the recent Zionist assaults on the Arabs and the truth," Peters wrote to all CAFS members in early September 1967. "The situation calls for creative thinking and handwork on the part of all us, for the Arabs have never been good publicists."[57]

Peters was central in building a national organization dedicated to Arab-Canadian rapprochement. On 4–5 November, eighteen delegates from Toronto, Ottawa, Edmonton, Hamilton, and London gathered in the residence of the recently immigrated Dr Salman Abu Sitta. Under the joint leadership of Peters and the Palestinian-born engineer, who had been recruited by the University of Western Ontario to work on Toronto's CN Tower, a handful of local societies constituted the Canadian Arab Federation (CAF). By design, recent Arab immigrants occupied the national organization's governing leadership. Dr Ibrahim Salti, a renowned physician formerly based at the American University of Beirut, and Abu Sitta were elected inaugural president and vice-president respectively.[58] The CAF's mandate echoed those of its constituent groups, like Peters's CAFS: the reorientation of relations between Canada and the Arab world. Above all, it hoped "to move Canada from its complicity in biased Western policies to one of neutrality, and then ultimately with the aid of the innate decency of Canadians, to win Canada's support for Arab aspirations to justice, unity, and prosperity." While understanding that "Canada is not a prime mover in oppressing the Arabs," CAF founders identified Canadian society as being part of a worldly tradition that denigrated Arabs on political, social, economic, and cultural levels and, as a result, lent credence to Zionism. Canada was "a Western puppet state" that followed in the imperial footsteps of Britain, France, and the United States.[59]

Peters, for his part, took on the executive position of head of the CAF's "important" anti-defamation committee. His chief role was to publicly critique Canadian Orientalism. Canada, the CAF insisted under his leadership, was compliant and complicit in the global dehumanization of Arabs. "The defamation of Arabs is constant," Peters remarked at the founding gathering in London, "especially during times of crisis." Canadian politicians and laypeople alike were not bystanders in the transnational crime of character assassination of the

Arabs; rather, as government policies and media clippings portrayed, they were accomplices. The 1967 war unearthed Canada's involvement "in the long history" of Orientalism "and its tradition persists."[60]

The power of Peters's anti-Orientalist pen dictated his hand. "The alienation of the Arab people is now a historical fact," he wrote to the new leader of the Liberal Party Pierre Elliott Trudeau in April 1968.[61] For evidence, the Canadian prime minister needed to look no further than the Canadian Broadcasting Corporation's (CBC) undiplomatic coverage of the 1967 Arab-Israeli crisis. Like Ottawa, the CBC was far from even-handed. News reports "often referred to the Arabs as the 'enemy,' showing a complete and lamentable identification with Israel." Many segments, per Peters, "looked as if they had been made by the government of Israel rather than by a neutral national broadcasting corporation of a neutral state." Tragically, the CBC was replete with "out-of-date stereotypes." Arab Canadians "wince in pain every time the CBC attempts to deal 'fairly' with Middle East affairs," he complained to CBC president George F. Davidson. Whether it purposely vilified Arabs or held "unconscious biases" was beside the point. *Grosso modo*, the CBC contributed "with alacrity to the sustained character assassination of the Arabs."[62]

Knowing full well that it had "its work cut-out," the CAF did not waste any time in planning its inaugural convention. Held in Toronto's Royal York Hotel on 17–19 May 1968, the national meeting united forty groups and 200 members across Canada with Arab diplomats and public intellectuals, as well as leading US anti-Orientalists.[63] As co-chair and president of the host society, Peters took centre stage. Following an opening presentation by Dr George Tomeh, Syrian ambassador to the United Nations, on "the historical meaning of the 1967 disaster," Peters gave his own talk on the history of "stereotypes created for us by others." The Arab Canadian leader did not disappoint. Canada, he argued, was complicit in global Orientalism. As such, Canadians needed to enlist with the burgeoning anti-Orientalist network; together, they needed to decolonize Canada. In conclusion, Peters asked the hundreds in attendance: "Is there any Canadian Arab here today who has not winced at what he has heard and read in the media? Who dares read the [Toronto] Star or Telegram without fear of another lie, another shock and the helpless anguish and frustration we feel disturb the normal tenure of our lives?" The CAF convention was a resounding success. By year's end, its membership doubled and member societies popped up "in every major Canadian city."[64]

When it came to the sensitive matter of Canada's dehumanization of Arabs, Peters served as an inspiration and guiding light. Equally vital, however, were his relentless decolonial effort and unique contribution to transnational anti-Orientalist thought. As an Arab Canadian, Peters was well situated to speak to the worldliness of Orientalism. The Palestine Liberation Organization's recently launched Institute of Palestine Studies in Beirut, Lebanon, thought so when it invited him to "write a short monograph on the relationship between Palestine and Canada" – which he reluctantly declined to do because he was drastically spread thin by his Canadian anti-defamation activities.[65] Orientalism's borders, Peters's writings and activism revealed, transcended imperial centers such as London, Paris, and Washington. Unexceptional within the Western world, the postcolonial Canadian example showed how imperialism was a global structure that superseded conventional relationships between colonized and colonizers. Canada, according to its own myth-making, was a so-called middle-power, which prided itself on the imagined distance it forged from its principal Western allies. Yet anti-Arab racism included Canada, even if Ottawa had not colonized Arab lands. "The West," he wrote in the CAF's newsletter *The Arab Dawn*, "regards Arabs as an inferior breed of mankind, lacking the virtues which the mother countries and her colonies possess."[66]

When sharpening his anti-Orientalist critique, the Arab Canadian leader targeted the spirit of Canadian liberalism, "solicitous of human rights and of human dignity." But Peters did not limit himself to the Liberal Party. Canada's Conservative Party was no different in his mind, as it claimed to seek "justice for all men, not only in [its] own country, but everywhere regardless of race or religion"; Zionism crossed the Canadian aisle.[67] In a letter to the Conservative leader John Diefenbaker, he shared his disgust with the latter's recent reception of an Israeli prize for humanitarianism, along with his controversial suggestion that Ottawa recognize Jerusalem as Israel's capital. Canada's inhumane treatment of Palestinians, Peters explained to the federal leader in an open letter, followed its treatment of Indigenous peoples in Canada. Diefenbaker, who had been raised in Treaty 6 Territory, publicly expressed "great concern for the Canadian Indians," like he did for the human rights of Palestinian refugees. Yet his deeds remained disconnected from his words. "Are Arabs not human beings?" Peters asked. "Apparently not as far as Western politicians are concerned. And you politicians of Canada are indifferent to their fate because they have so few votes in Canada, and a minority of them are Christians." Canada, he insisted, was equally responsible for "the problems of Palestine." Ottawa's refusal to denounce Israeli settler colonialism, furthermore, was inhumane and hypocritical. Canadian liberalists paradoxically had "right thoughts," but disregarded the universality of human rights.[68]

*   *   *

Jim Peters's anti-Orientalism continued beyond the 1960s, yet in private he often questioned its effectiveness. With the Arab-Israeli conflict unresolved, Ottawa's approach unchanged, and Canadians generally unmoved, Canadian Orientalism remained *l'ordre du jour*. "My efforts have seemed to be quite useless," he lamented to a young protégé. Orientalist stereotypes, like those implicit in *The Orgiastic Near East*, in the Toronto press, and in Canadian foreign policy, were not displaced from the Canadian public sphere. Yet despite feeling like "a crank," Peters refused to relent from his anti-Orientalist efforts to decolonize Canadian ways of seeing and being, both at home and in the world. He was "obliged to within [himself]." The Arab Canadian leader felt like he "*had* to do it."[69]

Jim Peters's activism in the 1960s entrenched the global process of Arab decolonization in Canada, while further globalizing an Arab-led anti-Orientalist critique. His offering to Canada-Middle East relations was straightforward: the Don Mills resident challenged Canada's character assassination of Arabs and connected the Canadian public sphere to the global flows of decolonial ideas. Through his writings, community engagement, networking, organizing, and mentoring, Peters sensitized Canadians to their undiplomatic conduct toward, (mis)representations of, and (in)difference for Arabs. Within a national container, he challenged inhumane frames of reference and sowed seeds of cross-cultural empathy and mutual understanding through his empowerment of Arab points of view. His public interventions allowed willing Canadians to contemplate Ottawa's approach to the Arab-Israeli conflict, along with its imagined peacekeeping identity in the world, during a key period in postcolonial history.

Jameel's journal, furthermore, offered a unique, place-based contribution to worldly anti-Orientalist thinking. Canada's direct connection to the globalizing tradition of Orientalism revealed that imperialism, driven by culture first and foremost, had no spatial limits. Its imperial ways of thinking and being were both relational and universal. Canadians did not need to formally colonize so-called foreign lands to partake in empire and its systems of human inequality. Anti-Arab prejudices and ensuing state and non-state (in)actions linked their country to global structures of imperialism. Canadian mindsets, Peters argued, mattered *because* they mirrored British, French, and US ones. Anti-Orientalists, as a result, better understood the developing predicament of Arab decolonization in the world. And Canadians were better positioned to critically reconcile their relationships with global discourses of difference, be they racial, religious, linguistic, gendered, class-based, or sexualized, as well as their ongoing, postcolonial relationship with imperialism's past, present, and future. Given his Arab heritage, Canadian experience, and Arab Canadian perspective, Peters felt they had to.

NOTES

1 Abdel Khalek Hassouna to Peters, 30 June 1968, James Peters Fonds (JPF), vol. 4, file 1, Library and Archives Canada (LAC).
2 Peters to US State Department, 6 May 1968, RG 25, vol. 9366, file 20-18-2-1, part 1, LAC.
3 Joseph Rosenfeld, *The Orgiastic Near East: A Psychological Study of the Sexual Customs of the Arab* (Canoga Park, CA: Viceroy Books, 1968), 5.
4 Edward Said, *Orientalism* (New York: Vintage, 1978), 190. For a more extensive analysis of the connection between sex and Orientalism, see Joseph Massad, *Desiring Arabs* (Chicago: University of Chicago Press, 2007); and Ann Stoler, *Race and the Education of Desire: Foucault's History of Sexuality and the Colonial Order of Things* (Durham: Duke University Press, 1995).
5 Massad, *Desiring Arabs*, 8.
6 Rosenfeld, *The Orgiastic Near East*, 157.
7 Ibid., 164–5.
8 Peters to US State Department, 6 May 1968, RG 25, vol. 9366, file 20-18-2-1, part 1, LAC.
9 Edward Said, *The World, the Text, and the Critic* (Cambridge: Harvard University Press, 1983).
10 Edward Said, "Traveling Theory," in *The Edward Said Reader*, edited by Moustafa Bayoumi and Andrew Rubin (New York: Vintage Books, [1982] 2000), 195–217.
11 See Thomas Brisson, "La critique arabe de l'orientalism en France et aux États-Unis: Lieux, temporalités et modalités d'une relecture," *Revue d'anthro-*

pologie des connaissances 2, no. 3 (2008): 505–21; Joseph Escovitz, "Orientalist and Orientalism in the Writings of Muhammad Kurd Ali, *International Journal of Middle East Studies* 15, no. 1 (1983): 95; and Zachary Lockman, *Contending Visions of the Middle East: The History and Politics of Orientalism* (Cambridge: Cambridge University Press, 2004), 183. Two strong examples of earlier Arab anti-Orientalist thought are: Anouar Abdel-Malek, "Orientalisme en crise," *Diogène* 44 (1963): 109–42; and A. L. Tibawi, "English-Speaking Orientalists: A Critique to Their Approach to Islam and Arab Nationalism," *The Muslim World* 53, no. 4 (1963): 298–313.

12 Said, *Orientalism*, 325.

13 Edward Said, *Reflections on Exile and Other Essays* (Cambridge: Harvard University Press, 2000), 202.

14 See Christopher Anderson, *"Métis": Race, Recognition, and the Struggle for Indigenous Peoplehood* (Vancouver: UBC Press, 2014); Sean Carleton, "Colonizing Minds: Public Education, the 'Textbook Indian,' and Settler Colonialism in British Columbia, 1920–1970," *BC Studies* 169 (2011): 101–30; Shahnaz Khan, "Race, Gender, and Orientalism: Muta and the Canadian Legal System," *Canadian Journal of Women and Law* 8, no. 1 (1995): 249–61; Christine Kim, *The Minor Intimacies of Race: Asian Publics in North America* (Urbana: University of Illinois Press, 2016); Renisa Mawani, *Colonial Proximities: Crossracial Encounters and Juridical Truths in British Columbia, 1971–1921* (Vancouver: UBC Press, 2009); Adele Perry, *On the Edge of Empire: Gender, Race, and the Making of British Columbia* (Toronto: University of Toronto Press, 2001); John Price, *Orienting Canada: Race, Empire, and the Transpacific* (Montreal: McGill-Queen's University Press, 2011); and Audra Simpson, *Mohawk Interruptus: Political Life across Borders of Settler States* (Durham: Duke University Press, 2014).

15 Houda Asal, *Se dire arabe au Canada: Un siècle d'histoire migratoire* (Montreal: Les Presses de l'Université de Montréal, 2016); Stephanie Bangarth, *Voices Raised in Protest: Defending North American Citizens of Japanese Ancestry, 1942–49* (Vancouver: UBC Press, 2008); Karen Dubinsky, *Babies without Borders: Adoption and Migration across the Americas* (Toronto: University of Toronto Press, 2010); Karen Dubinsky, Sean Mills, and Scott Rutherford, eds., *Canada and the Third World: Overlapping Histories* (Toronto: University of Toronto Press, 2016); Jenna Hennebry and Bessma Momani, eds., *Targeted Transnationals: The State, the Media, and Arab Canadians* (Vancouver: UBC Press, 2013); Sean Mills, *A Place in the Sun: Haiti, Haitians, and the Remaking of Quebec* (Montreal and Kingston: McGill-Queen's University Press, 2016); Mills, *The Empire Within: Postcolonial Thought and Political Activism in Sixties Montreal* (Montreal and Kingston: McGill-Queen's University Press, 2010);

Ryan Touhey, *Conflicting Visions: Canada and India in the Cold War, 1946–76* (Vancouver: UBC Press, 2015); and David Webster, *Fire and the Full Moon: Canada and Indonesia in a Decolonizing World* (Vancouver: UBC Press, 2009).

16 Peters to Keliele, 22 April 1975, JPF, vol. 6, file 1, LAC; and Peters to Rostom, 16 April 1987, JPF, vol. 8, file 5, LAC. James Peters was the name registered to him at birth and the one that he formally identified with. That said, "Peters" was not his true family name; "Qahwash" was. "Peters" comes from the surname of his Syrian father, Naseem Butrus Qahwash. "Butrus" translates into "Peter," which becomes "Peters" when applied as a family name.

17 An exception and a great, historical example of "Third World" anti-racism in Canada is: Seema Sohi, *Echoes of Mutiny: Race, Surveillance, and Indian Anti-colonialism in North America* (New York: Oxford University Press, 2014).

18 Peters to Rostom, 16 April 1987, JPF, vol. 8, file 5, LAC; Baha Abu-Laban, *An Olive Branch on the Family Tree* (Toronto: McClelland and Steward, 1980), 57; and Notes, April 1984, JPF, vol. 2, LAC.

19 Peters to Rostom, 16 April 1987, JPF, vol. 8, file 5, LAC; Muhammad Said Massoud, *I Fought as I Believed: An Arab Canadian Speaks Out on the Arab-Israeli Conflict* (Montreal: Ateliers des sourds, 1976); and Eliezer Tauber, "The Palestine Question in the 1940s and the Emergence of the Arab Lobby in Canada," *American Review of Canadian Studies* 40, no. 4 (2010): 530–40.

20 Biographical Outline, n.d, JPF, vol. 1, LAC.

21 Baha Abu-Laban, "Arab-Canadians and the Arab-Israeli Conflict," *Arab Studies Quarterly* 10, no. 1 (1988): 104–26.

22 David Bercuson, *Canada and the Birth of Israel: A Study in Canadian Foreign Policy* (Toronto: University of Toronto Press, 1985); Shira Robinson, *Citizen Strangers: Palestinians and the Birth of Israel's Liberal Settler State* (Stanford: Stanford University Press, 2013); and Elizabeth Tauber, *Personal Policy Making: Canada's Role in the Adoption of the Palestine Partition Resolution* (Westport, CT: Greenwood Press, 2002).

23 Memorandum, 21 February 1955, RG 25, vol. 6669, file 12158-40, LAC; and Gary D. Kennan, "Issa Fahel, A Man to Remember," https://www.canpalnet-ottawa.org/canpalissafahel.html.

24 Cunningham to Peters, 11 August 1960; and Fahel to Peters, 2 October 1960, JPF, vol. 1, file 1, LAC.

25 Meeting, 20 September 1960, JPF, vol. 1, file 1, LAC; Press Release, 6 November 1960, JPF, vol. 1, file 1, LAC; and Habeeb Salloum, "History of the Canadian-Arab Friendship Society," *Polyphony* (Summer 1984): 165–7.

26 Khalid Babaa, *Facts Versus Misstatements* (Ottawa: Arab Information Center, 1960), 37; Babaa to Diefenbaker, n.d, John Diefenbaker Papers, file: 045 ARAB, VI/393, University of Saskatchewan Archive [USA]; and Cunningham to Peters, 11 August 1960, JPF, vol. 1, file 1, LAC.

27 Babaa to Peters, 7 November 1960, JPF, vol. 1, file 1, LAC; and New York to Ottawa, 17 December 1962, RG 25, vol. 7061, file 7631-B-40, LAC.

28 "Ali Babaa's Grandson Pushing Arabs' Views from Office in Ottawa," *Ottawa Citizen*, 2 March 1960.

29 Letter, 20 December 1960 and Peters to Greene, 24 December 1960, JPF, vol. 1, file 1, LAC.

30 Jack G. Shaheen, *Reel Bad Arabs: How Hollywood Vilifies a People* (Northampton, MA: Olive Branch Press, 2009); Shaheen, *The TV Arab* (Bowling Green, OH: Bowling Green State University Popular Press, 1984); and Notes for Presentation at Unitarian Church of South Peel, 2 December 1961, JPF, vol. 1, file 1, LAC.

31 Babaa to Peters, 8 February 1961, JPF, vol. 1, file 1, LAC; and Giora Goodman, "'Operation Exodus': Israeli Government Involvement in the Production of Otto Preminger's Film *Exodus* (1960)," *Journal of Israeli History* 33, no. 2 (2014): 223.

32 Aziz Sahwell, *Exodus: A Distortion of Truth* (New York: Arab Information Center, 1960), 1–2.

33 Shaheen, *Reel Bad Arabs*, 209. See Amy Kaplan, "Zionism as Anticolonialism: The Case of *Exodus*," *American Literary History* 25, no. 4 (2013): 870–95; and Michelle Mart, *Eye on Israel: How America Came to View Israel as an Ally* (Albany: SUNY Press, 2006). For the Canadian Jewish context, see Harold Troper, *The Defining Decade: Identity, Politics, and the Canadian Jewish Community in the 1960s* (Toronto: University of Toronto Press, 2010).

34 Babaa to Peters, 8 February 1961, CFME Announcement, 17 March 1961, and Peters to Cunningham, 1 April 1961, JPF, vol. 1, file 1, LAC.

35 Peters to Cunningham, 18 March 1961, Babaa to Peters, 13 April 1961, and Massoud to Peters, 27 August 1962, JPF, vol. 3, LAC.

36 Peters to Abrams, 8 January 1961, JPF, vol. 1, file 1, LAC.

37 *Middle East Digest and Newsletter* 9 (July 1965): 7–8; David Taras, "From Passivity to Politics: Canada's Jewish Community and Political Support for Israel," in *The Domestic Battleground: Canada and the Arab-Israeli Conflict*, edited by David Taras and David Goldberg (Montreal and Kingston: McGill-Queen's University Press, 1989), 37; Peters to Cunningham, 11 May 1961, JPF, vol. 3, LAC; and Notes for Presentation at Unitarian Church of South Peel, 2 December 1961, JPF, vol. 1, file 1, LAC.

38 Peters to Greene, 18 September 1961, JPF, vol. 1, file 1, LAC; and James Peters, "A New Digest to Serve You," *Middle East Digest and Newsletter* 1 (January 1962): 1.

39 Harold Martin, "Seething Arab World," *Saturday Evening Post* (January 1962): 11–18.

40 James Peters, "Editorial: The Seething Arab World," *Middle East Digest*

and Newsletter 2 (March 1962): 1–2; and Editorial, n.d., JPF, vol. 1, file 1, LAC.

41 Peters, "Peters' Progress," *Middle East Digest and Newsletter* 5 (February 1963): 9–11; and Peters to Babaa, 28 October 1962, JPF, vol. 1, file 1, LAC.

42 Peters, "No Change," *Middle East Digest and Newsletter* 4 (November 1962): 1.

43 Peters, "He Made the Stone's Bloom," *Middle East Digest and Newsletter* 9 (July 1965): 7–8.

44 Peters, "Peters' Progress"; Doc 62; Peters to Hassouna, 1 November 1962, JPF, vol. 1, file 4, LAC; and James Peters, "Election Dilemma," *Middle East Digest and Newsletter* 3 (June 1962): 4–5.

45 Peters to Pearson, 1 November 1962, JPF, vol. 3, LAC; and Peters, "In the News," *Middle East Digest and Newsletter* 6 (July 1963): 1.

46 Sami Hadawi, *The Story of My Life: Memories and Reflections* (Amman: s.d., 1996), ix.

47 Hadawi, *Palestine: A Loss of a Heritage* (San Antonio, TX: Naylor, 1963).

48 Peters to Mehdi, 12 January 1965, JPF, vol. 1, file 7, LAC.

49 Alfred Lilienthal, *The Other Side of the Coin: An American Perspective on the Arab-Israeli Conflict* (New York: Devin-Adair Company, 1965), 203.

50 Shukrullah to Peters, n.d., JPF, vol. 1, file 4, LAC; Doc 77; Doc 85; Peters, "A Letter of Appreciation," *Middle East Digest and Newsletter* 9 (July 1965): 5; Lilienthal to Peters, 20 August 1965 and Peters to Wilmot, 28 December 1965, JPF, vol. 3, file 4, LAC.

51 For more on the myth of Canadian exceptionalism, see Colin McCullough, *Creating Canada's Peacekeeping Past* (Vancouver: UBC Press, 2016).

52 Maurice Jr. Labelle, "Not So Nobel: Arab Perceptions of Lester B. Pearson and Canada," in *Mike's World: Lester B. Pearson and Canadian External Relations, 1963–68*, eds., Asa McKercher and Galen Roger Perras (Vancouver: UBC Press, 2017), 168–88.

53 Troper, *The Defining Decade*, 126; and Peters, "What Are Arabs Really Like?" *Middle East Digest and Newsletter* 12 (April 1967): 12.

54 Press Release, 2 June 1967, JPF, vol. 1, file 24, LAC.

55 Walter Hixson, *The Myth of American Diplomacy: National Identity and U.S. Foreign Policy* (New Haven: Yale University Press, 2008); Labelle, "Not So Nobel"; and Cairo to Ottawa, 15 June 1967, RG 25, vol. 10052, file 20-1-2-ME, part 2, LAC.

56 Peters to Byfeld, 2 August 1967, JPF, vol. 3, file 6, LAC; and Labelle, "Not So Nobel."

57 Peters to editor of *Toronto Star*, 13 July 1967, JPF, vol. 3, file 6, LAC; Shukrullah to Peters, 11 March 1966, JPF, vol. 3, file 4, LAC; Peters to Tannous, 31

May 1967, JPF, vol. 3, file 6, LAC; and Peters to CAFS Members, 2 September 1967, JPF, vol. 1, file 24, LAC.

58 Report, 10 August 1968, JPF, vol. 4, file 2, LAC; No Author, "Canadian Arabs Form National Federation," *Middle East Digest and Newsletter* 13 (January 1968): 9; and Salman Abu Sitta, *Mapping My Return: A Palestinian Memoir* (Cairo: The American University of Cairo Press, 2016), 216, 220.

59 Draft, n.d., and Report, 10 August 1968, JPF, vol. 4, file 2, LAC.

60 Draft, n.d., JPF, vol. 4, file 2, LAC.

61 Peters to Trudeau, 21 April 1968, JPF, vol. 4, file 1, LAC.

62 Peters to Davidson, 6 March 1968, JPF, vol. 4, file 1, LAC.

63 Report, 10 August 1968, JPF, vol. 4, file 2, LAC; Peters to Batah, 26 February, and News Report, 22 May 1968, JPF, vol. 4, file 1, LAC.

64 Report, n.d.; Notes, "Defamation of the Arab Character," 18 May 1968; and Peters to Gardner, 26 May 1968, JPF, vol. 4, file 2, LAC; and no title, *L'aube arabe – The Arab Dawn* 1, no. 1 (November 1968): 1, 9.

65 Hafiz to Peters, 9 January 1969, and Peters to Sayegh, 13 June 1968, JPF, vol. 4, file 2, LAC.

66 No author, "Anti-Arab Racism," *L'aube arabe – The Arab Dawn* 1, no. 3 (February 1969): 9.

67 Speaking Notes, 19 January 1969, JPF, vol. 4, file 2, LAC.

68 Peters to Diefenbaker, 24 September 1968, John Diefenbaker Papers, file XI/B/1162 United Arab Republic, USA; and Speaking Notes, 19 January 1969, JPF, vol. 4, file 2, LAC.

69 Peters to Botrie, 25 May 1974; and Speaking Notes, 19 January 1969, JPF, vol. 5, file 5, LAC.

7

International Development and the State in Question: Liberal Internationalism, the New Left, and Canadian University Service Overseas in Tanzania, 1963–1977

WILL LANGFORD

From 1963, Canadian University Service Overseas (CUSO) – a non-governmental, volunteer-sending international development organization – delivered foreign assistance to Tanzania. Canadian volunteers motivated by idealism, the prospect of adventure, or humanitarian concern took up jobs in education or the civil service. They were ostensibly non-state actors, drawn to the issue of global inequality in a decolonizing and Cold War world, and active participants in transnational exchanges. In Tanzania, CUSO personnel, espousing either liberal internationalist or New Left principles, engaged with an attempt to forge self-reliant development and an African socialism. As a program position paper warned: "Involvement in development is involvement in a political process."[1]

Until recently, twentieth-century international history has largely been written with attention to the formal relationships between empires or national governments. Accordingly, the bulk of the literature on Canada's international dealings focuses on state diplomatic actors. Historian David Meren, in a recent historiographical essay, has commented on the resulting narrowness of Canadian international history.[2] Concurring, the editors of this volume have called for a revitalization and hybridization of the field by proposing that international histories take transnational, cultural, or social turns. But as historian Dominique Marshall points out in her vital reply to Meren, historians have been (perhaps not always explicitly) practising a new kind of international history for a decade or two. A Canada in the World scholarship already exists, found in work on humanitarian aid, migration, refugee policy, human rights activism, international adoption, and transnational interventions.[3] Recent studies have concretely sought to place Canada in a global context and to trace engagements with a wider world.[4]

For historians, there are choices to make within a more expansive and flexible Canada in the World field – as the varied contributions in this volume attest. "Undiplomatic History" can take different forms. First, the nation need not be the only, or even primary, concern. Transnational histories have rightly insisted on the necessity of looking beyond a reflexively national frame.[5] Second, politicians, military officials, and Foreign Affairs bureaucrats need not be the only actors. A range of Canadians have been active participants in international interactions. Third, diplomacy need not be the only subject of study, for Canadians have engaged with the world in diverse ways and made various ideological, cultural, social, and political connections.

My essay – on aspects of CUSO international development thought and practice in Tanzania in the 1960s and 1970s – joins an outward-looking Canadian scholarship that increasingly highlights the ways in which non-state participants have shaped international relations. My approach emphasizes the everyday politics conducted by ordinary people – a focus characteristic of a "new political history" informed by the insights of social and cultural history. But though the chapter turns away from state actors, I keep states and international relations in critical view. I examine how one set of Canadians – CUSO staff and volunteers – understood the position of their non-governmental organization relative to Canada, Tanzania, and development.

Decolonization, the Cold War, and the politics of poverty shaped the shared histories of Canada and the Third World from the 1950s. Historians have begun to explore the ways in which Canada and the Third World were caught up in global power relations as well as political, cultural, and intellectual exchanges.[6] A few historians have extended a diplomatic history approach to Canadian interactions with new nations, demonstrating that Canadian government actors were largely preoccupied with advancing anti-communism and maintaining North Atlantic alliances.[7] Certainly, shaped by American

hegemony, development assistance was one component of a geopolitical and liberal internationalist impulse that involved all First World
nations.[8] Development warrants study precisely because it was a wide
transnational project involving both Canadian state and non-state
actors. Recent histories have examined state provision of foreign aid,
Canadian technical experts abroad, mission contributions to development, and CUSO itself.[9] A contextualized study of CUSO in Tanzania
adds a dimension to newer work, especially as the role of non-governmental organizations (NGOs) in relation to foreign policy and
international development remains debated.[10]

I argue that between 1963 and 1977, CUSO personnel in Tanzania had
complex and changing understandings of the state, international relations, and the role of non-governmental organizations in international
development. If competing views coexisted, the political trajectory was
leftward. Implicitly subscribing to liberal internationalism, CUSO members initially believed that they should respect self-determination and
make short-term contributions to state-led development. However,
for some volunteers and field staff, support for Tanzanian socialism
and anti-colonialism demanded political commitment rather than
humanitarianism. The result was an organization ethos defining
development as liberation, though the ethos could be understood
in multiple ways. By the early 1970s, New Leftists reframed CUSO's
position in light of their neo-Marxist critique of global capitalism, international relations, and the Canadian and Tanzanian states.
My essay – as well as providing needed context – explores these
positions in turn, interpreting the shifting ways CUSO understood
the relationship between state, non-state activity, and international
development assistance.

CUSO, created in 1961, was the primary secular NGO for Canadians
travelling to the Third World to participate in technical assistance.
Placed at the request of foreign governments, volunteers were given
two-year contracts to work in public sector jobs. It was hoped that volunteers might contribute to social and economic development and
themselves "derive a richly rewarding educational experience."[11] CUSO
development practice turned on involving Canadians in postcolonial
national development efforts directed by state bureaucracy.

Ruth Compton Brouwer has shown that CUSO sent approximately
9,000 people abroad by 1981 – especially on teaching assignments for
which they had no prior experience. Most volunteers were in their
early twenties, from middle-class or skilled working-class back-

grounds, from white urban or suburban families, and from the Protestant or Catholic mainstream – all things typical of students at the Canadian universities from which volunteers had generally just graduated. Women were overrepresented. The volunteers wanted adventure, to put their idealism into action, and to do useful work.[12] Between 1963 and 1979, just over 350 volunteers worked as part of CUSO's program in Tanzania (CUSOTAN). About 150 of them taught in secondary schools.

Wherever CUSO intervened in the Third World, it contributed to two nation-building projects: a Canadian and a postcolonial one. That position was assured in both ideological and financial terms. Though an NGO, CUSO was overwhelmingly financed by the Canadian government after 1965. It was thus an ancillary part of Canadian foreign policy. Prime Minister Lester Pearson told CUSO members that foreign aid, in assuaging the misery and "rising expectations" of Third World peoples, could help avert "world-wide revolutionary violence and subversion."[13] More than simply contribute to a Cold War anti-communist imperative, volunteers were viewed – politically and popularly – as embodiments of a youthful Canadian idealism.[14] By subscribing to humanitarian concern, anti-poverty action, and liberal democratic capitalism, CUSO dovetailed with Canadian state interests and prestige abroad. Indeed, when the Canadian International Development Agency (CIDA) began to finance CUSO through a formal NGO program, it did so to "tap the enormous resources, experiences, expertise and knowledge that resided outside of government."[15] In 1973, 90 per cent of CUSO's budget came from CIDA.[16]

At the same time, CUSO activity abroad depended on the assent and subsidy of Third World governments. Unlike aid agencies such as CIDA (which paid the salaries of the technical experts they sent), CUSO volunteers were paid by foreign governments. These costs were external to CUSO budgeting. Yet a significant part of CUSOTAN's program – more than 50 per cent by a 1972 estimate – was borne by the Tanzanian government through the provision of salaries, housing, and health care to volunteers.[17] Volunteers assumed public sector jobs and CUSOTAN directly aligned itself with the postcolonial state project in Tanzania. Deference to state-led development was not simply a practical necessity, but a political commitment to national sovereignty in an era of decolonization. As one organization executive explained, "CUSO respects each country and its people's right to self-determination, which can take many unpredictable and un-Canadian forms."[18]

Liberal internationalist ideology was sufficiently malleable to accommodate both Canadian and Tanzanian nation-building roles.

As elsewhere, CUSO intervened in a complex postcolonial context in
Tanzania. Created in 1964, the country united Tanganyika, a British
colonial territory that had secured its peaceful independence in 1961,
and Zanzibar, an island where a leftist revolution had just ended
British rule. The new government unmade the tripartite racial order
and an ethnically based system of indirect political rule. But it retained many existing administrative structures, and, in response to an
early 1964 army mutiny, restricted civil society and installed a one-
party state. The postcolonial leadership also inherited a colonial development ethos increasingly informed by modernization theory.[19] Augmented cash crop agriculture, supported by improved services, might
boost exports and raise funds for industrialization. Development was
an attractive proposition in a country where the 9.5 million (and 95
per cent rural) population had a per capita income of $C60 in 1968.[20]

Julius Nyerere, Tanzania's president, hoped to remake postcolonial
society. His vision for an African socialism rested on *ujamaa*, a concept
best translated as "familyhood." Socialism, Nyerere insisted while
drawing on a Fabian tradition, was "an attitude of mind," rooted in fair
distribution rather than acquisitiveness and capitalist inequality. Such
a sensibility was exemplified by traditional, self-governing African villages that he characterized as devoid of exploitation.[21] In 1967, the
Arusha Declaration elevated the ideal to a national philosophy.
Designed to inspire the masses, the declaration charged the state with
eliminating poverty, ignorance, and disease. Suggesting that it was
"stupid" to rely on foreign money as the major instrument of development, the statement declared: "Independence means self-reliance."
The basis for self-reliant development would be increased agricultural production, as well as new agricultural processing and industry, and
would depend on hard work, land, and sound leadership.[22] However,
once key sectors of the economy had been nationalized, Tanzania
became an agrarian nation dominated by an undemocratic bureaucracy concentrated in the state, parastatal agencies, and the ruling
party. Authoritarian populism, not socialism, took shape.[23]

Self-reliance had been declared in part to guard against overdepen-
dence on foreign aid. Indeed, the popular understanding of development in Tanzania was self-sufficiency and freedom from non-African
economic forces. Ironically, state aims impressed observers, and international development assistance arrived from a variety of sources. Tan-

zania was a non-aligned country in the Cold War and donor nations on both sides of the conflict supplied capital, resources, and personnel.[24] For example, Canada – focusing loan provision on infrastructure, economic planning, and wheat-based agricultural development – provided $C208 million in bilateral aid to Tanzania between 1961 and 1981, and placed Canadians locally as civil servants, teachers, and military instructors.[25] United Nations agencies, the World Bank, American foundations, church groups, and international NGOs (like Oxfam and the Canadian Hunger Foundation) provided assistance. Volunteer-sending organizations from West Germany, Australia, Denmark, United States, Israel, Sweden, Liechtenstein, and Britain assigned personnel. Therefore, CUSOTAN formed part of a wider set of cosmopolitan, development-minded interventions in Tanzania.[26]

The Arusha Declaration decidedly politicized the role of foreign technical assistance personnel. For many CUSOTAN members, the situation demanded deeper commitment to Tanzanian development goals. Rudolph Carter made the point most clearly, reflecting in part on the Peace Corps' exclusion from the country in 1969 over American participation in the Vietnam War. The persistence of CUSOTAN, he felt, would depend on "the responsiveness of the CUSO organization in assuring that it remains a productive, integral manpower resource. In Tanzania, a productive resource with the context of the on-going cultural revolution and socialism is one that is positively identified with the direction of the country and that is not 'reactionary.'"[27]

Positive identification with national aims was an able description of the liberal internationalist aspirations of Canadians working in Tanzania. In 1968, CUSOTAN staff argued that their goal was "to supply manpower and related support to assist the country in achieving its goals," particularly by conforming to "the socialist direction of Tanzanian development."[28] Again in 1973, the aim was "to cooperate with the People, Party, and Government in their efforts to achieve a socialist, self-reliant society."[29] Official government policy became that of CUSOTAN. However, a number of considerations complicated the alignment.

Volunteers often recognized that racial, class, and cultural differences constrained their possible contributions to development. Once abroad – and not unlike Amanda Ricci's description in this volume of the experience of white Canadian feminists attending the International Women's Year Tribune in Mexico City in 1975 – CUSOTAN members reflected on inequality and were exposed to new political

discourses. As volunteer Hugh Winsor made clear: "The first distin-
guishing characteristic about a volunteer is that he is a white man.
Everybody can see that, so he has a lot of history to answer for."[30] The
continued presence of foreign personnel underlined that the African-
ization of the civil service had not yet been realized. Staff person
Shirley Baker tried to sum up the common Tanzanian view by
explaining: "They want Africans. We are white. Call it racialism, discrimination, what you will, this is one of the things African Independence is all about." Agreeing with other CUSOTAN members, Baker
supported government plans to progressively reduce reliance on temporary personnel procured from abroad. Once enough Tanzanians
had been trained, CUSOTAN might "consider its job done and phase
itself out."[31]

So long as they were inserted into public sector jobs, volunteers
enjoyed a middle-class position in Tanzanian society. In 1969, volunteers received 1,100 shillings a month when the average annual
income of Tanzanians was 386 shillings. Their income was boosted by
pay supplements and allowances provided by CUSOTAN.[32] Volunteers
also enjoyed government housing, disposable income sometimes
spent on status symbols like cars, and a social life often involving
interactions with fellow technical assistance personnel from various
countries.[33] Teachers Betty Palik and Michael Prupas never felt as if
they integrated into the "majority society." They commented that
"both what we got out of Tanzania and what Tanzania got out of us
were limited because we only operated within a certain stratum of the
population – those with a secondary school education or in the
process of getting one."[34] Socially distant from the rural majority, volunteers enjoyed a privileged position ensured by their employment
with the state.

Cultural difference was also a consideration. Directed at those
thought to undermine *ujamaa*, a racialized popular discourse around
"aliens," "enemies," and "parasites" emerged. It targeted the Indo-Tan-
zanian minority, which had long controlled domestic commerce. It
was also levelled at white foreigners who occupied positions of
authority associated with colonial rule, including teachers who might
influence youth with "alien habits and values."[35] Volunteer Richard
Carothers, with attention to cultural sensitivity, felt that "it would be
rather naive to think that teachers from outside can really do the job
as well as teachers from Tanzania. There are really quite a few differences in our cultural backgrounds and teachers from outside really, I

think, at times aren't going to understand the background of students, their family lives, their own lives, the way they are going to think and the problems they are going to have all the time in school."[36] Field staffer Chris Brown worried that CUSOTAN teachers, as "white, westerners, and usually middle-class non-socialists," would have limited effectiveness and relevance to the socialist project.[37] If still believing that CUSOTAN could make a worthwhile contribution to development, these commentators called attention to the outsider status of volunteers.

For those taking the Arusha Declaration seriously, being an outsider in no way precluded political commitment. Indeed, Tanzanian politics prompted growing CUSOTAN opposition to colonialism and minority rule in southern Africa. The Tanzanian government privileged anti-colonial unity, non-alignment, and Pan-Africanism. These principles were reflected in diplomatic dealings, an open-door refugee policy, and the allowance of southern African liberation movements to operate from Dar es Salaam.[38] Tanzania thus participated in what historian Christopher Lee has called the Bandung Spirit, the common cause of new nations pressing for human rights, self-determination, and world peace in international diplomacy.[39] Anti-colonial unity was exemplified by the Lusaka Manifesto, signed by Tanzania and twelve other African countries in 1969. The document denounced colonial and racial oppression in southern Africa and supported the right of all human beings "to participate, as equal members of the society, in their own government."[40]

CUSOTAN staff came to understand national liberation as a necessary condition for development. They decided to act in solidarity with southern Africans, and they took measures repositioning CUSO's relationship to several states, notably apartheid South Africa, South West Africa, and Southern Rhodesia, and the Portuguese colonies of Angola and Mozambique. First, in August 1969, all volunteer travel to southern Africa was forbidden. The ban ensured that CUSO observed the boycotts and diplomatic policies put in place by signatories of the Lusaka Manifesto.[41] Second, CUSO denounced colonial and minority regimes in southern Africa and upheld the legitimacy of liberation movements, coming to provide them with small-scale humanitarian assistance. Third, organization activists – as part of the human rights lobbying described in this collection by Stephanie Bangarth – began to speak out against Canadian complicity in imperialism. In 1971, CUSO delivered a statement before the Standing Committee on For-

eign Relations confronting Canada's ambivalent foreign policy position. CUSO lobbied the federal government to make its appeals to
"social justice" a reality by instituting standards of corporate behaviour in South Africa, assisting refugees, ending arms deals with Por-
tugal, and providing non-military aid to liberation movements.[42] In
sum, CUSOTAN activists believed that support for Tanzanian principles
ought to shift Canadian commitments as well. The Canadian state
could join its Tanzanian counterpart in rejecting the legitimacy of
racist and colonial southern African states by upholding the liberal
democratic principle of self-determination in international relations.

Volunteers, if generally thinking that going to Tanzania with CUSO
was the "right thing" to do, could be uninformed on political questions and mostly concerned with their jobs.[43] With turnover a built-
in part of the CUSOTAN program, field staff sought to build and sustain volunteer commitment to Tanzanian self-reliant development. In
April 1972, staff concluded that some sort of manifesto "along the
lines of the Arusha Declaration" was needed to clarify CUSO's role in
confronting global inequality.[44]

Barry Fleming drafted a development charter. Though informed by
Tanzanian political philosophy, the charter was more than a restate-
ment of CUSOTAN's deference to the policies of its host government.
Rather, cognizant of the influence of multinational corporations and
the neocolonial character of the international terms of trade, Fleming
wanted to identify the key elements of a CUSO commitment to development and to new nations.[45] Known as the Dar Declaration, the document argued that development was "the liberation of people, not
just from the constraints of poverty, hunger and disease, but also from
constraints which inhibit a person's control over his destiny, the pursuit of dignity and social equality." CUSO must aim "to participate in
the global struggle for justice, equitable development and human
progress." Volunteers should improve their awareness of "the root
causes of inequitable development in Canada and overseas," participate to the best of their abilities in culturally sensitive development
action, and identify "with oppressed peoples and further to recognize
that his own country is culpable in the continuing exploitation of one
people by another."[46] The Dar Declaration, attentive to global inequality, defined development as freedom. Yet it did so vaguely and in such
a way as to blur action for collective liberation and a defense of indi-
vidualistic, and indeed liberal, liberation.

The declaration served as the base text for a CUSO-wide Development Charter and Operating Principles, implemented in 1974.[47] However, the changed outlook was opposed by some within the organization. The CUSO committee in Sault Ste. Marie reasserted a humanitarian altruism and declared that it would stop supporting CUSO if members engaged in politics. The committee insisted: "Surely CUSO's basic humanitarian philosophy has been based on the concept that we can best help these people by helping to free them from disease, poverty, and ignorance. Free a man's mind from ignorance and you free him from oppression – because once he recognizes that he is being oppressed and exploited he will take steps to free himself – but leave him self-determination."[48] Others continued to endorse job-centrism. Volunteer G. Stewart asserted that CUSO should not waste its time trying to work on behalf of oppressed peoples, but rather focus on "doing effectively the job the government that requested their service wants them to do."[49] In these terms, CUSO made a worthwhile and ostensibly neutral contribution to state-led development in the Third World.

Despite the conflicting points of view, it was significant how the languages of liberation and of humanitarianism coexisted. After a trip through southeast Africa in 1974, CUSO Montreal coordinator Lance Evoy remarked that varied or ignorant volunteer views on liberation movements, development, political economy, and Canadian participation in aid and trade was "a reflection of CUSO and the type of classical liberalism which can accommodate any ideology and which works against any direction. This makes it impossible to touch any basic issues and simply allows factions to pass the buck."[50]

Liberal internationalism accommodated much. Though some volunteers sought to circumscribe their contribution to development by fulfilling their immediate jobs and eschewing political questions, other CUSOTAN personnel were drawn into a deepening engagement with matters of race, class, culture, and politics. Both Tanzanian political philosophy and southern African liberation movements inspired a liberationist organizational development ideal. Yet the core liberal internationalist proposition remained that CUSOTAN, responding to Canadian and Tanzanian nation-building precepts, could respect self-determination, temporarily fill civil service positions abroad, and thus contribute to state-led development within global capitalism.

The Dar Declaration, however, also signalled the emergence of a more radical politics within CUSOTAN. From the early 1970s, against a diffuse liberal ideology, New Left activists intervened in development debates. Some CUSOTAN personnel adopted a neo-Marxist analysis of international power relations as well as the Canadian and Tanzanian states. In doing so, they participated in a wider long-sixties anti-imperialist politics that is refracted, in other contexts explored in this volume, by Amanda Ricci in her essay on competing international feminisms and by Maurice Jr. Labelle in his study of transnational anti-Orientalism.

Between 1974 and 1977, staff person Richard Marquardt fomented a leftward shift in CUSOTAN ideas and practices. He wanted to further elaborate "the praxis of the liberation of man through the vehicle of a small, independent, government-funded, decentralized development agency."[51] Indeed, he agreed with those who wanted to transform CUSO from a placement agency into a development agency. The distinction was a bit ambiguous. But it tended to mean moving from the passive provision of technical assistance to empowering field staff, and volunteers, to prioritize what they themselves thought worked best for development. Although he was willing to continue filling short-term government manpower requests, Marquardt felt that those postings largely functioned to create a positive impression of Canada among Tanzanians. He believed that CUSOTAN needed a more activist program, one that sought out development opportunities.[52] To a certain extent, strict deference to Tanzanian government wishes and earlier caution about the role of foreigners abroad had fallen away. Instead, there was a sense that CUSOTAN itself could or should know what it was doing in development.

Marquardt's analysis departed from attention to Tanzania's position within an international political economy. He drew on dependency theory, whose Latin American articulators argued that development and underdevelopment were interrelated processes produced by global capitalism and geopolitics. Employing neo-Marxist thinking, Marquardt also insisted that Tanzania's underdevelopment would not be rectified by deeper involvement in international trade and capitalism. Even more so than the Tanzanian government, he supported efforts to build an internally integrated national economy.[53] For liberals within CUSO, technical assistance brought Canadians into a position where they could – albeit with some complication – help the Tanzanian state modernize society and overcome poverty. In Marquardt's New Left conception, development aid figured within an inequitable global capitalism that produced poverty and already linked Canada with Tanzania.

Marquardt's critique extended to the Canadian state and CUSO's own dependency. Citing New Left political economists Wallace Clement and Cy Gonick, he argued that the Canadian state served the interests of capital. Therefore, CIDA served the interests of Canadian capital abroad. It perpetuated underdevelopment by supporting Third World ruling classes and, in cooperation with aid organization, creating a charitable facade for the exploitative relationship between the Third World and multinational capital. He insisted that CIDA's subsidy of CUSO had to be understood in this light.[54]

CUSOTAN liberal internationalists, to the extent that they considered the Canadian state, criticized complicity in imperialism in southern African and lobbied for a more just foreign policy. New Leftists opposed capitalism and adopted a far more systematic neo-Marxist critique of the role and class character of the Canadian state. Both positions, in fact, raised the prospect that change might be better pursued in Canada than abroad. In 1972, a CUSO Development Education Department was set up to engage the Canadian public on Third World issues. And, across Canada, solidarity activism and social justice-minded development education supported demands for equitable relations between countries.[55] However, CUSOTAN remained a program delivering development assistance in Tanzania. Marquardt wrote about the irony of his position, musing: "In what other position could one denounce Canadian capital and still have so much of it to dispose of?"[56] Yet in a very real sense, despite the autonomy it retained, CUSOTAN was effectively an on-the-ground subcontractor of CIDA.

Marquardt also considered the Tanzanian state. Echoing the analysis of Tanzanian scholar Issa Shivji, Marquardt argued that the socialist project was failing: "Tanzania is not developing. This is because initiative and creativity has been stifled by a ruling class which does not trust its own people, which rules in an authoritarian and oppressive manner, and which is not progressive or dynamic because of its bureaucratic nature." Marquardt insisted that experience showed that state capitalism marshalled by an elite reliant on international capitalism was not the way out of underdevelopment.[57] Though calling attention to the gap between rhetoric and reality, Marquardt continued to ground CUSOTAN aims in official Tanzanian development ideals. Strikingly, he set out to realize the Arusha Declaration vision where the state was apparently falling short by moving "critically, consciously, humanely, in the direction of facilitating the development of socialism and self-reliance in Tanzania." CUSOTAN should avoid supporting "those actions and institutions serving to derail the Tanzanian revolution," especially a school system that remained elitist.[58] Instead, a development agency must seek "to identify the social classes within the host countries that have the potential to challenge the hegemony of international capital and its local agents, and to support these classes in their efforts to develop their analytical, organizational, and productive skills."[59]

The break with the Tanzanian state was partial at best. Field staff, appraising the effectiveness of different state departments and agencies, selectively responded to requests for personnel. And with the volunteer contingent shrinking, they devoted more attention to projects beginning in 1972. Projects – capital expenditure beyond the labour of volunteers – enabled staff to back development activities amenable to their own analysis, priorities, and political feeling. Still, most projects aligned with key elements of Tanzanian development thought, including self-reliance, productive skill, and rural development.[60] CUSOTAN delivered funds to boost agricultural productivity and small-scale industry, improve technical education, and contribute to rural health services. Most commonly, capital donations were made so that institutions, cooperatives, and *ujamaa* villages might purchase needed equipment, construct facilities, or acquire livestock. To give just a few examples, CUSOTAN money allowed a Dar co-operative to buy power tools for making jewelry, financed the purchase of medical reference textbooks for rural dispensaries, helped the Marangu branch of the National Union of Women of Tanzania acquire two goats for its daycare, and funded the expansion of the Ndiva Ujaama Village maize mill.[61]

In seeking to reach common people, CUSOTAN endorsed rural development and turned partly to *ujamaa* villages. In 1967, Nyerere launched a resettlement effort known as villagization. He wanted *ujamaa* villages – presumed sites of mutualism, common property ownership, hard work, and self-reliance – to serve as the basis of national social organization. In villages, agricultural advancement as well as improvements in rural services and industry might be achieved.[62] If migration was at first voluntary, coercion was exercised from late 1973. About six million people were relocated in all, though the scheme alienated rural residents and failed to raise output.[63] Marquardt could see the effects of forced villagization in the countryside and argued that the initiative contradicted the government's stated progressive aims. But, in figuring out how to proceed, practical considerations mattered. If CUSOTAN wanted to help rural people improve their conditions of life, *ujamaa* villages were where residents had been pushed.[64]

CUSOTAN bought livestock or funded the purchase of equipment for a number of village cooperatives. For examples, CUSOTAN funded the purchase of 100 chickens at the Ngorogo Ujamaa Village, assisted the Ikwiri Ujamaa Fishing Cooperative, and boosted a village-based carpentry cooperative near Arusha.[65] Yet to intervene in such projects was problematic. Compulsory villagization, scholar Michael Jennings has maintained, was abetted by the contributions of international development agencies and NGOs.[66] Did providing resources to boost local productivity strengthen a more intrusive state capitalism and top-down rural development? Or did cooperative industry empower ordinary people? Certainly, CUSOTAN plans accepted the official suggestion that development must come from *ujamaa* villages. Much of the critique of villagization centered on a sense that, stifled by bureaucrats, rural people did not have a sufficient opportunity to become genuinely self-reliant.[67] Field staff wanted *ujamaa* to live up to its rhetorical ideal. Yet CUSOTAN itself had no popular base and merely acted as a capital contributor. Its program, too, acted on rural people in ways only vaguely attached to grassroots activity and participatory democracy.

CUSOTAN had a left-wing critique of prevailing dynamics, but its mid-1970s activities scarcely stood out. That Tanzania required rural development was a state aim and an international consensus. CUSOTAN collaborated on projects with state agencies and institutions, domestic NGOs and cooperatives, aid agencies (like CIDA), and international NGOs. Therefore, through intermediaries, CUSOTAN selectively participated in existing initiatives directed at increasing the production of the masses and improving services.

CUSOTAN staff attempts to selectively support state-led development and to advance the interests of oppressed social classes nonetheless prompted a rebuttal. In 1978, Carleton University president Michael Oliver returned from a trip to Dar and wrote to CUSO's executive director to convey the views of Tanzanian university and government officials. According to Oliver, they were puzzled by, and critical of, CUSOTAN's insistence on deciding what development assistance was appropriate for Tanzania. Oliver expressed concern that CUSO's reputation was being undermined "by what is regarded by Tanzanians themselves as an incredibly arrogant piece of left-wing colonialism."[68]

CUSOTAN New Leftists had indeed adopted a radical analysis. They insisted that, within international capitalism and geopolitics, the class character of the Canadian and Tanzanian states served to reproduce global and domestic inequality. Marquardt felt that although CUSO-TAN was financially dependent on Canadian state funds, it might become an effective development NGO by enhancing the productive skill of Tanzanian popular classes hitherto dominated by an undemocratic, bureaucratic state. Yet not only did CUSOTAN continue to affirm Tanzanian political philosophy, it also supported some state-initiated, and internationally sustained, efforts to increase productivity and advance rural development within capitalism.

By the mid-1970s, executive director Murray Thomson suggested that CUSO was an organization divided between, first, those who wanted greater identification with the poor and oppressed as opposed to association with Third World elites, and, second, those who wanted simply to place Canadians in public sector jobs abroad. Thomson suggested that the factions nevertheless had common ground.[69] As the CUSOTAN story illustrates, there may have been agreement on the need for development in Tanzania. Yet liberal internationalists and New Leftists sharply disagreed on capitalism, and on what development was and what it entailed.

Within CUSOTAN, even as differing views coexisted, the leading political position on the state, international relations, and the role of NGOs in international development shifted leftward in the 1960s and 1970s. CUSOTAN practice was premised on the idea that a Canadian volunteer-sending international development NGO, underwritten by the Canadian and Tanzanian states, might contribute to state-led post-colonial development by temporarily placing volunteers in public sector jobs. The initial liberal internationalist ethos was rooted in a respect for self-determination and a belief that vast inequalities between nations were not only wrong, but a cause of subversion and conflict. Some volunteers subscribed to a purportedly neutral humanitarianism and focused on performing their immediate jobs, even amid questions concerning race, class, and culture. But following the Arusha Declaration, other CUSOTAN members committed themselves to supporting Tanzanian socialist philosophy and, by extension, southern African liberation movements. Indeed, with respect to southern Africa, CUSO activists lobbied Canada to amend its foreign policy and commit to social justice in the realm of international relations. When the Dar Declaration called for "the liberation of people" from all constraints on their autonomy, human dignity, and social equality, it did not wholly upend a pliable CUSOTAN liberal internationalism which accommodated multiple points of view. But, ascendant after 1973, CUSOTAN New Leftists rejected the prospect of a liberal liberation in Tanzania. They adopted a neo-Marxist critique of international capitalism and the Tanzanian and Canadian states. Field staff, in ways that were contradictory and often insubstantial, tried to turn CUSOTAN into a class-aware, activist development NGO seeking to effect progressive change. Securing greater global equality through development remained an unfulfilled goal. With the onset of economic crisis, structural adjustment, and neoliberalism over the course of the 1980s, the Tanzanian state was compelled to cut social spending. NGOs like CUSOTAN continued to operate, but increasingly supported depoliticized remedial efforts to forestall the erosion of the standard of living of common people.[70]

My case study has examined the different ways that CUSOTAN members viewed the relationship of their development NGO to the Tanzanian and Canadians states as well as international relations. I have not presumed to deliver the multi-sited, multi-archival research now preferred by many international historians. Given my source base, my historical narrative (though augmented by secondary literature) is largely contained within CUSO. The views of Canadian and Tanzanian state actors on CUSO are faintly heard, much less the voices of the secondary school students, co-operative members, or rural people impacted by CUSOTAN intervention.

That said, I have modelled an "Undiplomatic History" that broadens the frame to consider Canada's interconnections with the Third World, engaging the context of decolonization and demonstrating non-state participation in international relations beyond diplomacy. Development assistance was an issue of broad global significance during the 1960s and 1970s. By attending to CUSOTAN experience, I have shown how an important group of Canadian non-state actors engaged in the wider currents of development thought and practice. My approach has looked not simply beyond the state, but also at the everyday political debates that Canadians in postcolonial Tanzania had over state-led development and inequality, and at the international exchanges in which they consciously participated.

NOTES

1   Odetta Keating, Richard Marquardt, Mike Murphy, and David Perry, "CUSO
    Forum Supplement," *CUSO Forum* 5, no. 1 (1977): 13.

2   David Meren, "The Tragedies of Canadian International History," *Canadian
    Historical Review* 96, no. 4 (2015): 534–66.

3   Dominique Marshall, "Réponse à 'The Tragedies of Canadian International
    History': Un autre survol historiographique," *Canadian Historical Review* 96,
    no. 4 (2015): 583–9.

4   For example: Sean Mills, *A Place in the Sun: Haiti, Haitians, and the Remaking
    of Quebec* (Montreal and Kingston: McGill-Queen's University Press, 2016);
    Laura Madokoro, *Elusive Refuge: Chinese Migrants in the Cold War* (Cam-
    bridge, MA: Harvard University Press, 2016).

5   Karen Dubinsky, Adele Perry, and Henry Yu, "Introduction," *Within and with-
    out Nation: Canadian History as Transnational History* (Toronto: University of
    Toronto Press, 2016), 4–11.

6   Karen Dubinsky, Sean Mills, and Scott Rutherford, eds., *Canada and the
    Third World: Overlapping Histories* (Toronto: University of Toronto Press,
    2016).

7   David Webster, *Fire and the Full Moon: Canada and Indonesia in a Decoloniz-
    ing World* (Vancouver: UBC Press, 2009); Robin S. Gendron, *Towards a Fran-
    cophone Community: Canada's Relations with France and French Africa,
    1945–1968* (Montreal and Kingston: McGill-Queen's University Press, 2006);
    Asa McKercher, "Southern Exposure: Diefenbaker, Latin America, and the
    Organization of American States," *Canadian Historical Review* 93, no. 1
    (2012): 57–90; Ryan M. Touhey, "Dealing in Black and White: The Diefen-
    baker Government and the Cold War in South Asia, 1957–1963," *Canadian
    Historical Review* 92, no. 3 (2011): 429–54; Kevin A. Spooner, *Canada, the
    Congo Crisis, and UN Peacekeeping, 1960–64* (Vancouver: UBC Press, 2009);
    Michael K. Carroll, *Pearson's Peacekeepers: Canada and the United Nations
    Emergency Force, 1956–67* (Vancouver: UBC Press, 2009).

8   Nick Cullather, *The Hungry World: America's Cold War Battle against Poverty
    in Asia* (Cambridge, MA: Harvard University Press, 2011); Michael Connelly,
    Fatal Misconception: The Struggle to Control World Population (Cambridge, MA:
    Belknap Press, 2008).

9   On Canadian official development assistance, see David R. Morrison, *Aid and
    Ebb Tide: A History of CIDA and Canadian Development Assistance* (Waterloo,
    ON: Wilfrid Laurier Press, 1998); Jill Marie Sarah Campbell-Miller, "The Mind
    of Modernity: Canadian Bilateral Foreign Assistance to India, 1950–60" (PhD
    diss., University of Waterloo, 2014). On Canadian experts abroad, see David

Webster, "Modern Missionaries: Canadian Postwar Technical Assistance Advisors in Southeast Asia," *Journal of the Canadian Historical Association/Revue de la Société historique du Canada* 20, no. 2 (2009): 86–111. On mission contributions to development, see Peter Ernest Baltius, "Forging the Link between Faith and Development: The History of the Canadian Catholic Organization for Development and Peace 1967–1982" (PhD diss., University of Saint Michael's College, 2012); Ruth Compton Brouwer, *Modern Women Modernizing Men: The Changing Missions of Three Professional Women in Asia and Africa, 1902–69* (Vancouver: UBC Press, 2002); Catherine LeGrand, "L'axe missionnaire catholique entre le Québec et l'Amérique latine: Une exploration préliminaire," *Globe, revue internationale d'études québécoises* 12, no. 1 (2009): 43–66. On CUSO, see Ruth Compton Brouwer, *Canada's Global Villagers: CUSO in Development, 1961–86* (Vancouver: UBC Press, 2013).

10 Molly Kane, "International NGOs and the Aid Industry: Constraints on International Solidarity," *Third World Quarterly* 34, no. 8 (2013): 1505–15.

11 Minutes of the Meetings of the Executive Committee of Canadian University Service Overseas, held on Sunday and Monday, November 14th and 15th, 1965, in Room 304, 75 Albert Street, Ottawa, Ontario, Canadian University Service Overseas fonds, MG28 I 323, vol. 49, file 49-25, Library and Archives Canada (LAC).

12 Brouwer, *Canada's Global Villagers*, 2, 28–32, 36.

13 "Pearson Addresses Annual Meeting," *Cuso Bulletin* 4, no. 1 (November 1965): 2.

14 Brouwer, *Canada's Global Villagers*, 26.

15 Morrison, 69.

16 Ian Smillie, *Land of Lost Content: A History of CUSO* (Toronto: Deneau Publishers, 1985), 265.

17 Dennis September, "An Analysis of CUSO Involvement in Education in the Countries of East/Central/Southern Africa," 1972, MG28 I 323, vol. 13, file 13-28, LAC.

18 Hugh Christie, "Comment on CUSO Policy," *Cuso Bulletin* 5, no. 3 (June 1967): 2–3.

19 Nils Gilman, *Mandarins of the Future: Modernization Theory in Cold War America* (Baltimore: Johns Hopkins University Press, 2007); W.W. Rostow, *The Stages of Economic Growth: A Non-Communist Manifesto* (Cambridge: Cambridge University Press, 1960).

20 Cranford Pratt, *The Critical Phase in Tanzania, 1945–1968: Nyerere and the Emergence of a Socialist Strategy* (Cambridge: Cambridge University Press, 1976), 22–3, 28, 35, 43, 60–1; Andrew Coulson, *Tanzania: A Political Economy*

(Oxford: Oxford University Press, 1982), 4, 33–4, 43–7, 135, 176; Issa G. Shivji, "Nationalism and Pan-Africanism: Decisive Moments in Nyerere's Intellectual and Political Thought," *Review of African Political Economy* 39, no. 131 (2012): 104, 106; "East Africa, 1968–69," MG28 I 323, vol. 17, file 17-13, LAC; D. Barry Fleming and Wayne Mullins, CUSO Tanzania Country Plan 1973/74 and Situation Report, November 1972, MG28 I 323, vol. 19, file 19-25, LAC.

21 Julius K. Nyerere, "*Ujamaa* – The Basis of African Socialism [1962]," in *Freedom and Unity: A Selection from Writings and Speeches, 1952–65* (Oxford: Oxford University Press, 1967), 162–4, 166, 170; Priya Lal, *African Socialism in Postcolonial Tanzania: Between the Village and the World* (Cambridge: Cambridge University Press, 2015), 27–128.

22 TANU, "The Arusha Declaration," in Julius K. Nyerere, *Ujamaa: Essays on Socialism* (Dar es Salaam: Oxford University Press, 1968), 13–15, 28–35.

23 Shivji, 104, 107–8, 114; Ronald Aminzade, *Race, Nation, and Citizenship in Post-Colonial Africa: The Case of Tanzania* (Cambridge: Cambridge University Press, 2013), 139; Steven M. Feierman, *Peasant Intellectuals: Anthropology and History in Tanzania* (Madison: University of Wisconsin Press, 1990), 232–3.

24 Pratt, 231–2; Aminzade, 94, 98, 182; Coulson, *Tanzania*, 2.

25 Roger Young, *Canadian Development Assistance to Tanzania* (Ottawa: North-South Institute, 1983), 43–4.

26 Jamie Monson, *Africa's Freedom Railway: How a Chinese Development Project Changed Lives and Livelihoods in Tanzania* (Bloomington: Indiana University Press, 2009), 1; Michael Jennings, *Surrogates of the State: NGOs, Development, and Ujamaa in Tanzania* (West Hartford, CT: Kumarian Press, 2008), 91–4; Christine Zaccarelli to Rudy Carter, "Information About Other Volunteer Agencies in Tanzania," 28 August 1968, 1, LAC, MG28 I 323, Volume 20, file 20-5.

27 Rudolph Carter, "Education ... Tanzania's Cultural Revolution," *CUSO Forum*, no. 3 (Summer 1969), 4–5, MG28 I 323, vol. 103, 103-12, LAC.

28 CUSO Tanzania, "Appreciation of the Situation [1968]," MG28 I 323, vol. 17, file 17-12, LAC.

29 D. Barry Fleming, CUSO Tanzania Country Plan 1974/75 and Situation Report, November 1973, 1MG28 I 323, vol. 19, file 19-25, LAC.

30 "Hugh Winsor," in *Man Deserves Man: CUSO in Developing Countries*, edited by Bill McWhinney and Dave Godfrey (Toronto: Ryerson Press, 1968), 316–25.

31 Shirley Baker to Bob Olivero, Regional Report, 11 January 1969, MG28 I 323, vol. 17, file 17-17, LAC.

32 Dave Beer and Dennis September, "A Position Paper on the Possibility of

CUSO Paying Full Cost for Its Personnel in the East and Central Africa Programme," December 1969, MG28 I 323, vol. 17, file 17-16, LAC.

33 Richard Denham, *Once Upon a Time – in Africa: Honeymoon Adventures of a Canadian Couple in Tanzania* (s.l.: CreateSpace, 2014), 42–3, 50, 54, 85, 111–12; Courtney C.J. Bond, "His," in *Letters from Dar: His, Courtney C.J. Bond, Hers, Elisabeth S. Bond* (s.l.: s.n., 1995), 1, 6, 17, 31, 34, 48; Laura Fair, "Drive-In Socialism: Debating Modernities and Development in Dar es Salaam, Tanzania," *American Historical Review* 118, no. 4 (2013): 1089.

34 Michael Prupas and Betty Palik Prupas, "Termination Report," Dar es Salaam, 21 June 1973, 174–5, in *Readings in Education*, issued by CUSO Development Education, April 1974, MG28 I 323, vol. 44, file 44-20, LAC.

35 James R. Brennan, *Taifa: Making Nation and Race in Urban Tanzania* (Athens: Ohio University Press, 2012), 165; Nesta Wyn Ellis, "Complaints about Volunteers," *CUSO Forum*, vol. 2, no. 4 (June 1974): 7.

36 Quoted from Neil McKee, "Tanga Man" (Crawley Films Ltd.: 1973), MG28 I 323, Accession 1985-0255, item 310, LAC.

37 C.M. Brown, "Education Report," CUSO Tanzania Country Plan 1970, July 1969, MG28 I 323, vol. 19, file 19-26, LAC.

38 Daniel Ogweno Nyangani, "Tanzania's Foreign Policy: The Support for the Liberation of Southern Africa and the Quest for African Unity" (PhD diss., Boston University, 1986); Joanne Tague, "The War to Build the Nation: Mozambican Refugees, Rural Development, and State Sovereignty in Tanzania, 1964–1975" (PhD diss., University of California, Davis, 2012).

39 Christopher Lee, "Introduction," in *Making a World after Empire: The Bandung Moment and its Political Afterlives* (Athens: Ohio University Press, 2010), 15.

40 "The Lusaka Manifesto," April 1969, MG28 I 323, vol. 17, file 17-17, LAC.

41 Chris Brown to All CUSO Personnel in Tanzania, "Travel Restriction CUSO Personnel East and Central Africa," August 1969, December 1969, MG28 I 323, vol. 17, file 17-16, LAC.

42 "CUSO Brief on Southern Africa," MG28 I 323, vol. 50, 50-27, LAC.

43 Interview with Barry Fleming, 12 August 2015; interview with Richard Marquardt, 8 December 2016; Dennis September, "An Analysis," 44.

44 Minutes of the East and Central Africa Regional Meeting, Blantyre, Malawi, 20–26 April 1972, MG28 I 323, vol. 17, file 17-2, LAC.

45 Interview with Barry Fleming, 12 August 2015.

46 Minutes of the East and Central Africa Regional Meeting, Tanzania, 18–25 April 1973, MG28 I 323, vol. 17, file 17-9, LAC.

47 Odetta Keating, Richard Marquardt, Mike Murphy, and David Perry, "CUSO Forum Supplement – Appendix 1," *CUSO Forum*, vol. 5, no. 1 (1977), 16.

48 Sault Ste. Marie Local Committee, "cuso's Role: As We See It," *cuso Forum*, vol. 2, no. 1, (January 1974): 28.

49 G. Stewart, Suggestion, 27 February 1974, MG28 I 323, vol. 166, file 166-6, LAC.

50 Lance Evoy, Montreal Metro Co-ordinator, "Report on Trip to CUSO East, Central and Southern Africa Programme," April–May 1974, 12 June 1974, MG28 I 323, vol. 86, file 86-5, LAC.

51 Richard Marquardt to Colin Freebury, The Praxis of Liberation, 24 January 1975, 1, LAC, MG28 I 323, vol. 87, file 87-25, LAC.

52 Odetta Keating, Richard Marquardt, Mike Murphy, and David Perry, "cuso Forum Supplement," *cuso Forum*, vol. 5, no. 1 (1977), 14; Richard Marquardt, "cuso Tanzania: Some Thoughts on Strategy and Tactics," Tanzania Situation Report, April 1975, MG28 I 323, vol. 20, file 20-1, LAC.

53 Richard Marquardt, Termination Report, May 1977, MG28 I 323, vol. 14, file 14-20, LAC; interview with Richard Marquardt, 8 December 2016; minutes of CUSO ECSA Regional Meeting, held at Likabula House, Mulanje, Malawi, 5–12 April 1976, MG28 I 323, vol. 17, file 17-7, LAC; Ramon Grosfoguel, "Developmentalism, Modernity, and Dependency Theory in Latin America," *Nepantla: Views from the South* 1, no. 2 (2000), 347, 360.

54 Marquardt, Termination Report, 6–8, 14.

55 Sean Mills, "Popular Internationalism: Grassroots Exchange and Social Movements," in *Canada and the Third World*, 246–66; Jean Christie, "A Critical History of Development Education in Canada," *Canadian and International Education* 12, no. 3 (1983): 8–20; interview with Richard Marquardt, 8 December 2016.

56 Marquardt, Termination Report, 8, 14.

57 Minutes of CUSO ECSA Regional Meeting, 5–12 April 1976, 12. See Issa G. Shivji, *Class Struggles in Tanzania* (London: Heinemann, 1976).

58 Richard Marquardt to CUSOTAN Committee, "The Next CUSOTAN Plan," 28 August 1974, MG28 I 323, vol. 19, file 19-25, LAC.

59 Marquardt, Termination Report, 3.

60 Richard Marquardt, cuso Tanzania, Country Plan and Budget 1976–77, August 1975, MG28 I 323, vol. 14, file 14-17, LAC.

61 Evoy, 3; Richard Marquardt to Enid Hinchley, Discretionary Project Reports, 19 October 1976, MG28 I 323, vol. 146, file 146-16, LAC; Dennis Lewycky, Director, CUSO - Tanzania, to Ms Pat Oxley, High Commissioner, Canadian High Commission, Dar es Salaam, 10 January 1980, MG28 I 323, vol. 135, file 135-19, LAC; Marquardt, cuso Tanzania, Country Plan and Budget 1976–77, 20.

62 Julius K. Nyerere, "Socialism and Rural Development [September 1967]," in *Ujamaa: Essays on Socialism* (Dar es Salaam: Oxford University Press, 1968), 107–8, 120, 124, 143.

63 Lal, 15, 17, 79, 216; James C. Scott, *Seeing Like a State: How Certain Schemes to Improve the Human Condition Have Failed* (New Haven: Yale University Press, 1999), 223–47.

64 Interview with Richard Marquardt, 8 December 2016; minutes of CUSO ECSA Regional Meeting, 5–12 April 1976, 31.

65 Richard Marquardt to Projects Tanzania File, Project 616–18 – Ngorogo Ujamaa Village Youth Development, 22 August 1974, MG28 I 323, vol. 87, file 87-19, LAC; CUSO, Tanzania Situation Report for March 1977 Regional Meeting, March 1977, MG28 I 323, vol. 91, file 91-31, LAC; Tanzania Discretionary Projects [c. 1973], MG28 I 323, vol. 87, file 87-20, LAC.

66 Jennings, 64.

67 CUSO Tanzania, Country Plan and Budget 1977–78, August 1976, MG28 I 323, vol. 14, file 14-17, LAC.

68 Michael Oliver, president, Carleton University, to Robin Wilson, executive director, CUSO, 24 April 1978, MG28 I 323, vol. 14, file 14-18, LAC.

69 Murray Thomson, "CUSO Trends in 1974," *CUSO Forum*, vol. 2, no. 1 (January 1974): 2–3.

70 Peter Gibbon, "Merchantisation of Production and Privatization of Development in Post-*Ujamaa* Tanzania: An Introduction," in *Liberalised Development in Tanzania: Studies on Accumulation Processes and Local Institutions*, edited by Peter Gibbon (Uppsala: Nordiska Afrikainstitutet, 1995), 9–36; Tim Kelsall, "Donors, NGOs, and the State: Governance & 'Civil Society' in Tanzania," in *The Charitable Impulse: NGOs & Development in East & North-East Africa*, edited by Ondine Barrow and Michael Jennings (Bloomfield, CT: Kumarian Press, 2001), 133–48; Firoze Manji and Carl O'Coill, "The Missionary Position: NGOs and Development in Africa," *International Affairs* 78, no. 3 (2002): 567–83.

8

Making Global Citizens?
Canadian Women at the World Conference
of the International Women's Year,
Mexico City 1975

AMANDA RICCI

In 1975, the United Nations General Assembly proclaimed International Women's Year. With the prodding of non-governmental organizations, and facilitated by the Commission on the Status of Women, the UN sponsored three World Conferences on Women during the Decade for Women, 1976–1985. Held in Mexico City (1975), Copenhagen (1980), and Nairobi (1985), these unprecedented gatherings on gender justice brought together feminists from all over the world.[1] The conferences were each in fact two concurrent events: the first formal and official meeting was attended by government-appointed delegations, and the second meeting, referred to as the Tribune, was open to NGOs. The emerging scholarship on the meetings, however, brings to light some of the imperfect relations at the conferences, where the question of *how* to achieve gender equality was hotly contested both within and between nations, and the International Women's Year (IWY) themes of "Equality, Development, and Peace" were differently prioritized and understood among attendees.[2] This chapter focuses on Canada's contributions to the World Conference on International Women's Year in Mexico City, exploring the ways in which the official and unofficial delegations grappled with the competing definitions of feminism put forth by the other delegates, as well as by each other. It argues that this inaugural conference provides a window to understand Canadian women's engagement with the world in the postwar period, against a backdrop of Cold War tensions, decolonization struggles, and the quest of newly independent nations for a more just economic order.[3]

This chapter makes three historiographical interventions, tying in formal diplomatic structures, transnational processes, and social context. First, the study contributes to a feminist rethinking of Canadian international history. With the latter's emphasis on high politics – an arena of power where women are typically underrepresented – this branch of Canadian history lacks a gendered perspective. In fact, feminist scholars of international relations tend to lament the lack of gender-based analyses within their discipline, which, in the words of political theorist Annick Wibben, "has been one of the last fields to open up to feminism."[4] In Mexico City, the official Canadian delegation was women-led, thus raising questions regarding the role and contributions of "femocrats"[5] from this country in the global sphere. When representing the federal government abroad, these civil servants, for example, abstained from the "Declaration of Mexico," a document authored by seventy-seven developing countries which called for, among other points, a more equitable redistribution of the world's wealth. The chapter builds on the scholarship of historians such as Tarah Brookfield, Ruth Compton Brouwer, and Whitney Wood, who explore Canadian women's international engagement as well as their place within various transnational networks.[6]

Second, this chapter contributes to the international, interdisciplinary literature on transnational feminism. Broadly speaking, to cite sociologist Marilyn Porter, transnational feminism "refers to the coming together of non-governmental organizations to work across borders in coalitions and campaigns." The term "transnational," as opposed to "global," "reflects a means of recognizing both the continued significance and particularity of nations *and* their transcendence by feminist movements."[7] There are two major components to this paper – the positions of the official delegation, and the actions of the NGO representatives who attended the tribune. The latter spoke on their own accord in Mexico City, making them accountable to their respective women's organizations and communities rather than to the government of Canada.

Finally, "Global Citizens?" contributes to the literature on the "second wave" of feminism in Canada – that is, the upsurge in feminist

activism in the late 1960s and 1970s. The growing historiography
emphasizes its complexity, where women tapped into highly regional
as well as transnational social movement networks. Women organized
to combat sexism, in addition to racism, colonialism, homophobia,
militarism, and poverty. They were involved in various liberation
movements, from Red Power, to Black Power, to the Quebec liberation movement.[8] The chapter incorporates the UN World Conference
on Women into the broader equation of this social movement.
Despite the conferences' importance in the development of postwar
transnational feminist networks, until recently they have attracted
very little scholarly attention by historians.[9] For Canada, the results
are telling. Members of the official delegation toed the government
line in Mexico City, reinforcing Canada's position in the international political economy. Grassroots activists, in contrast, subverted official positions in front of an international audience: Indigenous wom-
en, for example, used the gathering as a forum to expose the country's
internal colonialism. By adopting a multi-scaled analysis of the
women's movement, this chapter advances a nuanced, complex, and
ultimately revamped understanding Canadian women's engagement
with the world.

I

The World Conference on Women of the International Women's
Year, held from 19 June to 2 July 1975, generated a broad-based level
of participation: 133 states took part alongside representatives from
UN bodies such as the United Nations Development Programme, the
World Food Programme, and the Economic Commissions for Asia
and the Pacific, Latin America, Africa and Western Asia. In accordance with UN practice, national liberation movements recognized
by the Organization of African Unity or by the League of Arab States
were invited to participate in the conference as observers, which
included the African National Congress (ANC, South Africa), the
Palestine Liberation Organization (PLO), and the African National
Council (ANC, Zimbabwe).[10] What was perhaps most striking, however, was that women delegates outnumbered their male counterparts
by about five to one, and prominent women were out in full force. A
number of "first ladies" were present at the gathering, for instance
Jahin Al Sadat of Egypt, Lea Rabin of Israel, Beverly Manley of
Jamaica, and Begum Nusrat Bhutto of Pakistan. Iran's Princess Ashraf

Pahlavi and Swaziland's Princess Masitsela headed their respective delegations.[11] After the opening speeches in front of a 5,000-person audience, where the Mexican president Luis Echeverria referred to women as "an enormous revolutionary reserve" whose increasing awareness of unequal treatment made them "natural allies in the struggle against oppression," the delegations set out to tackle an ambitious agenda – one that, in the words of Helvi Sipila, secretary-general of the conference, sought to "devise an appropriate strategy to overcome centuries of oppression and discrimination."[12] Delegates, then, set high hopes for the UN conference's role in promoting gender justice around the world.

But, first, countries such as Canada needed to develop their official positions. In the year leading up to the Mexico City gathering, the International Women's Year Secretariat, established in the Privy Council and headed by Martha Hynna, held a series of meetings in Ottawa, in order to discuss IWY action items and the conference's agenda with the representatives of prominent Canadian women's organizations. In its pre-circulated version, the substantive points of the agenda focused on UN policies and programmes, the involvement of women in strengthening international peace and eliminating racism, the major obstacles to be overcome in the achievement of equal rights and opportunities, and the integration of women in the development process as equal partners with men. The government of Canada also received a copy of the World Plan of Action, which was going to be voted on in Mexico City.[13] The extent to which the Secretariat listened to delegates' input during the consultative phase, however, remains unclear. By October, women's organizations were embittered by the consultations. Referring to the lack of follow-through on the part of Ottawa, Helen LaFountaine, from Women for Political Action, asserted that "sensitizing is the new word in Ottawa at the moment when it comes to women. The ever popular 'research study' has been rather overdone. Something had to be invented to fill the gap since we may have concluded that what follows logically after research is action." According to LaFountaine, delegates would have preferred to see the implementation of free, state-funded daycare, for example, over expensive conferences or advertising campaigns.[14]

Nevertheless, International Women's Year garnered no small amount of enthusiasm on the part of women's organizations across the country. Many mounted special projects with public funds, earmarked for IWY. For example, the Canadian Federation for University

Women compiled a "Roster of Qualified Women" with the aim of improving women's representation on boards and commissions. They then forwarded the list to the provincial and federal governments, expecting improvements.[15] When it came time to choose Canada's official delegation to Mexico City, women eagerly wrote in to the International Women's Year Secretariat putting forward potential candidates. In response to the UN's request to keep delegations small, Ottawa selected nine people to attend the official conference. With Coline Campbell, parliamentary secretary to the minister of national health and welfare and to the minister responsible for the status of women, at its head, the delegation consisted of Sylva Gelber (director of the Women's Bureau, Department of Labour), Freda Paltiel (special advisor, Status of Women, Health and Welfare), Richard Burkart (from the United Nations Economic and Social Affairs and Canada's Department of External Affairs), Hilda Bateman (liaison officer at the Canadian International Development Agency), Yvette Rousseau (from the Federal Advisory Council on the Status of Women in Ottawa), and D.R. Whelan (vice-consul at the Canadian Embassy, in Mexico). Ottawa also appointed Ethel McLellan (Women's Programs Division of Ontario's Ministry of Labour), Gene Errington (Office of Planning advisor to Cabinet, British Columbia), and Laurette Robillard (Conseil du Statut de la Femme, Quebec) in order to represent the provinces, choosing from a list of nominees from every region of the country.[16] The women of this contingent held powerful positions, exemplifying the strides women made in the civil service with the rise of "second-wave" feminism. There existed a gulf, however, between "femocrats" and their grassroots counterparts, which, as we will see, only widened.

Although Ottawa funded IWY projects and passed the Omnibus Bill on the Status of Women (Bill C-61) (which equalized, among others, the Canada Elections and Immigration Acts), the federal government – and by extension its official delegation – appeared mainly concerned with avoiding conflict or contentious positions in Mexico.[17] As recorded in the meeting minutes of another consultative meeting in April 1975, "Canada generally plays such conferences in a low key manner, thus avoiding much of the antagonism that often arises from developing countries who feel that the developed countries have no real perception of the important problems." With regards to Item 8 on the agenda, that is, the involvement of women in strengthening international peace and eliminating racial discrimination, the federal government believed that "it is not a status of women issue per se." As stated very explicitly in response to a question from the floor, "Since it is anticipated that this item will be handled in a political manner, Canada intends, as in the past, not to participate actively in such discussions." We can only hypothesize as to who asked the question that prompted this response; however, it is worth mentioning that Kay Livingstone from the Canadian Negro Women's Association, a group dedicated to racial and gender justice, was in the audience. At the same meeting, Richard Burkart, from the Department of External Affairs (DEA), spoke about the Charter of the Economic Rights and Duties of States, which proposed "a fundamental redistribution of wealth among developed and developing nations," in the context of "international politicking" as well as a potential source of "major political problems." According to the DEA, Canada hoped to "take a strong position in certain policy areas, but in others may play a mediating role between different bloc positions."[18] For the official delegation, gender inequality was marginally related to the global political economy and racism. "Femocrats" in turn adopted this stance.

While the federal government was consulting with the provinces and NGOs, UN-sponsored agencies organized a series of regional seminars around the world.[19] The proceedings from these meetings indicate the stark political differences informing these consultations in comparison to their Canadian equivalent. For example, the *Report of the Regional Seminar for Africa*, held in Mogadishu, Somalia from 3–5 April 1975, brought to light the role African women played in national liberation movements, as well as their ongoing struggles against neocolonialism. According to Fathia Bettahar, the Algerian secretary-general of the Pan-African Women's Organization, neocolonial structures kept the developing world in poverty. Although she insisted that the poor health and educational outcomes affected women more than men, Bettahar specified during her opening address that "1975 will enable us to demonstrate, first and foremost, that we share the concerns of our peoples and that we contemplate our own promotion only in connection with the promotion of our respective countries."[20] The proceedings of this pan-African gathering, albeit with delegations from Cuba, the Soviet Union, and the Women's International Democratic Federation (WIDF), highlight the salience of anti-apartheid movements for women's activists – where, for instance, the seminar recommended "an unflinching struggle" against all forms of apartheid, racism, and neocolonialism.[21] Perhaps unsurprisingly, these differing understandings of gender oppression quickly collided at the inaugural World Conference on Women, with the Canadian official delegation firmly on the side of their wealthy counterparts, that is, countries that pulled the most weight in the international political economy.

II

The World Conference on Women raises provocative questions regarding the rapport of "femocrats" with diplomatic structures. If women have been typically underrepresented in formal politics, and the state has been conceptualized as a patriarchal entity in feminist scholarship, the actions of civil servants in Mexico City push us to reflect on these characterizations.[22] When representing the government abroad, the Canadian women who were part of the official delegation reiterated government policy.[23] Participating in what historian Jocelyn Olcott aptly calls the "carefully scripted choreography of instructed delegations," MP Coline Campbell, as the head of the official Canadian contingent, gave an address to the thousands of people in attendance.[24] Overall, her speech lauded the federal government's efforts at redressing gender inequality in Canada, mentioning, for example, the establishment of the Royal Commission on the Status of Women in 1967 and the Advisory Council on the Status of Women in 1973. She adopted a distinctly celebratory, nationalistic tone, chalking up gender inequality to what she referred to as "attitudinal barriers" rather than state-informed social structures. Campbell made a mere mention of "regional disparities" but otherwise she presented the Canadian nation as homogeneous and unified (ironic, considering that Quebec neo-nationalism and the Red Power movements were both strong by the mid-1970s). She also paid lip service to Canada's support for developing "a more acceptable balance in basic human conditions throughout the world," which, when it came to voting, proved to be far more rhetorical than substantial.[25] In short, Campbell's speech, by no means exceptional in the broader context of the official conference, propped up Canada's already-existing place in the world, promoting federal policies and positions.

Two substantial documents came out of the IWY official meeting. For Canada's part, the country voted in favour of the World Plan of Action, which outlined a series of recommendations with regards to gender equity, from education to family planning to political participation. The document was "one of the major tasks and achievements of the conference," according to *Meeting in Mexico*, because of the "complexity of the questions and the strong views of the delegations."[26] The Canadian delegation then abstained from the "Declaration of Mexico, 1975," which was co-sponsored by a group of seventy-seven non-aligned developing countries (G-77). The G-77 was formed during the founding meeting of the United Nations Conference on Trade and Development to promote its members' interests.[27] That such a bloc emerged at the World Conference on Women, even if it was internally heterogeneous, speaks to the role of the unequal global political economy in creating political divisions among feminists. The first paragraph of the declaration pointedly argued that "the problems of women, who constitute half of the world's population, are the problems of society as a whole, and that changes in the present economic, political and social situations of women must become an integral part of efforts to transform the structures and attitudes that hinder the genuine satisfaction of their needs." The resolutions were even clearer. One emphasized that "under-development imposes upon women a double burden of exploitation," but added that "the national development policies designed to fulfill this objective are seriously hindered by the existing inequitable system of international economic relations."[28] According to the Declaration of Mexico, the problems of women were intrinsically related to highly structural socio-economic inequalities. Rather than simply a question of men's domination over women, this analysis of women's subordination in the developing world, most importantly, implicated their counterparts in richer countries, placing them in a dominant position.

As a North American country, most of Canada's population – though not all, as we will see below – benefited from comparatively favourable conditions, often living radically different lives than their counterparts in other regions of the world. Not unrelatedly, Canada played a neocolonial role in the world economy through its multinational corporations. Both of these issues came out at the conference. As Dr Lucille Mair of Jamaica explained, "We would like to see the position of women in developed and developing countries on a level of equality with men, but equally important, if not more important, we would like to see the conditions of these women brought closer together so that the appalling level of living of women in developing countries could be brought closer to that in developed countries." In the same interview, Mair pointed to the tensions that arose from the declaration's support of the "sovereign right of countries to nationalize their resources." As the Jamaican representative maintained, "Certainly one of the claims of developing countries is acknowledgement of their right to say 'this is my sand and sea, it's my bauxite, it's my copper, and therefore I claim the right to nationalize it.' This point of view had not yet proved acceptable to the countries who have been developing our resources."[29] Indeed, Canada has a long history of unequal economic ties with the Caribbean, investing heavily in the bauxite-alumina industry.[30] In Mexico, the country abstained on a number of other resolutions as well, namely relating to apartheid in South Africa, Namibia, and Southern Rhodesia on the basis that it was perceived as "extraneous" to a meeting on the status of women. The resolution urged all governments "to apply political, economic, social and military sanctions ... with the aim of isolating the minority and racist regimes."[31] Again, Canada's record vis-à-vis these racist regimes was less than stellar, an issue explored in Stephanie Bangarth's and Will Langford's contributions to this volume.

Finally, the official Canadian delegation – along with twenty-three others – opposed the paragraphs calling for the elimination of Zionism in the Declaration of Mexico. The controversial resolution, supported by sixty-one countries and abstained on by another twenty-five,[32] stated "that international cooperation and peace require the achievement of national liberation and independence, the elimination of colonialism and neo-colonialism, foreign occupation, *Zionism*, apartheid, racial discrimination in all its forms as well as the recognition of the dignity of peoples and their rights to self-determination."[33] During the conference and in its immediate aftermath, various civil action groups sent telegrams to the Canadian government, expressing their opposition to the negative references to Zionism in the Mexico declaration.[34] In the weeks following the event, minister of national health and welfare Marc Lalonde responded to some of these messages. In a letter to Rabbi Gunther Plaut, the acting chairman of the Canada-Israel Committee, Lalonde emphasized that "the Canadian government considered this conference in Mexico as being exclusively concerned with the improvement of the status of women throughout the world." Similarly, he went on to write, "We therefore instructed our Canadian delegates to avoid any involvement in political debate, and to dedicate their efforts to the promotion of the status of women," because, as Lalonde specified, the federal government did not consider resolutions relating to the Middle East question "appropriate to the conference."[35] The American position and rhetoric was similar. As Ambassador Barbara White argued, "I have no doubt that Israeli women and Arab women feel just as strongly about the issues of Palestine as the men of those two countries. One of the primary reasons why the US did not want the conference to concentrate on these political and economic issues was because there are plenty of other UN conferences to discuss these in. We wanted to concentrate this time on the particular problems of women."[36] Over and above the Israeli-Palestinian conflict, as well as the settler colonial ramifications of Zionist ideology (which Maurice Jr. Labelle explores more extensively in this volume), Canada's actions in this regard put the country at odds with many of the women-led delegations in Mexico whose liberation was intrinsically tied to national liberation. In short, Canada's abstention on the Declaration of Mexico can best be read in terms of its rapport with developing countries, rather than simply as a means to avoid – to go back to the words of Richard Burkhart – "international politicking."[37]

III

The International Women's Year Tribune, convened from 19 June to 3 July, was equally impressive in terms of participation relative to its official counterpart. Historians estimate that approximately 6,000 women from eighty-two different countries took part, with one-third of the participants each from Latin America, North America, and Europe. Mildred Persinger and Rosalind Harris, two Americans appointed by the UN Commission on the Status of Women, organized the gathering.[38] Yet the tribune as a body had no position on issues discussed at the official conference and did not adopt formal resolutions. Or, as the Australian National Advisory Committee, for example, put it, "A clever tyrant once diverted his subjects' demand for a share in Government by setting up *two* assemblies: one could discuss but not vote, and the other could vote but not discuss. This was an archetype of the IWY conference at Mexico with the Tribune (with no vote) and official United Nations conference (almost no communication)."[39] Betty Friedan, the infamous American author of the *Feminine Mystique* (1963), raised similar questions in a retrospective piece on the gathering: "Was it deliberate, situating the Tribune five kilometers across town from Tlatelolco so that the thousands of women who had come to Mexico really concerned about women's conditions couldn't get near where the real decisions were being made?"[40] The tribune's informality and ideological distance from the official conference, however, was perhaps its greatest strength. The event took on an ad hoc, grassroots, and internationalist character with participants able to speak beyond, and over, their national governments.[41] For instance, women organized presentations on "Trade Unions in Africa" and formed the International Lesbian Caucus. Chicanas and African-Americans, moreover, came together under the name of Coalition of Unrepresented Women (CUW) in order to criticize the mostly white, American delegations.[42] These are only a few examples. Therefore, the tribune was a site of contestation, where participants – Canadians among them – debated the very definition of feminism and its rapport with international governance.

The tribune hosted a wider range of women, in that national delegations at this gathering were far more diverse than their official counterparts. Yet the event – highly subversive in content and tone – would not have been made possible without $225,000 in donations from more than twelve sources, including the Canadian International Development Agency.[43] Mildred Persinger wrote a letter to the Canadian government in April of 1975, requesting funds with the explicit purpose of guaranteeing multiregional participation. As she explained to Marc Lalonde, "We are convinced that attendance from around the globe will make possible the kind of dialogue we believe so necessary between developing and industrializing country citizens if they are to play a role in supporting the process of development."[44] The federal government responded positively to Persinger's request, and also earmarked $5,000 for Canadian attendees. According to the memorandum, the Department of the Secretary of State sought to ensure that "the diversity of Canadian women's experiences" was represented at the tribune.[45] Nineteen people received a small travel bursary of several hundred dollars, in order to represent organizations such as the Federation of University Women, the Voice of Women, the Fédération des femmes du Québec, and the Canadian Negro Women's Association.[46] Another sixty to seventy women travelled to Mexico City at their own expense, although this number may have been higher. Among them was a contingent of Indigenous women from Kahnawake, Quebec, at the forefront of a battle to amend Article 12(1)(b) of the Indian Act in order to reclaim status for out-married women.[47] In Mexico, they called into question the type of feminism put forth by the federal government.[48]

Like in Canada, Indigenous women engaged in parallel political organizing in Mexico City. They also continued to tie their feminism to larger questions of self-determination. As reported in *Akwesasne Notes*, a Red Power newspaper, Indigenous women were either absent or tokenized at the first, official conference, where they were excluded from the official Canadian delegation, as were women of colour. The tribune, in contrast, brought together the likes of Kahnawake's Mary Two Axe Earley, the founder of Indian Rights for Indian Women (IRIW), and Yankton Sioux Reservation's Madonna Thunder Hawk, the prominent American Indian Movement (AIM) and Women of All Red Nations leader. As an early adherent of the Red Power movement, Thunder Hawk (née Gilbert) was known for her role in the occupation of Alcatraz and the Wounded Knee incident. In Mexico City, Indigenous women from North American territories participated in a panel on racism where leaders from South African, Zimbabwean, Namibian, Chicano, and Australian Aboriginal liberation movements "all identified the main problem of each native group as colonization by one or another European power." Since they were frequently perceived as disappearing peoples, Indigenous participants came to the gathering prepared to correct this erroneous assumption. The United States' Treaty Council Office published a booklet, which was reportedly very "useful for African and Asian women, who knew very little about native American peoples." According to *Akwesasne Notes*, the tribune was a success because the delegation made contacts with women "from all over the world." Women from Canada and the United States visited a Mexican Indigenous school. The Palestinian delegation also showed a great deal of interest in the situation of the Indigenous peoples of the Americas. The UN gathering thus offered an essential platform – one that was in fact part of a much larger strategy to promote "solidarity among all native peoples in this hemisphere" in order to gain "recognition by the rest of the world" and "the right to lands on which to live as sovereign peoples."[49] Stated otherwise, Indigenous women's politics in Mexico City aligned with African and Latin American approaches to women's liberation. Rather than adopting a liberal discourse of gender equality, women's fate was tied to that of their nations. In the words of Madonna Thunder Hawk, "We're fighting as a people for survival."[50]

Although Mary Two-Axe Early and her fellow activists inscribed the battle to amend the Indian Act into a broader quest for self-determination, they also fostered strategic linkages with powerful, mostly white feminist organizations, which carried over to Mexico City. For example, the Fédération des Femmes du Québec's (FFQ) dedication to reformist, anti-discrimination measures at the state level opened up room for contact between French-speaking and Haudenosaunee women.[51] Once FFQ members went to Mexico and were confronted with such radically different feminist discourses, they found reason to pause. Rather than speaking about themselves, and their perspectives, they decided to advocate for Indigenous women.[52] Perhaps ties between mostly white and Indigenous women's organizations were strengthened at the UN gathering. The Canadian delegation put forth a resolution to the tribune on behalf of Indigenous women, and sent a telegram to the ministries responsible for the status of women in Ottawa and Quebec City, the prime minister, and Chief Kirby of Kahnawake.[53] Therefore, non-Indigenous delegates, even if their own complicity in settler colonialism was left unexamined, worked to oppose the gendered ramifications of the Indian Act. They too, went against the federal government's policy in Mexico with regards to Article 12(1)(b). With a much lower profile than their American counterparts, who came under fire for speaking over attendees from other countries, Canadian women seemed to pass under the radar.[54] In the case of some, their naiveté, obliviousness even, speaks to the distance that existed between the world's women.

The tribune appeared to serve as a moment of reflection for many women from Canada who had the means, or acquired the means, to attend the gathering. By many accounts, discussions were both productive as well as contentious.[55] However, since the event was open to NGOs from around the world, and privileged discussions rather than voting, the tribune was successful in creating a platform for cross-cultural encounters. In the words of one delegate, "This whole experience crossed national, cultural, language and class barriers. It was fabulous."[56] Canadian (and Québécois) women were forced to grapple with their advantageous position in the global political economy, where, for instance, they demanded equal pay for equal work while their "Third World" counterparts focused on access to water.[57] Muriel Duckworth of the Voice of Women confirmed the gulf, writing, "Many North American women seemed to be hearing for the first time that development programs often widen the economic gap between men and women in developing countries, that imperialism compounds the acts of repression against women, including putting many behind bars, that rape is an act of war, that peace is essential."[58] In other words, they were put in the position of listeners and learners, and thus, as the FFQ's Ghislaine Patry-Buisson reflected, the gathering was "very enriching on the interpersonal and inter-organisational level." In order to pursue the conversation, the fédération requested money to host a conference back home.[59] Duckworth similarly recounted the strong representation of Latin American women, writing that the tribune provided "a place where they could speak to all of us and to each other."[60] Canadian participants then, came away from the tribune with a broadened view of gender inequality, at least in terms of women outside of Canada.

The impact of the UN gatherings on questions of difference among Canadian women remains one of the major questions of the much larger book project to which this chapter belongs. The written sources suggest that the tribune fostered a more positive rapport among English- and French-speaking Euro-Canadians. In a letter to Marc Lalonde, Azilda Marchand, the president of the Quebec-based l'Association féminine d'éducation et d'action sociale (AFEAS), wrote that

> les déléguées canadiennes, à part cette question de langue qui nous divise, ont fait un réel effort pour se regrouper. Elles croient qu'elles auraient pu faire davantage pour bien représenter leur pays, si leur participation avait été mieux organisée. Le Pays est grand … et la décision de participer à la Conférence a été tardive … Ce manque d'organisation ne favorisait pas des rencontres avec les déléguées d'autres pays. Seuls les échanges individuels furent possibles et enrichissants.[61]

In Canada, language differences among "second-wave" feminists were a point of contention. In Quebec, especially, where nationalism and feminism fed off one another, French-speakers' relative powerlessness shaped social relations within the movement.[62] In Mexico City, however, French was one of the three official languages of the conference, and, as Marchand commented, "the simultaneous translation was excellent."[63] Although she regretted that Canada did not provide more French-language pamphlets at the tribune – to which Marc Lalonde responded that the federal government was not invited to participate in this unofficial event – Marchand appeared to form genuine relationships with other Canadian delegates.[64] As she wrote, "Je fus très honorée d'être reçue par l'Ambassade canadienne à Mexico. J'ai apprécié d'avoir des contacts intéressants avec des membres de la délégation officielle canadienne, particulièrement avec Mmes Coline Campbell, Sylvia Gelber, Freda Partiel et bien sûr avec Laurette Robillard et Yvette Rousseau. Je tiens à leur remercier. "[65] In other words, French- and English-speaking feminists who were often socially and geographically distant appeared far closer in Mexico.

The Mexico City conference, however, does not tell the full story. Much has been written about Quebec's place in the world, including works by David Meren, Maurice Demers, and Sean Mills which collectively demonstrate the ways in which the nation's minority position within the Canadian federation informed its engagement with the world.[66] This parallel international history carried over to feminist politics. For instance, the Ligue des femmes du Québec, a communist group based in Montreal, attended the World Congress for International Women's Year held in Berlin in October 1975. There, the Marxist women's group used its presence "to publicize our national problem," making sure that they had the Quebec flag in view during the opening ceremony.[67] Indeed, North America-based leftist or radical feminist groups seemed to favour the East German conference.[68] Although beyond the scope of this paper, the Berlin gathering was, as historian Celia Donert writes, "the symbolic culmination of postwar campaigns by Soviet and East European states to internationalize a 'socialist' vision of women's rights."[69] According to the conference proceedings, "this Congress is a gathering of public organizations, a people's congress."[70] The ethos of the event, then, was different from its "bigger," "glitzier," and "more memorable" Mexican counterpart.[71] For example, Angela Davis, the infamous Black Panther and prison abolitionist, was in Germany for the occasion. For Canada's (or Quebec's) part, the women of Maison d'Haïti, a community organization based in Montreal, took the opportunity to continue their overseas opposition to the Duvalier dictatorship.[72] In Quebec, these same activists were part of the Congress of Black Women, which was represented in Mexico City. Founded in 1973, this bilingual, pan-Canadian organization was the outgrowth of the Canadian Negro Women's Association whose most prominent leader, Kay Livingstone, was at the tribune. However, Livingstone died suddenly on 25 July 1975; thus, her role in Mexico has yet to be uncovered.[73] Many Congress women were highly involved in transnational networks, from anti-apartheid activism to IWY.[74] Shortly after the Mexico City conference, Australian Elizabeth Reid, who emerged as a "feminist rock start" at the gathering, hosted a "Women and Politics" colloquium in Canberra. Its line-up included anti-imperialist lesbian Charlotte Bunch, lawyer and civil rights advocate Flo Kennedy, and the Jamaican-born, Congress of Black Women member and politician Rosemary Brown.[75]

From the perspective of Canadians, was the World Conference of the International Women's Year a success? The Report of the Canadi-an Delegation was tempered, stating that, "While the Conference pro-ceedings were at times highly politicized creating a sense of frustra-tion and even bitterness for many Conference participants, the very real progress made as reflected in the final approved texts of the Con-ference eclipses most of these political skirmishes."[76] Writing about her experiences in Mexico, Freda Paltiel, a member of the official del-egation, was, on the contrary, categorical: the conference had failed. In her view, "While there are those who felt the conference was a success because that flaw [the lack of emphasis on gender inequality] did not tear the conference apart and there were no major walkouts of any bloc, I do not share this view. The status of women in different parts of the world and strategies to improve their conditions were only a minor theme of the conference. Attempts to stress this theme were viewed as a hostile rejection of the 'main agenda,' a transformation of the world order."[77] Yet women who attended the tribune appraised the gathering differently. As Gwendolyn Black, the past president of Cana-dian Federation of University Women, maintained, "One thing is cer-tain: no one who attended the World Conference of Women in Mex-ico City will ever again relate to the women's movement in quite the same way as before. Our horizons were widened, our attitudes broad-ened, our enthusiasms aroused for new goals, our sympathies engaged for less fortunate women." With regards to the contentious undercur-rent pervading the discussions, she acknowledged, "Of course there were political tensions. The official government representatives were either civil servants or government appointees, well indoctrinated in national ideologies." According to Black, Coline Campbell's "ideal-ized summary of the opportunities available to Canadian women" evi-dently did not exempt Canadians from this classification.[78]

The Mexico City gathering was thus the site of "diplomatic" and "undiplomatic" relations for Canadian women. As this chapter points out, "femocrats," leading an official delegation to the United Nations for the first time, voted in a manner that placed them firmly on the side of the world's wealthy countries. Their actions suggest a femi-nism that was seen through the lens of their own advantageous position in the global community. The tribune, however, forces us to expand our analysis of Canadian women's rapport with the world during International Women's Year. Participants came back from Mexico transformed, with new insights and energies. They learned a lot at this crucial juncture in feminist activism, paving the way for the rest of the United Nations Decade for Women. Rather than minoritized, as they were in Canada, Indigenous women's perspectives and understanding of gender equality were given significant weight in Mexico where they were part of a plurality, if not a majority, of participants who tied their emancipation to genuine self-determination. They were able to use the United Nations to force the federal government to make changes in their favour. In fact, in 1981, the United Nations ruled against Canada, forcing the country to amend article 12(1)(b) of the Indian Act.[79] Circulating back to Canada, the effects of Indigenous peoples' engagement with the UN undermined – at least to a degree – the Canadian colonial project. The inaugural World Conference on Women was just the beginning of what appears to have been a shift in Canadian women's place in the world.

NOTES

1 The initial conferences generated so much momentum that a fourth was held in Beijing in 1995.
2 Angès Desmazières, "Negotiating Religious and Women's Identities: Catholic Women at the UN World Conferences, 1975–1985," *Journal of Women's History* 24, no. 4 (2012): 74–98; Kristen Ghodsee, "Rethinking State Socialist Mass Women's Organizations: The Committee of the Bulgarian Women's Movement and the United Nations Decade for Women, 1975–1985," *Journal of Women's History* 24, no. 4 (2012): 49–73; Jocelyn Olcott, "Empires of Information: Media Strategies for the 1975 International Women's Year," *Journal of Women's History* 24, no. 4 (2012): 24–48.
3 Historians such as Nancy Forestell have called for a further rethinking of feminism in Canada from a transnational perspective. For work on an earlier period, see, for example, Nancy Forestell and Maureen Moynagh, eds., *Documenting First Wave Feminisms: Volume II; Canada-National and Transnational Contexts* (Toronto: University of Toronto Press, 2013); Nancy Forestell, "Ms. Canada Goes Global: Canadian First Wave Feminism Revisted," *Atlantis* 30, no. 1 (2005): 7–20.
4 Annick Wibben, "Feminist International Relations: Old Debates and New Directions," *Brown Journal of World Affairs* 10, no. 2 (2004): 98. Of course,

there have been a number of recent additions over the years. See, for example: Tarah Brookfield, "Save the Children/Save the World: Canadian Women Embrace the United Nations, 1940s–1970," in *Canada and the United Nations: Legacies, Limits, Prospects*, edited by Colin McCullough and Robert Teigrob (Montreal and Kingston: McGill-Queen's University Press, 2017), 104–36; Vivien Hughes, "Women, Gender, and Canadian Foreign Policy, 1909–2009," *British Journal of Canadian Studies* 23 (2010): 159–78; and Janice Cavell, "Like Any Good Wife: Gender and Perceptions of Canadian Foreign Policy, 1945–75," *International Journal* 63 (2008): 385–403.

5 "Femocrat" is an informal term used to refer to government officials who advocate feminist policies.

6 See, for example, Brookfield, "Save the Children/Save the World"; Ruth Compton Brouwer, *New Women for God: Canadian Presbyterian Women and India Missions, 1876–1914* (Toronto: University of Toronto Press, 1990).

7 Marilyn Porter, "Transnational Feminisms in a Globalized World: Challenges, Analysis, and Resistance," *Feminist Studies* 33, no. 1 (2007): 44.

8 See, for example, Judy Tzu-Chun Wu, "Rethinking Global Sisterhood: Peace Activism and Women's Orientalism," in *No Permanent Waves: Recasting Histories of U.S. Feminism*, edited by Nancy A. Hewitt (New Brunswick: Rutgers University Press, 2010), 193–220; Lara Campbell, "'Women United against the War': Gender Politics, Feminism, and Vietnam Draft Resistance in Canada," in *New World Coming: The Sixties and the Shaping of Global Consciousness*, edited by Karen Dubinsky, Catherine Krull, Susan Lord, Sean Mills, and Scott Rutherford (Toronto: Between the Lines, 2009), 339–57; Nancy Janovicek, "'Assisting our own': Urban Migration, Self-Governance, and Native Women's Organization in Thunder Bay, Ontario, 1972–1989," *American Indian Quarterly* 27, nos. 3 and 4 (2003): 548–65; Judy Rebick, *Ten Thousand Roses: The Making of a Feminist Revolution* (Toronto: Penguin Canada, 2005).

9 Jocelyn Olcott, *International Women's Year: The Greatest Consciousness-Raising Event in History* (New York: Oxford University Press, 2017) stands out as an exception in this regard, even if, and quite reasonably, there is scant mention of the Canadian contingent. Previous to Olcott's book, very little historical scholarship existed on the conferences. As Jean Quataert and Benita Roth explain in a 2012 special issue of the *Journal of Women's History*, most of the writings on the conferences have been limited to participants' recollections published in women's studies journals, works by sociologists or political scientists, and scholars studying the impact of the UN meetings on mainstream development practices. See Jean Quataert and Benita Roth, "Guest Editorial Note: Human Rights, Global Conferences, and the Making of Postwar

Transnational Feminisms," *Journal of Women's History* 24, no. 4 (2012): 11–23, 12–13.

10 United Nations, *Report of the World Conference of the International Women's Year, Mexico City, 19 June – 2 July 1975* (New York: United Nations, 1976), (E/CONF.66/34), 120–2. There were also envoys, again in the capacity of observers, from, for example, the Organization of African Unity and the Organisation for Economic Co-operation and Development.

11 Canada at the World Conference on the International Women's Year, *Delegation Report on the World Conference of International Women's Year*, (Mexico City, 19 June – 2 July 1975), 1.

12 United Nations Centre for Economic and Social Development, *Meeting in Mexico: The Story of the World Conference of the International Women's Year (Mexico City, 19 June – 2 July 1975)* (New York: United Nations, 1975), 1.

13 List of Documents and Proposed Timetables of Meetings. 22 April 1975, RG 106, vol. 18, file 5, LAC.

14 H. Lafountaine, "Report on Ottawa Consultation," MG 28 I 196, vol. 13, file 13-23, LAC. The meeting took place on 22 October 1974 at the conference centre in Ottawa. An expensive advertising campaign was indeed part of the federal government's initial IWY programming. See *IWY Newsletter* 1, no.1 (1974): 1.

15 International Women's Year – 1975 Club Projects, "New Release, 30 June 1975, University Women Meet in Victoria," MG 28 I 196, volume 13, file 13-18, LAC.

16 "Canadian Delegation to the World Conference of the International Women's Year, Mexico City, 19 June to 2 July, 1975," RG 106 vol. 18, file 4, LAC.

17 For more on federal funding for IWY projects, see "Special Issue on Funding," *IWY Newsletter* 1, no.4 (November 1974): 1; "Speech by the Honourable Marc Lalonde on Second Reading of the Omnibus Bill on the Status of Women (Bill C-16), May 29, 1975, House of Commons," R-12590 174, file 174-5, LAC.

18 "Minutes of the Federal-Provincial Consultative Meeting about the World Conference of the International Women's Year, April 17, 1975," RG 106 vol. 18, file 1, LAC.

19 For example, one was organized in Bangkok, Thailand. See *Regional Consultation for Asia and the Far East on Integration of Women in Development with Special Reference to Population Factors. Plan of Action. Bangkok, Thailand, 13–17 1974* (New York: United Nations, 1975).

20 *Report and Proceedings of the Regional Seminar for Africa held in connection with International Women's Year, in Mogadishu April 3rd to 5th, 1975* (Women's Section of the Political Office of the Presidency of the Supreme

Revolutionary Council of the Somali Democratic Republic, October 1975),
12–14.

21 Ibid., 42, 114.

22 See, for example, the excellent work of Nira Yuval-Davis and Pnina Werbner,
Women, Citizenship, and Difference (New York: St Martin's Press, 1999) for a
thorough and nuanced reflection on women's rapport with the nation-state
with attention to race, class, and national origin.

23 Referring to transnational feminism in the Cold War context, historian
Francisca de Haan cautions against the characterization of women from
socialist countries as mere "puppets of the communist party or the socialist
state." On the contrary, she argues that "one should not homogenize state-
socialist women's organizations nor exaggerate the independence of US
women's organizations or delegates (nor that of representatives of other
western countries, for that matter." See "Eugénie Cotton, Pak Chong-ae, and
Claudia Jones: Rethinking Transnational Feminism and International Politics," *Journal of Women's History* 25, no. 4 (2013): 175.

24 Olcott, *International Women's Year*, 326.

25 "Speech by Coline Campbell – World Conference of the International
Women's Year – Mexico City – Wednesday, June 25, 1975," R-12590 174, file
174-12, LAC.

26 United Nations Centre for Economic and Social Information, *Meeting in
Mexico: The Story of the World Conference of the International Women's Year*
(New York: United Nations, 1975), 28.

27 Olcott, *International Women's Year*, 38.

28 Ibid., 53.

29 Ibid., 25–7.

30 Kari Levitt and Alister McIntyre, *Canada-West Indies Economic Relations*
(Montreal: Centre for Developing-Area Studies, McGill University, 1967), 18.

31 Canada at the World Conference on the International Women's Year, *Delegation Report on the World Conference of International Women's Year* (Mexico
City, 19 June–2 July 1975), 12.

32 Olcott, *International Women's Year*, 444.

33 Canada at the World Conference on the International Women's Year, *Delegation Report on the World Conference of International Women's Year* (Mexico
City, 19 June–2 July 1975), 10–11.

34 Telegram sent to Prime Minister Trudeau; Honourable Allan MacEachen
from Dorothy Reitman, National Council of Jewish Women of Canada, 7
July 1975, RG 106, vol. 18, file 5, LAC.

35 Letter from Marc Lalonde to Rabbi W. Gunther Plaut, n.d. [July 1975], RG
106, vol. 18, file 4, LAC.

36 United Nations Centre for Economic and Social Information, *Meeting in Mexico: The Story of the World Conference of the International Women's Year* (New York: United Nations, 1975), 27.

37 Since the 1980s, feminist scholars have indeed moved away from under-standings of "global feminism" that ignored inequalities and differences among women. The shift towards complex analyses of transnational process-es pointed to, as political scientist Leela Fernandes explains, the "ways in which women not simply were victims of their particular systems of patri-archy but also were placed in complex historical and material relationships with both men and women in other parts of the world." Leela Fernandes, *Transnational Feminism in the United States: Knowledge, Ethics and Power* (New York: New York University Press, 2013), 13.

38 Marisela Chavez, "Pilgrimage to the Homeland: California Chicanas and International Women's Year, Mexico City, 1975," in *Memories and Migrations: Mapping Boricua and Chicana Histories*, edited by Vicki Ruiz and John Chavez (Chicago: University of Illinois Press, 2008), 178.

39 Australian National Advisory Committee, *International Women's Year Confer-ence, Mexico City 1975*, International Women's Year, Canberra City, 1975, 1, RG 106 vol. 18, file 6, LAC.

40 Betty Friedan, *'It Changed My Life': Writings on the Women's Movement* (New York: Random House, 1974), 347.

41 Australian National Advisory Committee, *International Women's Year Confer-ence, Mexico City 1975*, International Women's Year, Canberra City, 1975, 14, RG 106, vol. 18, file 6, LAC.

42 Chavez, "Pilgrimage to the Homeland," 178, 181.

43 Ibid., 178.

44 Letter from Ms Mildred E. Persinger to Marc Lalonde, 2 April 1975, RG 106, vol. 18, file 5, LAC.

45 "Department of the Secretary of State: IWY Programme. 1 May 1975," MG 28 I25, vol. 154, file: International Women's Year, 1974–1975, LAC.

46 "Granting Activity – 1975/76 (approved as of June 10/75) International Women's Year. International Travel – IWY Tribune," RG 106, vol. 18, file 5, LAC. The listed organizations were the Federation of University Women, the Canadian Federation of Business and Professional Women's Clubs of Cana-da, the Voice of Women, the Fédération des femmes du Québec, National Action Committee on the Status of Women, United Nations Association in Canada, the Canadian Federation of Civil Liberties and Human Rights Associations, The Family Planning Federation of Canada, l'Association Fem-inine d'Éducation et d'Action sociale, the Canadian Negro Women's Associ-

ation, Canadian Commission for UNESCO, the Young Women's Christian Association of Canada, and SID.

47 With its origins in the 1960s, this struggle only ended in 1985, but in many respects continues to this day. See, for example, Pamela Palmater, "Genocide, Indian Policy, and Legislated Elimination of Indians in Canada," *Aboriginal Policy Studies* 3, no. 3 (2014): 36–7.

48 The number sixty to seventy is taken from Muriel Duckworth's report. Duckworth was at the tribune representing the Voice of Women. I suspect the actual number was higher; however, it is too early in the research process to say for certain. See Muriel Duckworth, "International Women's Day Tribune – Mexico City," *Newsletter of the Voice of Women*, November 1975, 3–4. Found in Newsletter of the Voice of Women 1974–1978, MG 28 I218, vol. 22, file 23-9, LAC.

49 "Native American Women Denied Voice at International Women's Year Conference," *Akwesasne Notes*, Early Winter 1975, 33.

50 Ibid. For more on Thunder Hawk, see Elizabeth Castle, "'The Original Gangster': The Life and Times of Madonna Thunder Hawk," in *The Hidden 1970s: Histories of Radicalism*, edited by Dan Berger (New Brunswick: Rutgers University Press, 2010), 267–83.

51 I have made this argument elsewhere; see for example "Contesting the Nation(s): Haitian and Mohawk Women's Activisms in Quebec" in *Women's Activism and "Second Wave" Feminism: Transnational Histories*, edited by Barbara Molony and Jennifer Nelson (London: Bloomsbury Press, 2016), 273–94.

52 Ghislaine Patry-Buisson, "Mexico: La grande rencontre des discriminées et des sur-discriminées," *Bulletin de la FFQ* (November 1975): 4.

53 Letter from Azilda Marchand to Marc Lalonde, 1 August 1975, RG 106, vol. 18, file 4, LAC.

54 *Xiolonen*, the tribune's daily newsletter, made scant reference to Canada. *Xiolonen* can be found in the *Women and Social Movements, International – 1840–Present* online database, located at Wilfred Laurier University.

55 See, for example, "Scene 11: The First Rule of Fight Club," in Oloctt, *International Women's Year*, 344–60.

56 United Nations Centre for Economic and Social Information, *Meeting in Mexico: The Story of the World Conference of the International Women's Year* (New York: United Nations, 1975), 38.

57 Ghislaine Patry-Buisson, "Mexico: La grande rencontre des discriminées et des sur-discriminées," *Bulletin de la FFQ* (November 1975), 4.

58 Muriel Duckworth, "International Women's Day Tribune – Mexico City," *Newsletter of the Voice of Women* (November 1975), 3–4.

59 Letter from Ghislaine Patry-Buisson to Hugh Faulkner, 22 September 1975, RG 106, vol. 18, file 4, LAC.

60 Muriel Duckworth, "International Women's Day Tribune – Mexico City," *Newsletter of the Voice of Women* (November 1975), 3–4.

61 Letter from Azilda Marchand to Marc Lalonde, 1 August 1975, RG 106, vol. 18, file 4, LAC.

62 See, for example: Sean Mills, *The Empire Within: Postcolonial Thought and Political Activism in Sixties Montreal* (Montreal and Kingston: McGill-Queen's University Press, 2010), 119–37.

63 Letter from Azilda Marchand to Marc Lalonde, 1 August 1975, RG 106, vol. 18, file 4, LAC.

64 Letter from Marc Lalonde to Azilda Marchand, 23 September 1975, RG 106, vol. 18, file 4, LAC.

65 Letter from Azilda Marchand to Marc Lalonde, 1 August 1975, RG 106, vol. 18, file 4, LAC.

66 David Meren, *With Friends Like These: Entangled Nationalisms and the Canada-Quebec-France Triangle, 1944–1970* (Vancouver: UBC Press, 2012); Maurice Demers, *Connected Struggles: Catholics, Nationalists, and Transnational Relations between Mexico and Quebec, 1917–1945* (Montreal and Kingston: McGill-Queen's University Press, 2014); Sean Mills, *A Place in the Sun: Haiti, Haitians, and the Remaking of Quebec* (Montreal and Kingston: McGill-Queen's University Press, 2016).

67 Report of the Canadian Delegation, *Equality, Peace, Development. World Congress for International Women's Year, Berlin, 1975, GDR* (Mississauga: Canadian Liaison Committee for International Women's Year, 1976), 6.

68 Olcott, *International Women's Year*, 248. Referring mainly to the American context, Olcott maintains that many radical feminists "dismissed" the Mexico City event as "too patriarchal."

69 Celia Donert, "Women's Rights in Cold War Europe: Disentangling Feminist Histories," *Past and Present* 218 (2013): 201.

70 *Documents of the World Congress for International Women's Year Held in Berlin 20–24 October 1975* (Berlin: National Organizing Committee of the GDR for the World Congress for International Women's Year, December 1975), 40.

71 Donert, "Women's Rights in Cold War Europe," 201.

72 RAFAC, *Femmes Haïtiennes* (Montreal: Maison d'Haïti: Carrefour International, 1980).

73 "Kay Livingstone Obituary," *New York Times*, 27 July 1975.

74 For example, the Congress of Black Women took a stand against apartheid. See Joella H. Gibson, ed., *Impetus – The Black Woman: Proceedings of the*

Fourth National Congress of Black Women of Canada (Windsor, Ontario, 19–21 August 1977), 51. LAC.

75 Olcott, *International Women's Year*, 473–4.

76 Canada at the World Conference on the International Women's Year, *Delegation Report on the World Conference of International Women's Year* (Mexico City, 19 June – 2 July 1975), 16.

77 "United Nations World Conference of the International Women's Year: A Personal Overview by Freda L. Paltiel, Canada's Representative, Committee II," RG 106, vol. 18, file 6, LAC.

78 International Women's Year Conference Mexico City, Canadian Federation of University Women, "Report on World Conference of Women in Mexico City, June 19, 1975 – July 2, 1975 by Gwendolyn Black, Past President, Canadian Federation of University Women," MG 28 I 196, vol. 13, file 13-22, LAC.

79 Judith Aks, *Women's Rights in Native North America: Legal Mobilization in the US and Canada* (New York: LFB Scholarly Publishing, 2004), 79.

Cold War and Peace

9

Dancing into Hearts and Minds: Canadian Ballet Exchanges with the Communist World, 1956–76

KAILEY HANSSON

Rudolf Nureyev, the Kirov ballet company's male lead, and one of the most charismatic dancers of his era, stunned the world when he defected to the West in 1961. The defection itself was one fit for a movie: Nureyev broke away from the company as it was preparing to board a plane at the Le Bourget Airport in Paris. The flight was headed for London, where the Kirov Ballet company was slated to begin a four-week run at the Royal Opera House in Covent Garden. Nureyev reportedly dashed to a police barrier where he then made his appeal for political asylum, with two Soviet police officers close on his heels.[1] The flare and intrigue of the event caused a stream of sensationalist reports in the North American media. *Globe and Mail* correspondent Robert Duffy described the event as Nureyev's "prodigious solo leap from Communism."[2]

Although Nureyev's defection undoubtedly gave the West a valuable point on its cultural Cold War scorecard, defectors were the exception. As David Caute has pointed out, Soviet dance companies regularly transported "hundreds of performers across the world and brought them all home."[3] What then was the motivation behind Nureyev's "leap to freedom"? According to Caute, the most "abrasive issue" in the world of ballet was less about politics and more about form. Western ballet companies had moved away from telling dramatic stories about heroes and villains, which remained standard fare in the Soviet repertoire. Instead, Western choreographers believed dance should be a "suggestive form of motion, mime, and gesticulation."[4] In short, abstract movement, like abstract paintings, became an important marker of artistic freedom and advancement.

However, while the battle between "modernism" and "realism" was certainly ever-present, it was not the only binary at work in the "culture wars." Also at stake was showcasing which system – either free enterprise or state-sponsorship – was more beneficial for the performing arts. This cultural "faceoff" began in earnest after the death of Joseph Stalin in 1953. According to Cadra Peterson McDaniel, Nikita Khrushchev understood the value of culture more fully than his predecessor. Under Khrushchev, the arts were to play a "crucial role in foreign policy" and were thought to be an "instrumental weapon in spreading Communist ideology."[5] The Soviets acted quickly to institute this new policy. Between 1953–55, the Kremlin increased by a factor of three the number of dance troupes, theatre companies, and musical groups it exported to other countries.[6]

The speed and potency of the Soviets' "cultural offensive" pushed American president Dwight Eisenhower to take dramatic action soon after taking office in 1953. As Kenneth Osgood points out, despite his reputation as a battle-hardened, fiscal conservative, Eisenhower understood that cultural export programs were essential if the West was to halt the worldwide spread of communist ideology.[7] In a letter to his brother, Eisenhower outlined the challenge facing the United States in developing a counteroffensive to the Soviet's cultural programs. Europeans, Eisenhower complained, had been taught that Americans were a "race of materialists" whose only diversions were "golf, baseball, horse racing, and an especially brutalized brand of boxing." What America needed to do was to convince audiences across the world that it could produce sophisticated, "worthwhile" cultural works.[8]

With the combined efforts of the State Department, the United States Information Agency (USIA), and private cultural organizations, the Eisenhower administration launched a full-on cultural assault aimed at the communist and non-aligned world. Initially, the high arts, such as classical music and ballet, figured prominently in the United States' cultural programs, largely because some of the strongest elements in the Soviet's cultural tradition were the classical works of famous Russian composers and dancers.[9] American officials reasoned that the United States needed to show that it could produce composers and dancers who were not only equal to their Soviet counterparts, but who could also showcase a creativity and ingenuity that was only possible under a liberal-democratic, free-enterprise system. As a result, some of America's most impressive orchestras and ballet troupes were launched at strategic cultural and political hotspots in Europe, Asia, the Middle East, and Latin America. In terms of ballet, every aspect of a troupe, including set designs, repertoire, costumes, choreography, and the physical appearance of the dancers themselves, became vehicles through which the sending nation sought to communicate their ideological values and beliefs. An evening at the ballet, then, was not just an occasion for entertainment – it was an opportunity to evaluate the strengths and failures of an entire ideological system.

Like the United States, Canada was ambivalent towards the Soviets' cultural offensive. Despite the possibility that cultural exchanges with the Soviets could expose Canadian society to dangerous and subversive propaganda, Canadian officials reasoned that cultural exchanges had the potential to expose people under communist rule to the freedom enjoyed by artists in the West. However, as this chapter will argue, Canada's ballet exchanges with the communist world revealed all that was lacking with Canadian ballet in particular and the development of the arts in general. Russian ballerinas were better paid than their Canadian counterparts; they also had their education and training subsidized by their government, and they could expect to receive a pension, something that was far from the reality for ballet dancers in Canada. In addition, there was far less commercial pressure on Soviet dancers, as Western "freedom" often meant conformity to a commercial logic that could be as confining as the diktat of a party boss. Far from showing the deficient nature of Soviet-style communism, Soviet ballet companies proved that the arts could thrive under communist rule. By comparison, the socio-economic well-being of dancers was a subject that Canada's cultural elites preferred to ignore.

The purpose of this chapter is to discuss Canada's ballet exchanges with the Soviet Union and thereby provide a look at Canadian cultural diplomacy – an overlooked area of Canada's international history, even as it has been a growth area in the field of the United States in the World, where scholars have also emphasized the impact of American culture on foreign policy-making.[10] It also engages directly with this volume's aim of pushing forward the boundaries of Canadian international history. Instead of focusing on the relationship between nation-states and state-centric policy-making, this chapter will emphasize non-state actors, cross-border cooperation, and the transmission of ideas and techniques across national boundaries. Canada's ballet exchanges can be characterized as "undiplomatic" in that they reveal less about Canada's relationship with the Soviet Union as expressed through high politics than they do about the lived experiences of individuals who had to navigate both the restrictions and possibilities of the Cold War period.

There are two major themes that run throughout this chapter. Firstly, through cultural exchanges with the communist world, Canadian government officials and cultural elites sought to make Canada more culturally distinctive. In terms of the country's relationship with the United States, there was a desire to promote Canada as the more tolerant, sophisticated country in North America. In a similar vein, Canada's cultural elites, as exemplified by the Canada Council, wanted to hone a Canadian cultural identity that was separate from the mass entertainment industry they associated with the United States. Secondly, Canada projected a very "high-culture" and "European" notion of itself. Unlike the United States, which embraced jazz as a uniquely American art form and made jazz musicians a central element of cultural diplomacy, Canada sought both to mirror and to project the classical performing arts of Europe and particularly the United Kingdom. For the most part, the complicated projection of a mainly "classical" Canada can be explained by a sense of confusion about the degree to which most North Americans' cultural preferences should factor into the Canadian cultural identity. But the rejection of popular culture as an acceptable cultural export highlighted Canadian officials' desire to present Canada as a country distinct from the United States.

The late 1950s and early 1960s were tumultuous years for the development of ballet in Canada. Canada's three main ballet companies – the Royal Winnipeg Ballet, the National Ballet of Canada, and Les Grands Ballets Canadiens – were all struggling to improve their artistic standards in the face of soaring expenditures and paltry government grants. What is more, the hope that ballet could be a symbol of Canadian cultural prowess was both eternal and perplexing. As the *Dauphin Herald* asked: "Can an art form born in Europe be transplanted here and find national expression?"[11] This chapter will explore the ways in which Canada's cultural elites tried to improve the state of ballet in Canada so that it could compete with the great companies of continental Europe. It will also explore the relationship between the private and public sectors, and their shared interest in using Canadian ballet companies as a tool of Cold War diplomacy. I suggest that the Canada Council's formula for successfully developing ballet in Canada functioned as a test case for the Western alliance's insistence that a capitalist, liberal democracy could lead to financial success and artistic freedom.

As ballet was beginning to get its footing in Canadian cultural circles, Canada Council members wanted to ensure that Canadian ballet did not become merely parochial. As the council declared in 1958, Canadian artists would inevitably be compared to their counterparts in Britain, France, and the United States. It was therefore necessary that Canadian artists reach for the same world-class standards that had already been set by artists in those countries. "Canada becomes every day a more mature nation and she can afford to take an adult attitude – accepting freely, using, and working with what is English, French, or American (or anything else) because it is good and not simply because it comes to us from abroad."[12] Canadian ballet was therefore encouraged to imitate techniques and styles from British, American, French, and, in some cases, even Soviet repertoires. Thus, from the outset, the Canada Council believed that Canadian ballet should, at least in the short term, mirror what had already been achieved on the international ballet scene.

Aside from an imported repertoire, there were other barriers to cultivating a truly "Canadian" form of ballet. Regionalism had, from the outset, fuelled a bitter rivalry among the nation's ballet companies. The National Ballet of Canada, for example, often drew the most criticism from the ballet community outside of Toronto for putting the word "Canada" in its name. However, as James Neufeld explains, the National Ballet Guild of Canada truly believed that Toronto was the best location for Canadian ballet to flourish. For the board members of the Royal Winnipeg Ballet, such an assumption typified the attitude of wealthy Torontonians, who had little regard for artistic initiatives outside central Canada. Though smaller than the NBC, the RWB had garnered a strong enough reputation in the early 1950s to perform for Queen Elizabeth II. The performance led to the company receiving a Royal proclamation. At the same time, however, a new, exciting company arrived on the ballet scene to contend for the country's dance loyalties. Founded in Montréal in 1953, Les Grands Ballets Canadiens de Montréal was initially established to perform for the Canadian Broadcasting Corporation (CBC). Its founder and artistic director, Ludmilla Chiriaeff, quickly earned the company praise for its innovative choreography. Within a decade, Les Grands Ballets Canadiens grew to be an important expression of Quebec's cultural identity. With regional interests at play in each company's identity, it became increasingly clear that a single, national ballet company was unlikely to emerge.

On the other side of the iron curtain, Soviet ballet companies were a world ahead of their Canadian counterparts. The Kirov Company, based in Leningrad, and the Bolshoi Company, based in Moscow, had enjoyed the benefits of full state sponsorship since 1917. Although both companies had been founded in the days of the Russian Empire, they remained important elements of cultural life in Russia after the revolution. The most observable difference between Soviet and Western ballet was in style and technique. Whereas Western directors such as George Balanchine had begun to experiment with intricate steps and short, stylized repertoires, the Kirov and Bolshoi favoured movements and stories that communicated strength and power. As Christina Ezrahi points out, the movements and expressions reflected the "heroic utopianism" propagated by the Soviet state. Soviet choreography thus favoured powerful jumps that enabled the dancer to cover the stage in mighty leaps.[13] Moreover, in a Cold War atmosphere that celebrated traditional conceptions of male bodies, the lean, perfectly chiselled bodies of male Soviet dancers redefined what power and strength could look like. As Linda Winer has suggested, one cannot dispute "the Russian influence on the West's acceptance – even idolization – of dancing men."[14]

However, until the mid-1950s, no Westerners, apart from the few who visited Moscow, had seen either the Bolshoi or Kirov perform. This changed after cultural exchange agreements were signed between the Soviet Union and the United Kingdom, and shortly thereafter with the United States. According to Ezrahi, Kremlin officials hoped that "the artistic mastery of Soviet ballet would stun the world, symbolizing the cultural peaks reached by Soviet civilization and proving not just the superiority of Soviet ballet but of the Soviet project as a whole."[15] The Bolshoi ballet's first multi-week tour in the West occurred in London in 1956. British prima ballerina Antoinette Sibley spoke of the impact of seeing Russian prima ballerina Galina Ulanova dance: "It was the sort of miracle that it is to have a baby ... This was exactly the same, theatrically, to me."[16] However, some critics also pointed out that the Bolshoi lacked innovative choreography. They also noted that the company's costumes and stage décor appeared run-down and heavy.[17] Nonetheless, the Bolshoi's visit to London succeeded in showing that ballet had hardly withered under communist rule. After having heard of the Bolshoi's success in Britain, North American audiences were eager to see the company first hand. According to Winer, the Bolshoi's historic American debut in 1959 was "one of the earliest signs of the Cold War thaw."[18] Reporting from New York for the *Globe and Mail*, Irving Spiegel declared that for three hours, the "East-West tension was forgotten." Sol Hurok, the colourful American impresario who was responsible for arranging the performance, quipped: "As long as they keep dancing and the diplomats keep talking, we'll have no war."[19]

Canada, on the other hand, was reluctant to enter into ballet exchanges with the Soviets. As Jamie Glazov has pointed out, the Diefenbaker government was reluctant to "move the state into cultural affairs."[20] Although no official cultural agreement was signed, External Affairs looked favourably on efforts by the private sector to negotiate with Gosconcert, the Soviets' centralized concert agency controlled by the Ministry of Culture; they saw it as an opportunity to expose Soviet dancers to the perks of Western society. Nicholas Koudriavtsev, Canadian impresario and president of Canadian Concerts and Artists Limited, was the man responsible for introducing Canadian audiences to the Bolshoi, following its scheduled eight-week tour of the United States in the spring of 1959. The *Globe and Mail* called the Bolshoi's impending visit to Toronto a "landmark event in the artistic life of this city."[21] The article also mused on the impact the Bolshoi's performance that spring would have on East-West relations: "The fact that [the Bolshoi] is now touring North America is striking proof of the way the Iron Curtain has parted, at least in cultural affairs. The cold war may still rage on the political and diplomatic fronts, but it is once again possible for the peoples of Russia and the West to sample and appreciate each other's artistic achievements. In the long run, that will make for better understanding."[22]

The Bolshoi's performances at the O'Keefe center drew rave reviews from Canadian arts critic Herbert Whittaker. While he noted that there were perhaps "too many" lifts and tosses – which, he added, were no doubt meant to impress the audience with the athleticism and power of the company's male leads – the entire performance was "dazzling."[23] Despite the artistic praise, the *Toronto Star* questioned whether Canadians could look past the Cold War implications of the

Bolshoi's visit. Could Canadian audiences give the Bolshoi a bad review if they thought it merited such a reaction? Or were all Canadians supposed to smile and applaud for the sake of diplomacy? "Though the prima ballerina falls flat on her tutu every couple of bars, still the audience must rise up in ovation rather than disturb the artist's compatriots back home, fingering their missile releases."[24] In this particular instance, however, the reaction among Canadian audiences seemed genuine. One individual told the *Globe and Mail* that the performance was "an outstanding highlight in a fairly long life."[25] The Soviet press also hailed the success of the exchange. *Pravda* declared that the Bolshoi's Canadian tour had been "a great step in the cause of developing cultural relations between the two countries." The Canadian people "welcomed the Soviet artists with extraordinary warmth and kindness and the artists themselves produced an unforgettable impression on the Canadian public."[26]

While a diplomatic success, the Bolshoi's performance served notice to Canada's cultural elite that the state of Canadian ballet was far from matching that of the Soviet Union. Instead of sending a Canadian ballet company to reciprocate, Koudriavtsev made plans to send Glenn Gould to Moscow for a second time, in addition to singers Maureen Forester and Jacques Beaudry.[27] While this can partly be explained by the Soviets' intense interest in Gould, Forester, and to a lesser extent Beaudry, it also suggests how little faith the entrepreneur had in Canadian ballet's capacity to impress the Russians.

It became increasingly obvious to the Canada Council that it would serve Canadian ballet well if the companies could interact with successful teachers and dancers from around the world. Ballet exchanges promised not only to boost box office sales but also invigorate the companies with new styles and techniques. Moreover, as Canada's cultural exchanges with the Soviet Union had gradually increased since 1959, it seemed an auspicious time for the private sector to arrange for bilateral exchanges with the major Russian companies. As a Russian name on a theatre bill was sure to fill an auditorium, all three Canadian companies were anxious to collaborate with the Russians. The Royal Winnipeg Ballet, for example, hoped that inviting Soviet dancers for a guest appearance would generate publicity ahead of its twenty-first anniversary celebrations. Gosconcert agreed, and sent two leading dancers from the Leningrad ballet, Askold Makarov and Olga Moiseev, to perform as guest stars. Here was a small cultural exchange, yet it loomed large locally: the city of Winnipeg made every effort to ensure that the Soviet guests were warmly embraced. Mayor Stephen Juba welcomed the dancers to the "friendliest city of the nation" and emphasized that Winnipeg was honoured to have them visit. By all accounts, the trip was a success. The *Winnipeg Free Press* quoted Makarov as saying, "We can already see we have made no mistake at all in coming here. You have been very friendly to us, and we hope the visit will be beneficial to all of us."[28]

The Soviets reciprocated by extending an invitation to artistic director Arnold Spohr to visit the Soviet Union as an observer. After receiving a $1,000 grant from the Canada Council, Spohr travelled to Moscow and Leningrad in the spring of 1962, where he observed teaching and production methods at the Kirov and Bolshoi companies. When he returned, Spohr told the *Winnipeg Press*: "I decided that after we brought those Russian dancers here to perform, that I wanted to study at first-hand the system which produced such fantastic dancing." The visit was instructive for Spohr, who reported that the state of ballet in the Soviet Union was far better than in Canada. "Ballet stars over there are treated like Hollywood actors here. A dancer in Russia is a Rock Hudson. They are part of the elite and are highly respected. Everyone vies for a chance to be a dancer. They live very well."[29]

But why was ballet struggling in Canada? For starters, Spohr noted, Canada lacked a reliable audience. The Russians, on the other hand, encouraged a passion for the arts from childhood. "In Leningrad, I saw an opera performed entirely for children. Most of them were only five or six years old, but they sat enthralled for four hours and took it completely in their stride."[30] Spohr also noted the appreciation and gratitude that Soviet children seemed to have for high culture. "For them, it's a rare privilege to be taken to the opera or ballet. It's what they seem to live for." Compared to Canadian children, whose daily entertainment was tied closely to consumerism, Soviet children seemed to have a greater appreciation for cultured, mature forms of art and entertainment.

Spohr also suggested that the widespread hunger for the high arts could be explained by Soviet subsidies. "Money is no object," he told the *Globe and Mail*. "The state pays for everything. The Bolshoi has 2,500 workers, including 300 musicians and 240 dancers. If any company wants 120 dancers for a ballet, they just go ahead and get them." Despite the usual arguments that the costs of living in a closed society outweighed the benefits, Spohr thought the opposite might be true. Although he did not ask the dancers how much they made,

Spohr believed their pay was quite good. After dining at the home of Rimma Karelskaya, one of the Bolshoi stars, he wrote: "It was a lovely apartment, and the dinner lasted from 7 to 11:30, complete with vodka and champagne. Everything they say about Russian hospitality is true." Spohr's perception of Russian ballet life was prejudiced by the first-class treatment he received as a visitor. However, he was adamant that the Soviets had succeeded at elevating the arts to a place of importance in society: "The artists have prestige. They're honoured people." In Canada, "the only way a ballet dancer achieves an admired position is by being a star. But our companies haven't toured enough and Canadian dancers haven't been seen enough to build up any star system."[31]

For the Royal Winnipeg Ballet a similar kind of stardom began in 1965 when the company hired J. Sergei Sawchyn as its general manager. A native of Winnipeg, Sawchyn believed in combining intensive touring with high-powered marketing to strengthen the company's brand on both the domestic and international scene.[32] His dynamic and assertive style made him an effective cheerleader and pitbull for the company. According to Mark Crabb, Sawchyn was responsible for convincing Prime Minister Lester Pearson to send the RWB, as opposed to the National Ballet or Les Grands Ballets Canadiens, to represent Canadian ballet at the Commonwealth Arts Festival in London.[33] As there existed a fierce rivalry between the three companies, Sawchyn's move was bold and risked backfiring. However, Pearson approved the proposal and sent the RWB on its way. Despite his considerable efforts behind the scenes, when asked why the RWB had been chosen, Sawchyn boasted, "we like to think it is a matter of quality."[34] The RWB received widespread praise for its performance at the festival. David Pulver of the *Winnipeg Free Press* reported that the "exuberant and exhilarating group brought in a breath of tangy Canadian air into the somewhat heavy atmosphere of classical ballet that is London's usual autumn fare."[35]

Hoping to seal the RWB's image as a company of truly "international" calibre, Sawchyn worked hard to win the company an invitation to the 1968 Paris International Ballet Competition. He also travelled with Koudriavtsev to Moscow, in order to request an official invitation from the Soviet Ministry of Culture for the company to perform in Moscow and Leningrad after the company's Paris engagement. Sawchyn succeeded on both counts and the company embarked on its first continental European tour in November 1968.

Both locations offered their own challenges. In Moscow and Leningrad, there was the risk that audiences would not take well to the company's "youthful" and modern repertoire. As for the French capital, although not the ballet epicenter it had once been, Paris was still considered a city of sophistication and high culture, and therefore one that expected performances of the highest calibre.

French audiences, however, proved to be very receptive to the RWB's style. Along with winning the gold star for best company, Winnipeg's prima ballerina, Christine Hennessy, won the gold star for best female dancer. On top of these accomplishments was the fact that the company had won such acclaim with its repertoire of largely original works, thanks in part to the contributions of its choreographer, Canadian Brian MacDonald. As the *Globe and Mail* noted, the RWB's innovative repertoire luckily coincided with the "period of decadence" that was sweeping across France. "The fresh creative spirit running through North America is what the French most need and admire."[36] The RWB's success seemed to announce to the international community that Canadian ballet had finally arrived.

Once the RWB got to Leningrad, however, the mood changed. Their performances received "polite applause," but it was apparent that the Russian audience did not feel that the Canadians deserved "their famous standing ovations." Although the performances were described by one Leningrad newspaper as "original," the *Globe and Mail* explained that such a descriptor was not necessarily a compliment. "Originality can be a political sin, and should be more nearly equated with strange or unorthodox." One critic explained the conundrum in this way: "The Russians are academic and traditional rather than sophisticated. They have seen very little dance from outside Communist countries, and almost nothing from New York, except in movies such as West Side Story. Russian dancers on tour are eager to see American work, but the general public doesn't begin to understand it."[37]

Of more concern to officials in Ottawa were a series of faux pas in the company's publicity campaign following its return to Canada. Sawchyn had created a "newspaper," distributed to Canada's missions abroad, that was part of the company's promotional package. When the "newspaper" arrived in Moscow at the Canadian embassy, Ambassador Robert Ford wrote a strongly worded memo back to Ottawa lamenting the "poor judgment that was exercised" in issuing such a publication. The "paper" irreverently used the original heading of the

CPSU Central Committee newspaper *Pravda*, complete with Lenin's medallion and appropriate wording in Russian. The heading was off-set by the statement, "There really is a difference – we're free!" together with a cartoon drawing of the RWB's prima ballerina Christine Hennessey standing next to Lenin's portrait.[38]

According to Ford, the text of the paper criticized various aspects of life in the USSR. The food was described as "greasy, cold, and unpalatable," and the company's Russian hosts had apparently "made no attempt to socialize."[39] As Ambassador Ford had spent an inordinate amount of time paving the way for Canadian-Soviet cultural exchanges, he was particularly frustrated at the possible strain in relations the newspaper could cause. "The Russians are very sensitive to any criticism and should be all the more vexed by criticism of the conditions surrounding the Royal Winnipeg Ballet tour, when a real effort was made in this country to assure the Canadian company's success here." Ford predicted that the publicity-oriented paper would get wide circulation in Winnipeg. It was therefore "probable" that it would find its way into the hands of the Soviet embassy in Ottawa, "if it had not done so already."[40] As the Department of External Affairs had become reliant on impresarios and concert managers to nurture good ties with Gosconcert and Soviet cultural officials, he considered the incident most unfortunate. Although no serious harm was done to Canadian-Soviet cultural relations, the incident showed how the private sector's desire for commercial publicity could chafe with the business of diplomacy.

Aside from his occasional disregard for diplomatic protocol, Sawchyn was largely responsible for intertwining the activities of the company with the foreign policy goals of the Canadian government. Like Koudriavtsev, Sawchyn showed External Affairs how the private sphere could help project a positive image of Canada to a foreign audience. Undoubtedly his drive was fuelled by a commercial desire to make the RWB an internationally recognized brand. However, according to Michael Crabb, Sawchyn was also dedicated to making the company "Canada's best known touring attraction, at home and abroad, and he wanted its Canadian identity at the forefront." As Sawchyn proudly announced in July 1971, "We don't see ourselves as a Royal Winnipeg Ballet. We see ourselves as Canada's oldest ballet, as a national ballet and one of the nation's treasures."[41]

The National Ballet of Canada did not have a larger-than-life personality to match the RWB's Sawchyn. Nor was it particularly useful as a touring company, given that its repertoire largely included full-length performances that required a greater volume of set pieces and costumes. It did share the RWB's drive to connect with international audiences. More specifically, as James Neufeld has argued, its artistic and financial salvation came about as a result of a "Russian invasion" of repertoires, dancers, and choreographers in the early to mid-1960s. The arrival of Russian-born dancer Galina Samsova played a particularly significant part in putting the National on the international ballet map. Samsova had received her training with the Kirov school where she met Ukrainian-Canadian dance teacher Alexander Ursuliak. After the two married, Samsova immigrated to Canada in 1961. Two years after joining the National Ballet Company, she was asked to perform the title role of *Cinderella* at the International Dance Festival in Paris in 1963. Samsova danced the role every day for a month and finished the festival by winning the gold medal for a female dancer.

As Samsova was an unknown on the ballet scene, her performance had a bombshell effect on the sophisticated French capital. Toronto painter and designer Lillian Sarafinchan witnessed Samsova's Paris performance. According to Sarafinchan, "She just popped out of nowhere as far as the Parisians were concerned." "Suddenly, whoops, here is this marvellous dancer, and nobody knows anything about her."[42] The publicity director at the National Ballet Guild contacted the major dailies in Ontario and Quebec to ensure that there was Canadian press coverage of Samsova's Parisian "triumph." The National Ballet of Canada was, of course, eager to show Canadians, and the world, how its resources and training had helped hone such a great talent as Samsova. The hope was that her successes on the international stage would generate greater interest among Canadians for ballet, and, perhaps more importantly, attract greater funding from the public sector and private investors.

While the Canadian press hailed her as an immigrant success story, some members of the press emphasized the degree to which Samsova represented the "Other." The Toronto *Telegram*, for example, featured a large photo of Samsova that declared she had an "exotic Garbo look."[43] Like the Swedish actress, Samsova had blonde hair that was often remarked upon by the press as an indicator of her physical beauty. But the emphasis on Samsova's "exoticism" complicated her new status as Canada's latest "sweetheart." *Canadian Weekly* declared that Samsova was Canada's "newest star" while simultaneously mentioning that her face was "unmistakably Russian, with its wide-set eyes and high-

sculpted cheekbones."[44] This scrutiny of Samsova's physical characteristics suggests a nascent distrust for immigrants of Slavic descent.
While there was a desire to celebrate defections and, in the case of
Samsova, legal immigration to Canada from the Soviet Union, the
degree to which these newcomers were real "Canadians" was consistently challenged.

Although Galina Samsova's acceptance as a "Canadian" cultural
export was at times ambiguous and problematic, there is little doubt
that her decision to join the National Ballet elevated the status of the
company.[45] However, Samsova was the first high-profile star who
could provide first-hand and credible comparisons about life as a
dancer in the Soviet Union versus Canada. *Maclean's* magazine pro-
filed Samsova in 1963, and the dancer described her life in Canada.
Far from praising the West for its luxuries and comfortable standard
of living, Samsova confessed that she was "shocked" by the contrast
between a dancer's life in Canada and in Russia. As first soloist (one
step below prima ballerina) for the Kiev company in the Ukraine,
Samsova had earned a monthly salary of 1,600 rubles (roughly \$C650)
for a minimum of nine performances a month. She also earned the
same amount during the summer months when the theatre was
closed. After dancing for twenty years, Samsova could expect to retire
and continue receiving 80 per cent of her salary.[46] Samsova provided
an equally honest portrayal for the Toronto *Telegram*. Dancers in Kiev
worked no more than eight hours a day, Samsova reported, and travelled only once a year, to Moscow, for a ten-day visit. For Samsova, "It
is a more normal life."[47]

According to Samsova, the respect accorded artists in the Soviet
Union made it a desirable profession: "In Kiev my sister, Luba is an
engineer, yet my salary was higher than hers. But here a worker earns
more money than I do. At least twice my salary."[48] Hired by the
National Ballet for only seven months a year, which was a typical contract, Samsova earned anywhere between \$62.50 per week for
rehearsals and \$127 per week while on tour in the US. According to
Maclean's, this money had to stretch to cover the cost of hotels, meals,
clothes other than her costumes, medical expenses, and living expenses for the five months of the year when she was not dancing with the
company. Furthermore, there was no pension plan in place for Samsova, or any dancer for that matter. "When I think about what will
become of me in 10 years," she told *Maclean's*, "I am very worried."[49]
Although Samsova was Canada's first bona fide prima ballerina, even

she could not escape the financial uncertainty faced by the majority of Canadian dancers. Her interview showed that Cold War cultural diplomacy could have unpredictable consequences.[50]

The Russian "invasion" began when the Bolshoi Company arrived in 1963 at the O'Keefe Center in Toronto for a series of performances. Accompanying the Bolshoi was former prima ballerina Galina Ulanova; she was invited to give lessons at the National Ballet School that same week. Any anxiety felt by the students was dispelled after Ulanova praised the quality of their training. "The dancers' arms are very bad in America. That is not true here. Here they are very good. This school is serious and knows what it is about." As Herbert Whittaker remarked, for a ballerina of Ulanova's stature, that was "praise indeed for the budding National Ballet school."[51] Ulanova's visit initiated a series of exchanges between the National and the Bolshoi and Kirov companies. For example, Eugen Valukin, a highly regarded teacher at the Bolshoi Ballet, undertook several extended visits to Canada beginning in 1963, when he accepted an invitation to be a guest instructor at the National Ballet School.

According to Oliphant, the students and other ballet teachers were "besotted" with Valukin; they praised his "superb" teaching and were captivated by his "magnetic personality."[52] On a political level, Valukin's visit provided a significant opportunity for both the Soviet and Canadian governments to overcome the tensions caused by the Cuban Missile Crisis. Herbert Whittaker characterized the relationship as "cultural exchange on a quiet but still potent level."[53] What emerged from Valukin's time in Toronto were the outlines of an alliance of artists that would flourish over the next decade. For example, in 1965, Betty Oliphant, dance instructor and principal of the National Ballet School, accepted an invitation to visit Moscow and Leningrad. The visit provided Oliphant with a rare opportunity to study Russian dance instruction first hand and to rekindle her friendship and working partnership with Valukin. As different as each teacher was in terms of their training styles and approaches, each emerged from the exchanges as passionate advocates for ballet exchanges between Canada and the Soviet Union.

Such exchanges were highly significant from an artistic standpoint. There is little debate among historians of Canadian ballet that the artistic influence of Valukin helped the National Ballet achieve a new level of artistic recognition, both domestically and internationally. The "Russian invasion" revitalized the National's repertoire and introduced the techniques and style that had made Russian ballet dancers so successful on the world stage. But the relationship was not a one-way street. The opportunity for Ulanova and Valukin to teach in Canada provided the kind of artistic freedom that was denied to dancers in the Soviet Union. As much as Soviet bureaucrats wanted to show the West that Soviet ballet was beyond reproach, Soviet dancers and choreographers understood that exchanging ideas and techniques with Western ballet companies was the only way to keep the art of ballet evolving, on both sides of the Iron Curtain.

CONCLUSIONS

Other than amateur sports, ballet saw the greatest number of defections during the Cold War. The list featured such big names as Nureyev and Mikael Baryshnikov, who defected to Canada in 1974, along with dozens of other Soviet and Cuban dancers. Based on the number of defections, Canada could seemingly claim that its combination of free enterprise, government subsidy, and box office sales was superior to state sponsorship. The reality, however, was much more complicated. The Canada Council admitted to the poor socio-economic prospects faced by Canadian ballet dancers in 1967. "Sometimes dancers unable to afford a room have had to sleep in a corridor of the artistic director's apartment … Rehearsals have been in places where you get sweaty and where the showers are abominable. Companies have moved about in buses that boil you alive or perish you to death." Despite ballet's substandard conditions nation-wide, the council noted acidly that some Canadian dancers who had been "nurtured with awards to help their development have vanished into foreign companies, and at Christmas time they remember us with cards and a twinge of conscience."[54]

It was hardly surprising that some Canadian dancers left for greener pastures. The promise of more money, better facilities, and greater international exposure was enough to tempt any young Canadian dancer to seek out better conditions in another country. On the other hand, ballet in the Soviet Union thrived thanks to huge injections of state funds, in addition to a culture of acceptance that made dance a vital marker of national pride and prestige. In addition, ballerinas in Russia had access to a stable income, housing, and a guaranteed pension, along with the star status that was accorded members of the national ballet. While deficient human rights and political hardships made life in communist countries far from ideal, the success of the performing arts in these countries made it more difficult to describe either side as the Cold War's clear winner or loser.

In many ways, the repertoires, choreography, and the dancers themselves eschewed national definition, which complicated their role as ideological "tools." Cultural exchanges in the late 1950s and early 1960s allowed the ballet community to see itself and the art form it practised as necessarily "transnational." Neither side could claim ignorance of the improvements and evolutions in artistic expression and choreography happening on both sides of the Iron Curtain. The contacts that were made during tours of so-called enemy territory opened the door for future collaborations and the eventual transmission of ballet styles and techniques. Betty Oliphant, a former dance instructor with the National, recalled the effect of the "Russian invasion" upon the National Ballet School and the company in a special to *The Globe and Mail* in 1993. According to Oliphant, the outcome of Russian influences was a distinctive Canadian style of dance, one that drew upon both Russian and British schools. In essence, the National Ballet Company's style, aesthetics, and expression became distinctly, and inescapably, transnational.[55] Therefore, despite the Canadian and Soviet governments' attempts to use ballet exchanges as a means of obtaining tangible victories on the ideological and cultural playing fields of the Cold War, the dancers and choreographers – and techniques and styles – on both sides of the Iron Curtain refused to be labelled. In short, ballet proved stronger and more resilient than the political ideologies that had tried to contain it.

NOTES

1 "Flees Soviet, Dances in Paris," *Toronto Star*, 19 June 1961.

2 Robert Duffy, "Russian Dancer's Prodigious Leap," *Globe and Mail*, 23 June 1961.

3 Daivd Caute, *The Dancer Defects: The Struggle for Cultural Supremacy during the Cold War* (Oxford: Oxford University Press, 2003), 468.

4 Ibid.

5 Cadra Peterson McDaniel, *American-Soviet Cultural Diplomacy: The Bolshoi Ballet's American Premiere* (New York: Lexington Books, 2015), xix.

6 Jonathan Rosenberg, "'To Reach ... into the Hearts and Minds of Our

Friends:' The United States Symphonic Tours and the Cold War," in *Music and International History in the Twentieth Century*, edited by Jessica C.E. Gienow-Hecht (New York: Berghahn Books, 2015), 153.

7 Kenneth Osgood, *Total Cold War: Eisenhower's Secret Battle at Home and Abroad* (Lawrence: University of Kansas Press, 2006), 217–18.

8 Michael L. Krenn, *The History of United States Cultural Diplomacy, 1770 to the Present Day* (New York: Bloomsbury Academic, 2017), 147.

9 Ibid., 154.

10 On Canadian cultural diplomacy, see: Graham Carr, "'No Political Significance of Any Kind': Glenn Gould's Tour of the Soviet Union and the Culture of the Cold War," *Canadian Historical Review* 95 (2014): 1–29; Kailey Hansson, "An Ancillary Weapon: Cultural Diplomacy and Nation–Building in Cold War Canada, 1945–1967" (PhD diss., Queen's University, 2015). On US Cold War culture and cultural diplomacy, see: Christina Klein, *Cold War Orientalism: Asia in the Middlebrow Imagination, 1945–1961* (Berkeley: University of California Press, 2003); Penny M. Von Eschen, *Satchmo Blows Up the World: Jazz Ambassadors Play the Cold War* (Cambridge, MA: Harvard University Press, 2004); Melani McAlister, *Epic Encounters: Culture, Media, and U.S. Interests in the Middle East since 1945* (Berkeley: University of California Press, 2005); Naima Prevots, *Dance for Export: Cultural Diplomacy and the Cold War* (Hanover: University Press of New England, 1998).

11 "Internationally Recognized Artist: First Canadian to Head Ballet," *Dauphin Herald*, 27 January 1965.

12 *First Annual Report of the Canada Council, to 31 March 1958* (Ottawa: Canada Council, 1958), 22.

13 Christina Ezrahi, *Swans of the Kremlin: Ballet and Power in Soviet Russia* (Pittsburgh: University of Pittsburgh Press, 2012), 158.

14 Linda Winer, "Dance: Defections; Weighing Merits and Minuses on the Ballet Scale," *Chicago Tribune*, 23 September 1979.

15 Ezrahi, *Swans of the Kremlin*, 139.

16 Ibid., 137.

17 "The Bolshoi ... Westward in Tights," *Globe and Mail*, 25 April 1959.

18 Winer, "Dance Defections."

19 Irving Spiegel, "Bolshoi Packs Met: Cold War Mellows," *Globe and Mail*, 9 July 1962.

20 Jamie Glazov, *Canadian Policy toward Khrushchev's Soviet Union* (Montreal and Kingston: McGill-Queen's University, 2002), 84.

21 "The Bolshoi in Toronto," *Globe and Mail*, 11 June 1959.

22 Ibid.

23 Herbert Whittaker, "Bolshoi Highlights Top Each Other," *Globe and Mail*, 13 June 1959.

24 Eric Nicol, "The Lighter Side: When Russian Artists Perform Here Are We Cheering Art or Politics," *Toronto Star*, 28 December 1959.

25 P. Lockwood, "Bolshoi and Boorishness," *Globe and Mail*, 23 June 1959.

26 David Johnson, trans., *Pravda*, 22 June 1959, RG25, 10438-V-6-40, pt. 2.2, LAC.

27 David Johnson to External Affairs, 16 March 1959, RG25, 10438-V-6-40, pt. 2.1, LAC.

28 "Heart the Source of Russian Ballet Appeal?" *Winnipeg Free Press*, 20 December 1960.

29 Pat Clayton, "A Russian Ballet Adventure," *Winnipeg Free Press*, 14 July 1962.

30 Charles Taylor, "Arnold Spohr's Flight into a Fabulous Land for the Dance," *Globe and Mail*, 2 June 1962.

31 Ibid.

32 Michael Crabb, "Arnold Spohr: the Great Director," *DCD The Magazine* 54 (2002): 6.

33 Michael Crabb, *An Instinct for Success: Arnold Spohr and the Royal Winnipeg Ballet* (Toronto: Dance Collection Danse Press, 2002), 111.

34 Kathryn Thomas, "Royal Winnipeg Ballet on Tour: Three-Work Overseas Trip," *Winnipeg Free Press*, 11 September 1965.

35 David Pulver, "Royal Winnipeg Ballet at Arts Festival," *Winnipeg Free Press*, 9 October 1965.

36 "From Paris Love to Russian Silence," *Globe and Mail*, 7 December 1968.

37 Ibid.

38 Promotional newspaper, Royal Winnipeg Ballet, June 1969, RG25, 55-17-RWB, pt. 4.2, LAC.

39 "To Russia with the Royal Winnipeg Ballet."

40 Robert Ford to the Under-secretary of State for External Affairs, 8 July 1969, RG25, 55-17-RWB, pt. 4.2, LAC.

41 Crabb, *An Instinct for Success*, 113–14.

42 Alan Harvey, "Canadian Ballet Dancer Is Taking Paris By Storm," *Charlottetown Patriot*, 18 December 1963.

43 Stasia Evasuk, "The Ballerina Is Just Beat," *Toronto Telegram*, 6 July 1963.

44 "A Russian Becomes Canada's Newest Star," *Canadian Weekly*, 4 April 1964.

45 Also significant was the company's acquisition of two rare works from the Russian repertoire – the pas de six from famed Georgian ballet dancer Vakhtang Chabukiani's *Laurencia* and the pas de deux from Leonid Lavrovsky's *Walpurgis Night*. Both works played no small role in elevating the artistic stature of the National Ballet Company. See Neufeld, 111.

46 Wendy Michener, "Profile: Canadian Ordeal of a Russian Ballet Star," *Maclean's*, 15 July 1961.

47 Helen McNamara, "Samtsova: Local Talent From Kiev," *Toronto Telegram*, 28 March 1964.

48 Ibid.

49 Michener, "Canadian Ordeal."

50 As Penny Von Eschen argues, while the jazz tours were designed to counter Soviet charges of American racism, they were more successful in projecting the "optimism and vitality of black American culture throughout the globe." Rather than being instruments of the state, the jazz ambassadors crafted and championed their own message. See Von Eschen, *Satchmo Blows Up the World*.

51 Herbert Whittaker, "Ulanova at the National Ballet," *Globe and Mail*, 15 December 1962.

52 Betty Oliphant, *Miss O: My Life in Dance* (Winnipeg: Turnstone Press, 1996), 154.

53 Herbert Whittaker, "Russian Teacher Charms as He Teaches," *Globe and Mail*, 2 December 1963.

54 Ibid.

55 Betty Oliphant, "Russian Influence at the National Ballet School," *Globe and Mail*, 7 August 1993.

10

The Elephant in the Room:
Rethinking Cruise Missile Testing
and Pierre Trudeau's Peace Mission

SUSAN COLBOURN

In March 1982, news broke that the Liberal Party might allow the United States Air Force to conduct cruise missile tests at the Canadian Forces Base at Cold Lake, Alberta. The announcement divided Canadians and galvanized the Canadian peace movement, which had been mostly in hibernation since the end of protests against the Vietnam War.[1] Thousands responded, taking to the streets in record numbers to oppose the possible tests. Chanting slogans like "Don't cruisify Canada," protestors conveyed their anxieties about the prospect of nuclear war and their "fear of frying."[2] Prime Minister Pierre Trudeau, despite his support for cruise missile testing, expressed similar concerns about the possibility that a nuclear war might break out given the heightened tensions between the superpowers. "The choice we face is clear and pressing," he told a Montreal audience in November 1983. "We can without effort abandon our fate to the mindless drift toward nuclear war. Or we can gather our strength, working in good company to turn aside the forces bearing down on us, on our children, on this Earth."[3] During the winter of 1983–84, Trudeau tried to do just that. He visited sixteen countries in three months on a self-appointed Peace Mission, hoping to rebuild confidence between East and West.

Both the debates over cruise missile testing and Pierre Trudeau's ensuing Peace Mission encouraged Canadians to think about the image they wished to project of themselves and their country to the world. Taken together, the two issues highlighted traditional concerns in Canadian foreign relations: anxieties about relations with the United States and the country's related efforts to carve out a role for itself as a "middle power."[4] Canadian debates, as illustrated in the pages that follow, repeatedly returned to these ideas. In the spirit of considering a "new" Canadian international history, this chapter explores these two traditional themes and the limits thereof.

Canada's decision to test the cruise missile in the 1980s – an issue that lingered for the next decade – has predominately been situated in longer narratives about continental defence arrangements and the impact of such agreements on Canada's sovereignty.[5] Cruise missile testing fits neatly in a trajectory from the creation of the Permanent Joint Board on Defence in 1940 to the debates over ballistic missile defence in the 2000s. Similarly, Trudeau's Peace Mission can be situated in a larger narrative about the tumult of US-Canadian relations during the early 1980s, marked by squabbles over everything from Central America to Canadian economic policies. US reactions to the Trudeau Peace Mission feature prominently in scholarly treatments of the prime minister's diplomatic efforts. Even the ever-popular question – was the Peace Mission a success? – is often shaped by the assumption that the only real measure of success was whether Trudeau managed to influence Ronald Reagan's policy with a "diplomacy of constraint" for the 1980s.[6] Greg Donaghy flipped the script, suggesting that the only success that could be claimed for the initiative is that it "delighted most Canadians, reinforcing their skepticism about American claims to exclusive leadership" in the West.[7]

Certainly, the United States played a central role in Canadian debates over cruise missile testing and in Trudeau's Peace Mission, both in the initiative's framing and its reception. But, in thinking about the future of Canadian international history, these topics serve as illustrative examples of the possibilities going forward. It is tempting to focus on relations with the United States to the exclusion of other issues, returning to traditional themes in Canadian foreign relations history, such as the debates over sovereignty and continental defence. Canadian concerns in the early 1980s, be they Trudeau's diplomatic efforts or grassroots demonstrations against cruise missiles, fit in a much larger international landscape of public anxiety about the prospect of nuclear war and the bombastic rhetoric emanating from Washington following the election of Ronald Reagan. As historians increasingly turn their attention to the peace movement as a domestic, transnational, and international phenomenon, there is ample opportunity to consider Canada's relationship to these narratives.[8] In so doing, the existing literature on Canada-US relations can be contextualized by considering how Canadian views echoed or differed from those of other US allies, and Canadians' concerns about the style and substance of Washington's policies.

Much of the new international history in Canada and abroad emphasizes the need to situate the global in the local and, to be sure, Trudeau's Peace Mission is a prime showcase for this approach in the Canadian context. But historians, even international ones, must also account for domestic influences. Fredrik Logevall, as part of an influential 2009 forum in the *Journal of American History* on the study of the United States in the World, urged international historians to look inward since so much of US foreign policy is driven by domestic considerations.[9] The same can easily be said of Canada. Cruise missile testing and the Trudeau Peace Mission were domestically contentious issues, debated by a variety of actors from peace activists to politicians. The language used in these debates points to the centrality of national identity (both real and perceived) in understanding the controversies of the early 1980s.[10] Canadians across the political spectrum appealed to images of the country's foreign policy in making the case for their preferred policy. Discussions and debates invoked Canada's role as a middle power, an honest broker, and a champion of peace in the international system, from the legacies of peacekeeping to arms control and disarmament advocacy. Some Canadians harkened back to a (non-existent) tradition of national neutrality, while others highlighted the country's fundamentally Western orientation. Each of these images reflected a long-simmering debate over Canada's role in the world, a debate that was intimately linked to the way Canadians saw themselves and how they wished to be seen in the world. Ultimately, as in so many other instances, the influence that many Canadians envisioned for themselves in the world in the early 1980s tended to be out of step with the realities of international affairs and with how Canada's role was perceived from the outside.[11]

CRUISE CONTROL

Anti-nuclear protestors often described cruise missile testing as something fundamentally un-Canadian. Canada should "refuse the cruise [and] show the Canadian spirit," as one Vancouver protestor put it.[12] If Canada agreed to test the cruise missile, critics charged that the country would abandon its traditional role as an advocate for arms control and disarmament.[13] Accepting the tests would be, in the words of the United Auto Workers' Canadian director Bob White, "destroying whatever credibility Canada has with other nations as an advocate of an end to the insane buildup of military power."[14] Canadian anti-nuclear activists tended to view the choice as black and white. If Trudeau agreed to let the United States test the cruise missile in Canada, he would be "an accomplice" helping to perpetuate the nuclear arms race. "In effect," as one activist charged, "we will be telling the world that we support the Reagan administration's suicidal nuclear policies."[15]

Trudeau and his cabinet justified the cruise missile tests as part of Canada's responsibilities as a member of NATO. Canada was "unique among [the] Western allies." It had the physical space, terrain, and climate to conduct "realistic" tests of the cruise missile's guidance system.[16] Put another way, western Canada's wide open spaces and snow-covered ground resembled parts of the Soviet Union, a fact that did not escape Soviet officials and propagandists.[17] Canada's transatlantic responsibilities became the Trudeau government's common refrain. Behind the scenes, Trudeau's cabinet remained divided on the testing issue.[18] But for the prime minister, the choice was a simple one: either Canada agreed to test the cruise missile or the country should leave NATO entirely.[19]

Trudeau's government justified testing with NATO's 1979 Dual-Track Decision, the alliance's commitment to modernize allied theatre nuclear forces while simultaneously pursuing arms control talks with the Soviet Union. In real terms, the Dual-Track Decision meant that the United States would deploy Pershing IIs and ground-launched cruise missiles to Western Europe (collectively referred to as intermediate-range nuclear forces or INF), and it would be Washington who negotiated with Moscow. Protestors explicitly linked their objections to a global struggle against the arms race: "Canadians must join with the millions world-wide who are demanding an end to this military madness!," one demonstration flyer announced.[20] "Refuse the cruise," the protestors' slogan of choice, linked Canadian activists to their counterparts in the United States and Western Europe seeking to prevent the INF deployments in the fall of 1983.

Opponents of cruise missile testing largely dismissed Trudeau's references to transatlantic obligations. "It is a bilateral agreement between

Canada and the United States; it is not part of Canada's role in NATO," the Canadian Disarmament Information Service succinctly put it.[21] A decision in favour of the tests reflected, in the words of long-time peace activist Ursula Franklin, nothing less than the "economic and political complicity of Canada as a US client state."[22] These critics had a point: the tests themselves would be handled as a bilateral matter. When the tests did ultimately go ahead, a joint Canada-US test team observed each of the tests, and communications plans divided public relations responsibilities between agencies on both sides of the border.[23] Trudeau's transatlantic appeals were accordingly dismissed as nothing more than a transparent ploy to change the conversation.[24]

Both the protestors and Pierre Trudeau knew cruise missile testing was more than a bilateral question. Even as they disagreed and debated relations with the United States, they tapped into a global conversation about the dangers of nuclear weapons. Canadian conversations bore clear similarities to those taking place across the West. By virtue of the US security guarantee, NATO's structures singled out the United States for criticism. The structure of the Dual-Track Decision did little to diminish these concerns: the United States shouldered the primary burden for deploying INF and for the success (or the failure) of the INF talks. Perceptions of Ronald Reagan and his foreign policy only stoked fears. His loose talk about nuclear weapons, his anti-communist rhetoric, and his emphasis on increasing defence spending were all seen as evidence of the administration's desire to fight – and win – a war with the Soviet Union. Reagan's policies in Central America, which were deeply unpopular in Canada, led some to conclude that the administration was blinded by an obsession with communism.[25]

Trudeau's earlier policies had stoked the Canadian public's desire for "a distinct Canadian foreign policy which gives expression to Canadian values and aspirations."[26] To be distinct often meant being distinct from the United States. The Third Option, which had been adopted by the Trudeau government in 1972, tried to diversify the country's trade, moving away from its reliance on the United States and introducing measures to protect Canadian culture. Launched in 1980, the National Energy Program looked to increase Canadian ownership of the energy sector, meaning, in real terms, a corresponding decrease in US ownership. The Foreign Investment Review Agency, set up in 1973, screened potential foreign investors in Canada, most of whom came from the United States. Together, these policies spelled

out a more nationalist outlook, a reflection of public attitudes during
the era.[27] Trudeau visibly broke with the United States on several foreign policy issues, such as recognizing the People's Republic of China
and visiting Fidel Castro's Cuba. Agreeing to test the cruise missile
seemed a complete about-face from these efforts to develop a more
independent, home-grown foreign policy. Trudeau's government, Project Ploughshares's Ernie Regehr wrote, seemed to have "forfeited the
role of formulating an indigenous national security policy." "We're acting as a branch plant of the Pentagon," one protestor remarked, borrowing the language of economic nationalism.[28]

Cruise missile testing clearly played on Canadian anxieties about
the United States and its ability to shape Canadian policy. Concerns
about outsized US influence could be seen, as much of the existing literature illustrates, in debates over bilateral defence cooperation and
the preservation of Canadian sovereignty dating back to 1940.[29] In
one *Financial Post* column debunking the "fallacies" surrounding
cruise missile testing, David Frum, then a young neoconservative
political activist, clarified that cruise missile testing was not a viola-
tion of Canadian independence.[30] Yet the perception of Canadian
subservience persisted. After Vice President George H.W. Bush visited
Ottawa in March 1983, one political cartoon (figure 10.1) showed the
prime minister handing over a "parting gift": the keys for the weapons
testing range at Primrose Lake.[31] Existing scholarship, too, displays
the same fears: on the very first page of John Clearwater's *"Just Dummies": Cruise Missile Testing in Canada*, he argues that "the structure of
politics and the military in Canada is set up to serve the military
requirements of the United States."[32]

Before Bush's visit to Ottawa, the Canadian ambassador in Washington, Allan Gotlieb, warned him that the press would likely
describe his trip "as an exercise in arm-twisting." Bush, having made
the rounds in Western Europe to address public opposition to the INF
deployments, quipped that he was already used to it.[33] Once in
Ottawa, Bush faced a hostile audience. Secretary of State for External
Affairs Allan MacEachen, looking to improve his own political position for the post-Trudeau era, invited those members of cabinet
opposed to the tests to meet with Bush. Trudeau's insistence that
Canada test the cruise missile, Gotlieb wrote in his diary, ended Liberal plans to use the issue to secure another electoral mandate. The
logic was simple: if Trudeau accepted the tests, he could not be "a
super-peacenik sticking it to the Yanks."[34]

Figure 10.1   And as a Parting Gift to you, Mr Vice-President, Here's the Key to Primrose Lake!

Throughout the spring of 1983, Trudeau pointed to the hypocrisy of many protestors. "They're eager to take refuge under the American umbrella," he wrote in an open letter to Canadians, "but don't want to hold it up."[35] Trudeau returned to this theme in a "fireside" chat with the *Toronto Star*, reminding readers of his record on nuclear issues. He appreciated and shared their concerns about the dangers of nuclear war, but opposition to cruise missile testing went beyond these legitimate fears. Much of the opposition reflected, in Trudeau's estimation, an underlying anti-American sentiment made worse by Reagan. "They are demonstrating against what they see as the policy of an American president who has, rightly or wrongly, been perceived as warlike or hostile against the Soviet Union that he can't be trusted," Trudeau argued.[36] "Prime Minister Trudeau," the Toronto Disarmament Network responded, "either misunderstands the issues involved in the question of cruise testing, or else he is deliberately attempting to mislead the Canadian public."[37] What Trudeau understood was that his support for US cruise missile testing blackened his record as anti-nuclear campaigner and hurt his popularity with many of the leftward leaning Canadian nationalists whose views he had long championed. It was no surprise, then, that he launched a peace initiative meant to burnish his reputation at home.

TRUDEAU ON TOUR

On 15 July 1983, Trudeau's government officially announced that the cruise missile tests would go ahead. "The decision surprises no one," that night's report on CBC's *The National* opined, "but it's still filled with controversy."[38] But Trudeau's support for the tests did not mean that the prime minister and his advisors failed to appreciate the public's broader concerns about the nuclear arms race and the prospect of nuclear war.

Already, on an April 1983 visit to Washington, Trudeau emphasized the damage caused by Reagan's bombastic, anti-Soviet tone. When the time came to make a final decision on the cruise missile tests, he told Vice President Bush, evidence of the administration's commitment to arms control would matter.[39] Canadians, like citizens throughout the Atlantic alliance, needed to be convinced that Reagan intended to negotiate with the Soviets in earnest. After the government announced its final decision to test the missiles that July, MacEachen sent a clear message to George Shultz, Reagan's secretary of state: "Now that we have agreed to participate in the development of a major weapons system we believe that Canada has an even greater obligation to join in the search for a secure peace."[40]

Addressing an audience at the University of Guelph on 27 October 1983, Trudeau followed through on that promise. He warned of the "dangerously confrontational" relationship that had emerged between the Cold War superpowers and lamented the current "rhythm of crisis" in global affairs. The events of the preceding few weeks – the Soviet downing of a passenger aircraft, Korean Airlines flight 007; the bombing of US and French outposts in Beirut, Lebanon; and the US invasion of Grenada – all underscored Trudeau's central message about the need for peace:

> The risk of accident or miscalculation is too great for us not to begin to repair the lines of communication with our adversaries. The level of tension is too high for us not to revive a more constructive approach to the containment of crises. The degree of

mutual mistrust is too intense for us not to try to re-build confidence through active political contact and consultation.

He reaffirmed the principles laid out in the G7's Williamsburg Declaration that May, promising again "to devote our full political resources to reducing the threat of war."[41]

After kicking off his Peace Mission in Guelph, Trudeau travelled to Western Europe. There, the prime minister hoped he might be able to "encourage his NATO friends and allies to engage themselves in the search for a more confident peace" and to create the conditions for greater dialogue in East-West relations.[42] Trudeau then gave a speech in Montreal, expanding on his peace initiative by laying out a series of concrete arms control and disarmament proposals. He called for a five-power conference of the nuclear weapons states, and measures to strengthen the Non-Proliferation Treaty.[43] Above all, Trudeau's team hoped the speech would convey the prime minister's optimism, confidence, and ability to make a difference: as one aide wrote, Trudeau "had the MO" and he "ain't alone" in his concerns.[44] Trudeau's globe-trotting continued. Before November was through, the prime minister made stops in Tokyo, Dhaka, New Delhi (for the Commonwealth Heads of Government Meeting), and Beijing. He headed to Washington in December and then to Prague, East Berlin, and Bucharest early in the new year.

Trudeau received broad statements of support at stop after stop – hardly surprising, as few politicians go on the record to speak out against peace – but his specific proposals met considerable opposition. Not one of the five countries implicated in his proposed conference of nuclear powers, for instance, supported the plan.[45] The CIA's Ottawa station chief reported that "Canadian jokes" were now commonplace in the corridors at NATO headquarters.[46] Some setbacks were self-inflicted bureaucratic mix-ups. After Trudeau's stops in Eastern Europe, a member of the prime minister's task force on the peace initiative, Gary Smith, was dispatched to brief Bonn on the talks. When Smith added a stop in Paris to his itinerary, Ottawa entirely overlooked the possibility of adding a stop in London. The oversight left the Foreign and Commonwealth Office "smarting" over being briefed by their French counterparts about an initiative undertaken by a fellow member of the Commonwealth.[47]

Trudeau returned from Eastern Europe to announce an end to his peace initiative in February 1984. Wrapping up his Peace Mission before the House of Commons, Trudeau pointed to a series of new, promising signs that had emerged in the West: British Prime Minister Margaret Thatcher's recent visit to Hungary, the moderate tone of Reagan's 16 January 1984 address (his now-famous "Ivan and Anya" speech), and NATO's recent calls for "a balanced and constructive relationship and for genuine détente" with the East.[48] He optimistically noted the multilateral talks now underway in Stockholm, the Conference on Confidence- and Security-Building Measures in Europe. All of these recent developments contributed to his central objective of building confidence between East and West in the hopes of stabilizing the Cold War.[49] Having (albeit tenuously) declared his Peace Mission a success, Trudeau topped the whole thing off with a trip to the Soviet Union for Soviet General Secretary Iuriĭ Andropov's funeral and talks with his successor, Konstantin Chernenko.

THE TYRANNY OF GEOGRAPHY

When Trudeau launched the Peace Mission, sticking it to Washington was certainly how many interpreted the prime minister's initiative. The US Embassy in Ottawa dismissed it as an attempt to "stir up anti-Americanism" prior to the next federal election campaign. They likened the current state of Canada-US relations to the infamous Johnson-Pearson showdown after Pearson's 1965 speech at Temple University. Once again, the Canadians were "pissing in their garden."[50] Similar criticisms could be heard at home, too. "I noted with interest that his activities are applauded by the anti-cruise groups and other movements hostile to the United States," one concerned citizen wrote to MacEachen.[51]

Geography made – and still makes – the United States a near-constant presence in Canada and its history. Activists in British Columbia certainly understood these realities when they demonstrated against US Trident nuclear submarines stationed just over the border in Bangor, Washington.[52] But Canadian anxieties about the United States can diminish other significant connections and influences. Canadian debates over nuclear questions in the early 1980s took place under Washington's long shadow. Critics of the Trudeau government's decision to allow the cruise missile tests accused the prime minister of being too close to the United States and a handmaiden to US militarism and imperialism. Trudeau's invocations of transatlantic obligations were dismissed as mere eyewash. Instead, conversations about cruise missile testing were dominated by perceptions of the United States – and in particular, Reagan's foreign policy – as bombastic and dangerous. Trudeau's Peace Mission, clearly inspired by the contentious domestic debates over cruise missile testing, reflected similar concerns about Washington's approach to the Cold War.

There are numerous other avenues that can and should be considered alongside these bilateral questions. Former West German chancellor Helmut Schmidt, to give one such example, played a central role in convincing Trudeau of the need to approve cruise missile testing.[53] Disentangling the global, the transatlantic, and the bilateral is difficult, if not impossible. Observers in the Reagan White House, for instance, concluded that most Canadians almost completely equated NATO and the United States.[54] Perceptions of the United States mattered, but so too did Ottawa's transatlantic connections. Telling an entangled, intertwined history of the two illustrates the competing visions that Canadians had of their role in the world, both real and idealized.[55]

Thinking about the future of Canadian international history is not just about moving away from the debates of the past. The controversies over cruise missile testing and Trudeau's Peace Mission cannot be discussed without some reference to the United States or to anti-Americanism as a potent force in Canadian politics. But these issues can and should be situated in a broader landscape.

Most anti-nuclear demonstrations in Canada, at least the majority of those recorded and archived, occurred in large urban centres. Sheer numbers helped protests make the headlines. Some city dwellers may have been self-interested, given that missiles would target these urban centres, but considerable controversy also surrounded the cruise missile testing site itself. *The Nuclear North*, published in 1983, highlighted the potential damage to Indigenous populations living in the sparsely populated area. Activists seized the opportunity, using the cruise missile tests and the contested boundaries on the testing site to draw attention to ongoing land claims disputes.[56]

Canadian fears about the possibility of nuclear war were stoked by popular culture that transcended borders. Like tens of millions of Americans, they watched a nuclear attack destroy Lawrence, Kansas, in the made-for-TV movie *The Day After*, and like millions of people across the world, they listened to the West German pop group Nena sing about an accidental nuclear strike triggered by ninety-nine red balloons.[57] Canadians, too, contributed to this body of work: for instance, *If You Love This Planet*, an Oscar award-winning film about the dangers of the arms race, was produced by the National Film Board.[58] Many of those who spoke out against cruise missile testing operated in a transnational milieu, swapping tactics, slogans, and arguments. Others took an interest in Canada's peace movement: during one 1983 stop in Toronto, E.P. Thompson, the co-author of the 1980 *Appeal for European Nuclear Disarmament* (and prominent historian), encouraged the Canadian movement and appealed to Canada's role as the first non-proliferator as a source of legitimacy.[59] Furthermore, Canadian activists can be situated in larger narratives about the role of gender in shaping anti-nuclear activism, considering the Canadian peace group Voice of Women alongside the advocacy of the Australian campaigner Dr Helen Caldicott or the Women's Peace Camp at Greenham Common in the United Kingdom. Similar connections can be drawn out regarding students, unionized labour, religious organizations, and scientists.

Trudeau can also be situated in a broader trend. He was far from the only political leader concerned about the lack of dialogue between East and West in 1983–84. Canadian efforts to reduce Cold War tensions were one initiative among many. High-ranking Australian, British, French, and West German officials, for example, all headed to Moscow in the summer of 1984 to try and cultivate a more constructive dialogue between East and West.[60] The group Parliamentarians for World Order called on a number of world leaders – including Trudeau – to form "a peace team" to push for a two-year moratorium on missile deployments.[61] Trudeau declined, but the Five Continent Peace Initiative went ahead without him, insisting that "peace is too important to be left to the White House and the Kremlin."[62] All of these connections reinforce the point that Trudeau's Peace Mission was not simply an isolated Canadian response to the dangers of the late Cold War, designed (depending on one's perspective and level of cynicism) to salvage his reputation, irritate the Americans, or chart a course to reduce international tensions. Trudeau's efforts cannot be understood in isolation; without the global context of nuclear fears and worried politicians, Trudeau's diplomacy risks being seen as either a prescient Canadian corrective or a diplomatic wildcard.

PEARSON'S LONG SHADOW

Like so many Canadian prime ministers, Pierre Trudeau was forced to wrestle with the legacy of Lester Pearson, Canada's Nobel Peace Prize-winning foreign minister (1948–57) and later prime minister (1963–68).[63] Prior to entering politics, Trudeau famously referred to Pearson as the "defrocked priest of peace" after he agreed to accept US BOMARC missiles, nuclear warheads and all, in 1963.[64] Having decried Pearson's plans to accept US nuclear weapons on Canadian soil and pushing to denuclearize the Canadian Forces, Trudeau ended his own career by accepting US missiles – though, as Trudeau's team reminded critics, these missiles were not armed with nuclear warheads during testing. The Peace Mission illustrated the same shift in Trudeau's foreign policy, which Robert Bothwell and J.L. Granatstein dubbed his "pirouette."[65] By undertaking the Peace Mission, the journalist Michael Valpy wrote the day after Trudeau's Guelph speech, "he has taken up the role of international political craftsmanship that he so scorned 15 and 20 years ago when former Prime Minister Pearson played that part." "Echoes of Pearson," the headline read.[66] Comparisons to the Suez Crisis were commonplace, too, in the winter of 1983–84. CBC's *The Journal*, reporting on Trudeau's Peace Mission following the prime minister's December stop in Washington, showed footage of Lester Pearson addressing the United Nations. "Not since the Suez Crisis," the broadcast went on, "has Canada tried to play such a mediating role."[67] And just as Pearson's approach proved controversial, so too did Trudeau's search for peace.

Some derided the Trudeau peace initiative as naive and poorly conceived. His stops east of the Iron Curtain aroused particular concern, not least from Eastern European diasporic communities and organizations within Canada.[68] One constituent letter, penned after Trudeau's stops in Czechoslovakia, the German Democratic Republic, and Romania, put it bluntly: "I would like to know if you honestly feel that countries with a foreign power's tanks stationed in their forests have any real chance of influencing that foreign power, or are we to take your remark in the spirit of good honest fun that this latest joke by the Prime Minister is meant?"[69] To many, the peace initiative seemed nothing more than a public relations stunt or a last hurrah before Trudeau retired, this time for good.[70] But to the prime minister and his supporters, the Peace Mission would improve

Trudeau's legacy, and perhaps even secure the next Canadian Nobel Peace Prize.[71] Even the French foreign ministry viewed Trudeau's Peace Mission in these terms.[72]

The Liberals' rhetoric often relied on Pearson's earlier achievements to frame current policy. When Allan MacEachen addressed the Committee on Disarmament in February 1983, he opened his remarks by recalling Pearson's acceptance speech for the 1957 Nobel Peace Prize. Pearson had warned of the problems inherent in the nuclear age: "a choice between peace and extinction." These problems, MacEachen argued, had only increased in the intervening decades.[73] Activists appealed to the same Pearsonian legacies of peacekeeping and peace-making. "Canada's role as a peacekeeper may never have been quite so significant as Mr Pearson's Nobel Prize and Canadian folklore suggest," Ernie Regehr wrote in July 1982, "but it remains a prominent element within Canadian mythology – a myth that becomes increasingly difficult to sustain in the face of alliance politics and defence policies."[74] At the University of Toronto, students arranged a mock funeral to demonstrate against the cruise missile, asking attendees to dress in head-to-toe black to mourn "the death of Canada as a peacemaker."[75]

It is hardly novel to suggest that Canada's peacekeeping past and its commitment to internationalism – real or imagined, "Pearsonian" or not – shaped the country's national identity. Canadian nostalgia for the so-called golden age of diplomacy is well-chronicled, as is the affection for peacekeeping as part of Canadians' "genetic code."[76] Pearson's Suez solution, however, was fundamentally Western in orientation, motivated by concerns about allied unity.[77] These transatlantic elements were certainly contested in the early 1980s. Placards and flyers called for Canada to get out of NATO and NORAD. One Toronto highschooler pointed to the cruise missile as "a tool of Reagan" to unify NATO. Camping in Queen's Park, he was "willing to get arrested to protest the Orwellian super-country of NATO."[78] Others suggested that cruise missile testing would violate an image of Canadian neutrality. "Canada has always been able to remain neutral in the eyes of the world," one schoolteacher in Grand Centre, Alberta put it.[79] Statements like these ignored the realities of Canada's past, to be sure, but illustrated a desire to reframe Canada's role in the world that animated many peace activists.

Critics accused Pierre Trudeau of the same neutralist tendencies. His frequent, critical remarks about Reagan's foreign policy suggested some sort of equidistance between the two Cold War superpowers.

US officials resented Trudeau's willingness to blame both the Soviet Union and the United States for the poor state of East-West relations. Brian Mulroney, the leader of the Progressive Conservatives, objected to Trudeau's Peace Mission on similar grounds. While he supported the initiative's overarching goals, Mulroney accused Trudeau of presenting Canada as "a sort of neutral observer," rather than a member of the Western Alliance.[80] "We are prepared to accept neither the inexorable Finlandization of Europe nor a neutralist Canada," the future prime minister insisted.[81]

CONCLUSION

Given the hold that both ideas have on conceptions of Canadian foreign policy, it is not particularly groundbreaking to suggest that Canada's relations with the United States and the contested legacies of its Pearsonian past were up for debate in the early 1980s. But, as the cruise missile test debates and the Trudeau Peace Mission illustrate, they are only one part of the story.

Pierre Trudeau's Peace Mission involved stops across the globe, not just in Washington. Few of the existing studies have made use of relevant archival materials to consider other perspectives on the Trudeau Peace Mission, leaving ample left to be considered and reconsidered.[82] Trudeau's actual proposals were wide-ranging, part of a larger effort on the part of his government to reduce the nuclear menace. Canadian policy-makers prided themselves on the few inroads that the Peace Mission proposals did make. Ideas from Trudeau's "decalogue" of principles, some argued, inspired West German foreign minister Hans-Dietrich Genscher's public statements on East-West relations in the spring of 1984 and NATO's Washington Declaration on the same subject.[83]

For all the international connections, the domestic ones are just as significant: the way many Canadians thought about and debated cruise missile testing and the Trudeau Peace Mission ultimately began at home. Liberal Party strategists were keen to burnish their nationalist credentials (particularly when this meant striking a different chord from Reagan's belligerence), whereas Brian Mulroney saw the Peace Mission as a prime example of the Trudeau government's failures, especially in managing Ottawa's relations with its NATO allies. Anti-nuclear activists, too, saw clear domestic political implications. Some interpreted Trudeau's whirlwind diplomacy as nothing more than an attempt to undermine the peace movement, given its recent resurgence.[84]

Cruise missile testing and Pierre Trudeau's Peace Mission reflected the messy "intermestic" realities of foreign policy, as they were bound up in local, national, and global politics simultaneously. At their core, though, were near-existential questions about Canada's identity. What was Canada's role in the world and what should it be? Were Canadians complicit in what some deemed the "containment militarism" of the Reagan administration?[85] Should Canada seek out a role as a helpful fixer? There were countless answers to these questions in the early 1980s, as now. But the sheer frequency with which Canadians appealed to foreign policy traditions and images of Canada's role in the world as they debated cruise missile testing and assessed Trudeau's peace initiative is telling in its own right. Conversations over these issues were often marked by emotional appeals to both the past and the future, as foreign policy served as yet another arena in which Canadians might shape their desired image of Canada.

And what of a "new" Canadian international history? Here, cruise missile testing, the Peace Mission, and the intersections between the two offer a crucial reminder. Not all histories need be "undiplomatic." If we envision the field's future as one of Canada and the World, this approach should not simply toss out the old in favour of the new. Instead, it can enable the so-called traditional issues of diplomatic history – high politics, economic issues, and security questions – to be part of a broader dialogue about Canada (and Canadians) in the world.

NOTES

1 One December 1983 poll showed an almost even split: 48.6 per cent of respondents insisted that Canada must test the cruise missile, while 49.9 per cent thought the country should not. Decima Quarterly 16, 16 December 1983.

2 *Pacific Tribune* photograph, "End the Arms Race rally against cruise testing, Robson Square," 23 July 1983, *Pacific Tribune* Photograph Collection, Simon Fraser University Archive (SFUA), http://digital.lib.sfu.ca/pt-2536/end-arms-race-rally-against-cruise-testing-robson-square; *Pacific Tribune* photograph, "End the Arms Race march against cruise missile, Jericho Park to Vanier Park," 22 October 1983, *Pacific Tribune* Photograph Collection, SFUA, http://digital.lib.sfu.ca/pt-2771/end-arms-race-march-against-cruise-missile-jericho-park-vanier-park.

3 Pierre Trudeau, "A Global Initiative to Improve the Prospects for Peace," 13
   November 1983, Department of External Affairs, *Statements and Speeches*,
   no. 82/20.
4 Petra Dolata recently named two traditional perspectives in understanding
   Canada's place in the world: its relations with the United States and its multilateral, "middle power" approach: Dolata, "Canada and/in the World,"
   Canadian Journal of Political Science/Revue canadienne de science politique 50,
   no. 1 (2017): 351.
5 Brian Bow, "Defence Dilemmas: Continental Defence from Bomarc to
   BMD," *Canadian Foreign Policy Journal* 15, no. 1 (2009): 40–59; J.L. Granatstein, "Staring into the Abyss," in *Towards a New World: Readings in the Histo-
   ry of Canadian Foreign Policy,* edited by J.L. Granatstein (Toronto: Copp
   Clark Pitman, 1992), 53; Patrick Lennox, *At Home and Abroad: The Canada-
   US Relationship and Canada's Place in the World* (Vancouver: UBC Press,
   2009), 56–70.
6 Adam Bromke and Kim Richard Nossal, "Trudeau Rides the 'Third Rail,'"
   International Perspectives (May/June 1984): 1; Beth A. Fischer, "The Trudeau
   Peace Initiative and the End of the Cold War: Catalyst or Coincidence?,"
   International Journal 49, no. 3 (1994): 613–34; Richard Gwyn and Sandra
   Gwyn, "The Politics of Peace," *Saturday Night* (May 1984), 30. On the "diplomacy of constraint," see Denis Stairs, *The Diplomacy of Constraint: Canada,
   the Korean War, and the United States* (Toronto: University of Toronto Press,
   1974), and Timothy Andrews Sayle, "A Pattern of Constraint: Canadian-
   American Relations in the Early Cold War," *International Journal* 62, no. 3
   (2007): 689–705.
7 Greg Donaghy, "The 'Ghost of Peace': Pierre Trudeau's Search for Peace,
   1982–84," *Peace Research* 39, nos. 1–2 (2007): 39.
8 For some of the recent literature on anti-nuclear activism in the 1980s, see
   Eckart Conze, Martin Klimke, and Jeremy Varon, *Nuclear Threats, Nuclear
   Fear and the Cold War of the 1980s* (Cambridge: Cambridge University Press,
   2017); Kyle Harvey, *American Anti-Nuclear Activism, 1975–1990* (Houndmills:
   Palgrave Macmillan, 2014); William M. Knoblauch, *Nuclear Freeze in a Cold
   War: The Reagan Administration, Cultural Activism and the End of the Arms
   Race* (Boston: University of Massachusetts Press, 2017); Holger Nehring and
   Benjamin Ziemann, "Do All Paths Lead to Moscow? The NATO Dual-Track
   Decision and the Peace Movement – A Critique," *Cold War History* 12, no. 1
   (2012): 1–24; Leopoldo Nuti et al., eds., *The Euromissile Crisis and the End of
   the Cold War* (Washington, DC: Woodrow Wilson Center Press, 2015); Paul
   Rubinson, "The Global Effects of Nuclear Winter: Science and Antinuclear
   Protest in the United States and the Soviet Union during the 1980s," *Cold*

War History 14, no. 1 (2014): 47–69; Angela Santese, "Ronald Reagan, the Nuclear Freeze Campaign, and the Nuclear Scare of the 1980s," *The International History Review* 39, no. 3 (2016): 496–520; Giles Scott-Smith, "A Dutch Dartmouth: Ernst van Eeghen's Private Campaign to Defuse the Euromissiles Crisis," *New Global Studies* 8, no. 1 (2014): 141–52; Gerhard Wettig, "The Last Soviet Offensive in the Cold War: Emergence and Development of the Campaign Against NATO Euromissiles, 1979–1983," *Cold War History* 9, no. 1 (2009): 79–110.

9 Fredrik Logevall, "Politics and Foreign Relations," *Journal of American History* 95, no. 1 (2009): 1074–8.

10 Brett Thompson briefly alluded to the Peace Mission's connection as a debate about Canada's understanding of its place in the world. Thompson, "Pierre Elliott Trudeau's Peace Initiative: 25 Years On," *International Journal* 64, no. 4 (2009): 1137.

11 See, for other examples of this disconnect between perceptions and realities, Ryan M. Touhey, *Conflicting Visions: Canada and India in the Cold War World, 1946–76* (Vancouver: UBC Press, 2015), esp. 1–8. On the staying power of images in Canadian foreign policy more broadly, see Adam Chapnick, "The Canadian Middle Power Myth," *International Journal* 55, no. 2 (2000): 188–206.

12 *Pacific Tribune* photograph, "End the Arms Race Rally against Cruise Testing, Robson Square," 23 July 1983, *Pacific Tribune* Photograph Collection, SFUA, http://digital.lib.sfu.ca/pt-2536/end-arms-race-rally-against-cruise-testing-robson-square.

13 M.V. Naidu, "Cruise Missiles in Canada: Suffocation Through Rejuvenation?," *Peace Research* 15, no. 1 (1983): i; Science for Peace, BC Chapter, "The Cruise Missile: A Canadian Perspective," January 1983, Campaign for Nuclear Disarmament fonds, box 1, file "Science for Peace," University of Toronto Archives (UTARMS).

14 "UAW Opposes Testing of U.S. Weapons in Canada," William Ready Division of Archives and Research Collections, Canadian Peace Congress fonds, box 18, file "Other Organizations – Circulars + Printed – Cruise Missile," McMaster University Library (MUL).

15 "Network replies to Trudeau," *The Peace Calendar* 1, no. 5 (1983); Neil MacDonald, "A Deadly Missile," *The Peace Calendar* 1, no. 3 (1983).

16 "Excerpt from Communications Plan presented to Cabinet," July 1983, RG 25, vol. 18617, file 27-8-USA-3 LAC.

17 Moscow to External Affairs, "Missiles de Croisiere," 5 Nov. 1984, RG 25, vol. 18617, file 27-8-USA-3, LAC.

18 J.L. Granatstein and Robert Bothwell, *Pirouette: Pierre Trudeau and Canadian Foreign Policy* (Toronto: University of Toronto Press, 1990), 363.

19 Allan Gotlieb, *The Washington Diaries, 1981–1989* (Toronto: McClelland and Stewart, 2006), 139.

20 Flyer for 30 October 1982 demonstration, "Stop the Cruise Missile!," Canadian Peace Congress fonds, box 18, file "Demonstrations – Ottawa Oct. 30 [1982] – Cruise Missile," MUL.

21 "Network replies to Trudeau," *The Peace Calendar* 1, no. 5 (1983).

22 Franklin to Thomson, 13 February 1984, Ursula M. Franklin fonds, box 45, file "Trudeau's 1983 Peace Initiative and response from the peace community 1983–1984," UTARMS.

23 Draft US press release, "U.S. News Release to be Used on Successful Completion of Test Flight," 18 December 1985, and "ALCM Test Launch: Public Affairs Guidance," 18 December 1985, RG 25, vol. 18617, file 27-8-USA-3, LAC.

24 Harald van Riekhoff and John Sigler, "The Trudeau Peace Initiative: The Politics of Reversing the Arms Race," in *Canada Among Nations 1984: A Time of Transition*, edited by Brian W. Tomlin and Maureen Appel Molot (Toronto: Lorimer, 1985), 54.

25 A great many Canadians, it should be noted, held a largely positive view of the United States and of Canada's relations with the US during the early Reagan years. In one April 1982 poll, for example, 84.3 per cent of respondents favoured "very close" or "somewhat close" relations with the United States as being in Canada's best interests. As part of this same survey, 11.7 per cent of those polled expressed a "very favorable" view of President Reagan and an additional 40.4 per cent characterized theirs as "somewhat favorable": Environics Focus Canada 1982–83, April 1983.

26 Discussion paper, "Canada/USA Relations," July 1982, RG 25, vol. 28840, file 20-1-2-USA, LAC.

27 See Stephen Azzi, "The Nationalist Moment in English Canada," in *Debating Dissent: Canada and the 1960s*, edited by Lara A. Campbell, Dominique Clément, and Greg Kealey (Toronto: University of Toronto Press, 2012), 213–30.

28 Ernie Regehr, "The Canadian Churches Respond to Militarism," *International Review of Mission* 71, no. 283 (1982): 357; "19 Arrested at Protest Rally against Cruise Missile Plant," *Globe and Mail*, 7 August 1982.

29 Bow, "Defence Dilemmas"; Granatstein, "Staring into the Abyss"; Lennox, *At Home and Abroad*, 56–70.

30 David Frum, "'Many Fallacies over the Cruise Missile Issue," *Financial Post*, 21 May 1983.

31 Kaufmanis cartoon, 25 March 1983, LAC, online MIKAN no. 2841852.

32 John Clearwater, *"Just Dummies": Cruise Missile Testing in Canada* (Calgary: University of Calgary Press, 2006), 1. Joseph Jockel, in a review of Clearwater's book, called this "polemical overdrive": Jockel, "Review," *Scientia Canadensis* 31, nos. 1–2 (2008): 202.

33 Washington to External Affairs, "Bush Visit – Mtg with Vice President," 18 March 1983, RG 25, vol. 28591, file 20-1-2-USA, LAC.

34 Gotlieb, *Washington Diaries*, 139–40.

35 Pierre Elliott Trudeau, "Canada's Position on Testing Cruise Missiles and on Disarmament: An Open Letter to all Canadians by the Right Honourable Pierre Elliott Trudeau," 9 May 1983, Department of External Affairs, *Statements and Speeches*, no. 83/8.

36 "A 'Fireside' Chat with Trudeau," *Toronto Star*, 14 May 1983.

37 "Network Replies to Trudeau," *The Peace Calendar* 1, no. 5 (1983).

38 The National broadcast, "Cruise Missile Testing Coming to Canada," 15 July 1983, CBC Digital Archives, http://www.cbc.ca/archives/entry/1983-cruise-missile-testing-coming-to-canada.

39 Fowler memorandum, "Report of a Meeting between Prime Minister Trudeau and Vice President Bush," RG 25, vol. 28591, file 20-1-2-USA, LAC.

40 MacEachen to Shultz, 15 July 1983, RG 25, vol. 18617, file 27-8-USA-3, LAC.

41 Trudeau remarks, "Reflections on Peace and Security," 27 October 1983, Department of External Affairs, *Statements and Speeches*, no. 83/18. MacEachen made a similar reference to the Williamsburg Declaration in a July 1983 letter to Shultz: MacEachen to Shultz, 15 July 1983, RG 25, vol. 18617, file 27-8-USA-3, LAC.

42 Trudeau-Thatcher memorandum of conversation, 15 November 1983, RG 25, vol. 25337, file 28-6-1-TRUDEAU PEACE MISSION, LAC.

43 The five powers were France, the People's Republic of China, the Soviet Union, the United Kingdom, and the United States. "Notes for Remarks by the Prime Minister on Peace and Security," 13 November 1983, RG 25, vol. 25337, file 28-6-1-TRUDEAU PEACE MISSION, LAC.

44 Hancock to Fowler, "Draft PM Initiative Speech, Mtl, 13 Nov," 9 November 1983, RG 25, vol. 25337, file 28-6-1-TRUDEAU PEACE MISSION, LAC.

45 Trudeau's proposal was for a conference of the five nuclear powers recognized by the Non-Proliferation Treaty: China, France, the Soviet Union, the United Kingdom, and the United States.

46 Bartleman to Shenstone, "Canada/US Relations," 10 February 1984, RG 25, vol. 26958, file 28-6-1-TRUDEAU PEACE MISSION, LAC.

47 London to External Affairs, "PM Initiative: De-briefing on Eastern European Visit," 10 February 1984, RG 25, vol. 26958, file 28-6-1-TRUDEAU PEACE MISSION, LAC.

48 "Declaration of Brussels," 9 December 1983, Archives of the North Atlantic Treaty Organization (NATO), http://www.nato.int/cps/en/natohq /official_texts_23216.htm?.

49 Trudeau remarks, "Initiatives for Peace and Security," 9 February 1984, Department of External Affairs, *Statements and Speeches*, no. 84/2.

50 Smith to Delvoie, "PM Initiative: USA Embassy Views," 15 February 1984, RG 25, vol. 26958, file 28-6-1-TRUDEAU PEACE MISSION, LAC.

51 Kollar to MacEachen, 31 January 1984, RG 25, vol. 26958, file 28-6-1-TRUDEAU PEACE MISSION, LAC.

52 Pacific Life Community pamphlet, "From Trident to Life," Canadian Peace Congress fonds, box 9, file "Disarmament – Circulars + Printed," MUL.

53 Pierre Elliott Trudeau, *Memoirs* (Toronto: McClelland and Stewart, 1993), 334; Sheldon Gordon, "Cruise Missile Test Vital, Schmidt Says," *Globe and Mail*, 17 May 1983.

54 Memorandum for Steiner, "Canadian Attitudes towards NATO," Dennis C. Blair Files, RAC box 4, file Public Diplomacy 1982 (09/1981-02/1982), Ronald Reagan Presidential Library (RRPL).

55 Bow and Chapnick make a similar argument in their recent survey on the study and teaching of Canada-US relations, suggesting that scholars consider the connections between bilateral relations and broader global dynamics: Brian Bow and Adam Chapnick, "Teaching Canada-US Relations: Three Great Debates," *International Journal* 71, no. 2 (2001): 311.

56 Carole Giangrande, *The Nuclear North: The People, the Regions, and the Arms Race* (Toronto: House of Anansi Press, 1983); P. Whitney Lackenbauer, *Battle Grounds: The Canadian Military and Aboriginal Lands* (Vancouver: UBC Press, 2011), 214.

57 Nena's "99 Red Balloons" spent twenty-two weeks on the top singles charts in 1984: "RPM Weekly," 2 June 1984, RPM vol. 40, no. 13, Item No. 3971, LAC.

58 National Film Board of Canada, "If You Love This Planet," available at: https://www.nfb.ca/film/if_you_love_this_planet/.

59 Beth Richards, "E.P. Thompson Tells Toronto Audience: Canada Can Be Leader," *The Peace Calendar* 1, no. 8 (1983).

60 Simon Miles, "Engaging the 'Evil Empire': East-West Relations in the Second Cold War," (PhD diss., University of Texas at Austin, 2017), 217–35.

61 The proposed team included Indian prime minister Indira Gandhi, Swedish prime minister Olof Palme, Tanzanian president Julius Nyerere, Greek prime minister Andreas Papandreou, general secretary of the Romanian Communist Party Nicolae Ceauşescu, Mexican president Miguel de la Madrid, and Trudeau: DMF to IDDZ, "PM's Initiative: The Future," 11 February 1984, RG 25, vol. 26958, file 28-6-1-TRUDEAU PEACE MISSION, LAC.

62 Olafur Grimsson and Nicholas Dunlop, "Indira Gandhi and the Five Conti-
nent Initiative," *Bulletin of the Atomic Scientists* 41, no. 1 (1985): 46; Lawrence
S. Wittner, *The Struggle against the Bomb, Volume 3, Toward Nuclear Abolition:
A History of the World Nuclear Disarmament Movement, 1971 to the Present*
(Stanford: Stanford University Press, 2003), 310.

63 On Pearson's legacy, see Asa McKercher and Galen Roger Perras, "Introduc-
tion: Lester Pearson and Canadian External Affairs," in *Mike's World: Lester
B. Pearson and Canadian External Affairs*, edited by Asa McKercher and Galen
Roger Perras (Vancouver: UBC Press, 2017), 3–23.

64 Pierre Elliott Trudeau, "Pearson ou l'Abdication de l'Espirit," *Cite Libre*
(Apr. 1963): 7.

65 Granatstein and Bothwell, *Pirouette*.

66 Michael Valpy, "Echoes of Pearson," *Globe and Mail*, 28 October 1983.

67 The Journal broadcast, "Pierre Trudeau's Push for Cold War Peace,"
15 December 1983, CBC Digital Archives,
http://www.cbc.ca/archives/entry/trudeaus-push-for-cold-war-peace.

68 Corn and Boucek to Trudeau, 19 January 1984, RG 25, vol. 26958, file 28-6-1-
TRUDEAU PEACE MISSION, LAC.

69 Schindler to MacEachen, 7 February 1984, RG 25, vol. 26958, file 28-6-1-
TRUDEAU PEACE MISSION, LAC.

70 John Gray, "Desperation an Ingredient of Trudeau's Peace Mission," *Globe
and Mail*, 28 November 1983.

71 The prospect of another Canadian Nobel Peace Prize weighed heavily. "I've
been working for Canada in and around its foreign policy for almost thirty
years, and we are still searching for a Canadian role or, more accurately, the
big Canadian initiative, the one that's going to win our minister, whoever
he is, a Nobel Peace Prize," Gotlieb wrote in his diary in December 1985:
Gotlieb, *Washington Diaries*, 339.

72 MAE memorandum, "La mission de paix de M. Trudeau," 2 January 1984,
1930INVA/5643, file "Canada," Archives Diplomatiques (AD).

73 MacEachen remarks, "Mutual Security: Negotiations in 1983," 1 February
1983, Department of External Affairs, *Statements and Speeches*, no. 83/1, 1.

74 Ernie Regehr, "The Canadian Churches Respond to Militarism," *International Review of Mission* 71, no. 283 (1982): 357.

75 U of T Campaign for Nuclear Disarmament/United Campuses to Prevent
Nuclear War letter to members, 28 January 1983, Campaign for Nuclear
Disarmament fonds, box 001, file "Corresp.," UTARMS.

76 Carol Off, *The Lion, The Fox, and the Eagle: A Story of Generals and Justice in
Yugoslavia and Rwanda* (Toronto: Random House Canada, 2000), 2. Countless works have been written on internationalism in Canadian foreign poli-

cy and its ties to Pearson. Stephen Harper's tenure did nothing to stem this tide, nor did Justin Trudeau's 2015 assertions that "we're back." For some recent examples, see: Colin McCullough, *Creating Canada's Peacekeeping Past* (Vancouver: UBC Press, 2016); Hector Mackenzie, "Golden Decade(s)? Reappraising Canada's International Relations in the 1940s and 1950s," *British Journal of Canadian Studies* 23, no. 2 (2010): 179–206; Roland Paris, "Are Canadians Still Liberal Internationalists? Foreign Policy and Public Opinion in the Harper Era," *International Journal* 69, no. 3 (2014): 303–6; Claire Turenne Sjolander, "Through the Looking Glass: Canadian Identity and the War of 1812," *International Journal* 69, no. 2 (2014): 155–7.

77 Gerald Wright, "Managers, Innovators and Diplomats: Canada's Foreign Ministers," in *Canada among Nations 2008: 100 Years of Canadian Foreign Policy*, edited by Robert Bothwell and Jean Daudelin (Montreal and Kingston: McGill-Queen's University Press, 2009), 64.

78 John Pendegrast, "A Concrete Vacation," *The Peace Calendar* 1, no. 7 (1983).

79 Larry Donovan, "US Cruise Missile Gets Rough Ride in Western Canada," *The Christian Science Monitor*, 25 January 1983.

80 Transcript, "CBC The National – 09 February 1984 Prime Minister Trudeau's Peace Initiative," 10 February 1984, RG 25, vol. 26958, file 28-6-1-TRUDEAU PEACE MISSION, LAC.

81 External Affairs to all posts, "PM Initiative: House of Commons Debate 9 Feb," 10 February 1984, RG 25, vol. 26958, file 28-6-1-TRUDEAU PEACE MISSION, LAC.

82 I have written at greater length elsewhere about the connections between the Peace Mission and transatlantic relations in the early 1980s. See Susan Colbourn, "'Cruising toward Nuclear Danger': Canadian Anti-Nuclear Activism, Pierre Trudeau's Peace Mission, and the Transatlantic Partnership," *Cold War History* 18, no. 1 (2018): 19–36. There are also ample things that might be reconsidered from the Canadian perspective as well. Records at Library and Archives Canada on the Peace Mission have only recently been declassified, thanks to Access to Information requests. Records released from the file series 28-6-1-TRUDEAU PEACE MISSION are remarkably detailed, totalling nearly 10,000 pages of correspondence and clippings. Moreover, the publication of many of the interviews conducted by Robert Bothwell and Jack Granatstein while writing *Pirouette* offers another source to revisit. Robert Bothwell and J.L. Granatstein, *Trudeau's World: Insiders Reflect on Foreign Policy, Trade, and Defence, 1968–1984* (Vancouver: UBC Press, 2017), esp. 351–73.

83 BNATO to External Affairs, "Etude Est/Ouest," 17 May 1984, RG 25, vol. 16394, file 27-4-NATO-1-14, LAC; Delvoie to IFB, "East-West Relations: An FRG Prescription," 1 May 1984, RG 25, vol. 16394, file 27-4-NATO-1-14, LAC.

84 Thomson report, "Report to the Ploughshares Board of Sponsors," 23 Nov. 1983–6 Mar. 1984, Murray Thomson fonds, box 10, file "Project Ploughshares – 1979–1984," MUL.

85 F.H. Knelman, *Reagan, God, and the Bomb: From Myth to Policy in the Nuclear Arms Race* (Toronto: McClelland and Stewart, 1985), 14–15.

11

Cold War Endings:
The Canadian Peace Congress and the
Transnational Peace Movement, 1977–91

STEVEN HUGH LEE

The historiography on the late Cold War has illuminated the role of peace groups in contesting the power politics of the two superpowers.[1] Researchers have drawn particular attention to the transnational and transcontinental ties between peace organizations, as well as their interactions with state actors linked to the capitalist and communist worlds.[2] Transnational disarmament actors and civil society organizations, especially American scientists concerned with the intensified arms race after the mid-1970s, were at the forefront in shaping the ideas and strategies of key policy-makers, notably in the Soviet Union after 1985.[3]

Leopoldo Nuti rooted the late Cold War peace movement in what he termed a "crisis of détente,"[4] one underpinned by Warsaw Pact and North Atlantic Treaty Organization (NATO) force modernization projects from the latter 1970s. Even before the Soviet Union garrisoned SS-20 missiles in Eastern Europe in 1976, however, American secretary of defense Donald Rumsfeld had recommended to President Gerald Ford that the US station in Europe so-called precision tactical nuclear weapons. He supported the neutron bomb, which had a smaller explosive power than other nuclear weapons, but a lethal radiation that would penetrate Soviet armoured divisions.[5] The characteristics of this new bomb fuelled big protests in Holland, Germany, and elsewhere, and in 1978 President Jimmy Carter postponed deployment of the weapon.[6]

Central to the 1980s transatlantic crisis over nuclear weapons was the 1979 "dual track" decision by NATO to, by 1983, counter Soviet SS-20 missiles by equipping military bases across Western Europe with new intermediate ballistic missiles, the Pershing II and the land-based cruise missile. The Carter administration advanced this agenda in NATO, whose members demanded open arms limitations negotiations with the Soviet Union during the four-year period that the weapons were under manufacture. As one group of historians have pointed out, 1983 became the year that defined the dramatic yet peaceful climax of the Euromissile Crisis.[7]

Studies of transnational actors in the peace movement have tended to focus on mainstream liberal or social democratic actors. The role of communists has been interpreted largely within a framework tied to the ideology and practices of the Cold War: the far left were doing Moscow's bidding, and therefore needed to be distanced from the broader campaign in order to preserve its integrity and independence. Such arguments were central to the ideological debates within the transatlantic peace movement in the 1980s, ones which engaged Canadian activists. In Canada, the Canadian Peace Congress (CPC), an affiliate of the pro-Soviet World Peace Council, was at the centre of these controversies. An examination of the activities and goals of the congress will therefore shed light on the dispute from a Canadian perspective. It will also provide a more nuanced understanding of the operations of the CPC, which collaborated with a wide range of Canadian peace groups and played a leading role, in conjunction with a number of other civil society organizations, in shaping the broader movement.

Historians have written cogent critiques of the operations of the World Peace Council, which was tied to the Soviet Union's global foreign policy objectives and which provided guidance to organizations like the Canadian Peace Congress.[8] As Holger Nehring and Benjamin Ziemann have pointed out, however, these critiques are also based on assumptions about Soviet propaganda, not about the agency of the actors associated with the council. According to Nehring and Ziemann, researchers "hypothesize about the impact of propaganda, when it would be much more apposite to discuss social movement activism."[9] Another weakness of existing literature is a tendency to marginalize the histories of Western-based communists within the peace movement. Lawrence Wittner's work on the international struggle against atomic weapons, despite its very impressive synthetic strengths, tends to isolate the far left from the mainstream movement. In the case of the United States, this perspective is appropriate, given the US Peace Council's apparent lack of linkages with other organizations. But in Holland, for example, Wittner downplayed the important role that Dutch communists played in mobilizing public opinion in the late 1970s, including the decision by the Interchurch Peace Council (IKV), an organization dominated by Christians, to work with the communists.[10] Similarly, the dominant coalition of peace groups in Belgium, the Flemish Action Committee Against Nuclear Weapons (VAKA), included the Belgian Communist Youth, with political input from the Belgian Communist Party.[11] This background is absent in Wittner's analysis, as are the working ties between Christians, socialists, and communists in Britain's Campaign for Nuclear Disarmanent (CND).[12] Nerhig and Ziemann have shown that West German activists embraced communist organizers to transcend Cold War binaries across a divided Germany.[13] Within Western democracies, communists rarely played key roles in the peace movement in the 1980s. For historians to marginalize their position within the movement, however – especially in the era of reform and political possibility that the later 1980s represented – overlooks an important dynamic of the international movement of the time, one which was also present in Canada. Recovering the history of the Canadian Peace Congress in the era thus illuminates not only how the Canadian movement navigated the end of the Cold War, but also the wider history of the conflicts, as well as the alliances within civil societies in their efforts to redefine global processes associated with democracy, governance, power, and the present and future of the international system. Furthermore, a study of the Canadian Peace Congress's activities underlines ways in which the organization embraced reform and peaceful transitions (albeit unevenly) in the Cold War. Indeed, the activities of the Canadian Peace Congress both illuminate, in a new way, the "traditional" debate surrounding the end of the Cold War, and provide rich material for an alternative "undiplomatic" international history of Canada.

The roots of the organization, for example, lay at the intersection of global affairs and domestic Canadian politics in the early Cold War – specifically, in Canadian and European initiatives to counter the diplomacy of policy-makers from the North Atlantic region designed to mobilize resources against the perceived "communist" threat. The congress drew support from a coalition of the Canadian left, including members of the Communist Party of Canada, trade unionists, people who had been active in anti-fascist campaigns in the 1930s and 1940s, and religiously inclined individuals. The first president of the congress, James Endicott, was a United Church minister and socialist peace activist who had been born in China to missionary parents.[14] He presided over the organization when it was the leading peace group in the country. The organization established a central coordinating body in Toronto, which sent out directives and policy to affiliates in towns and cities across Canada. The numbers of people involved in the congress and related councils across the country is difficult to ascertain because membership lists were not kept by the organization. Furthermore, some councils did not last very long, and new ones were set up over the course of the period studied. A rough estimation would be a core of about ten people in Toronto with another sixty across the country. Beyond Toronto, there were particularly active councils in Vancouver, Manitoba, and Regina.[15]

Most of the policies recommended by the Canadian Peace Congress contested the official government position in the Cold War, offering a radical alternative world view that showed some sympathy for Soviet initiatives and diplomatic goals in the international system, and which sought to reorient Canadian governmental policies away from militaristic activities and towards greater spending on public social welfare projects. In the early Cold War, under the influence of Endicott and reflecting early solidarity with the Sino-Soviet alliance, the congress oriented its activities to East Asia as well as the North Atlantic region. Over the 1950s, 1960s, and 1970s, its members engaged in a wide array of international issues, including support for national liberation struggles in the Global South, decolonization, an end to apartheid, and the civil rights movement in the United States. During major crises in the communist world, as in Hungary in 1956 and in Czechoslovakia in 1968, some members of the movement criticized Soviet actions. In the aftermath of the 1956 crises, the executive of the Peace Council argued that states should not use their military forces to intervene in the politics of other countries: "we believe this holds true in Egypt, Hungary or any of the other countries of the world where foreign troops are stationed."[16] Domestically, the organization campaigned against Canadian engagement in Cold War alliances and agreements, especially NATO and NORAD, and demanded an end to Canada's direct or indirect support for wars in Korea and

Vietnam. It did support Canadian foreign policy initiatives that members felt promoted peace, including Lester Pearson's peacekeeping initiatives at the United Nations after the Suez Crisis.[17] The organization's definition of "peace" shifted over time, but, at the outset of the 1980s, it included an important psychological dimension of supporting initiatives designed to end the legacies of colonialism and imperialism, structures of power that its members argued reinforced poverty and inequality.

In 1971, John Hanly Morgan succeeded Endicott as president of the national organization and remained titular head of the congress until 1986. Like Endicott, Morgan had a background as a religious leader. Born and educated in the United States, Morgan had attended Harvard Divinity College and was a member of the American Unitarian Church, a non-denominational syncretic religious organization involved in progressive political causes. In the 1950s, Morgan had served with the South Bend Unitarian Church in Indiana, and in the 1960s he moved to Toronto to lead the First Unitarian Congregation of that city.[18] There were significant differences in world view between Endicott and Morgan, including the legacies of the Chinese revolution, the meaning of the concept of "God," and the role of the Soviet Union in the international system.[19] Both leaders, however, agreed that the United States was an imperial state whose policies led to war, undermined world peace, and threatened Canadian sovereignty.

An overview of the history of Canada and the Cold War, delivered by Morgan at a biennial congress meeting in Toronto in 1980, is instructive as an introduction to the organization at the outset of that decade, as well as to Morgan's eclectic ideology and world view. In his address, he referred to the Marshall Plan as a strategy designed to "deflect the European peoples away from what seemed to be almost great changes in the social structure of their societies toward ... socialism, whatever term you want to use." Morgan argued that the early postwar era was also when then-foreign minister Lester Pearson was "chosen by those who run and own the United States to be the front man in the organization of NATO," suggesting that the Canadian political elite lacked agency and was subordinate to American strategic and economic interests. From the point of view of the peace movement, however, Pearson's decision to accept nuclear weapons on Canadian territory soon after the 1963 general election also informed Morgan's perspective. Morgan recalled "the McCarthy horror" of the early 1950s, but also the social struggles for racial equality during that decade. He pointed approvingly to the late 1950s as an era tied to the emergence of national liberation movements around the world, as well as to "the insurgent United States Black movement, which had an immense impact on U.S. society, the era of Martin Luther King and afterwards." Race was thus also an important analytical framework within which he viewed the momentum of progressive politics. There were elements of liberal ideology in Morgan's thinking, and his respect for Martin Luther King reflected, in part, his admiration for a preacher motivated by progressive social action. Within the international system, Morgan viewed the Soviet Union as the big power best suited to battle imperialism, to contain American military adventurism, and to promote social equality. He warned his audience that the congress would be ill advised to increase the size of its supporters by taking the view that there were two superpowers in the world. This perspective represented a "false image of balance," since it portrayed "the peace states as basically aggressive and imperialistic." There were not two superpowers that threatened the world, but only one, "the U.S. transnational government."[20]

In the same speech, Morgan admitted the challenges the congress faced in dealing with the Soviet role in Afghanistan. The situation was "temporarily hard for some of our people," he stated, which indicated the conflicting opinions within the organization. Despite these difficulties, emphasized Morgan, Afghanistan should not revert to the pre-1979 era, with an existing infant mortality rate of 50 per cent, polygamy practised by 10 per cent of the population, and "the bitterly reactionary aspects of the Afghan-Muslim movement, tied in with feudal land-owning and other repressive structures." From his viewpoint Soviet intervention was not part of an imperial expansion, but represented a modern sense of "progress" and an advancement of Afghanistan's socio-economic conditions. "What will be established in Afghanistan," he forecast, would be "another centre of stability, with people slowly building out of the nightmare and the horror that the poor experienced there." The country would be "linked in with a healthy system that interacts industrially, economically, culturally: an area of stability, an area of peace."[21]

It is hard to gauge, based on evidence from the era, the degree to which Morgan embraced the Soviet model of government. In a retrospective memoir published in 2001 discussing his role as president of the Canadian Peace Congress, Morgan referred to some of the faults of the Soviet political system. During the Cold War, he reflected, most people in the West were ill-equipped to understand the history of either the Soviet Union or Russia, especially the latter's "800 year history of authoritarian rule with attitudes that had been largely carried into the approach to the building of socialism." When, in the past, he had been confronted with the point that the Soviet Union lacked political freedom, Morgan's answer was that as a Unitarian minister he was intimately knowledgeable about democratic values: "You don't need to tell me about civil liberties, human rights, group dynamics. They are the life-blood of our denomination."[22] Philosophically, Morgan believed that, as a Unitarian, he was a humanist, one who thought that the leaders of the Soviet Union would be able to "move away from the massive waste of military production" and "slowly mend their many faults."[23] Morgan's view of the international system as fundamentally unipolar, however, informed his understanding of debates in the World Peace Council in the 1980s, and he tended to be critical of Soviet officials in that body who advocated for reform. This position put him at odds with some of the congress executive, and was likely an important reason for his release from the presidency of the organization. Thus, although members of the congress did not publicly articulate criticisms of the Soviet Union, and generally believed the USSR was the leading force for progressive social and political action around the world, there were also important differences within the organization regarding the best way to approach 1980s reform in both the Soviet Union and the World Peace Council.

The congress tended to define peace in a broadly inclusive manner, to include not only efforts to limit the arms race, but also to support societal goals and political movements that ended exploitative systems, especially colonialism in its various forms. Themes such as decolonization, apartheid, the Vietnam War and its legacies, and the status of the newly independent states remained important issues for the congress's membership in the early 1980s. One difference between the ideas of the congress and the more mainstream liberal peace movements of the era was that for most members of the congress, the idea of peace was closely tied to goals broader than ending the arms race – for example, overturning colonialism and its associated violence. In 1980 Morgan welcomed the newly won independence of "peace governments" in places like Mozambique, Angola, Guinee Bissau, South Yemen, Ethiopia, and Vietnam. Some of these countries had to fight "to establish control in the face of often withering reaction from within – the old exploitative order – and from without by foreign interests manipulating and assisting the reaction – often with armed assistance."²⁴ What impressed a workshop at the conference tasked with discussing liberation movements was the qualitative change in those countries as they developed mass social movements. This phenomenon was particularly true in South Africa, the workshop participants noted, where the white population had begun to join with Africans in a struggle where liberation "has become a fight against a military and economic oppressor rather than just a fight against apartheid." The Canadian Peace Congress contributed to the liberation movements, the group agreed, because it was able to contextualize their struggles and understand that they were "an attempt to get free from violent oppression." Canadian organizations and people should "continue using demonstrations, vigils, letters to MPs, letters to [Prime Minister Pierre] Trudeau, letters to the editor – all means possible – to make the necessary arguments."²⁵

In articulating positions about international peace, broadly defined, the members of the Canadian Peace Congress were guided by the broader foreign policy goals of the Soviet Union and its allies. Significantly, the congress described itself as "affiliated to the World Peace Council" in its letterhead and advertising. The council had been established in Warsaw in November 1950, during the US-led UN offensive against North Korea in the Korean War. A distinguished French scientist, Frederic Joliot-Curie, who had earlier played a leading role in similar congresses in Warsaw and Paris in 1948 and 1949, became the council's first president. The council articulated a critique of American foreign policy, rejected the possibility of a non-aligned peace movement, and passed resolutions against all weapons of mass destruction (including the atomic bomb), in support of North Korea in the Korean War, and in relation to a number of other critical issues in the early Cold War era.²⁶

Throughout the Cold War, the leaders of the Canadian Peace Congress took part in World Peace Council (WPC) meetings and conferences, normally held in eastern or northern Europe. In 1981, for example, the Canadian attendees of a WPC-sponsored "Conference against the Arms Race and For Disarmament in Europe," held in Stockholm in early June, included Dr James Foulks, the head of the Department of Pharmacology at the University of British Columbia; Lee Lorch, FRSC; and Mac Makarchuk of the NDP.²⁷ These Canadians were connected to, or worked with, local peace councils of the Canadian Peace Congress. Two other members of the delegation, Jean Fortin and Jean

St Denis, were members of the Conseil Québécois de la Paix. The discussions at the conference were shaped by the 1979 decision to implement the "dual track" policy of NATO and President Reagan's 1980 order to proceed with production of the neutron bomb.

In the month before the WPC conference, Soviet premier Leonid Brezhnev gave a secret speech in Moscow in which he had argued that the two big powers were very close to nuclear conflict. Yuri Andropov, the Soviet KGB head at the time, told the gathering that the United States might even be aiming to launch a pre-emptive strike on the Soviet Union and its allies.[28] Soviet officials responded to the American challenge by planning for a possible conflict and increasing military preparedness while also trying to intensify anti-war sentiment around the world through the peace council and its international affiliates.

The council's informational campaign reached Canadian delegates at the conference, which emphasized the need for an American and Soviet moratorium on the deployment of medium-range nuclear weapons in Europe. Soviet academics and officials wanted a freeze on all further missile modernization in Europe, which included Pershing II and cruise missiles. Speaking at the conference, Lev Semeiko, a senior associate of the Institute of US and Canadian Studies at the Soviet Academy of Sciences, argued that Soviet nuclear policy did not overturn the global strategic balance because Soviet SS-20 missiles could not reach the United States. On the other hand, the proposed new NATO missiles did threaten the USSR directly but also did not contribute to Western security. He pointedly remarked that "to turn West European countries into launching sites for Pershings and Tomahawks puts those countries in mortal danger." NATO had a "vast nuclear potential in Western Europe," now well understood as a "nuclear powder keg." The West was only making the danger worse. "Who needs this absurd policy?" Semeiko exclaimed.[29]

A memorandum produced by the World Peace Council in October 1981, and circulated to affiliated national peace organizations, emphasized the importance of encouraging participation "in national events connected with the worldwide campaign against the danger of nuclear war."[30] The object was to foster "mass activities for the Prevention of Nuclear War," in part by exposing "the myth of limited nuclear war and the notion that a nuclear war can be won" and "to disseminate widely information on the horrors of nuclear war." Planners should organize marches, demonstrations, petitions, marathons, and bicycle events. Campaigns could include bans on weapons testing, reduction in military forces, support for international disarmament campaigns (including the UN Special Session on Disarmament), and the creation of "nuclear weapon-free and peace zones." The council recommended that peace groups establish more ties with NGOs and mobilize "intellectuals, parliamentarians, trade unionists, religious forces, women, scientists, physicians, and artists against the war danger."[31]

The goal of the World Peace Council in the early Cold War had been to bring "the masses" into the peace movement as a means of preventing a world war.[32] While the repressive politics of fear in the 1950s had prevented such a coalition from developing, the early 1980s was a period when the peace movement, at least as an anti-nuclear war protest, began to evolve into a popular movement. Furthermore, in Canada, the congress increased its linkages with other peace groups in the country and made some limited efforts to build a peace coalition. In 1981 and 1982 the CPC was involved in a number of national and local initiatives, and expanded its ties with various non-governmental charities. One of these activities was the circulation of a petition, "Peace is Everybody's Business," to be sent to Prime Minister Trudeau. The congress welcomed Trudeau's 1978 proposal, to the UN Special Session on Disarmament, to "suffocate" war by ending research and development of weapons of mass destruction. Now it was up to Canadians, argued *Peace News*, the mouthpiece of the congress, "to make Canada a force for world peace."[33] The petition demanded that Canada press America to sign SALT II and begin negotiations on limiting medium range missiles in Europe; work to dissolve military alliances; and convene a conference on European disarmament.[34] Councils across the country were tasked with obtaining signatures, which they would forward to the head office in Toronto. The petition differed from a separate letter sent to the prime minister by the organization in that it was more moderate in tone, as a means of gaining more public support. The campaign collected over 150,000 signatures, well short of the goal of a million, but still a sign of the growing momentum of the Canadian peace movement. Prominent Labour organizers and unions endorsed the petition, including the BC Federation of Labour, Dennis McDermott of the Canadian Labour Congress, and Bob White, the international vice-president of the United Automobile Workers. The two versions of the appeal to the Canadian government, however, raised the ire of John Harker of the CLC, who wrote a memo in February 1982 that was circulated to the presidents and secretaries of Labour Councils. The memo stated that the CPC's petition had been endorsed by "a number of prominent trade unionists," but that the organization was unfairly associating the petition with its own statement to the Canadian prime minister, which, "not surprisingly, is totally one-sided, conveying the impression that the USSR is indeed peace-loving while the USA is bent on aggression." Harker recommended that workers look to the International Confederation of Free Trade Unions and its position on disarmament for a more "balanced" position on the issue.[35] The Peace Congress appealed to Harker and the CLC executive, explaining the misunderstanding[36] and formally resolving the conflict, but the tensions had highlighted important philosophical differences between the conservative and left-leaning labour movement, as well as some of the difficulties faced by the congress in its efforts to coordinate a broader coalition in the early 1980s. On the other hand, the incident also underlined the Peace Congress's decision to engage in mainstream reformist pressure group activities, as part of its larger effort to focus public attention on the issue of nuclear weapons and disarmament.

Members of the congress and its local affiliates also got involved in municipal debates about nuclear weapons, and in efforts to establish nuclear weapon-free zones. Wittner's work on the world disarmament campaign in Canada notes the importance of Operation Dismantle and Project Ploughshares in these initiatives, but does not detail the role of the Canadian Peace Congress, possibly because of his belief that the American Peace Congress was not much involved in the broader peace movement. The situation in Canada, however, was different from the United States. A notable success for the organization occurred in the summer of 1981, when the Vancouver City Council passed a resolution introduced by Rob Yorke, a member of the Canadian Communist Party, that the American government reconsider its decision to stockpile the neutron bomb. In the lead-up to the debate in late August, the BC Peace Council organized a public demonstration at the US consulate in Vancouver; sent a telegram urging External Affairs Minister Mark MacGuigan to condemn Ronald Reagan's decision to produce the neutron bomb, "a new threat to the survival of humanity"; announced Yorke's motion at Vancouver City Council; and noted the Fraser Valley Peace Council's telegram to the Canadian government criticizing the weapon's contribution to the arms race. A few days later the BC Council asked the US Consul General in Vancouver, Robert Moore, to convey to Reagan that the neutron bomb "only adds to the deadly spiral and accelerated the danger of a nuclear holocaust."[37]

The following spring, Toronto's city council voted to hold a referendum on global nuclear disarmament; it distributed, to all households, a public health report on the impact of nuclear weapons and warfare on humans. Prior to the vote in November, the Canadian Peace Congress participated in "Disarmament Week," organized a demonstration under the theme "No to the Cruise," coordinated a "Youth for Peace" program, and brought in a prominent speaker, Nino Pasti, a former general from Italy and NATO deputy supreme allied commander for nuclear affairs who had become a vocal critic of the Brussels-based organization, and especially of US nuclear policy.[38] The Peace Congress coordinated activities with other non-governmental organizations in Toronto, including Operation Dismantle, the Cruise Missile Conversion Project, the Christian Movement for Peace, and Science for Peace.[39] By the autumn of 1982 the executive secretary of the congress, Jean Vautour, wrote about the "tremendous upsurge in peace activities" across the country, a sign of public concern at the mounting tension of the "second Cold War" of the early 1980s.[40] On 8 November, 78 per cent of Toronto voters approved a resolution advocating "a world free from nuclear weapons" and demanding the federal government negotiate "the earliest possible achievement of this goal."[41]

The Peace Congress also continued to show solidarity with other social reform organizations, including women's organizations, on the theme of peace. In April 1982, the secretary of the Congress of Canadian Women, Jeanne McGuire, wrote to the Peace Congress, amongst other "friends," stating that the CCW was organizing a rally "to commemorate the origins of Mother's Day, a day originally called for peace – a Mother's Day for peace." McGuire argued that while commercial businesses might want society to forget the meaning of the day, the "C.C.W. (Toronto) believes motherhood should be honoured, truly honoured by making motherhood a personal decision, not an economic choice." The group reflected that "the renewal of life accords with peace and is incompatible with war." To remember the day, the CCW planned a rally at Toronto City Hall to highlight "the hypocrisy of employers and governments who pay lip service once a year to those who produce society's children and for the rest of the year punish those same women through the denial of paid maternity leave and quality, accessible daycare." On 22 April the executive director of the congress, Gordon Flowers, wrote back to the CCW that the Peace Congress was "pleased to support this special event," one that promised "to become a future recognition of how to truly celebrate Mother's Day."[42] The Peace Congress's support for this event again distinguished its peace activities from those of other more narrowly defined peace groups. It also offers insights into the broader social dynamics of the peace movement in Canada in the 1980s, and how the theme of "peace," broadly interpreted, could be used to further the political and social goals of non-governmental organizations across the country.

Another women's organization the Peace Congress worked with was the Voice of Women, whose position on Canadian foreign relations often accorded with the opinions of the Peace Congress. One area of common concern, for example, related to the two organizations' position on the Canadian role in the North American Air Defence Agreement. As a VOW brief on NORAD pointed out, "Canada should not renew the NORAD agreement." This stance was even more important in the early 1980s than it had been in the late 1960s, VOW argued, because "the United States is committed to a 'first strike' policy, through Presidential Directive 59, without consulting her allies." The continental defence cooperation also undermined Canada's contribution "as a peace-maker in lessening today's extremely crucial world tensions." In placing part of the country's military forces under American command, the agreement also "seriously impairs Canada's territorial and political integrity."[43] Loss of Canadian sovereignty was a theme that the Peace Congress literature also emphasized.

In the early 1980s, the linkages that the Canadian Peace Congress established with other NGOs tended to lack depth, and were often created out of a perceived short-term common goal. On a number of occasions, the initiative for cooperation came not from the Peace Congress but from one of the other advocacy groups. For example, the president of Operation Dismantle, T. James Stark, wrote John Morgan in February 1982 to say that his organization was interested in "talking coalition" with a number of proponents of disarmament. Stark realized that the proposed meeting "may not result in a national coalition," but he believed that "with goodwill and effort" the group would improve their ability to assess areas for additional study "before a national coalition could become a realistic possibility."[44] Flowers responded to Stark's reply favourably, and asked Stark also to invite to the meeting the congress's "sister organization" in Quebec, Le Conseil Québécois de la Paix.[45]

Stark's 1982 letter represented an early attempt to create a broader network of peace organizations that eventually led to establishment of the Canadian Peace Alliance in 1985, a decentralized organization designed to help facilitate communication and coordination amongst a large number of peace groups across the country. Efforts to build peace coalitions were complicated by differences between various groups over ideology, approach, platform, and the large number of organizations and personalities that were involved. The activities of the Canadian Peace Congress were occasionally singled out as being particularly problematic for the peace movement, largely because of concerns about the organization's lack of independence vis-à-vis the World Peace Council and the Soviet Union. A debate emerged amongst various peace groups, starting in 1983, and continued to appear over the next decade, until the Peace Congress disbanded in the aftermath of the fall of the Soviet Union. This debate was informed by transatlantic perspectives on the role of the peace movement in the context of the Cold War and the two superpowers.

A key starting point for this debate was E.P. Thompson, the English historian who played a major role in creating European Nuclear Disarmament (END) in the spring of 1980.[46] In a series of articles in *The Nation* in early 1983, beginning with "Sleepwalking into a Trap: END and the Soviet 'Peace Offensive,'" Thompson outlined the challenges posed to the European and American movements by Soviet foreign policy. Expressing concern that Soviet policy would take advantage of the protests in the West to force the NATO governments to give up their cruise and Pershing missiles, Thompson exclaimed that neither "moralism nor fellow-travelling sentimentalism can be of any service in guiding the peace movement in its difficult relations with the Communist states." The problem with the Communist rulers, he argued, was that "they are the ideological look-alikes of their opposite numbers in the West, thinking in the same terms of 'balance' and security through 'strength.'" It was "futile" to place trust "in any heavily armed state, and especially in one where the information available to its citizens is strictly controlled and where public opinion can scarcely influence the rulers." Those in the West advocating for peace were "novices" in the big power game: "the cards are marked, and the game will end – as it always does with popular movements – in our being sold down the river by our partner."[47] When Thompson visited Canada later that year he remarked to an audience at the University of Toronto that what was being tested in Canada was not cruise missiles but Canadians. The peace movement was significant in global terms, he pointed out, as Canada was one of a small number of countries that had the ability to produce nuclear weapons but which had "democratically decided not to do so. Canadians should be proud of that decision and follow its logical consequences through. You should not sell yourselves short." Although Thompson argued that it was important to maintain dialogue with Soviet policy-makers, he had also "shunned the recent peace conference in Prague," considering it a "stage show, unrepresentative of the international peace movement." Beyond peace itself, one of the founding objectives of END was the "breaking up the NATO/Warsaw Pact bloc system, as a requisite for the break-down of the Cold War."[48]

Thompson's perspective was rooted in an European imaginary, though one which anticipated the end of the Cold War. The goal was to create an independent non-nuclear Europe, transcending the Soviet bloc. The vision was part of a broader strategy for a democratic Europe in the absence of superpower rivalry. This outlook on the two big power blocs and their alliance systems made sense for Europe, but what END and its many sympathizers failed to take into account was, first, that NATO was an organization with a global scope, at least in its "threat assessments," consultation, and planning; and, second, that isolating the organization within one region, albeit the most important one for the alliance, failed to situate the perceived global interests of its main backer, the United States.[49] NATO extended its field of military operations after the end of the Cold War partly for this reason, unlike the Warsaw Pact, which crumbled with the end of the Soviet sphere of influence in Eastern Europe.

Despite the apparent unity of the NATO alliance in implementing the 1979 dual track policy, this era was destabilizing for NATO as well as the Soviet bloc. One element of this uncertainty was delays in implementing NATO policy. The governments of Holland and Belgium, for example, regularly postponed the decision to station the missiles, and the ruling in Holland to deploy them in 1988 was preempted by the 1987 INF Treaty between the Soviet Union and the United States. In Canada, six members of parliament, representing the three major political parties, signed a statement in April 1982 departing from official defence and external policy. They found "kinship" with the 188 members of the US Congress, led by Republican Mark

Hatfield and Democrat Edward Kennedy, calling on the Soviet Union and the United States "to achieve a mutual and verifiable freeze on the testing, production and further deployment of nuclear warheads, missiles, and other delivery systems."[50] Politicians who had supported the 1979 decision were also very concerned about security on the continent. In Germany, for example, Chancellor Helmut Schmidt "feared that the United States would either give up Western Europe, or use it as a nuclear battleground," and he thus "shared some concerns with peace movement activists."[51]

Within the World Peace Council there were also public discussions that impinged on policy positions. A relevant issue was the linkages between the council and peace groups in the West. Just as European Nuclear Disarmament leaders debated ties with official peace councils in Eastern Europe, the World Peace Council evaluated its linkages with peace organizations in the West. In 1982 council vice president Yuriy Zhukov criticized END. Yet members of the International Department of the Soviet Communist Party, including Yevgeniy Primakov, later recruited by Premier Gorbachev, favoured cooperation with all peace groups, irrespective of ideology. Primakov gained a voice on the World Peace Council after the "World Assembly for Peace and Life, against Nuclear War," organized in Prague in June 1983, laid the groundwork for his election as a vice president. He replaced Zhukov, who continued his criticisms of END in the media.[52]

In the December 1983 issue of *Peace Calendar*, a national publication of the peace movement, Gordon Flowers, the executive director of the Canadian Peace Congress, protested Thompson's depiction of the World Assembly for Peace and Life, against Nuclear War as a "stage show." Flowers had attended the meeting, along with "72 other Canadians representing church, labour, women, youth, peace groups, elected civic and provincial officials of diverse views." Possibly hinting at Primakov's appointment, he contended that an objective person would not take such a position, if they read the minutes and conclusions of the discussions. Over the decade, Flowers and the leadership of the Canadian congress embraced the policy of engaging peace groups, and welcomed the reforms in the council, in support of Gorbachev's reform agenda. Flowers echoed Zhukov's concerns about END's role in dividing the peace movement, but also emphasized the willingness of the Prague meeting to allow divergent voices in the forum. This position contrasted with the END meeting in Berlin, he argued, which refused to let organizations from Eastern and Western Europe attend its conference.[53] Flowers did not engage Thompson on the broader issue of how each of their respective organizations defined "independence," for the Canadian Peace Congress also articulated what it called an independent foreign policy for Canada, one which remained silent on Canada's relationship with the Soviet bloc, but which campaigned for a Canada that withdrew from the NATO alliance.

Several weeks after Thompson's article countering the Soviet peace initiative appeared in *The Nation*, the US president delivered a speech in which he announced America's next new military program: the so-called "Strategic Defence Initiative," commonly known as "Star Wars." This missile defence system, to be partly based in outer space, became the focus of the next phase of the disarmament campaign organized by the Peace Congress. E.P. Thompson described Star Wars as "the ultimate break-down of deterrence theory, an attempt by the U.S. nuclear establishment to return to the womb of Hiroshima."[54]

It was during this period, from late 1983 to 1985, that peace groups across Canada held negotiations to discuss and formulate plans for a national alliance. In early February 1984 Gordon Flowers participated in a "National Strategy Conference" in Winnipeg to consolidate ties between labour unions, peace groups, and NGOs representing women, First Nations, students, youth, ethnic groups, and disarmament organizations. The meeting also planned the coordination of the Peace Petition Caravan Campaign. The latter sought signatures across the country for a statement, to be presented to the Trudeau government in Ottawa, in favour of ending Canada's support for the cruise missile, declaring Canada a nuclear weapons-free zone, reorienting government spending away from military to social spending, and allowing debate in the House of Commons on these topics without any direction from party leaders.[55] The planners of the petition drive, including the Peace Congress, sought not only to put pressure on the government, but also to direct public attention toward this popular issue at the time of the impending national election.

At the opening session of the conference, Simon Rosenblum, of Project Ploughshares, castigated the Canadian Peace Congress along the lines of E.P. Thompson's critique the previous year.[56] A dismayed Flowers said that he regretted the "divisive and counterproductive" debate, remarking that the movement was still "too narrow" in its base and that "attempts to exclude groups will definitely reduce the effectiveness of the [Peace Petition Caravan] Campaign."[57]

Rosenblum elaborated on his concerns in the next issue of *The Peace Calendar*, questioning whether the national peace coalition should include organizations "such as the Canadian Peace Congress and its affiliates, who are clearly pro-Soviet. This problem has nothing to do with ideology but rather involves perspectives relating to the arms race itself." The attack, however, was ideological, based on a critique of Rosenblum's understanding of the Soviet Union as a "communist" state: "In all other Western countries, the Soviet-inspired Peace Congress groups are not an integral part of the peace movement. Only in Canada you say? Pity."[58] What Rosenblum did not take into account, however, was the contribution that the Canadian group was making to the peace campaign in the country. As one respondent to Rosenblum's appeal wrote, the Canadian movement "calls for multilateral nuclear disarmament. If groups such as the Canadian Peace Congress, and indeed the Communist Party of Canada, are willing to march with us under banners calling for 'Disarmament East and West,' then we should welcome them. Their presence does not mean that we agree with their support of the Soviet system; it means that they agree with our call for disarmament."[59]

Discussions and meetings toward a loose coalition of peace groups continued over the spring and summer of 1984. The failure of the campaign to change government policy and the election of Brian Mulroney's Progressive Conservative Party in September 1984 further galvanized the peace leadership to improve their organizational capacity. At a November gathering in Ottawa of forty groups tied to the Peace Petition Caravan Campaign, peace activists including Flowers articulated strong support for a national coordinating body tied to the Canadian peace movement. The meeting agreed to establish a planning conference that would facilitate the creation of a national conference to build the coalition. The planning conference would be open to all interested groups, pay respect to regional diversity, and would encourage communication with the grassroots of organizations.[60]

Throughout the discussions, the Peace Congress representative, backed by the membership of the national organization, attempted to establish a "united and diverse coalition around common aims and goals toward a new independent Canadian foreign policy." Many of these objectives focused on Canada-US relations, convincing the Canadian government to withdraw from its bilateral and multilateral commitments with the United States, but starting with policies that would see Canada backing away from supporting issues tied to nuclear conflict. At the national meeting of the congress in May 1985, for example, the board agreed to participate in a peace coalition that would be open to everyone and work for "basic common demands," using slogans including "NO TO STAR WARS; REFUSE THE CRUISE; MAKE CANADA A NUCLEAR WEAPONS FREE ZONE; ESTABLISH A NUCLEAR FREEZE; JOBS NOT BOMBS; SIGNING OF A NUCLEAR WEAPONS TEST BAN TREATY."[61]

In April 1985, Canadian peace activist Bob Penner wrote an article in *Peace Magazine* announcing the decision by peace organizations across the country to establish a new national organization designed to promote the peace movement.[62] The founders held several meetings that year, and the new organization emerged as a decentralized institution designed to allow groups to maintain their autonomy and identity. There was no central spokesperson assigned for the Alliance, and the new organization did not endorse any particular group or event. As the founding document noted, the main goal of the organization would not be to run campaigns or establish policy for the national movement, but to "facilitate the launching of campaigns by some or all of its member groups."[63] A key element of the alliance was the steering committee, designed to implement the plans of the organization as determined at its annual convention. The committee was to meet up to four times annually, in different locations across the country, with the committee makeup linked both to regional and provincial representation, and with one representative from each of a dozen or so national peace organizations. A major longer term goal was to inject disarmament and anti-nuclear war issues into national politics so as to impact the next federal election.

The Peace Congress viewed the "structure document" that emerged from the meetings in August as a positive development. In a circular letter to the Canadian Peace Councils and its affiliates, Flowers pointed to the document's adoption of a number of positions of the congress, claiming that the new coalition permitted "involvement in broader foreign policy issues such as Nicaragua, foreign aid, etc., – a very positive development." He disliked the use of the word "superpowers" in a sentence that read: "All nuclear weapons states and especially the two superpowers have a special responsibility to end the arms between them," and he was critical of efforts to "raise the question of equal responsibility and the so-called human rights issue," referring to criticisms of the Soviet Union and its eastern bloc allies' repressive policies in Europe. On the whole, however, it was the congress's opinion that "we can live with this Statement of Unity."[64]

The creation of the Peace Alliance in 1985 opened up new opportunities for the Canadian Peace Congress, though it continued to face opposition from various quarters for its support for Soviet foreign policy and Soviet hegemony in Eastern Europe. The year also witnessed the emergence of Mikhail Gorbachev as leader of the Soviet Union, and in October the congress issued a press release supporting Gorbachev's diplomatic offensive to avert a space race, ban chemical weapons, and cut intermediate missiles in Eastern and Western Europe.[65] A turning point had arrived in the congress's relations with the Soviet Union and its position in the World Peace Council. In this transition, the national group embraced Gorbachev's foreign policy agenda, though there were dissenting voices, and leading members of the Peace Congress continued to view the United States as the big power responsible for the conflict and tensions of the Cold War.

One of the major initiatives that Gorbachev undertook in 1985 was a test ban on nuclear explosions. The idea for the test ban was rooted not in the Soviet Union itself, but in the interactions between Soviet academics and their transnational networks, especially the American bureau of the International Physicians for the Prevention of Nuclear War. Arguments about a unilateral Soviet comprehensive ban, independent of American governmental actions, were also circulating among people affiliated with the World Peace Council. In Toronto, at a meeting of the Canadian Peace Congress in the mid-1985, Hans Blumenfeld urged the congress to inform the Soviet Peace Committee of the importance of adopting a unilateral nuclear freeze on testing. In the event, the congress, despite having sympathy for the idea, decided not to push the Soviet body with their own initiative.[66] At the same time, the secretary of the World Peace Council from 1980 to 1985, Tair Tairov, heard similar suggestions from the council membership and sent messages to the Soviet Peace Committee and high-ranking Soviet officials who recommended the same policy. The Soviet Peace Committee rejected the message, but his second effort pleaded that "thousands of people from Australia to Canada are waiting" for the moratorium.[67] Tairov's recommendations reinforced a policy decision that would have been taken anyway, but the process demonstrated a willingness from within the World Peace Council, at the outset of Gorbachev's premiership, to advance innovative initiatives to the Soviet leadership.[68]

In 1986, the Canadian Peace Congress continued to support Gorbachev's diplomatic peace initiatives. In late January, Flowers wrote Prime Minister Mulroney that the congress "fully supports" Gorbachev's recent "proposal for the complete elimination of nuclear weapons throughout the world" by the end of the century. He added that the organization urged the governments of both Canada and the United States "to join with the Soviet Union in a moratorium on nuclear weapons testing."[69] Flowers sent the letter to local councils and affiliates across the country asking members to write similar letters to the leaders of the three national political parties and to lobby members of Parliament to withdraw from NORAD.[70]

The momentum of change in the World Peace Council continued at the council meetings in Sofia, Bulgaria, in the spring of 1986, when officials from the Soviet Peace Committee demanded that the Indian president of the council, Romesh Chandra, initiate a reform in the structure and policies of the organization and announce the need for such changes in his speech at Sofia. Although Chandra refused to accede to these requests and legitimized the existing work of the institution in his speech, the council bureaucracy published as the official record the reform speech that he was asked to give.[71]

The dispute initiated a major rift in the organization and its membership around the world about the future of the council. The conflict was mirrored within the Canadian Peace Congress, and was one factor in the decline of the activities of the national organization and many affiliates in the late 1980s and early 1990s. The main body of the national organization endorsed the reform, which would have democratized the institution by allowing more input from national group members. In the aftermath of the Sophia conference the Canadian Peace Congress forwarded to its supporters the council's April 1986 declaration, "To Safeguard Peace on Earth," advising them to study the document closely to understand the "present international situation."[72] The document outlined the Gorbachev-Reagan "Geneva Summit" meeting in November 1985, the first meeting of the two world leaders, and described it in positive terms as an event that "created the opportunity to normalize US-Soviet relations and the international situation as a whole." The declaration also stressed the importance of working with all peace groups around the world, but in a way that was meant for a more liberal policy towards peace groups located in Western Europe and the capitalist world. In the context of threats to human survival posed by nuclear weapons, the council "holds out the hand of friendship to all organizations and movements working for peace. We propose an open and constructive dialogue leading to mutual understanding and cooperation. The issue that unites us today in the face of imminent disaster is more important and transcends all differences."[73]

For President John Morgan, on the other hand, the era of Gorbachev's reforms was disastrous for the council, and he described his participation at the meeting in Sofia in 1986 as the "saddest day of my international work."[74] Morgan sided with Chandra, as did many of the members from the Global South. In his memoirs Morgan wrote disparagingly of Gorbachev's reforms, and intimated that the head of the US Peace Council, Rob Prince, who supported the World Peace Council reform while working for the organization at Helsinki, was a spy for American and NATO intelligence services.[75] It is significant that 1986 was the last year that Morgan retained the title of president of the congress. He retired later that year, becoming honorary president of the organization. Over time, the Conseil Québécois de la Paix also sided with those who preferred the status quo, and its leadership appears to have stopped cooperating with the Peace Congress in late 1989, partly as a result of "serious differences over the World Peace Council."[76]

By 1986, disarmament activists and public figures in Canada were more prepared than they had been in the early 1980s to work with a broad range of peace groups in the country, irrespective of ideology. This tendency was evident in the lead-up to the autumn of 1986 Copenhagen conference organized by Danish peace lobbyists, World Federalists, and the World Peace Council as part of the United Nations' "Year of Peace." To advertise the event the Peace Congress worked with campaign strategist David Kraft of the Toronto Disarmament Network. He was a strong supporter of the Canadian Peace Alliance who, in late 1985, had argued that the key to a successful movement was "the existence of a broadly-based popular movement ... Our future success will depend on our ability to build a well-informed, active, and truly mass-based movement."[77]

The Copenhagen conference attracted support from politicians of each of the major Canadian parties, three of whom signed a public "Appeal for Participation in the World Congress Consecrated to the International Year of the Peace." The three parliamentarians were Warren Allmand of the Liberals, Vincent Della Noce of the Conservatives, and Dan Heap of the New Democrats. Their collective statement underlined several themes that the congress had been advocating during the decade, though without a formalized critique of NATO or NORAD. The trio recognized the "inter-dependence of peace, economic development and social progress"; the urgency for "disarmament and for the prevention of a nuclear catastrophe"; the need for peace "as a condition for the satisfaction of human needs such as food, lodging, health, education, work and a healthy atmosphere"; and the importance of global cooperation, dialogue, and mutual understanding "in the maintenance of peace with the participation of governments, of parliaments and of non-governmental organizations." The environmental, economic, and human problems of the world demanded "that we consecrate at least part of the immense efforts and resources, (to these problems), now being used in preparation for war." The recent Geneva summit, however, represented "a new hope" and it was "the responsibility of the peace forces of the entire world to give this process a decisive character and to render it irreversible by means of the world congress." The event in Copenhagen "will be the occasion to unite North and South, East and West, parliamentarians, representatives of the actual peace movements, of political parties, religious groups, women, youth, the retired people, artists, veterans, professional associations trade unions." It was to be the meeting place "where every adversary" of the arms race "can exchange and discuss the means to reverse the present trend and to undertake a solution of the many, serious problems of our world." For Canadians, geographically situated between the two superpowers, a reduction in tension would bolster "the traditional peace policy of Canada" and have "positive impact on our own sovereignty and independence."[78]

In important ways, the statement represented a high point for the Canadian Peace Congress, as the organization sought to encourage broad participation in the activities of the World Peace Council. The joint statement reflected a willingness to overcome the Cold War barriers and rigid ideological posturing that had characterized relations between the Eastern bloc and NATO countries. At the same time, the latter part of the 1980s were years of decline for the peace movement, particularly the Canadian Peace Congress. The organization was already suffering from shortages of funds and an aging membership. Several key figures who had played leading roles in the organization and its affiliates retired in the 1980s after many decades of dedicated activism. Meetings of the national organization during this period referred to the need to recruit younger people, but such efforts failed as younger peace activists were attracted to organizations of more recent provenance.[79]

The negotiations between Premier Gorbachev and President Reagan in 1986 and 1987, from the meetings in Reykjavik to the successful negotiation of the 1987 INF Treaty, also weakened the perceived need to maintain the momentum for peace. The reform movement in the World Peace Council also failed in 1988, as a reaction set in and conservatives purged reformers.[80] The Canadian Peace Congress fought for continued reform, protesting the purges and demanding that the council return to its 1986 position and allow much greater roles and initiative for national groups. In January 1989 Gordon Flowers discussed the dispute in the council in the official organ of the Canadian Communist Party, the *Canadian Tribune*. He noted that "well before the 1986 meeting in Sophia, we were aware of the need to bring the activities of the World Peace Council into accord with the new world situation." Pointing out that the council's *Peace Courier* was now a "first rate publication," he complained that new rules in the organization "will not improve or make the WPC more democratic, but, in fact, do quite the opposite ... Unfortunately, our expectations for an open and democratic process have been jeopardized by undemocratic and old style administrative measures." The body needed a radical restructuring, one in which the national committees would come to the fore: "It should streamline its structure to be more democratic with all bodies elected by, and directly responsible to national committees. All WPC organs should improve like the Peace Courier."[81] In making these points, Flowers echoed some of the concerns aired publicly in July 1988 by Tair Tairov, now a member of the Soviet Peace Committee. Tairov spoke of END in positive terms and argued that the council "remains authoritarian and hierarchal." Members of the organization were "very nice" but were "afraid to criticize ... Such people are still waiting, but for what? For new commands, new instructions? They are going to have to change themselves – this is the meaning of glasnost."[82]

Within Canada, the Regina Peace Council was not afraid to criticize, and responded to Tairov's comments in a letter written by Ed Lehman to the national body. Lehman acknowledged that Tairov's point that the World Peace Council "spoke exclusively for Soviet foreign policy had some elements of truth, but he wrote that Tairov's critique was "far too negative and absolute [*sic*]. It turns everyone in the world working under the leadership of the W.P.C. into mindless robots who didn't know what they were doing without talent and creativity, who simply followed the Soviet line." The Regina Council agreed with the congress position that the international council should play a more important role in the peace movement and "undertake more independent campaigns." Significantly, the Regina group wanted to avoid being "another support group for what one particular and or dominant group desires."[83]

The World Peace Council did not respond to the demands of the Canadians and other groups, however, and abandoned the 1986 reform project. In 1990 the congress produced a report noting that the council now faced a major financial crisis, and that support from Western Europe and North America was unlikely because of the "few half-hearted, minor measures and with a leadership basically carrying on in the same old way." In this context, the congress executive in Toronto recommended that they "not place special emphasis on our affiliation with the WPC." The organization had reached a breaking point. In January 1991 it issued a letter to President Gorbachev criticizing him for ordering the use of military force against the newly created Lithuanian Republic, arguing that he had violated the demands of a government that had been elected democratically: "The right to self-determination and sovereignty rests with the people of individual nations, and not others who may be affected by exercise of these rights."[84] Such a declaration would have been impossible before Gorbachev, and reflected the major changes that had occurred in both the international arena and the thinking of the congress executive in Toronto. Although the national organization continued to operate for a few more years, the congress, already in significant decline, became unable to reconstitute itself with the collapse of the Soviet Union in 1991.[85]

The history of the Canadian Peace Congress in the 1980s highlights several themes surrounding the end of the global Cold War. It is fair to criticize the members of the congress for not acknowledging the failures of the Soviet model of governance, but the history of their activities also demonstrated an understanding that the two superpowers were not on equal footing, and that the global dimensions of American hegemony separated and differentiated the two big powers within the international system. In other words, despite its flaws, the congress was able to articulate, compared to other peace groups at the time, a more holistic critique of American power in the international system, one that identified the militaristic character of US power overseas and counterrevolutionary tendencies of American foreign policy in the late Cold War.

The congress's critical perspective changed in the second half of the decade, as the Soviet Union, under Gorbachev, sought to normalize relations with the United States as part of a goal of ending the arms race and reducing the danger of nuclear conflict. As the Soviet Union withdrew from the Global South in the 1980s, the Canadian Peace Congress, too, paid less attention to those regions of the world. The global analytical framework of congress policy thus receded in the 1980s, as it became more fixated on nuclear weapons in the North Atlantic and European worlds. Yet its membership did critique American foreign policy actions into the late 1980s – for example, in opposing the US bombing of Libya in 1986 and American efforts to bring military technologies into outer space.

The congress was active in the wider peace movement in Canada and established ties and good working relationships with a number of organizations at the local and national levels. The body was the centre of high-profile transatlantic debates about the role of groups that supported Soviet foreign policy. Some Canadians in the disarmament movement called for a boycott of the congress, but others worked with the organization as part of their commitment to a larger peace project. With the advent of Mikhail Gorbachev, there was some convergence of views between the Peace Congress and other activists and politicians in Canada, represented best in the declaration issued by Warren Allmand, Dan Heap, and Vincent Della Noce in 1986. Their view of peace incorporated a range of social, environmental, and political issues and was compatible with the notions of peace articulated by members of the congress. This convergence was not the product of the influence of the Peace Congress, but rather the effort by campaigners on both sides to overcome the constraints and confines of the Cold War. In this project the successes of both sides were flawed, and, for the congress, the contradictions of change were too much for the leadership to manage. In this context activism in Canada continued at the local level in the absence of a national coordinating body, demonstrating the importance of the grassroots ties that some peace councils had established in the late Cold War. But the congress, along with affiliated groups, had vigorously, even passionately, engaged in the events of the day and contributed to the broader anti-war history of the long and eventful decade between the late 1970s and the early 1990s.

NOTES

1 See William M. Knoblauch, *Nuclear Freeze in a Cold War: The Reagan Adminis-tration, Cultural Activism, and the End of the Arms Race* (Boston: University of Massachusetts Press, 2017); Christoph Becker-Schaum, Philipp Gassert, Mar-tin Klimke, Wilfried Mausbach, and Marianne Zepp, eds., *The Nuclear Crisis: The Arms Race, Cold War Anxiety, and the German Peace Movement of the 1980s* (New York: Berghahn Books, 2016); Beatrice Heuser, *Nuclear Mentalities? Strategies and Beliefs in Britain, France, and the FRG* (New York: St Martin's Press, 1998); and Vladimir Tismaneanu, ed., *In Search of Civil Society: Indepen-dent Peace Movements in the Soviet Bloc* (New York: Routledge, 1990).

2 For example: Eckart Conze, Martin Klimke, and Jeremy Varon, eds., *Nuclear Threats, Nuclear Fear and the Cold War of the 1980s* (Cambridge: Cambridge University Press, 2017); Leopoldo Nuti, Frederic Bozo, Marie-Pierre Rey, and Bernd Rother, eds., *The Euromissile Crisis and the End of the Cold War* (Stan-ford: Stanford University Press, 2015); Lawrence Wittner, *Toward Nuclear Abolition: A History of the World Nuclear Disarmament Movement, 1971 to the Present* (Stanford: Stanford University Press, 2003); and Gerd-Rainer Horn and Padraic Kenney, eds., *Transnational Moments of Change: Europe 1945, 1968, 1989* (Lanham, MD: Rowman and Littlefield, 2004). For a general survey, consult April Carter, *Peace Movements: International Protest and World Politics since 1945* (New York: Routledge, 1992).

3 On the leading role of transnational actors and organizations in shaping the ideas of leading figures in the Soviet Union, especially Premier Mikhail Gor-bachev and his advisors, see Matthew Evangelista, *Unarmed Forces: The Transnational Movement to End the Cold War* (Ithaca: Cornell University Press, 1999). See also Evangelista's "Transnational Organizations and the Cold War," in *The Cambridge History of the Cold War*, vol. 3, edited by Melvyn P. Leffler and Odd Arne Westad (Cambridge: Cambridge University Press, 2010), 400–21.

4 Leopoldo Nuti, ed., *The Crisis of Detente in Europe: From Helsinki to Gorbachev, 1975–1985* (Abingdon: Routledge, 2009).

5 The idea of the neutron bomb was conceived during the Korean War, when its inventor, Samuel Cohen, witnessed the second fall of Seoul in early 1951 during a secret mission for the Department of Defense and began to think about ways of defeating an enemy's army without destroying cities. See Bruce Cumings, "Nuclear Threats against North Korea: Consequences of the 'Forgotten' War," *The Asia-Pacific Journal – Japan Focus* 3, no. 1 (2005): 5.

6 On the neutron bomb's role in shaping the peace movement in the 1970s see Holger Nehring and Benjamin Ziemann, "Do All Paths Lead to Moscow? The NATO Dual-Track Decision and the Peace Movement – A Cri-

tique," *Cold War History* 12 (2012), 9–12. It was in this era in Canada that
several disarmament peace organizations emerged, including Project
Ploughshares and Operation Dismantle, both in 1977.

7 Nuti et al., eds., *The Euromissile Crisis and the End of the Cold War.*

8 See, for example, Gerhard Wettig, "The Last Soviet Offensive in the Cold
War: Emergence and Development of the Campaign against NATO Euromissiles, 1979–1983," *Cold War History* 9 (2009): 79–110.

9 Nehring and Ziemann, "Do All Paths Lead to Moscow?," 2–3.

10 After 1980, the role of the communists declined within the movement, but
Wittner described the IKV as "the leading force within the world peace
movement for bypassing national governments and generating 'détente
from below.'" Wittner, *Toward Nuclear Abolition,* 140.

11 For a comparison of the Dutch and Belgian movements and the difficulties
of their relationships with peace groups in East Germany, consult Matthijs
van der Beek, "Beyond Hollanditis: The Campaigns against the Cruise Missiles in the Benelux (1979–1985)," *Dutch Crossing* 40 (2016): 39–53.

12 Nehring and Ziemann, "Do All Paths Lead to Moscow?," 7; see also Jeremy
Tranmer, "Odd Bed-fellows: British Christians and Communists in the Strug-
gle for Peace," *Revue LISA/LISA* 9, special issue, "Religion and Politics in the
English-Speaking World: Historical and Contemporary Links" (2011), 170–87.

13 Nehring and Ziemann, "Do All Paths Lead to Moscow?," 14.

14 On Endicott, see Ian McKay and Jamie Swift, *Warrior Nation: Rebranding
Canada in an Age of Anxiety* (Toronto: Between the Lines, 2012), chap. 4.

15 By the late 1980s membership declined significantly, and many councils
stopped functioning.

16 Stephen Endicott, *James G. Endicott: Rebel Out of China* (Toronto: University
of Toronto Press, 1980), 326. According to Stephen Endicott, the majority of
the membership felt that the events in Hungary were a counterrevolution
provoked by the United States. The Hungarian Revolution split the Canadian left. In 1968 James Endicott signed a petition calling for the withdrawal
of Soviet troops in Czechoslovakia, part of his growing disillusionment with
Soviet foreign policy. According to Stephen, "the Soviet Union began to
emerge in [James] Endicott's eyes as a new imperialist superpower aggres-
sively contending for domination and spheres of influence with the older
American imperialism" (ibid., 343). James Endicott submitted his resigna-
tion to the congress in 1971, which voted by a majority of two to reject the
letter, but Endicott still resigned. Ibid., 352.

17 Ibid., 326.

18 Canada Peace Congress Fonds (hereafter CPC), box 14, file CPC Congresses
Biennial, McMaster University Archives.

19 These differences in opinion account for part of the reason for the transition in leadership in the organization in 1971, as Endicott embraced an ideological and international position more compatible with Maoism and China's perspective on the Sino-Soviet split.

20 Ibid.

21 Ibid.

22 John Hanly Morgan, *Pursuing the Dove: Reminiscences of the Present Peace Struggle* (Peterborough: Wellseley and Gardens, 2001), 26–7.

23 Ibid., 26.

24 CPC, box 14, speech by Morgan.

25 Ibid., "Workshop on Liberation Movements and the Struggle for Peace," 9 March 1980.

26 Lawrence Wittner, *One World or None: A History of the World Nuclear Disarmament Movement through 1953* (Stanford: Stanford University Press, 1993), chap. 10. The Canadian Peace Congress sometimes referred to its affiliation to the "World Peace Congress," the conference jointly held in Paris and Prague in April 1949. The congress had been the main body tied to the Stockholm Peace appeal of 1950, which called for the prohibition of the use of the atomic bomb and its international control. Wittner criticizes the appeal for sidestepping several issues, including the nature of international control of the bomb.

27 CPC, box 16, file Conferences – Int. Conf. Against Arms Race, Stockholm.

28 Lawrence Wittner, *Confronting the Bomb: A Short History of the World Disarmament Movement* (Stanford: Stanford University Press, 2009), 144. Wittner discounts the role of the council, arguing that its members remained out of touch with the emerging peace movements in Europe and the United States. See ibid., 165, and also chap. 11 of *Toward Nuclear Abolition: A History of the World Nuclear Disarmament Movement, 1971 to the Present* (Stanford: Stanford University Press, 2003).

29 CPC, box 16, file Conferences – Int. Conf. Against Arms Race, Stockholm, "Europe: A Moratorium on Medium-Range Nuclear Systems with the Beginning of Negotiations," n.d. Semeiko, a retired colonel, had been exposed to Western NGO critical thinking on the global nuclear balance. He stated that Pugwash was not taken seriously by the West, but "for us it was very enriching. My first time was 1976. There were top foreign scientists, so many arguments, and interesting ideas, in contrast to the boilerplate of our side's officially approved positions." Cited in Robert D. English, *Russia and the Idea of the West: Gorbachev, Intellectuals, and the End of the Cold War* (New York: Columbia University Press, 2000), 300n201.

30 CPC, box 18, file "World Peace Council Draft Programme of Action – 1982," October 1981.

31 Ibid.

32 Stalin had argued at the time of the creation of the council that its goal was
not to "overthrow capitalism and establish socialism." S.A. Smith, ed., *The
Oxford Handbook of the History of Communism* (Oxford: Oxford University
Press, 2014), 326.

33 *Peace News* (February 1981), British Columbia Peace Council (hereafter
BCPC) records, box 4, file Peace News, University of British Columbia Special Collections and University Archives. For a recent study of Trudeau's
proposal, see Paul Meyer, "Pierre Trudeau and the 'Suffocation' of the
Nuclear Arms Race," *International Journal* 71 (2016): 393–408.

34 Ibid..

35 William Smalley, Regional Director of CLC enclosing letter to presidents
and secretaries of all BC Labour Councils and ICFTU position paper, 24 February 1982, CPC, box 18, file Correspondence General. The ICFTU had been
established in 1949 after unions broke with the socialist and communist-ori-
ented World Federation of Trade Unions.

36 The Peace Congress argued that Harker had misinterpreted the meaning of
the decision to print the Peace Congress's statement to the PM on one side of
a bill and the more moderately worded national petition on the other side.
The congress had done so, argued the campaign director, Nick Prychodko,
out of a need to save money on printing costs, and Harken should have contacted the congress before sending out the unwelcome memo. Ibid., letter
from Prochkyo to John Harker, 22 April 1982. The congress petition that likely angered Harker read: "That the government [of Canada] accept the offer of
the USSR never to use nuclear weapons against any state which does not produce, import, or deploy nuclear arms, and confirm this mutual obligation by
a formal treaty with the USSR." "Statement to Prime Minister Trudeau and the
Canadian Parliament," n.d. [1981], CPC, box 18, file Circulars and Printed.

37 BC Peace Council, "Press Release," 14 August 1981, and letter to Robert
Moore, 19 August 1981, BCPC, box 4, file Neutron Bomb. Yorke's resolution
was altered in a way to which the author objected: a clause demanding that
the Soviet Union withdraw its soldiers from Afghanistan.

38 JD to Kelly North, 1 October 1982, CPC, box 18, file Correspondence General. Morgan quoted Pasti in a letter to the Liberal minister of labour, Charles
Caccia: "The terrifying aspect of the involution of U.S. military policy is the
attempt to convince U.S. public opinion that it is possible to wage a strategic war, that it is possible to win it and that the price of 20 to 30 million
U.S. dead, leaving aside the hundreds of millions of dead in other countries,
is an equitable and acceptable price to pay for the destruction forever of the
Soviet Union and communists in the world." 22 September 1982.

39 Ibid., "Public Concern for Consequences of Nuclear War for the City of Toronto," draft by Gordon Flowers, executive director of the CPC, n.d.

40 Vautour to C. Stewart, 13 September 1982, CPC, box 18, file Correspondence, General. The word "tremendous" was omitted from the typed letter, but present in the handwritten letter addressed to Stewart.

41 "Making Peace in Toronto: Timeline of City of Toronto Actions & Proclamations," Hiroshima Nagasaki Day Coalition, http://hiroshimadaycoalition.ca/data/uploads/Making%20Pe ace%20in%20Toronto%20(Timeline%20&%20City%20Proclamations).pdf

42 Jeanne McGuire, for the executive of the CCW, Toronto, 7 April 1982; Gordon Flowers to Congress of Canadian Women, 22 April 1982, CPC, box 18, file Correspondence.

43 "Summary of Voice of Women Brief on NORAD," submitted to the Standing Committee on External Affairs and National Defence, October 1980, BCPC, box 4 file NORAD. The US document referenced by VOW, NSC-59, has been mostly declassified, with the exception of one or two sentences. What has been released does not refer to a first strike policy, but the new policy was meant to provide greater flexibility for US nuclear policy in the event of war. NSC-59 called for the possibility of an automatic response from the US in the event that the USSR launched its own first strike.

44 Stark to Morgan 8 February 1982, CPC box 18, file Correspondence – Disarmament.

45 The CPC had no formal presence in Québec, but worked with le Conseil, headed by Jean St-Denis, which pursued similar kinds of strategies as the congress did in English Canada, including letters to the prime minister and marches for peace and disarmament. In 1982 the Conseil organized a large demonstration on 5 June which saw about 10,000 people participate in Montreal. Like the Canadian Peace Congress, le Conseil was affiliated with the World Peace Council.

46 For a discussion of Thompson's involvement in the peace movement see Bryan D. Palmer, E.P. Thompson: Objections and Oppositions (Verso: London, 1994), chap. 5. Palmer pointed out that "Thompson's protests for peace reached back decades and encompassed opposition to the Korean War, support for the World Peace Council's Stockholm Appeal to outlaw nuclear weapons, and dogged resistance to the imperial crusades of Britain, France, and others in Malaya, Cyprus, Kenya, Algeria, and British Guiana, all dutifully backed by the Cold War's respectable social democrats in the Labour Party," 127.

47 E.P. Thompson, "Sleepwalking into a Trap: END and the Soviet 'Peace Offensive,'" The Nation (26 February 1983), 233, 235.

48 Beth Richards, "E.P. Thompson Tells Toronto Audience: Canada Can Be Leader," *The Peace Calendar* (September 1983).

49 In some senses NATO was a global organization from its inception, with the inclusion of Algeria in its scope, and other countries and regions that were not part of the North Atlantic world: Italy, Greece, and Turkey. The Korean War was intimately tied to NATO, and formed the key to the military mobilization of the organization in the 1950s. The Vietnam War, decolonization, and the 1980s war in Afghanistan were part of the international frame within which NATO members debated and discussed strategic and foreign policy issues. Even though there were often significant differences in opinion about how to deal with the Global South it is not possible to separate the geographical scope of the organization from the global issues that its membership engaged.

50 Canada, "Security and Disarmament: A Minority Report," April 1982, CPC, box 18, Correspondence, Canadian Government House of Commons. The six MPs were Pauline Jewett, Bob Ogle, Walter McLean, Douglas Roche, Paul McRae, and Terry Sargeant.

51 Nehring and Ziemann, "Do All Paths Lead to Moscow?," 12. Neither did the Canadian government blindly follow Reagan's Star Wars lead. In 1985, Prime Minister Brian Mulroney announced that Canada would not take part in the Space Defence Initiative, though Canadian companies would not be barred from seeking defence contracts associated with the program.

52 United States Department of State, Foreign Affairs Note on "Soviet Active Measures: The World Peace Council," April 1985, 1–8. The US note interpreted the discussion as a debate within the Peace Council, but to some extent the positions of Zhukov and Primakov were complementary.

53 Gordon Flowers, "Letter," *The Peace Calendar* (December 1983). Flowers advised that Thompson's opposition would "only create division in the peace movement and assist the supporters of a return to the Cold War."

54 E.P. Thompson, "The Real Meaning of Star Wars," *The Nation* (9 March 1985), 275.

55 Eudora Pendergast, "National Conference Stresses Issues, Goals," *The Peace Calendar* (March 1984); Wittner, *Toward Nuclear Abolition*, 200.

56 He also criticized the decision by Operation Dismantle and others to bring a court case against the Canadian government, based on violating the Charter of Rights, for allowing the testing of the cruise missile on Canadian soil.

57 Martin Zeilig, "The Views of the Delegates," *The Peace Calendar* (March 1984).

58 Simon Rosenblum, "Soviet Apologists," *The Peace Calendar* (March 1984).

59 Matthew Clark, "Letters to the Editor," *The Peace Calendar* (April 1984).

Clark was a member of the Toronto Disarmament Network and a member of the Toronto Peace Petition Caravan Campaign Steering Committee.

60 Bob Penner and Christopher Ross, "Caravaners Plan Coalition Conference," *The Peace Calendar* (November 1984). Representatives on the planning committee included: David Delaunay, Ploughshares Sudbury; Leyla Raphael, President Québec PPCC; Jamie Scott, coordinator of the Election Priorities Project; Michael Manolson, coordinator of the PPCC; Lynn Connell, Performing Artists for Nuclear Disarmament; Jim Stark, Operation Dismantle; Gordon Flowers, executive director, Canadian Peace Congress; Chris Ross, Psychologists for Social Responsibility; Walker Jones, Women's International League for Peace and Freedom, Ottawa; David Langille, Peaceworks; Andrew Van Velzen, Cruise Missile Conversion Project; Joan Rentoul, Guelph Disarmament Committee; Andre Jacob, Conseil Québécois Pour la Paix; John Wilkinson, Brockville; Kristin Ostling, Ottawa.

61 "Canadian Peace Congress National Board Meeting 10–12 May 1985 Toronto Action Resolutions," BCPC, box 1, file Canadian Peace Congress.

62 Penner, "Peace Alliance Underway," *Peace Magazine* (April 1985): 23.

63 CPC, box 42a, file F9 "Canadian Peace Alliance – Structure Document, 1985."

64 BCPC, box 1, file Canadian Peace Congress.

65 Ibid., Canadian Peace Congress Press Release, 10 October 1985.

66 Ibid., box 11, file National Board Meetings 1988, 26–8 February 1988.

67 David Cortright, *Peace Works: The Citizen's Role in Ending the Cold War* (Boulder: Westview Press, 1993), 209; Evangelista, *Unarmed Forces*, 270–1. Tairov wrote a long letter to Gorbachev outlining his critical views of the World Peace Council, and on which Gorbachev wrote: "Check into this and get back to me with whatever you find out." See Metta Spencer, *The Russian Quest for Peace and Democracy* (New York: Lexington Books, 2010), 10.

68 In 1988, recalling Blumenfeld's recommendation, Gordon Flowers lamented that the congress had not adopted the suggestion. He stated that the lesson was that "we must accept or reject all ideas and proposals on their intrinsic merit, whether they advance the cause of peace or not, whether they contribute positively or negatively to the growth of our movement." Board Meetings, 26–8 February 1988, BCPC, box 11, file National Board Meetings 1988.

69 Gordon Flowers to Brian Mulroney, 27 January 1986, BCPC, box 11, file Canadian Peace Congress Correspondence.

70 Flowers to Councils and Affiliates, "OUT OF NORAD," 19 February 1986, BCPC, box 11, file Canadian Peace Congress Correspondence.

71 Wittner, *Toward Nuclear Abolition*, 363.

72 "Circulars," National Board to Peace Councils, 16 May 1986, CPC, box 26, file F11.

73 Ibid., Declaration of the World Peace Council, "To Safeguard Peace on Earth," adopted at the World Peace Council meeting in Sofia, 24–7 April 1986.

74 John Morgan, *Pursuing the Dove*, 142.

75 Ibid., 146–7. Prince worked closely with Flowers and there is correspondence between them discussing policy issues at this time.

76 "Canadian Peace Congress State of the Organization," n.d. [likely 1993], BCPC, box 11, file Canadian Peace Congress: National Board Meeting 1989.

77 *Peace Magazine* (November 1985): 26.

78 "Appeal for Participation in the World Congress Consecrated to the International Year of Peace," August 1986, CPC, box 26, file F26, Conferences World Congress Peace Appeal.

79 Carmela Allevato of Vancouver was one example of this dynamic at work. She briefly served as head of the BC Peace Council in Vancouver, but soon quit and dedicated her activism to the operations of End the Arms Race (EAR). Allevato, however, continued to coordinate her work in EAR with the BC Peace Council.

80 Wittner, *Toward Nuclear Abolition*, 364–6.

81 "Discussions Underway to Strengthen Work for Peace," *Canadian Tribune* (30 January 1989), 7. Italics missing in original.

82 "Disarmament Campaigns: An Interview with Tair Tairov," *Peace Magazine* (December 1988–January 1989): 30.

83 Regina Peace Council memo to Congress, signed by Ed Lehman, January 1989, BCPC, box 11, file Canadian Peace Congress: National Board Meeting 1989. In March 1992, the Regina Council, under President Jaki Russell, wrote Rosaleen Ross that her council had "good working relations with the WPC prior to and immediately after the Gulf War." As a result they were investigating the possibility of having direct ongoing relations with the WPC." Ibid., Lehman to Ross, 17 March 1992. In 2017 Lehman remained active in the organization as president of the Regina Peace Council, commenting on a wide range of international issues pertaining to Canada's role in the world.

84 Ibid., Canadian Peace Congress to President Gorbachev, 18 January 1991.

85 Most of the local councils also ended their activities in the early 1990s, though some, including Manitoba (established in the mid-1980s in Winnipeg) and Regina, continued their local community and peace work. The World Peace Council was significantly reorganized in 1996 and a new Canadian Peace Congress re-emerged in 2006, in a substantially altered interna-

tional system and age of conflict and violence. John Hanly Morgan sent a written letter of welcome as he was too ill to attend the meeting, but he was elected honorary president. For the current organization's activities, which are shaped by Cold War legacies and big power rivalries, visit http://www.canadianpeacecongress.ca/. Information on the 2006 meeting is available at http://www.simpsonsask.ca/PeaceNews14-2.html.

SECTION FIVE

Human Rights, Corporate Rights

12

Canadian Corporate Social Irresponsibility: A History

STEPHANIE BANGARTH

"I must say that I feel the whole Canadian policy to be very hypocritical. We talk a good game but then proceed to act inconsistently by promoting trade with the countries whose policies we denounce."

F. Andrew Brewin to Miss Hazel-May Brooks, 1 February 1974[1]

The year was 1974 and the issue of Canadian trade with South Africa was making the headlines. It reflected the increasing awareness of and support for human rights in Canadian foreign policy during the late 1960s and the early 1970s. The period ushered forth a wave of foreign policy emergencies and human rights challenges. Conflict in India, Pakistan, and South America (principally Chile and Argentina), alongside refugee issues in Czechoslovakia, Chile, and Uganda, as well as the ongoing problem of Rhodesia and South Africa concerning apartheid, occupied the foreign policy landscape. These issues prompted significant debate in Canada about the relationship between economic assistance – notably foreign aid, Export Development Corporation credits, tariff concessions, and multilateral development bank loans – and Canada's support of foreign governments engaging in human rights violations. As a result, there was a concerted effort on the part of some parliamentarians and civil society groups to enact legislation to prohibit the Canadian government or its agencies from providing economic aid to such regimes. These efforts by concerned Canadian parliamentarians exemplified an attempt to move Canada away from its traditional posture of divorcing economic aid from considerations of human justice, and enshrine human rights as a fundamental tenet of Canadian foreign policy. But despite these efforts, and contrary to the assertions of some human rights scholars, the 1970s were no watershed for human rights, certainly not with respect to Canada's foreign and trade policies.

This paper begins a conversation on the origins of efforts to legislate government and corporate social responsibility in Canadian human rights history.[2] From the pinnacle of Canada's principled stand on apartheid in the 1980s to the nadir of the largest arms contract in Canadian history signed recently with Saudi Arabia, it is important to highlight how the defense of human rights has been articulated and circumvented in the relationship between commerce and rights. Activist historians would do well to revisit this history and remind Canadians of the many attempts to prohibit the Canadian government – and by extension its Crown corporations and Canadian banks – from using their resources to assist countries that consistently violate the basic human rights of their citizens. This chapter makes the assertion that corporate social responsibility is as much the purview of the Canadian government and its Crown corporations as it is that of the private sector. The federal government engages in corporate social irresponsibility when it allows its Crown corporations to act in an "undiplomatic" fashion, as this chapter will demonstrate, thus broadening the work that "traditional" diplomatic historians have done in the field of corporate and government irresponsibility.

As a broader historical trend, more attention is now paid toward humanitarianism in international affairs.[3] But in general, Canadian history, and particularly international history, has remained relatively silent on Canadian corporate social irresponsibility.[4] Corporate Social Responsibility ("CSR"), as defined by Global Affairs Canada, is "the voluntary activities undertaken by a company to operate in an economic, social and environmentally sustainable manner."[5] Non-shareholder stakeholders in this context are expanded to include the governing values of the society at large. This broad definition poses a challenge for scholars, lawyers, and those who run corporations. This chapter will explore mid-twentieth-century Canadian efforts to link corporate social responsibility, human rights, and economic development, via three examples in "undiplomacy": nuclear proliferation, apartheid South Africa, and the arms trade. In this way, this chapter contributes to the new international history by moving beyond "high" politics and elite actors and the traditional focus on economic and security issues. More than "history from below," this chapter also reflects the larger volume's aim of envisioning Canadian internation-al history from a multiplicity of viewpoints, which in this case involves the voices of civil society actors, concerned citizens, and opposition politicians whose concern for human rights in Canadian foreign policy drove their actions in the period under study. It also adds nuance to the field of human rights history in international rela-tions more generally.

CANADA AND NUCLEAR PROLIFERATION

As early as the mid-1970s controversy erupted when over 7,000 Chilean and other Latin American refugees were admitted to Canada after the violent 1973 overthrow of Salvador Allende's democratically elected Socialist-Communist government. Chilean and non-Chilean supporters of the old regime had fled the oppression of Chile's new military ruler, General Pinochet, in the wake of the coup. Thousands escaped to neighbouring Argentina where, under its own right-wing military dictatorship, it became a dangerous place for the Chilean exiles. Although Canada took the refugees in, it did so grudgingly – at least at first.[6]

Around the same time, Argentina was considering the purchase of CANDU nuclear reactors. Atomic Energy of Canada Limited (AECL) in 1972 submitted a bid to Argentina's equivalent nuclear oversight body, the CNEA. The Canadian government provided a $129.45 mil-lion concessionary loan from the Export Development Corporation, payable over twenty-five years, with repayment starting only when the reactor entered service, which it did in 1983. At a time when Canadi-ans were concerned over nuclear proliferation and the safety of nuclear energy, the sale of the CANDU 6 reactor to a right-wing mili-tary government naturally raised the ire of a good many Canadians. Alongside the context of Argentina's treatment of the Chilean and Uruguayan refugees, it appeared to many Canadians that the Liberal government under Prime Minister Pierre Trudeau was turning a blind eye to a number of problematic issues. It is worth noting that in Feb-ruary of 1977 the US government cut military aid to Argentina due to evidence of human rights violations presented to Congressional hear-ings on Argentina.[7]

In Canada, the Inter-Church Committee on Chile (under the aus-pices of the Canadian Council of Churches), in addition to the Soci-ety of Friends, OXFAM, and other civil society actors, pressured the government to yield on its strict immigration concerns. However, these groups also mobilized on the issue of economic support to the junta and coordinated their efforts closely with the NDP's Foreign Affairs critic, F. Andrew Brewin, who spoke frequently in the House of Commons and to the Standing Committee on External Affairs and National Defence.[8] In particular, the Inter-Church Committee on Chile issued a fact-finding report that urged the Trudeau government to stop economic and military aid to the Argentine military dictatorship and to hold a referendum in Parliament on the sale of the CANDU reactor "to this unstable and militaristic government."[9]

In response, the NDP had Brewin draft and attempt to pass a bill on the issue of fair trade and human rights. In 1978, Bill C-71, a private member's bill, was Brewin's effort to have principles of human rights recognized in Canadian trade operations. It would fail: the bill died on the floor of the House of Commons, voted down by the majority Liberals. Other attempts included Bill C-371, an act to prohibit aid to foreign countries consistently violating human rights (1977), recast as Bill C-272 in 1978. Both bills embodied the NDP's position that the Canadian government and Canadian banks should not have been using their resources to assist countries that consistently violated the basic human rights of their citizens. In the late 1970s all the major chartered banks in Canada, either directly or indirectly through international consortia of banks, were funding the apartheid government of South Africa, and some banks were involved in loans to Chile and Nicaragua. Bill C-371/C-272 was intended to prevent the Canadian government and Canadian banks from aiding these regimes if it was established by the information provided by reputable international agencies that they were violating human rights.[10]

As noted above, Canada has had a questionable history with respect to the sale of Canadian nuclear technology, facilities, and material. Duane Bratt has noted this particularly in the 1960s and the 1970s, with sales to dictatorships with very poor human rights records (Pakistan and Taiwan in the 1960s, and Argentina, South Korea, and Romania in the 1970s).[11] On 18 May 1974, India exploded a twelve-kiloton fission weapon at the Pokhran site in the Rajasthan desert. The land for the test was acquired in 1966 after 200,000 people were forcibly displaced.[12] The weapon was made with plutonium from the CIRUS reactor that Canada had transferred to India on the condition that it be used for peaceful purposes, but external inspections were not required. The reactor was donated by Canada in 1956 under the

Commonwealth "Colombo Plan" aid program, which sought to promote economic and social development in South and Southeast Asia.[13] The gift helped pave the way for future reactor sales: Canada sold India two CANDU reactors in 1963 and 1966.

Although Canada advised India that plutonium from the reactor could not be used for nuclear explosives, India claimed that the agreement did not exclude nuclear explosions "for peaceful purposes." Following the 1974 explosion, India stuck to its story that the test was a "peaceful nuclear explosion." As India's high commissioner to Canada noted, "any device can be used for good or for evil depending upon the motivation."[14] Or, as External Affairs Minister Alan MacEachen maintained, if Canada did not sell its reactors abroad, another country would anyway.[15]

As David Martin has noted, the Indian nuclear test was a crippling blow to the myth of the peaceful Canadian nuclear program. Canada had received many warnings that India was moving towards nuclear weapons production, but had done little about it. Pierre Trudeau had even visited India in 1971 to discuss the matter personally with Indira Gandhi.[16] However, in the wake of the test and following years of pressure by the NDP and non-proliferation activists, on 22 May 1974, then-secretary of state for foreign affairs Mitchell Sharp stated, "The Canadian government has suspended shipments to India of nuclear equipment and material and has instructed the Atomic Energy of Canada Limited, pending clarification of the situation, to suspend its cooperation with India regarding nuclear reactor projects and the more general technological exchange arrangements which it has with the Indian Energy Commission."[17]

At the height of the nuclear debate, in Canada and elsewhere, the export of nuclear reactors added a new and terrifying dimension. With the aid of a Canadian supplied reactor, the famous CANDU reactor, anti-nuclear and peace activists argued that it was impossible to separate the question of nuclear exports from that of nuclear arms proliferation.[18] At a keynote address during Canada Week at St Lawrence University in upstate New York, Rev. David MacDonald (MP Egmont, PEI), a long-time human rights parliamentarian activist, Progressive Conservative, and collaborator with Brewin, noted that Canada had been involved in building nuclear reactors in four countries that had yet to ratify the Nuclear Non-Proliferation Treaty – India, Pakistan, South Korea, and Argentina.[19] MacDonald and many others, including the Voice of Women, called on nations to promote the development of renewable and indigenous energy sources. But above all, Canadians were concerned about the ethics of nuclear proliferation. Many activists asserted that, in ratifying the Nuclear Non-Proliferation Treaty, Canada was in effect declaring that it would participate in serving as a "moral watchdog" committed to the development of world peace. As MacDonald noted, "the causes of war lie not in the implements of destruction, but in the underlying tensions brought on by such problems as we face today in the disparities among the common inhabitants of Earth."[20] Activists and parliamentarians called on the government to engage in an export moratorium of all nuclear materials.[21]

In December 1974, a new proliferation policy was partially revealed. First, it required a binding assurance that Canadian nuclear material, equipment, and technology would not be used for a nuclear explosive device, and it rejected the excuse of "peaceful nuclear explosions." Second, the policy prohibited in the "contamination clause" the use of Canadian-supplied technology for nuclear explosive devices. Third, exporters of nuclear technology and materials had to go through the Department of Industry, Trade and Commerce, and the Atomic Energy Control Board.[22] These three points were actually part of an eight-point program approved by Cabinet in December 1974, but not made public until 1975. The other safeguards included "a binding recognition of Canada's right of prior consent over: transfers to third countries; reprocessing of Canadian-origin material; and enrichment of uranium beyond 20%. As well, Canada maintained the right to apply fallback safeguards on reprocessing and enrichment should IAEA safeguards cease to be applied for any reason. Finally a binding commitment required the provision of adequate physical protection for Canadian-origin material."[23]

For two years after the Indian nuclear test, Canada continued with negotiations in order to convince India to accept the new safeguards. However, India remained obdurate, and on 18 May 1976 Canada formally terminated nuclear cooperation as India agreed to safeguard only the two Rajasthan reactors. In December 1976, the Canadian government announced a further upgrading of its non-proliferation policy when it decided that nuclear trade would be restricted to those countries which had signed the Non-Proliferation Treaty.[24] The fundamental problem with paper safeguards is that agreements can simply be ignored. This was clearly seen in the original transgression of India in the use of plutonium from CIRUS despite a bilateral agreement. The repercussions of Canada's nuclear trade with India extended elsewhere in the region. Canada sold a 125-megawatt reactor to Pakistan in 1959 and a CANDU heavy-water nuclear reactor in 1964. After India's nuclear test in 1974, Canada wanted Pakistan to promise never to build a bomb using plutonium from Canadian reactors, but Pakistan, which went to war with India in 1965, refused. Pakistani prime minister Zulfiqar Ali Bhutto declared that Pakistan would build the bomb "even if we have to eat grass or leaves or to remain hungry."[25]

CANADA AND APARTHEID SOUTH AFRICA

It is likely that most Canadians are unaware that Canada largely supported apartheid in South Africa, and that South Africa looked to Canada for guidance for its own odious policies. Many scholars have indicated how Canada's policies towards First Nations, and in particular residential schools, informed South Africa's approach towards apartheid.[26] Canada, not unlike many Western governments of the day, expressed its abhorrence for apartheid while being unwilling to place meaningful economic or diplomatic pressure on South Africa. According to Linda Freeman, "this 'having your cake and eating it too' policy became known as a policy of 'balance,' giving something in theory to questions of social justice and human rights and a lot in practice to the Canadian corporate sector."[27] In fact, *Foreign Policy for Canadians*, the Trudeau government's foreign policy master plan published in 1970, said as much, noting that "Canadian interests would be best served by maintaining its current policy framework on the problems of Southern Africa which balances two policy themes [Economic Growth, Social Justice] of importance to Canadians."[28] More than a decade before that, however, John Diefenbaker refused to cancel the 1932 Canada-South Africa trade agreement, an earlier indication of how the Canadian government practised its duplicitous policy of stating opposition to apartheid yet continuing to do business with the former British Dominion.[29] Western investment in South Africa came under fire over the course of the early 1970s, especially following Adam Raphael's articles in the *Guardian* in which he exposed how many British firms paid their black workers at rates below the Poverty Datum Line (which refers to subsistence rather than a minimum living wage). In June of 1973, Hugh Nangle wrote a series of articles in the *Montreal Gazette* that investigated six Canadian firms with subsidiaries in South Africa. Of the six, only one, Ford, compensated its workers above the Poverty Datum Line.[30] Whereas Britain would establish a parliamentary inquiry to investigate the conduct of British corporations in South Africa, Mitchell Sharp, the secretary of state for external affairs, merely urged Canadian companies operating there "to act as good corporate citizens in ways that will make the Canadian people proud of them."[31] Frankly, as Azeezah Kanji has remarked, Canada "spent too long on the wrong side of apartheid."[32]

Amidst such hypocrisy, concern over apartheid was expressed officially by the forerunner to the NDP, the Co-operative Commonwealth Federation (CCF), in its National Executive Resolutions of 1952. The CCF declared that the policy of segregation and repression followed by D.F. Malan's Nationalist government was in direct contravention of the Universal Declaration of Human Rights and to the principles of the United Nations. It called upon the Canadian government to take its stand firmly in the UN in opposition to the South African government's policy of apartheid.[33] At its federal convention in Vancouver in July 1973, the NDP adopted a series of resolutions on South Africa and Rhodesia, including calling on the Canadian government to provide guidelines to all corporations operating or investing in Southern Africa in order to "end Canadian investment in oppression."[34]

By the early 1970s the Canadian government began to show some initial and tentative points of unease with the blatant promotion of economic relations with South Africa. For example, it would waver in its approach towards Crown corporations that were directly involved in South Africa. In April of 1970 the government advised Polymer, a Crown corporation, to divest its $4 million holding in Sentrachem, a South African synthetic rubber company. This move seemed to set a general precedent to the effect that, although the government would not step into the affairs of the private sector, no Crown Corporation could be seen to profit from trade with South Africa. Still, Canada maintained Commonwealth tariffs for the benefit of South Africa; it banned military exports but continued to export spare military parts to the country. On 16 October 1970, it became public knowledge that Air Canada, a Crown corporation, had signed a sales agreement with South African Airways. An Air Canada spokesman heralded this as a "normal, standard agreement."[35]

The Air Canada/South African Airways tour package itself seemed a magnificent affair and promised much in the way of incredible traditional touristic delights. From the big city lights of Johannesburg and Capetown, to cultural sights in Salisbury, Rhodesia, to the featured highlights of Kruger National Park and the Hluhluwe Game Reserve, the twenty-five-day tour guaranteed to be a whirlwind of impressive South African hospitality.[36]

The members of the Committee for a Just Canadian Policy Towards Africa (CJCPTA) did not view the Air Canada/SAA Agreement that way. It was a representative group of generally socially conscious elites, many of whom had longtime interests and involvement with an independent Africa. The concerns expressed over the agreement were threefold: that it involved the sale by Air Canada of package tours to South Africa which in fact could not be available to Canadians who were not white; that the tours included a stay in Rhodesia, a *prima facie* offence under the United Nations Rhodesian Sanctions Order-in-Council; and that the federal government was willing to permit Air Canada to enter into direct commercial relations with a South African public corporation after announcing that it had asked Polymer to divest itself of its South African investment. In and of itself, the Air Canada brochure was wholly misleading, as it indicated that no visa would be required of holders of Commonwealth passports. But according to the South Africa information manual at the time, only Canadian passport holders *"of pure European descent"* required no visa. It also promised accommodation in hotels which could not be made available to non-white Canadians. Moreover, as the trip included a hotel stay in Rhodesia, funds paid by Canadian tourists through Air Canada would have to be transferred to hoteliers in Rhodesia, which was contrary to Article 13 (2) of the UN Rhodesian Sanction Regulations.

Mitchell Sharp initially received the brunt of the organized opposition, both in letter form and through in-person meetings with select committee members. Sharp was unbending, and maintained that the deal was strictly a sale arrangement, "relating only to the selling of tickets and cargo space." Critics refused to accept this reasoning and increased their efforts to change government and corporate policy. To that end, Brewin was instrumental in getting the CJCPTA and other sympathetic groups such as CUSO and the YWCA a hearing before the Standing Committee on External Affairs, of which he was a long-standing member.[37]

Letters were also sent to Yves Pratte, chief executive and chairman of the board of Air Canada. Pratte, in particular, was urged to reconsider "the implications of this agreement to Canada's relations with independent Africa." Air Canada's official response to the CJCPTA came over five months later in late April 1971. It largely skirted the direct issue, hiding behind a description of the company's involvement in the International Air Transport Association.[38] In addition to appealing directly to the federal government via Sharp, to Air Canada executives, and to sympathetic opposition MPs, the CJCPTA studied other options, including challenging Air Canada for publishing misleading advertising. The committee also considered a test case: a Mr and Mrs Lawrence Cummings of Toronto offered to be a Canadian couple of mixed race who would attempt to purchase tickets for the package tour. The CJCPTA investigated an appeal to the Ontario Human Rights Commission based on the aforementioned test case, but this option was quashed when the committee was advised that the jurisdiction of the Ontario Human Rights Commission covered matters only within provincial jurisdiction.[39]

These efforts also paralleled similar ones taking place in the US which did not go unnoticed by Canadian activists. Brewin kept a close correspondence with Senator Edward Kennedy regarding such issues. In 1972, the Comprehensive Anti-Apartheid Act had its initial introduction. Sponsored by Senators Richard Lugar, William Roth, and Mitch McConnell, the CAAA was the first United States antiapartheid legislation. The act was initiated by Congressman Ronald V. Dellums. The legislation banned all new US trade and investment in South Africa and spurred similar sanctions in Europe and Japan. Direct air links were also banned, including South African Airways flights to US airports. The act also required various US departments and agencies to suppress funds and assistance to the then proapartheid government.

Canadian anti-apartheid activists ultimately found success in their campaign to stop Air Canada from offering its vacation of a lifetime to South Africa and Rhodesia. In a letter to Brewin, Robert Matthews of the Committee for a Just Canadian Policy towards Africa noted that

> As far as I am able to discern at present, Air Canada has dropped all tours to Rhodesia and South Africa, though it still remains linked to South Africa Airways through the sales agreement. We feel, as I'm sure you do, that this agreement is undesirable and implicitly associates the Government and people of Canada with South Africa's policy of apartheid. In fact, the Government has sought to avoid complications over different entry

requirements for black and white Canadians. In a Press Release issued on May 21, 1971, the Passport Office of the Department urges all Canadians visiting South Africa to "check their individual visa requirements." Surely by so passing the buck to the South African Embassy the Government cannot hope to escape its own involvement.[40]

Eventually bowing to public and opposition pressure, the Trudeau government, via the Department of External Affairs (DEA), exerted its influence to halt Air Canada-South African Airways tours to Rhodesia, but maintained Air Canada's right to offer tours to South Africa. Thus, Canadians of "pure European descent" would still be the only group permitted a visa to travel to South Africa, leaving the Canadian government complicit in the participation of sales of services available on the basis of "race" to select Canadians. While Canadians expressed their "broad revulsion" at the Trudeau government's active and unnecessary identification with racial discrimination via the Air Canada-South African Airways deal, officials in the DEA described the reciprocal sales agreement between the two airlines as "a very normal commercial agreement" and noted that it was "quite natural for some people to protest." Claude Taylor, Air Canada's vice president for government and industrial affairs, even went so far as to say that although the race policies in South Africa precluded some Canadian citizens from obtaining visas, that was "no reason not to sell to the people who can."[41]

Air Canada would try again to promote its tours to South Africa, only to be stopped in October of 1986. NDP MP Howard McCurdy discovered that Air Canada flew sixty-four Canadians to London as part of the first leg of their Air Canada/South African Airlines tour of South Africa. In response, External Affairs Minister Joe Clark moved to tighten a loophole in the London sanctions that enabled Air Canada to continue its general sales agreement with South African Airways.[42]

CANADA AND THE ARMS TRADE

The issue of support for repressive regimes via foreign aid, Export Development Corporation credit, tariff concessions, and multinational development bank loans continued into the 1970s. Opposition parliamentarians unrelentingly crafted private members' bills to address this, which again mimicked legislation passed by Congress in the US. In 1977 David MacDonald tabled Bill C-404, "An Act to Prohibit Aid to Foreign Countries Violating Human Rights." It would prohibit the Canadian government or its agencies from providing any economic aid or benefit to repressive regimes but would exempt assistance supplied through international relief agencies. Bill C-404 closely reflected three amendments to the US trade and aid legislation passed by Congress (US Foreign Corrupt Practices Act) which were then used to prevent certain loans to Chile and the USSR.[43]

The American efforts came about with the election of Democrat Jimmy Carter as president in 1976, which brought a new emphasis, based on Carter's personal ideology, to US foreign policy. Carter believed that the nation's foreign policy should reflect its highest moral principles – a definite break with the policy and practices of the Nixon administration. By the end of 1977, the Department of State established the Bureau of Human Rights and Humanitarian Affairs (now known as the Bureau of Democracy, Human Rights, and Labor). But in Canada in the late 1970s, such sentiments were not in evidence. Like Brewin's earlier efforts, Bill C-404 was voted down in the House of Commons by the majority Trudeau Liberal government.

This was neither the first nor the last time that commercial interests and government human rights statements clashed. Canada has a long history of exporting military equipment around the world and authorizing trade with problematic regimes.[44] In the past twenty-five years Canada sold $5.8 billion worth of weapons to countries with questionable human rights records. Algeria, for example, received $28 million worth of Canadian-made military gear despite being embroiled in a vicious civil war and being classified as a dictatorship by the Washington, DC-based think tank Freedom House.[45] The Gulf War cemented Canada's relations with Saudi Arabia, which purchased $227 million worth of Canadian military equipment in 1992.[46] By the mid-1990s, Canada sold more than 1,600 light armored vehicles to the human rights-violating Gulf kingdom. In 2014, Canada – via the Canadian Commercial Corporation, a Crown corporation – signed a $15 billion deal to sell military vehicles built by General Dynamic Land Systems in London, Ontario. The vehicles in the current deal are in fact meant to replace the ones sold to Saudi Arabia in 1986. In 1986, Joe Clark, then minister of foreign affairs for the Conservative government under Brian Mulroney, travelled to Saudi Arabia and brokered a deal for LAVs worth an estimated $250 million. The company making the vehicles at that time was GM Defense (bought by General Dynamics Land Systems in 2002). Then, the fear was over the potential use of the vehicles, equipped with arms, against Israel. Concerns were raised in the House of Commons, including by John Brewin (NDP MP for Victoria), the party's defence critic and Andrew Brewin's son. The sale ultimately went through when the Saudis convinced Clark that the LAVs would only be used domestically. In 1986 the deal was as contentious as it is today. Brewin and other critics successfully managed to get the government to agree to a special Commons study of arms export policy. This study eventually led Lloyd Axworthy, minister of foreign affairs for the Liberal government under Jean Chretien, to bring in a progressive policy a few years later. The "human security" concept would be at the heart of Liberal foreign policy for much of the 1990s.[47]

Saudi Arabia is a country internationally singled out for its problematic human rights record. Initially Prime Minister Stephen Harper, International Trade Minister Ed Fast, and former London mayor Joe Fontana all touted the deal's economic benefits for London, but little mention was made of Saudi Arabia's poor human rights record until just before the federal election in 2015. Project Ploughshares has since established that at the time that the Saudi deal was announced in February 2014, the required export permits had not been issued. This is especially significant, as a key element of the export permits is a human rights assessment to determine that the deal in question does not contravene Canada's export control policies. The government should have enforced, from the very beginning, the strict export regulations that guarantee that our military equipment is not used against civilians. More ethical questions needed to be asked from the outset, particularly as Canada's arms industry increases its sales to clients in the Middle East. Linking our military sales to progress made on improving the Saudi regime's human rights record is only one "effective" solution.[48] Prime Minister Justin Trudeau and former foreign affairs minister Stephane Dion must have been studying the approach of Trudeau Sr and Mitchell Sharp, as they were deaf to sustained criticism.

"Canadian support of international human rights tends to hit a hard wall when it comes to the arms trade," Srdjan Vucetic noted recently in a discussion about Foreign Affairs Minister Chrystia Freeland's April 2017 announcement that Canada would finally sign the Arms Trade Treaty (ATT), and that her government was introducing new legislation to harmonize Canadian laws with the new treaty.[49] This long-overdue measure means that although the ATT cannot stop members from selling weapons to whomever they deem fit, deals with human rights-abusing buyers are more costly politically. Under the ATT, Canada and its weapons-producing companies, from large to small, will have to provide more transparency with respect to its exports – which may reveal the extent of Canada's impact on the global arms trade. Perhaps this may lead Minister Freeland to follow the lead of Swedish foreign minister Margot Wallström, who gained international headlines for her "feminist foreign policy."[50]

CONCLUSION

Throughout the 1960s and the 1970s, Brewin, MacDonald, and other concerned members of Parliament believed that Canada should not only be opposed to the practices of human rights-violating countries but that the federal government should take concrete action to ensure that Canadians would not even indirectly support them. Indeed, Brewin's justifications, noted in a letter to a constituent in 1979, hold as true today as they did then:

> The fact of the matter is that Canada, along with other nations, has in the United Nations supported resolutions containing condemnations of South Africa for its apartheid policies and its denial of basic rights such as free trials, freedom of speech, etc. Canada has expressed its abhorrence of these practices but has continued to extend aid through government grants and indirectly through encouraging Canadian corporations to invest in these countries. The same reasoning applies to various countries in South America where methods of terrorism and torture have been maintained to keep governments in power. In my view, and I share this with many other Canadians, if we condemn certain practices we should not assist them but discourage them.[51]

This examination of the Canadian state's undiplomatic approach to corporate social responsibility, and the efforts of opposition state and non-state actors serves to bridge human rights history, the study of social movements, and the efforts of the political left with international history. This is important for many reasons, not the least of which is that an examination of protest and human rights is largely (although not completely) absent from traditional Canadian international history. It is important to understand that individuals in and outside of government wanted Canada to be viewed as clearly opposed to those situations where the violations of human rights reached such proportions that they were unacceptable to the international community. In short, a wide array of actors in Canadian society wanted the Canadian government and its Crown corporations to cease "undiplomatic" activity.

While the current Liberal government is also at odds with the views of Canadians on the sale of armoured vehicles to Saudi Arabia, it remains unlikely that the deal brokered by a Canadian Crown corporation will be cancelled. History provides some directions for a way forward but yields very little by way of precedent. It is important to remember that a conflicted truth cannot and should not be hidden by historians of Canada's international affairs, including our assessment of "undiplomatic history." The examples described herein remind us that the arc of the moral universe does not bend towards justice by itself (apologies to Dr Martin Luther King, Jr); it required help from concerned Canadians, then as it does today.

NOTES

1 F. Andrew Brewin fonds, MG32 C26 vol. 91, file 91-15, LAC.
2 This paper will not deal with the mining industry as the scope of this sector requires lengthy and special treatment.
3 David Forsyth, "International Humanitarianism in the Contemporary World: Forms and Issues," in *Multilateralism Under Challenge: Power, International Order and Structural Change*, edited by Edward Neuman, Ramesh Thakur, and John Tirman (Washington: Brookings Institution Press, 2006), 237-8.
4 Some exceptions include Jon Weier and Stephanie Bangarth, "Merchants of Death: Canada's History of Questionable Exports," *Active History*, 18 April 2016, http://activehistory.ca/2016/04/merchants-of-death-canadas-history-of-questionable-exports/; Stephanie Bangarth, "'Vocal but Not Particularly Strong'? Air Canada's Ill-Fated Vacation Package to Rhodesia and South Africa and the Anti-Apartheid Movement in Canada," *International Journal* 71, no. 3 (2016): 1-10.
5 Government of Canada, Global Affairs Canada, "Corporate Social Responsibility," http://www.international.gc.ca/trade-agreements-accords-commerciaux/topics-domaines/other-autre/csr-rse.aspx?lang=eng.

6 Francis Peddie, *Young, Well-Educated and Adaptable: Chilean Exiles in Ontario and Quebec, 1973–2010* (Winnipeg: University of Manitoba Press, 2014); Stephanie Bangarth, "Citizen Activism, Refugees, and the State: Two Case-Studies in Canadian Immigration History," in *Canada since 1945*, edited by Catherine Briggs (Don Mills: Oxford University Press, 2014), 17–30.

7 Letter, Group for the Defense of Civil Rights in Argentina to F. Andrew Brewin, 28 February 1977, MG32 C26 vol. 74, file 2, LAC.

8 Excerpt from Minutes of Proceedings and Evidence of the Standing Committee on External Affairs and National Defence, 11 March 1975, MG32 C26 vol. 78, file 11, LAC.

9 Letter "Dear Sir" from Group/Committee for the Defense of Civil Rights in Argentina, 25 October 1976, MG32 C26, vol. 74, file 1, LAC.

10 Bill C-371: "An Act to prohibit aid to foreign countries consistently violating human rights." First reading 31 October 1977, MG32 C26 vol. 53 file 53, LAC; Bill C-272; "An Act to prohibit aid to foreign countries consistently violating human rights." First reading 30 October 1978, MG 32 C26 vol. 89, file 14, LAC.

11 Duane Bratt, *The Politics of CANDU Exports* (Toronto: University of Toronto Press, 2006): 78–80.

12 Thijs de la Court, *The Nuclear Fix: A Guide to Nuclear Activities in the Third World* (World Information Service on Energy, 1982), 296.

13 Bratt, *The Politics of CANDU Exports*, 104–14.

14 Letter, U.S. Bajpai to Andrew Brewin, 25 November 1974, MG32 C26, vol. 86, file 86-16, LAC.

15 Notes for an Address by Rev. David MacDonald, MP, 12 April 1976, MG32 C26, vol. 86, file 86-15, LAC.

16 David Martin, *Exporting Disaster: The Cost of Selling CANDU Reactors* (Campaign for Nuclear Phaseout, 1996), 53.

17 Ron Finch, *Exporting Danger* (Montreal: Black Rose Books, 1986), 84. It took two years for the government to clarify the situation.

18 Editorial, "The Nuclear Arrogance," *Globe and Mail*, 10 February 1976.

19 Notes for an Address by Rev. David MacDonald, MP, 12 April 1976, MG32 C26, vol. 86, file 86-15, LAC.

20 Ibid.

21 Ibid.; Voice of Women Statement, October 1975, MG32 C26, vol. 69, file 20, LAC; Brief presented to the Hon. Alan MacEachen on behalf of the Canadian Friends Service Committee, the Canadian Council of Churches, the United Church of Canada, the Korean United Church, the Coalition for Nuclear Responsibility, 26 February 1976, MG32 C26, vol. 86, file 86-17, LAC.

22 Statement by the Hon. Donald S. Macdonald, Minister of Energy, Mines and

Resources, 20 December 1974, MG32 C26, vol. 86, file 86-18, LAC; Finch, *Exporting Danger*, 86–7.

23 Statement by the Hon. Donald S. Macdonald, Minister of Energy, Mines and Resources, 20 December 1974, MG32 C26, vol. 86, file 86-18, LAC; Finch, *Exporting Danger*, 87.

24 Finch, *Exporting Danger*, 96–8.

25 Mahleeha Lohdi, "We'll Eat Grass but Build the Bomb," *Sunday Guardian*, 23 April 2017. Years later, it would be revealed that a Pakistani scientist sold nuclear secrets to Iran, Libya, and North Korea: "The Spider's Stratagem," *The Economist*, 3 January 2008.

26 Linda Freeman, *The Ambiguous Champion: Canada and South Africa in the Trudeau and Mulroney Years* (Toronto: University of Toronto Press, 1997), 16; Ron Bourgeault, "Canada Indians – The South African Connection," *Canadian Dimension* 21, no. 8 (January 1988): 6–10; John S. Saul, "Two Fronts of Anti-Apartheid Struggle: South Africa and Canada," *Transformation* 74 (2010): 135–51.

27 Linda Freeman, "Lessons from the Past: Canada and South Africa Then and Now," *South Africa Review* 11, no. 1 (1995): 3. See also Peter Henshaw, "Canada and the South African 'Disputes' at the United Nations, 1946–1961," *Canadian Journal of African Studies* 33, no. 1 (1999): 1–52.

28 Government of Canada, *Foreign Policy for Canadians* (Ottawa: Queen's Printer, 1970).

29 Brian Tennyson, *Canadian Relations with South Africa: A Diplomatic History* (Washington, DC: University Press of America, 1982): 170.

30 Ibid., 196–7. The six corporations investigated were Ford, Aluminium Company of Canada, Massey-Ferguson, Falconbridge, Bata, and Sun Life.

31 Tennyson, *Canadian Relations with South Africa*, 197; Canada, House of Commons, *Debates*, 9 July 1973.

32 Azeezah Kanji, "Canada Spent Too Long on the Wrong Side of Apartheid," *Toronto Star*, 6 April 2017.

33 CCF National Council Resolutions, 1952, MG32 C26, vol. 8, file 1, LAC.

34 Resolutions Passed by the New Democratic Party at the Federal Convention in Vancouver, July 1973, MG32 C26, vol. 91, file 14, LAC.

35 "Air Canada in Sales Pact Talks," *Globe and Mail*, 16 October 1970. Air Canada was privatized in 1988.

36 "The Black Paper: An Alternative Policy for Canada towards Southern Africa," *Canadian Journal of Africa Studies* 4, no. 3 (1970).

37 Letter, Pratt to Sharp, 25 November 1970, MG32 C26, vol. 89, file 11, LAC.; Letter, Sharp to Pratt, 23 December 1970; Letter, Pratt to Brewin, 27 May 1971; Letter, G.K. Helleiner to Brewin, 2 June 1971.

38 Letter, R.C. Pratt to Yves Pratte, 25 November 1970, MG32 C26, vol. 89, file 11, LAC; Letter, Claude Taylor, VP Government and Industry Affairs, Air Canada to Pratt, 23 April 1971.

39 Gerald Helleiner and R.C. Pratt, "Air Canada: South African Airways Agreement," May 3, 1971, MG32 C26, vol. 89, file 11, LAC.

40 Letter, Robert O. Matthews to Brewin, 24 June 1971, MG32 C26, vol. 91, file 9, LAC.

41 "Air Canada Drops South African Brochure, but Will Continue Selling Tours to Country," *Globe And Mail*, 3 June 1971; "Package Tour to Rhodesia And South Africa No Longer Sold or Promoted by Air Canada," *Globe and Mail*, 4 June 1971.

42 House of Commons, *Debates*, 22 October 1986, 612; 24 October 1986, 704–5 (as noted in Freeman, *The Ambiguous Champion*, 363n108); "Clark to Probe Charges Air Canada Broke Sanctions," *Ottawa Citizen*, 23 October 1986.

43 International Human Rights Bill, March 3, 1977, MG32 C26, vol. 53, file 11, LAC; Letter, David MacDonald to "Dear Colleague," 8 March 1977.

44 For an excellent explanation of the history of Canada's arms exports, see David Webster, "Episodes in Canada's Arms Trade: 1946 and 2016," *Active-History.ca*, 20 April 2016, http://activehistory.ca/2016/04/episodes-in-canadas-arms-trade-1946-and-2016/.

45 Srdjan Vucetic, "What Joining the Arms Trade Treaty Means for Canada," *opencanada.org*, 19 April 2017, https://www.opencanada.org/features/what-joining-arms-trade-treaty-means-canada/.

46 Norman Hillmer and J.L. Granatstein, *Empire to Umpire: Canada and the World to the 1990s* (Toronto: Copp, Clark, 1994), 318.

47 Lloyd Axworthy, Notes for an Address by the Honourable Lloyd Axworthy Minister of Foreign Affairs to the Woodrow Wilson International Center For Scholars, http://www.peace.ca/axworthyaddresstwoodrow.htm.

48 Erika Simpson, "Canada's Arms Deal with Saudi Arabia," *Political Science Publications* paper 123 (2016); Weier and Bangarth, "Merchants of Death."

49 Vucetic, "What Joining the Arms Trade Treaty Means for Canada."

50 Reid Standish, "How Sweden Is Pursuing Its 'Feminist Foreign Policy' in the Age of Erdogan, Putin and Trump," *Foreign Policy*, 29 July 2016.

51 "R" Miscellaneous. Letter, Brewin to Abdullah Rahman, 8 February 1979, MG32 C26. vol. 65, file 65-16, LAC.

13

Legislating Hate: Canada, the UN, and the Push to Ban Hate Propaganda, 1960–70

JENNIFER TUNNICLIFFE

In 1970, Canada became one of the first nations to criminalize hate propaganda. This decision coincided with the adoption at the United Nations of instruments containing articles to prohibit expressions of racial hatred. Both developments were a response to pressure for legal mechanisms to protect against racial discrimination resulting from a global outburst of anti-Semitism in the early 1960s. This chapter examines the parallel campaigns to ban hate propaganda, in Canada and at the UN, exploring the relationship between domestic and international efforts to protect human rights. It argues that, in order to successfully pressure federal policy-makers to enact hate provisions into the criminal code, campaigners in Canada had to engage with an international movement in a way that was not typical for Canadian rights activists at this time, placing domestic incidents of racial hatred into a broader global context. In doing so, individuals and groups advocating for legislative change at home also shaped Canadian diplomacy toward the UN's efforts to combat hate. Canadian policy toward human rights initiatives at the UN, and in this case the hate provisions specifically, were therefore intimately tied to domestic developments driven not by governments or diplomats, but by non-state actors and changing cultural attitudes.

As the introduction to this collection acknowledges, histories of Canadian foreign policy and diplomacy have tended to be state-centric; research focuses on a small group of state actors and the national interests that have historically guided foreign relations. The existing literature largely ignores, or denies, the influence of human rights principles or of domestic rights activism on foreign policy.[1] Even in studies of Canada's foreign policy toward the UN's human rights activities, scholars have too often neglected the role of cultural attitudes, rights advocacy, or non-state actors more generally in shaping Canadian diplomacy.[2] Similarly, the recent historiography on international human rights emphasizes the broad global forces that have shaped conceptualizations of rights. In a quest to locate the origins of human rights as an idea, or critique human rights at the UN as a form of political or ideological project, international human rights scholars have often sidelined domestic histories.[3] Yet efforts to define rights were not limited to debates at the UN or the discussions of high-level diplomats. More often, they were fought at the level of civil society, involving non-state actors struggling against their personal experiences with inequity, discrimination, and in some cases violent repression.

To reflect this, the growing field of Canadian human rights history stresses the central role that grassroots activists, minority groups, and social movement organizations have played in pushing provincial and federal policy-makers to expand rights protections, effectively demonstrating that the state has not been the primary driver of Canada's rights revolution.[4] The overall focus of this body of work, however, has been on the "made in Canada" solutions to the problems of prejudice and discrimination. While there has been work on the transnational forces that have influenced domestic human rights developments, very little has been done to situate Canada's experience into the broader global movement for human rights, to connect Canadian foreign policy and human rights history, or to look at how domestic rights activism in Canada influenced the development of international human rights law.[5]

To bring diplomatic history into closer conversation with human rights history, this chapter has two main goals. First, to look beyond state actors in understanding what has historically shaped Canadian diplomacy, in this case regarding Ottawa's participation in debates at the UN over international treaties that included provisions to ban hate speech. Second, to explore the intersections between Canadian understandings of the reasonable limits to freedom of speech, expression, and association; domestic campaigns to combat racial hatred; and the UN's efforts to eliminate racial discrimination. In the process, this "undiplomatic history" also highlights the contributions of Canadians to the development of international human rights law.

THE "SWASTIKA EPIDEMIC"
AND THE PUSH FOR LAWS TO COMBAT HATE

International efforts to regulate hate began as a response to a growing number of anti-Semitic incidents that took place in the winter of 1959–60, known as the "swastika epidemic."[6] This wave of hate propaganda began in West Germany, and quickly spread across Western Europe, into the Americas, and beyond. In total, more than thirty-four states reported incidents of public daubing of swastikas and anti-Semitic slogans, as well as physical attacks on Jewish property.[7] As the first global outburst of anti-Semitism after the Second World War, these attacks prompted Jewish leaders, heads of state, non-governmental organizations, and rights activists to demand that the UN take action.[8] In December 1960, the UN General Assembly unanimously adopted a resolution calling on member states to "take all necessary measures to prevent all manifestations of racial, religious and national hatred."[9]

International Jewish organizations, supported by US officials and the Israeli government, seized this opportunity to launch a campaign for an international treaty to ban anti-Semitism. They worked through the Sub-Commission on the Prevention of Discrimination and the Protection of Minorities, a sub-body of the UN Commission on Human Rights (UNCHR). By the early 1960s, this commission had become increasingly focused on the related issues of racial equality and decolonization. The Sharpeville massacre of March 1960 forced member states of the UN to reconsider their position toward apartheid policies in South Africa, and to question the idea that the promotion of human rights was the sole responsibility of states.[10] This emphasis, combined with the concerns about the rise in anti-Semitic hate propaganda, led to the adoption of two UN instruments: the Declaration on the Elimination of All Forms of Racial Discrimination in 1963, and a convention of the same name two years later. Both of these instruments included articles specifically prohibiting the promotion of racial hatred and the incitement of racial violence.[11]

The swastika epidemic affected Canada as well. In January 1960, newspapers reported on anti-Semitic vandalism in cities such as Montreal, Vancouver, Winnipeg, and Toronto.[12] Identifiably Jewish buildings, monuments, and tombstones were defaced with swastikas, and several prominent Jewish citizens received threatening letters.[13] Prime Minister John Diefenbaker and other federal politicians spoke publicly of their revulsion toward the acts.[14] Diefenbaker's government was in the process of adopting the first national bill of rights, but while the proposed bill prohibited discrimination based on "race, national origin, colour, religion or sex," there were no plans to include articles relating to hate propaganda.[15] The immediate response to the swastika epidemic by the Jewish establishment in Canada was one of caution. The Joint Public Relations Committee (JPRC) of the Canadian Jewish Congress (CJC) told members that there was no need for panic: any cases of swastika daubing should be reported to police, but no unnecessary publicity should be given to the incidents.[16] The practice of Canadian Jewish organizations at this time was to "quarantine" hate propaganda, with the idea that refusing to publicize incidents took away their power and prevented their spread.[17] In relation to the specific acts of 1960, the CJC stated that, "while these incidents may be inspired by the example of neo-Nazism in Germany, they appear to be the acts of a lunatic fringe – a form of imitative hooliganism – and should not be taken as the work of an organized anti-Semitic movement in Canada."[18] Not everyone in the Canadian Jewry agreed with this assessment. In the *Canadian Jewish News*, editor Meyer Nurenberger, who himself was subject to threatening letters, wrote in depth about the swastika epidemic. He argued that it was not a German issue, or a Jewish issue, but a matter that "constitutes a threat to freedom and human dignity the world over ... The incidents are minor, but the significance is of major importance."[19] Local Jewish and labour groups in Montreal organized a public meeting in February 1960 with the theme "Anti-Semitism – A Threat to Democracy."[20] Both Nurenberger and the organizers of the Montreal meeting attempted to link hatemongering in Canada to the wider history of anti-Semitism, fascism, the Holocaust, and other genocides, claiming that anti-Semitic hate propaganda had serious implications for all Canadians. The swastika epidemic lasted only a few months, however, so these ideas did not gain traction at this time.

Beginning in 1963, Canada experienced a second wave of hate propaganda, this time inspired by Nazi and white supremacist organizations in the United States.[21] In November, leaflets published by the American Nazi Party entitled "Hitler Was Right" and "Communism Is Jewish" were thrown from buildings onto citizens attending a Remembrance Day ceremony in Toronto.[22] Swastikas and slogans such as "Jews die" were painted on synagogues and stores in Toronto, Winnipeg, and Vancouver.[23] Over the next few years, anti-Jewish and anti-black propaganda became more widespread, especially in Ontario and Quebec. Hate literature was disseminated through the public mail system or in the streets. A cross was burned on the main street of Amherstburg, Ontario, and the primarily black First Baptist Church was desecrated with a warning that "the Klan is coming."[24] Such incidents generated enormous media coverage. Unlike the swastika epidemic, this wave of hate propaganda was prolonged. As it went on, the Jewish Labour Committee (JLC) abandoned its quarantine policy in favour of a public campaign, which demanded federal legislation to make it illegal to incite violence against a group based on that group's race, religion, colour, or national origin.[25] In its campaign, the JLC used the same arguments that Nurenberger had used only a few years earlier: that hate propaganda constituted a threat to all Canadians, not just those of African or Jewish ancestry, and for that reason, it must be banned. For more than five years, citizens, activist groups, minorities, and government officials debated how Ottawa should respond to the spike in incidents of racial hatred. Finally, in 1970 the federal government amended its criminal code to outlaw the public promotion of hatred against an identifiable group.

The global swastika epidemic and the subsequent rise of hate propaganda in Canada therefore led to two parallel campaigns to ban hate literature, one domestic and one international. These campaigns overlapped; members of the UNCHR were debating the form and content of the Declaration on the Elimination of All Forms of Racial Discrimination, including the article on inciting racial hatred, just as Canada was experiencing its second wave of hate propaganda. Canada was an active member of the UNCHR at the time. The UN Convention on the Elimination of All Forms of Racial Discrimination (ICERD) was introduced in early 1964, just as the Canadian Jewry was working to gain support from rights activists and other voluntary and professional organizations for amendments to the criminal code. For the next two years, the question of how to regulate hate speech was openly debated both at the UN and in Canada. Studies of Ottawa's policies toward the international instruments to combat hate are therefore incomplete without considering the possible influence of Canada's rights movement on its participation at the UN. Similarly, a history of the Canadian campaign for hate speech laws must take into account how domestic activists connected to the international movement to gain support for their cause.

THE CAMPAIGN FOR HATE PROPAGANDA LAWS IN CANADA

The public campaign for laws to ban hate propaganda in Canada must be considered in light of the fundamental changes that took place in postwar Canadian society concerning how citizens understood rights and freedoms. Historically, Canadians used the term "civil liberties" to describe a set of customary rights and freedoms inherited from the British political tradition, including property rights, legal rights, and the protection of an individual's right to formulate or express an opinion and act freely upon it in the private sphere.[26] These rights were reserved for certain citizens, however. The Canadian legal system privileged white, British, middle-class, Protestant males, and, in the period after Confederation, federal and provincial parliaments used their legislative powers to adopt legislation that protected this group of subjects above others. Governments put laws in place regulating areas such as property ownership, employment, education, voting, and immigration that disadvantaged Indigenous populations, women, the lower classes, and religious and racialized minorities. Canadian society was structured around "common sense" attitudes that reflected ideas of a racial hierarchy, whereby certain races were considered unfit to participate equally in Canadian society or to qualify for all of the rights and privileges inherent to Canadians of European ancestry.[27] As late as the 1940s, there was virtually no legislation in Canada to prohibit discrimination against these marginalized groups, or to explicitly promote rights and freedoms. Over the next two decades, however, there was a shift in the relationship between rights and the law, as legislative developments at the provincial and federal levels helped set the foundations of Canada's human rights state. These developments came as a result of the hard work of minority groups and rights activists.

A limited form of rights activism developed in Canada in the 1930s, leading to the establishment of the first civil liberties associations. Members of ethnic, religious, libertarian, and other organizations began to call for expanded rights protection, focusing on the ways in which governments in Canada violated the rights of their subjects, challenging discrimination in the courts, distributing petitions calling for the repeal of unfair laws, and supporting labour activism to push for expanded citizens' rights.[28] While Nazi atrocities and examples of overt racism in Canada throughout the Second World War heightened sensitivity to the idea of racial discrimination, in the postwar period most Canadians continued to see incidents of prejudice at home as isolated events rather than common behaviour. Such perceptions undermined the ability of Canada's early rights movement to gain widespread support, and so activists began to employ new strategies. The first of these was to form coalitions, bringing together groups with diverse interests to broaden the scope of the movement and help legitimize the argument that rights activism was not driven by specific groups seeking to gain privilege. Minority groups such as African Canadians, Japanese Canadians, and Jewish Canadians played a particularly vital role in increasing public awareness of the reality of prejudice and discrimination in Canadian society, challenging the idea that racist acts were aberrations, and gaining public support for the idea that governments had a role to play in prohibiting discrimination in areas such as employment, housing, and the provision of services.[29] Language also became a tool as activists began to more commonly use the phrase "human rights" in place of "civil liberties." While activists in the 1950s did not fully engage with the international human rights movement, they did begin to adopt the language of key UN documents such as the Universal Declaration of Human Rights. Other UN terminology used to describe rights, such as "inalienable," "natural," or "universal," also began seeping into the domestic discourse. As a result of these strategies, by the end of the 1950s most jurisdictions in Canada had passed fair employment and fair accommodation practices legislation, and several had also enacted equal pay laws.[30] This was the result of what historian James Walker has described as "organized" and "sustained" campaigns by citizen activists.[31] By the 1960s, human rights legislation had expanded to include a national bill of rights, as well as human rights codes and commissions in several provinces. Public support for human rights principles was cascading in Canada; in this period human rights ideas were diffused from elite intellectuals, human rights organizations, and minority groups activists to Canadian society more broadly, primarily through public education and the growth of human rights-related committees in other voluntary organizations. Cultural attitudes towards rights and freedoms had changed significantly, as citizens began to expect that government would take an active role in their promotion.

With this in mind, the push to ban hate propaganda can be understood as an extension of Canada's domestic human rights revolution. Campaigners argued that a ban would protect the rights of members

of identifiable groups not to be subjected to hatred, and they built on
the strategies they had used to pressure governments to enact anti-discrimination laws in the 1950s. Historian James Walker and legal scholar William Kaplan have examined the crusade to enact hate laws in
the 1960s, with Walker arguing that the criminal code provisions of
1970 were "a very deliberate product of a deliberate campaign, conducted with care and an immense amount of organization."[32] The CJC
led the public crusade, but in order to establish that this was not merely a Jewish issue, it worked to rally broader support. Beginning in
1963, church groups and a variety of professional and voluntary organizations, including the Manitoba Bar Association, the Canadian Federation of University Women, the UN Association of Canada, the
National Convention of the Royal Canadian Legion, the Canadian
Federation of Mayors and Municipalities, the National Council of
Women, the Canadian Citizenship Council, and organized labour, all
supported the campaign.[33] The CJC encouraged members of these
organizations to contact their local MPs and media outlets, expressing
their desire that Ottawa take legislative steps to stop the spread of hate
literature. Two members of Parliament introduced related private
members' bills into the Legislature: Milton Klein, a Liberal member
from Montreal, introduced a law relating to genocide, and David
Orlikow, the national director of the Jewish Labour Committee and
an NDP member from Winnipeg, introduced a bill restricting the use
of the public mail system to distribute hate propaganda.[34]

There was strong opposition to the idea of criminalizing hate propaganda in Canada – from many government officials, among citizens, and even within the human rights movement itself. Those who
spoke against anti-hate laws denounced the anti-Semitic and anti-
black hatemongering being reported, but they challenged the argument that criminalizing public statements of hatred was the solution.
These opponents used their own discourse of human rights, claiming
that hate speech laws would violate freedom of expression, freedom of
speech, and freedom of association, each of which had a long tradition in Canada. They argued that Canada's existing laws, and in particular sedition laws, were sufficient to deal with any public displays
of hate without the unnecessary restrictions on individual rights. Central to their argument was the claim that any spike in incidents of hate
propaganda was the product of marginal, extremist individuals and
groups, and that the risk of its ideas spreading to the mainstream of
Canadian society was too low to warrant intrusion, either by criminal

law or later by human rights commissions or tribunals.[35] The debate over anti-hate provisions therefore became one of how to balance two conflicting types of rights: an individual's right to freely express him or herself versus the right of an identified group to live free from expressions of racial hatred.

As Walker argues, in order to gain support for anti-hate laws, advocates had to "redefine the public interest": they had to show the importance of including protection for individuals as members of a definable group, and present the anti-hate provisions not as a restriction on, but an enforcement of, an individual human right.[36] To do this, campaigners had to first convince the public and government officials that hate propaganda posed a serious threat to Canadian society, and that existing laws were insufficient to deal with this threat. This required a different approach than was traditionally used to advance domestic rights legislation. In the campaigns for the anti-discrimination laws of the 1950s, minority groups and rights activists worked hard to educate the public about prejudicial laws, customs, and beliefs in Canada. They did so by highlighting the daily experiences of discrimination experienced by marginalized Canadians. While individuals and groups within Canada's early rights movement certainly connected with activists beyond their own borders, borrowing strategies and supporting similar causes, for the most part they were intent on finding legislative solutions to the particular problems of discrimination in Canada.

Cases of hate propaganda, while highly publicized, were certainly not as pervasive as individual experiences with discrimination at work or in the provision of services. With this in mind, opponents of hate laws argued that the problem was not significant enough in Canada to require legislation. To counter this argument, advocates of these laws worked to situate what was happening at home in relation to developments elsewhere, to show that incidents of hate propaganda had implications far beyond the pain they caused their targeted audience. Throughout the campaign, groups such as the CJC spoke of hate propaganda as a global phenomenon, pointing to examples from around the world. They argued that racial hatred had a long history that ignored national boundaries, and that tolerance for any level of hate propaganda was a slippery slope. To drive home this point, they explicitly linked incidents in Canada to the example of the rise of fascism and Nazism. The fact that most of the hate literature to be found in Canada originated out of American Nazi and white supremacist groups made this connection easier. For example, to convince the public of the severity of the threat of hate speech, activists cited the National White Americans Party's threat to execute or sterilize all Jews, which was reminiscent of the Holocaust.[37] These examples helped to generate public support for the campaign for anti-hate laws.

Canadian media coverage of the campaign reinforced the connection between the domestic and international, often employing Nazi or fascist tropes to capture public attention. In reporting on anti-Semitic acts in August 1966, the *Toronto Star* quoted Michael Rubinstein, the national president of the Jewish Labour Committee, who declared, "It has become clear that there is a revival of a Nazi international."[38] Newspapers across the country, from Moncton to Sault Ste. Marie to Vancouver, repeatedly tied the question of hate propaganda laws to the spread of fascism in Europe, the history of the Holocaust, or genocides more generally.[39] In an editorial entitled, "Hate Literature and Neo-Nazism," the *Montreal Star* reported that, "in our lifetime, Nazi barbarism has challenged the entire tradition of Western civilization. It is imperative that the Western democracies should cope with its remaining works by legal means in peace, as they have coped with Nazi barbarism itself, by means of force in war."[40] Articles like these framed hate propaganda as a global threat to peace and democracy.

By 1964, the citizen activists pushing for hate laws had gained enough public support to pressure the Canadian government to take some action. Unwilling to introduce any new laws, Minister of Justice Guy Favreau agreed to establish an extra-parliamentary committee to advise the government on how to suppress hate speech while balancing it with considerations of free speech.[41] Maxwell Cohen, dean of McGill University's law school, became the chair of this committee, whose mandate was to study the nature and extent of hate propaganda in Canada, to consider whether legal measures were necessary for its control, and if so to make appropriate recommendations.[42] The process by which the Cohen commission explored the question of hate speech, and generated its recommendations to the federal government, again reflected recognition of the important relationship between domestic and international human rights law. Rather than holding public hearings and taking submissions from the public, the committee insisted that the problem of hate propaganda could only be understood by placing it into a broader social, political, and legal context, including looking outside of Canada for answers as to how to best balance legislation prohibiting hateful speech with freedom of speech, association, and belief. The commission conducted a number of studies. One examined Canada's existing laws in relation to those in the US, Britain, and other common law nations. Another study explored international developments, considering how global issues such as apartheid, colonialism, and anti-Semitism might apply to the subject of hate speech. A third considered the socio-scientific implications of racial hatred, on individuals and on societies.[43] The committee also discussed in detail developments at the UN, including the 1965 adoption of the ICERD.

After ten months of study, the Cohen committee released a report drawing several important conclusions: that prejudice is a culturally learned condition; that given the proper circumstances, humans can be persuaded to believe almost anything; and that hate propaganda and racially motivated crimes have a tragic consequence on target audiences.[44] The report concluded that existing Canadian law was insufficient to deal with the hate propaganda of the 1960s, and recommended that the federal government amend the criminal code to include provisions banning hate speech. The Cohen report justified the need for hate speech provisions in the criminal code on the basis of the civil disorder that could come out of victim reaction to hate speech, and it argued that a ban would send a positive message to minorities in Canada.[45] Ultimately, the committee recommended the criminal code be amended to restrict hate speech, arguing, "Canadians who are members of any identifiable group ... are entitled to carry on their lives as Canadians without being victimized by the deliberate, vicious promotion of hatred against them. In a democratic society, freedom of speech does not mean the right to vilify."[46]

Despite the recommendations of the Cohen commission, the debate over how to balance free speech and protections from hateful speech continued. Several proposed bills were introduced into the Senate following the release of the Cohen report, but it was not until 1969, under the leadership of Pierre Elliott Trudeau, that the Liberals introduced a bill to restrict hate propaganda into the House of Commons.[47] Throughout 1969, the government heard extensive witness testimony, from NGOs, activist groups, and interested citizens, both in favour of and opposed to the legislation. Finally, on 11 June 1970, Bill C-3 received royal assent. The new sections added to the criminal code, Sections 318 and 319, criminalized the promotion of genocide, along with the public communication of statements deemed to incite or willfully promote hatred against an identifiable group.[48]

The activists who had openly campaigned for the criminalization of hate propaganda were seeking a legislative solution to the problem of racial hatred in Canada. In order to gain the support they needed for their cause, they had to connect hatemongering at home to global developments, including the UN's efforts. While this put pressure on the federal government to amend the criminal code, it also shaped Ottawa's policies toward the UN instruments as it became increasingly difficult for federal officials not to support human rights measures generally, and anti-hate provisions specifically.

CANADA AND THE ICERD

In and of themselves, Ottawa's active participation in the debates over the ICERD and its membership on the UNCHR attest to the influence of Canada's growing human rights movement on foreign policy. Throughout the 1940s and 1950s, the Canadian government had opposed efforts for an international bill of rights, resisting the adoption of the Universal Declaration of Human Rights (UDHR) in 1948 and subsequent efforts to draft the two International Covenants on Human Rights (the ICCPR and the ICESCR). It did so because Canadians had a very narrow understanding of civil liberties that conflicted with the expansive definition of "human rights" coming out of the UN.[49] Canadian federal policy-makers also had a strong desire to keep the international community from interfering in Canadian domestic affairs. As a result, Canada worked to stay on the periphery of any efforts to expand international human rights law. By the 1960s, however, a growing domestic rights movement, the adoption of a number of rights-related laws, and increased public support at home for human rights principles forced federal policy-makers to re-examine their position toward the international bill of rights, and the UN's human rights activities more generally.

The Department of External Affairs (DEA) began to consider ways in which Canada could increase its engagement with human rights at the UN.[50] One suggestion was to apply for the vacant seat on the UNCHR. Members of the DEA argued that, while Canada had historically avoided being a representative on this committee, growing interest in the field of human rights among Canadian citizens, and increased pressure from rights activists for Canada to participate more actively in the UN's human rights programs, made it an opportune time for Canada to apply.[51] Canada was successful, and began a three-year term in January 1963. This coincided with the drafting and adoption of the Declaration on the Elimination of All Forms of Racial Discrimination, and with the more lengthy debates and adoption of the ICERD. Canada's involvement with the UNCHR allowed it to participate actively in these debates.

The primary Canadian representative on the UNCHR was Margaret Aitken, a former Progressive Conservative politician from Toronto. The debate over the ICERD lasted for four weeks, and Canada's participation was influenced generally by a growth in public support for human rights at home, and more specifically by the debates taking place over hate propaganda. While Canada worked with Britain and the United States, it did not always support their positions, revealing that there were divisions in the way in which "Western" states envisioned rights, and understood reasonable limits to freedom of expression. The United States resisted the idea of international laws that would restrict free speech or freedom of expression.[52] Britain, which was in the process of adopting its first law to prohibit racial discrimination, was more supportive.[53] Aitken provided a uniquely Canadian perspective on the international convention. The different contributions of these states, all of whom were considered "Western," contribute to our understanding of how global human rights laws were shaped by local and national understandings of rights.

In his study of Canada's historic participation in the UNCHR, Andrew Thompson argues that Ottawa was ambivalent about using international instruments to protect against racial discrimination. He states that, despite resistance from its allies, the Canadian government voted in support of both the declaration and the convention because it "understood the broader significance of the treaties to the developing world," and it worried that Western opposition to these treaties would damage relations with those countries, thereby benefitting the Soviet Union.[54] While it is true that these considerations shaped Canada's position, an examination of the substance of the Canadian delegation's contributions to the debates over the ICERD reveals striking similarities to the debates taking place at home over the proposed amendments to the criminal code. This provides a strong example of how diplomacy at the UN cannot be considered only in relation to perceived national interests, but needs also to be examined in the context of domestic developments.

An analysis of the communications between Aitken and the DEA reveals that Canada was, in fact, prepared from the start to give its full support to the adoption of the ICERD. In February 1964, at the beginning of the session in which the UNCHR was debating the draft convention, the Canadian delegation called on states to "seek to achieve an instrument that will cover as much ground as possible both in terms [of] situations to which it will apply and of extension to its application. We should strive to have a well-balanced instrument sufficiently broad in its wording as to be ratified by as many Member States as possible to ensure its universal application."[55] This was a significant departure in language and tone from the response to the introduction of other UN human rights instruments, such as the UDHR; at that time, Canada had refused to commit to the idea of international human rights laws. Policy-makers within the DEA did have ideas as to how to amend the ICERD, hoping to narrow the obligation on states to intervene and to restrict freedom of expression. Aitken urged the commission to "avoid language which, whilst intended to protect against the abuse of discrimination, tends to neglect and sometimes even run against other fundamental rights enshrined in the Universal Declaration [of Human Rights]."[56]

Canada's proposed amendments to the draft ICERD were all connected to issues brought forth in the debates over its own domestic legislation: the question of regulating public versus private matters; the distinction between hateful thoughts and acts; and the need to balance any defence against racial hatred with the protection of free speech, expression, and association. In the first example, the DEA wanted to limit the extent to which UN treaties would obligate states to interfere into the private interactions of individuals. This reflected a long-standing debate within Canada's human rights movement over the relationship between individuals, groups, and the state. Aitken reported to the DEA that Article 1 of the draft convention defined "racial discrimination" in a way that restricted it to the field of "public life," and so Ottawa was satisfied that this would not permit unnecessary intervention.[57]

A second major concern taken up by the Canadian delegation was the extent to which any provisions on hate speech would distinguish between what individuals or groups did versus what they thought. The initial draft of the UN Declaration on the Elimination of All Forms of Racial Discrimination had proposed obligating governments to criminalize both the propagation of ideas of racial superiority *and* the incitement of racial hatred. The Canadian delegation argued this could be used to infringe on freedom of expression, and so wanted the text to reflect the link between racial hatred and violence by only criminalizing the incitement of racial hatred.[58] Again in the debates over the ICERD, the Canadian delegation argued that only in taking action should individuals or groups be subject to punishment. Delegates argued that only actions or specific incitements to racial hatred were the proper subject for criminal law, and that in this case the incitements would need to be in specific language. The delegate stated, "When the law departs from these principles and attempts to outlaw speech publication and association in the absence of any acts whatsoever, it paves the way to grave abuses by authorities in deciding which opinions are punishable and which are not."[59]

The final area of concern for Canada was that the proposed convention could be used to inappropriately restrict not only free speech and expression, but freedom of association as well. Again, this was a core aspect of the public debates taking place in Canada over the JLC's proposed hate propaganda provisions. In March 1964, the Canadian delegation intervened in the debates at the UNCHR, disagreeing with a proposed amendment that would "declare illegal any organization which, in the authorities' view, utters sentiments which they think might appear to promote racial discrimination."[60] The Canadian delegate emphasized that, as a convention, the instrument would essentially be a legal document, and that giving states the authority to prosecute or outlaw speech in this way could run contrary to freedom of association and be susceptible to abuse. Penalties should apply to the responsible officials within an organization, not to the organization itself, as guilt should be personal and not by association. Canada also supported an American proposal to narrow the obligations of states to intervene to cases in which "organizations, *or* the activities of organizations, promote *and* incite racial discrimination."[61] In its report to DEA, the delegation stated that this would safeguard against unnecessary limits on free expression and freedom of association.

Throughout the four weeks of the twentieth session of the UNCHR, the Canadian delegation actively participated in shaping the final format of the ICERD. Aitken reported to DEA that the delegation was much happier with the final format of the convention than it had been with the original draft. In its final form, Article 4 of the ICERD imposed a positive duty on all states party to the convention to "condemn all propaganda and all organizations which are based on ideas or theories of superiority of one race or group of persons of one colour or ethnic origin, or which attempt to justify or promote racial

hatred and discrimination in any form."⁶² Once the debate at the
UNCHR was complete, the commission submitted the draft conven-
tion first to ECOSOC and then to the General Assembly. In both cases,
Canada voted to support the document, which was adopted on 21
December 1965.⁶³

Ottawa's general support for the ICERD was driven both by perceived national interests and by a sense that the legislative and cultural changes taking place in Canada were closely linked to a shift in
how Canadian citizens understood rights and freedoms – whether
those were language rights, political rights, social rights, or the right
to live free from discrimination.⁶⁴ The substance of the Canadian delegation's participation in the actual debates, and in particular Canada's contributions to articles on hate propaganda, was influenced by
its own domestic campaign to ban hate speech. This, combined with
Canada's membership on the UNCHR, allowed Canada to play an
active role in the development of the UN's first instruments banning
the incitement of racial hatred.

CONCLUSIONS

By 1970, both the UN and Canada had adopted measures outlawing
hate propaganda. In fact, Canada's ratification of the ICERD took place
only six months after the federal government finally amended the
criminal code to include Sections 318 and 319. Any history of the
Canadian campaign that led to these amendments is incomplete
without recognizing the ways in which domestic activists worked to
place the threat of racial hatred in Canada into a global context, and
how the process to enact domestic laws relied on international developments. In the same way, Canada's willingness to actively participate
in the development of the ICERD is better understood in light of the
domestic activism that was taking place surrounding hate propaganda. In both cases, legislative developments and policy were shaped by
the efforts of citizen activists who campaigned to change understandings of rights in postwar Canada, and to create a new expectation that
government would take an active role in protecting the rights not
only of individuals, but also of identifiable groups.

The debate over restrictions on hate speech did not end in 1970.
Over the next two decades, Canadian provincial and federal human
rights codes expanded to include hate propaganda provisions, and several high-profile cases on the willful promotion of hatred began to

make their way through the courts.[65] Opposition to hate propaganda laws in Canada has remained strong, and debates over hate speech have become increasingly internationalized. In the contemporary political climate, the conflict between freedom of expression and the right to live free from racial hatred seem more relevant than ever. Claims of Islamophobia, white supremacist rallies, incidents involving the desecration of mosques or synagogues, all bear a striking resemblance to the rise in anti-Semitism that provoked the campaigns to ban hate speech in the 1960s. For this reason, we need to continue to historicize public debates over the reasonable limits to free speech, to consider the relationship between domestic and international human rights law, and to better understand the important role that civil society can play in shaping policy at both levels.

ACKNOWLEDGMENTS

This research for this paper was supported by a Social Sciences and Humanities Research Council of Canada postdoctoral fellowship, hosted at the University of Waterloo. I would also like to acknowledge James Walker for his contributions to this work.

NOTES

1 Some exceptions include: David Webster, "Self-Fulfilling Prophesies and Human Rights in Canada's Foreign Policy: Lessons from East Timor," *International Journal* 65, no. 3 (2010): 739–50; David Webster, "Canada and Bilateral Human Rights Dialogues," *Canadian Foreign Policy Journal* 16, no. 3 (2010): 43–63; Asa McKercher, "Sound and Fury: Diefenbaker, Human Rights, and Canadian Foreign Policy," *Canadian Historical Review* 97, no. 2 (2016): 165–94; Dominique Clément, "Human Rights in Canadian Domestic and Foreign Politics: From 'Niggardly Acceptance' to Enthusiastic Embrace," *Human Rights Quarterly* 34, no. 3 (2012): 751–78.

2 For example: William A. Schabas, "Canada and the Adoption of the Universal Declaration of Human Rights," *McGill Law Journal* 43, no. 2 (1998): 403–41; A.J. Hobbins, "Eleanor Roosevelt, John Humphrey and Canadian Opposition to the Universal Declaration of Human Rights: Looking Back on the 50th Anniversary of the UDHR," *International Journal* 53, no. 2 (1998): 325–42; Michael Behiels, "Canada and the Implementation of International Instruments of Human Rights: A Federalist Conundrum, 1919–1982," in *Framing Canadian Federalism: Historical Essays in Honour of John T. Saywell,*

edited by Dimitry Anastakis and P.E. Bryden (Toronto: University of Toronto Press, 2009), 151–84.

3 Samuel Moyn, *The Last Utopia: Human Rights in History* (Cambridge, MA: Belknap Press, 2010); Roland Burke, *Decolonization and the Evolution of International Human Rights* (Philadelphia: University of Pennsylvania Press, 2010); Mark Mazower, *No Enchanted Palace: The End of Empire and the Ideological Origins of the United Nations* (Princeton: Princeton University Press, 2009); Bonny Ibhawoh, *Imperialism and Human Rights: Colonial Discourses of Rights and Liberties in African History* (Albany: State University of New York Press, 2007); Roger Normand and Sarah Zaidi, *Human Rights at the UN: The Political History of Universal Justice* (Bloomington: Indiana University Press, 2008); Brian Simpson, *Human Rights and the End of Empire: Britain and the Genesis of the European Convention* (Oxford: Oxford University Press, 2001).

4 Some examples include: James W. St.G. Walker, "The 'Jewish Phase' in the Movement for Racial Equality in Canada," *Canadian Ethnic Studies* 34, no. 1 (2002): 1–29; Carmela Patrias and Ruth A. Frager, "'This Is Our Country, These Are our Rights': Minorities and the Origins of Ontario's Human Rights Campaigns," *Canadian Historical Review* 82, no. 1 (2001): 1–35; Ross Lambertson, *Repression and Resistance: Canadian Human Rights Activists, 1930–1960* (Toronto: University of Toronto Press, 2005); Christopher MacLennan, *Toward the Charter: Canadians and the Demand for a National Bill of Rights, 1929–1960* (Montreal and Kingston: McGill-Queen's University Press, 2003); Stephanie Bangarth, *Voices Raised in Protest: Defending North American Citizens of Japanese Ancestry, 1942–49* (Vancouver: UBC Press, 2008); Dominique Clément, *Canada's Rights Revolution: Social Movements and Social Change, 1937–1982* (Vancouver: UBC Press, 2008).

5 Some examples include: Bangarth, *Voices Raised in Protest;* Carmela Patrias and Ruth Frager, "Human Rights Activists and the Question of Sex Discrimination in Postwar Ontario," *Canadian Historical Review* 93, no. 4 (2012): 583–610; Rosanne Waters, "African Canadian Anti-Discrimination Activism and the Transnational Civil Rights Movement, 1945–1965," *Journal of the Canadian Historical Association* 24, no. 2 (2013): 386–424.

6 Egon Schwelb, "The International Convention on the Elimination of All Forms of Racial Discrimination," *International and Comparative Law Quarterly* 15, no. 4 (1966): 997. For other analyses, see: Howard J. Ehrlich, "The Swastika Epidemic of 1959–1960: Anti-Semitism and Community Characteristics," *Social Problems* 9, no. 3 (1962): 264–72; Oscar Cohen, *The Swastika "Epidemic" and Anti-Semitism in America* (New York: Anti-Defamation League of B'nai B'rith, 1960); and David Keane, "Addressing the Aggravated

Meeting Points of Race and Religion," *Maryland Law Journal of Race, Religion, Gender and Class* 6 (2006), 371.

7   Ehrlich, 264.

8   James Loeffler, "The Swastika Epidemic: Global Antisemitism and Jewish Politics in the Cold War 1960s," paper presented to the Kluge Center, Library of Congress, 11 December 2014.

9   United Nations General Assembly Resolution 1510 (XV), 12 December 1960.

10   Andrew Thompson, *On the Side of the Angels: Canada and the United Nations Commission on Human Rights* (Vancouver: UBC Press, 2017), 38.

11   Jewish organizations called on the CHR to include religious intolerance in its declaration and convention. Instead, member states proposed separate instruments relating to religious discrimination. These instruments proved too controversial, and were never adopted. See Thompson, 40–1.

12   For example, "Swastikas in Canada," *Globe and Mail*, 9 January 1960; "Will Ban Race Bias in Public Place," *Winnipeg Free Press*, 7 January 1960.

13   For example, Meyer J. Nurenberger, editor of the newly founded *Canadian Jewish News*, received verbal threats and a swastika painted on his garage door; his daughter walked to school with a police escort for some time. See Ira Robinson, *A History of Antisemitism in Canada* (Waterloo: Wilfrid Laurier University Press, 2015).

14   Canada, House of Commons, *Debates*, 24th Parliament, 3rd Session: Vol. 1 – 335-6 Mr. L.D. Crestohl (Cartier).

15   Canadian Bill of Rights, S.C. 1960, c. 44. 10 August 1960.

16   Franklin Bialystok, *Delayed Impact: The Holocaust and the Canadian Jewish Community* (Montreal and Kingston: McGill-Queen's University Press, 2000), 99.

17   James Walker, "Toward Equal Dignity: Canadian Jewry and the Hate Law of 1970," paper presented to the Jerusalem Conference on Canadian Studies, 1 July 2004, 4–5.

18   "Governments Move to Check Swastika Epidemic," *Jewish Telegraphic Agency*, 14 January 1960. See also Bialystok, *Delayed Impact*, 99.

19   Magdelena Kubow, "Kanada? The Canadian Jewish News and the Memory of the Holocaust in Canada," *Holocaust Studies* 19, no. 3 (2013).

20   Bialystok, *Delayed Impact*, 99.

21   P. Rosen, *Hate Propaganda* (Ottawa: Library of Parliament, 1989), 1. See also Thomas David Jones, *Human Rights: Group Defamation, Freedom of Expression, and the Law of Nations* (The Hague: Martinus Nijhoff Publishers, 1998), 206.

22   The American Nazi Party published the pamphlets. James Walker, "Toward Equal Dignity"; Bialystok, *Delayed Impact*, 112.

23 Robinson, *A History of Antisemitism*, 133.

24 Richard B. Parent and James O. Ellis III, "Right Wing Extremism in Canada," Working Paper Series, Canadian Network for Research on Terrorism, Security and Society, No. 14-03, May 2014, http://tsas.ca/wp-content/uploads/TSASWP14-03_Parent-Ellis10.pdf.

25 Robinson, *A History of Antisemitism*, 134. Also Walker, "Toward Equal Dignity," 5–6.

26 Walter Tarnopolsky, "Address to the Conference of Human Rights Ministers," 8 November 1974, Walter Tarnopolsky Papers, file 14, vol. 31, MG31 E55, Library and Archives Canada (hereafter LAC).

27 James W. St.G. Walker, *"Race," Rights and the Law in the Supreme Court of Canada: Historical Case Studies* (Toronto: Osgoode Society, 1997), 13.

28 Ross Lambertson, *Repression and Resistance: Canadian Human Rights Activists, 1930–1960* (Toronto: University of Toronto Press, 2005), chap. 1.

29 Patrias and Frager, "'This Is Our Country, These Are Our Rights.'"

30 For an outline of the development of provincial anti-discrimination laws, see Brian Howe, *Restraining Equality: Human Rights Commissions in Canada* (Toronto: University of Toronto Press, 2000), 8.

31 James W. St.G. Walker, "Decoding the Rights Revolution," in *Taking Liberties: A History of Human Rights in Canada*, edited by David Goutor and Stephen Heathorn (Don Mills: Oxford University Press, 2013), 29–58.

32 Walker, "Toward Equal Dignity," 16; and William Kaplan, "Maxwell Cohen and the Report of the Special Committee on Hate Propaganda," in *Law, Policy, and International Justice: Essays in Honour of Maxwell Cohen*, edited by William Kaplan and Donald McRae (Montreal and Kingston: McGill Queen's University Press, 1993).

33 Walker, "Toward Equal Dignity," 5–6; Allyson M. Lunny, *Debating Hate Crime: Language, Legislatures, and the Law in Canada* (Vancouver: UBC Press, 2015), 38.

34 Walker, "Toward Equal Dignity," 3–4.

35 Canadian Human Rights Commission, "Special Report to Parliament: Freedom of Expression and Freedom from Hate in the Internet Age," Minister of Public Works and Government, June 2009, http://publications.gc.ca/collections/collection_2009/ccdp-chrc/HR4-5-2009E.pdf.

36 Walker, "Toward Equal Dignity," 17.

37 Ibid., 7.

38 "Ask Hate Propaganda Bar," *Toronto Star*, 13 August 1966, 18.

39 Examples: "Council Berates Haters," *Sault Ste. Marie Daily Star*, 10 November 1964; "City Asked to Reject Fascists," *Montreal Star*, 25 November 1965;

"Hate Mail Hits Our Mails Once More," *Toronto Telegram*, 19 November 1965.

40 "Hate-Literature and Neo-Nazism," *Montreal Star*, 23 December 1966.

41 Lunny, *Debating Hate Crime*, 31.

42 Canada, Minister of Justice, *Report to the Minister of Justice of the Special Committee on Hate Propaganda in Canada* (Ottawa: Queen's Printer, 1966). Hereafter "Cohen report."

43 Walker, "Toward Equal Dignity," 8–9; Lunny, 30.

44 Cohen report.

45 Ibid.

46 Ibid.

47 Trudeau himself was a member of the Cohen commission in 1966.

48 Under s. 318, everyone who advocates or promotes genocide is guilty of an offence punishable by five years' imprisonment. Under s. 319(1), anyone who communicates statements in a public place and thereby incites hatred against an identifiable group where such incitement leads to a breach of the peace is guilty of an indictable offence punishable by two years' imprisonment or a summary conviction offence. Section 319(2) makes it a crime to communicate, except in private conversation, statements that willfully promote hatred against an identifiable group.

49 Jennifer Tunnicliffe, "'The Best of a Bad Job': Canadian Participation in the Development of the International Bill of Rights, 1945–1976" (PhD diss., McMaster University, 2014).

50 "Report of the Fourteenth Session of the Third Committee of the General Assembly," Department of External Affairs, Canada, 1959, file 5475-W-15-40, vol. 6928, RG 25, LAC.

51 Department of External Affairs Memo to the Minister, re: Canada's candidature for the Human Rights Commission, file 5475-W-40, vol. 6924, RG 25, LAC.

52 The United States did not ratify the ICERD until 1994, and did so with officially stated reservations.

53 United Kingdom, *Race Relations Act*, 1965.

54 Thompson, *On the Side of the Angels*, 38–9.

55 "Report of the Canadian Delegation to the 20th Session of the UN Commission on HR – NY," Department of External Affairs, Canada, 17 February–8 March 1964, file CB 10-2-2/15, vol. 319 119, RG 6, LAC.

56 Ibid., 3.

57 United Nations, *International Convention on the Elimination of All Forms of Racial Discrimination*, 21 December 1965. See also "Report of the Canadian Delegation to the 20th Session of the UN Commission on HR," 4.

58 Thompson, *On the Side of the Angels*, 42.

59 "Report of the Canadian Delegation to the 20th Session of the UN Commission on HR," 3–4.

60 Telegram from DEA to the Canadian Delegation in Paris, re: speech for delegate to give to 20th Session of HR Commission re: Article 4 of the Draft CERD, 4 March 1964, file CB 10-2-2/15, vol. 319 119, RG 6, LAC.

61 "Report of the Canadian Delegation to the 20th Session of the UN Commission on HR," 7.

62 UN, *International Convention on the Elimination of All Forms of Racial Discrimination.*

63 The ICERD was adopted by 106 votes in favour, none against, and one abstention.

64 Member of DEA talked about this in relation to both the adoption of the two Covenants on Human Rights, and the ICERD, in the 1960s. Memo from the UN Division to the Legal Division, Department of External Affairs, re: Canadian Position on Draft International Covenants on Human Rights, 25 January 1962, file 5475-W-15-40, vol. 5118, RG 25, LAC.

65 See Canada (Human Rights Comm.) v. Taylor (1990), 13 C.H.R.R. D/435 (S.C.C.) and R. v. Keegstra, [1990] 3 SCR 697.

Contributors

STEPHANIE BANGARTH is an associate professor of history at King's University College at Western University. Her work focuses on human rights, social movements, and immigration/refugee policy in Canadian political and social history.

SUSAN COLBOURN is a Henry Chauncey Jr '57 postdoctoral fellow at International Security Studies at Yale University. Her research focuses on transatlantic relations and the politics of nuclear weapons during the Cold War, and she is currently completing a book manuscript on NATO and the Euromissiles Crisis.

KAILEY HANSSON completed her doctoral studies at Queen's University where she specialized in Cold War cultural diplomacy. Her articles have appeared in the *Canadian Journal of Latin American and Caribbean Studies* and CPD *Perspectives in Public Diplomacy*. She is currently completing a book manuscript, *An Ancillary Weapon: Cultural Diplomacy and Nation-Building in Cold War Canada*.

SCOTT JOHNSTON received his PhD from McMaster University with a thesis entitled "The Construction of Modern Timekeeping in the Anglo-American World, 1876–1913." He is currently working as an independent researcher, and his work focuses on science, technology, and society in a global context.

MAURICE JR. LABELLE is an assistant professor of history at the University of Saskatchewan, located in Treaty 6 territory and the Homeland of the Métis nation. Articles of his have been published in *Diplomatic History*, *The Journal of Global History*, and *Radical History Review*. His current book project examines how Lebanon came to see the United States as an imperial power in the Middle East.

WILL LANGFORD is a SSHRC postdoctoral fellow in the Department of History at Dalhousie University. His research examines twentieth-century Canadian social movements and everyday politics in their transnational contexts. His recent work has explored anti-poverty activism, development programs, and democracy.

STEVEN LEE is associate professor and co-chair of the International Relations Program at the University of British Columbia. He is the author of *Outposts of Empire: Korea, Vietnam, and the Origins of the Cold War in Asia, 1949–1954* (McGill-Queen's University Press, 1995) and *The Korean War* (Longman, 2001). With Yun-shik Chang, he is the co-editor of *Transformations in Twentieth Century Korea* (Routledge, 2006). He is currently writing a global history of the long twentieth century for Wiley-Blackwell.

DANIEL MACFARLANE is assistant professor in the Institute of the Environment and Sustainability at Western Michigan University. He is the author of *Negotiating a River: Canada, the US, and the Creation of the St. Lawrence Seaway* and co-editor of *Border Flows: A Century of the Canadian-American Water Relationship*, and has forthcoming books on Niagara Falls and the International Joint Commission.

LAURA MADOKORO is a historian and assistant professor in the Department of History and Classical Studies at McGill University, which is on land that has long served as a site of meeting and exchange among Indigenous peoples, including the Haudenosaunee and Anishinabeg nations. She is the author of *Elusive Refuge: Chinese Migrants in the Cold War* (Harvard University Press, 2016), and the co-editor of *Dominion of Race: Rethinking Canada's International History* (UBC Press, 2017). She is currently at work on a transnational history of sanctuary practices in the Americas.

ASA MCKERCHER is assistant professor of history at the Royal Military College of Canada. He is the author of *Camelot and Canada: Canadian-*

American Relations in the Kennedy Era and co-editor of *Mike's World: Lester B. Pearson and Canadian External Affairs.*

AMANDA RICCI was a postdoctoral fellow at McMaster University's L.R. Wilson Institute for Canadian History from 2016 to 2018. She completed her doctoral studies at McGill University where she specialized in transnational social movements, gender and women's studies, and international migration. She is currently working on her manuscript, *There's No Place Like Home: Solidarity, Difference, and Belonging in Montreal's Second-Wave Feminist Movement.*

JENNIFER TUNNICLIFFE is an assistant professor with the Wilson Institute for Canadian History at McMaster University. She is the author of *Resisting Rights: Canada and the International Bill of Rights, 1947–76.*

PHILIP VAN HUIZEN is assistant professor of history in the Department of History at Western Washington University. His research focuses on energy and the environment in the North American West and has appeared in *The Pacific Historical Review*, BC *Studies*, and the edited collection *Powering Up Canada*. He is completing a book manuscript on the Canadian-US High Ross Dam controversy.

DAVID WEBSTER is an associate professor of history at Bishop's University. He is the author of *Fire and the Full Moon: Canada and Indonesia in a Decolonizing World*, and the editor of *Flowers in the Wall: Truth and Reconciliation in Timor-Leste, Indonesia and Melanesia*. He has published several articles on Canadian church-based coalitions' foreign policies, and continues to research in this area.

WHITNEY WOOD is an Associated Medical Services postdoctoral fellow in the Department of History at the University of Calgary. Her research interests include the histories of women's bodies, health, reproduction, and pain in late-nineteenth-and twentieth-century Canada. Her work has appeared in the journals *Social History of Medicine* (2018), *British Medical Journal: Medical Humanities* (2018), and *Canadian Bulletin of Medical History* (2014), as well as the edited collections *Perceptions of Pregnancy from the Seventeen to the Twentieth Century* (2017) and *Pain and Emotion in Modern History* (2014).

Index